**We go to gain a little patch of ground that hath in it
no profit but the name.**

William Shakespeare, *Hamlet*

GWYNNE DYER

WA

CARROLL & GRAF PUBLISHERS
NEW YORK

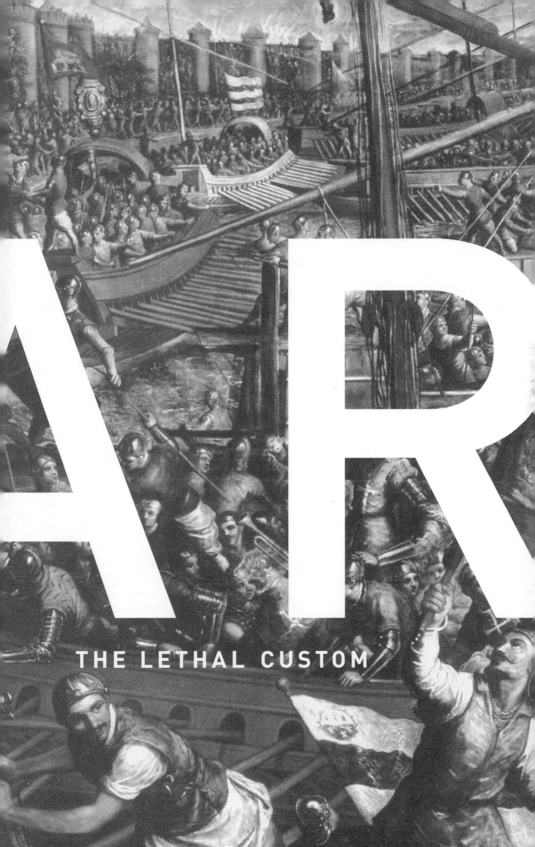

THE LETHAL CUSTOM

WAR
The Lethal Custom

Carroll & Graf Publishers
An Imprint of Avalon Publishing Group Inc.
245 West 17th Street
11th Floor
New York, NY 10011

AVALON
publishing group incorporated

Revised edition copyright © 2004 by Gwynne Dyer
Original copyright © 1985 by Gwynne Dyer

First Carroll & Graf edition 2005

Published by arrangement with Random House Canada, a division of
Random House of Canada Limited.

Library of Congress Cataloging-in-Publication Data is available.

ISBN: 0-7867-1538-3

9 8 7 6 5 4 3 2 1

Printed in the United States of America
Distributed by Publishers Group West

TO THE OLD FIRM

Contents

Acknowledgements

THE FIRST EDITION OF THIS BOOK, PUBLISHED ALMOST TWENTY years ago, grew out of the making of a television series, and quotations in the text from people who were then alive, unless otherwise indicated, are generally from interviews conducted for that series.

Television is not generally thought to be the most hospitable environment for ideas, but they flourished nevertheless. Some of them were mine, but many were not. For a long time before I got involved in the *War* series I had worked entirely alone as a freelance journalist, and I had forgotten—or maybe never knew—how much could be accomplished by a group of talented and intelligent people working on the same project every day (and many nights) for a couple of years. What emerged at the end was a perspective that none of us had when we started.

I haven't seen most of these people for twenty years, but even now there is still much of them in the book, so they need to be—not thanked, exactly, because they weren't doing it for me, but recognized as shapers of the perspective: the directors and editors Paul Cowan, Donna Dudinsky, Hannele Halm, Doug Kiefer, Judith Merritt and Barbara Sears; the people who worked on location, especially Bev Davidson, Mike Mahoney, Kent Nason, Hans Oomes and Liudmila Peresvetova; the executive producer, Barrie Howells; and the network producer, Paul Wright. It's the nature of the media business that people come together for a while, collaborate on some project, and then go their separate ways, but for me, at least, that was one where something valuable was happening.

Above all, there are Michael Bryans and Tina Viljoen, who should have their names on this book because so much of it comes from them. They weren't just good directors (though one of the films they made got an Academy Award nomination). The series was originally Michael's idea, and Michael and Tina were the only people who read and criticized each chapter of the first edition of this book. They have done it again for this edition, as have my sons Evan and Owen, now both journalists themselves, and my daughter Melissa, who also tracked down all the references I had managed to lose. I hope they realize how much I depend on them to keep me from going off the track—I am fortunate in my family and my friends.

The first edition of this book was published by Crown in New York, and I owe a lot to Jim Wade, then a senior editor there and still a dear friend. Holly Dressel in Montreal did the picture research for the original book and much other research besides; Ian Cowman, now back in Australia, did much of the historical research for the book while he was in London. Anne Collins, publisher at Random House in Toronto, was the person who suggested that I do a new edition of the book, and Susan Renouf has shepherded it through to completion. If it were always this painless, I'd seriously consider switching from newspaper columns to books.

London, 2004

Introduction

WHEN I WROTE THE FIRST EDITION OF THIS BOOK IN THE mid-1980s, the Cold War was nearing its second climax and the world lived in fear of an all-out nuclear war: ten thousand nuclear warheads exploding more or less simultaneously over all the main cities of Europe, North America, and Asia, destroying not only hundreds of millions of lives but most of the cultural heritage and capital stock accumulated over five thousand years of civilization. Five years later, we were granted a reprieve: a wave of non-violent democratic revolutions took us completely by surprise and swept away the governments on one side of that long and terrifying confrontation.

Now, for the moment, we are safe. The only kind of international violence that worries most people in the developed countries is terrorism: from imminent heart attack to a bad case of hangnail in fifteen years flat. We are very lucky people—but we need to use the time we have been granted wisely, because total war is only sleeping. All the major states are still organized for war, and all that is needed for the world to slide back into a nuclear confrontation is a twist of the kaleidoscope that shifts international relations into a new pattern of rival alliances.

That time may not come for another decade or so, but unless we can build institutions that move us decisively away from the old great-power game, sooner or later it surely will. And then at some later point, great-power war will also return: the megatons will fall, the dust will rise, the sun's light will fail, and the race may perish. We may inhabit the Indian summer of human history, with nothing to look forward to but the "nuclear winter" that closes the account.

It is now seen as rather alarmist to talk like this, but since the scientific and organizational abilities that make nuclear weapons and other as-yet-undeveloped weapons of mass destruction possible cannot be unlearned, the human race has to figure out a way of running our affairs that dispenses with war altogether. The starting point must be to see the institution of war as a whole and to understand how it works.

For most of history, war has been a more or less functional institution, providing benefits for those societies that were good at it, although the cost in money, in lives, and in suffering was always significant. Only in the past century have large numbers of people begun to question the basic assumption of civilized societies that war is inevitable and often useful, as two mutually reinforcing trends have gained strength.

One is moral: for all the atrocities of the twentieth century (or perhaps because of them), it was a time when people began to imagine that war—that is, killing foreigners for political reasons— might be simply wrong. The same explosion of new technologies that has made modern war so destructive has also made the whole world instantly and continuously visible. To see our "enemies" on television is not necessarily to love them, but it gets very hard to deny that they are human beings like ourselves. Even if morality is no more than the rules we make up for ourselves as we go along, one of those rules has usually been that killing people is wrong.

The other factor is severely practical: we will almost all die, and our civilization with us, if we continue to practise war. The deadline has been postponed but it has not been cancelled, and a civilization with the prospect of a major nuclear war in its future does not need moral incentives to reconsider the value of the institution of war. It must change or perish.

This does not mean, of course, that we will change or that we will survive. The universe does not give guarantees. But change is certainly possible, provided that we understand the nature of the institution we are trying to change and are willing to accept the consequences of changing it.

1

The Nature
of the Beast

If the bombardment [of London by V-bombs] really becomes a serious nuisance and great rockets with far-reaching and devastating effect fall on many centres . . . I may certainly have to ask you to support me in using poison gas. We could drench the cities of the Ruhr and many other cities in Germany in such a way that most of the population would be requiring constant medical attention.

Winston Churchill to the Chiefs of Staff Committee, July 1944

The rain of large sparks, blowing down the street, were each as large as a five-mark piece. I struggled to run against the wind but could only reach a house on the corner of the Sorbenstrasse. . . . [We] couldn't go on across the Eiffestrasse because the asphalt road had melted. There were people on the roadway, some already dead, some still lying alive but stuck in the asphalt. They must have rushed onto the roadway without thinking. Their feet had got stuck and then they had put out their hands to try to get out again. They were on their hands and knees screaming.

Kate Hoffmeister, then nineteen, on the firestorm in Hamburg in 1943[1]

THE CONCLUSION WAS GETTING HARD TO AVOID EVEN BEFORE the advent of nuclear weapons: the game of war is up, and we are going to have to change the rules if we are to survive. The brief, one-sided campaigns of well-armed Western countries against dysfunctional Third World autocracies kill in the tens of thousands, and the genocidal ethnic conflicts of fragile post-colonial states are local tragedies, but during the last two years of World War II, over one million people were being killed *each month*. If the great powers were to go to war with one another just once more, using all the weapons they now have, a million people could die each minute. They have no current intention of doing that, but so long as the old structures survive, Big War is not dead. It is just on holiday.

It is technology that has invalidated all our assumptions about the way we run our world, but the easiest and worst mistake we could make would be to blame our current dilemma on the mere technology of war. Napalm, nerve gas, and nuclear weapons were not dropped into our laps by some malevolent god; we put a great deal of effort into inventing and producing them because we intended to fight wars with them.

> A lot of people know that seventy thousand died at Hiroshima, but few people know that two hundred and twenty-five thousand died in Tokyo, as a result of only two raids with conventional bombs. I was a bomber pilot a long time ago. I bombed Hamburg. Seventy thousand people died there when the air caught fire. Eighty thousand or so died at

Dresden. And if you want to talk about numbers, one hundred and twenty-three thousand died at Iwo Jima . . . and so the problem is war, not nuclear war.

Man in the street in Washington, D.C.

The essential soldier remains the same. Whether he was handling a sling-shot weapon on Hadrian's Wall or whether he's in a main battle tank today, he is essentially the same.

Gen. Sir John Hackett

The soldier was one of the first inventions of civilization, and he has changed remarkably little over the five thousand years or so that real armies have existed. The teenage Iranian volunteers stumbling across minefields east of Basra in 1984 or the doomed British battalions going over the top in the July Drive on the Somme in 1916 were taking part in the same act of sacrifice and slaughter that destroyed the young men of Rome at Cannae in 216 BC. The emotions, the odds, and the outcome were fundamentally the same. Battle, the central act of civilized warfare, is a unique event in which ordinary men willingly kill and die as though those extraordinary actions were normal and acceptable. Changes in weapons and tactics have not altered those essential elements of its character.

However, the *consequences* of war can and do change. Force is the ultimate argument, and once it has been invoked, the only effective reply is superior force. The internal logic of war has frequently caused it to grow far bigger in scale than the importance of the issue originally at dispute would justify. In our time, the likely consequences of major war have grown drastically and irreversibly, so that they potentially include the destruction of the entire human habitat. Yet modern soldiers do not behave any more ruthlessly than their ancestors.

The residents of Dresden and Hiroshima in 1945 suffered no worse fate than the citizens of Babylon in 680 BC, when the city fell to Sennacherib of Assyria, who boasted: "I levelled the city and

Another day, another city. Assyrians looting and destroying an Egyptian city; bas-relief from Nineveh, Palace of Ashurbanipal.

its houses from the foundations to the top, I destroyed them, and I consumed them with fire. I tore down and removed the outer and inner walls, the temples and ziggurats built of brick, and dumped the rubble in the Arahtu canal. And after I destroyed Babylon, smashed its gods and massacred its population, I tore up its soil and threw it into the Euphrates so that it was carried by the river down to the sea."[2] It was a more labour-intensive method of destruction than nuclear weapons, but the effect (at least for an individual city) was about the same.

Most of the major cities of antiquity sooner or later met a fate similar to Babylon's—some of them many times—when the fortunes of war eventually left them exposed to their enemies. The difference between ancient military commanders and those who control the ultimate weapons of today (apart from a strikingly different approach to public relations) is more in the technologies and resources at their disposal than in their basic approach to the job. Soldiers often prefer to cloak the harsh realities of their trade in idealism or sentimentality, as much to protect themselves from the truth as to hide it from the rest of us, but at the professional level they have never lost sight of the fact that the key to military success is cost-effective killing. The relentless search for efficiency in killing that ultimately led to the development of nuclear weapons was just as methodical when the only means of introducing lethal bits of metal into an enemy's body was by muscle power. Consider the following instructions on the use of a sword in a Roman army training manual:

> A slash cut rarely kills, however powerfully delivered, because the vitals are protected by the enemy's weapons, and also by his bones. A thrust going in two inches, however, can be mortal. You must penetrate the vitals to kill a man. Moreover, when a man is slashing, the right arm and side are left exposed. When thrusting, however, the body is covered, and the enemy is wounded before he realises what has happened. So this method of fighting is especially favoured by the Romans.[3]

"A thrust going in two inches . . . can be mortal." Detail from the Ammendola Sarcophagus.

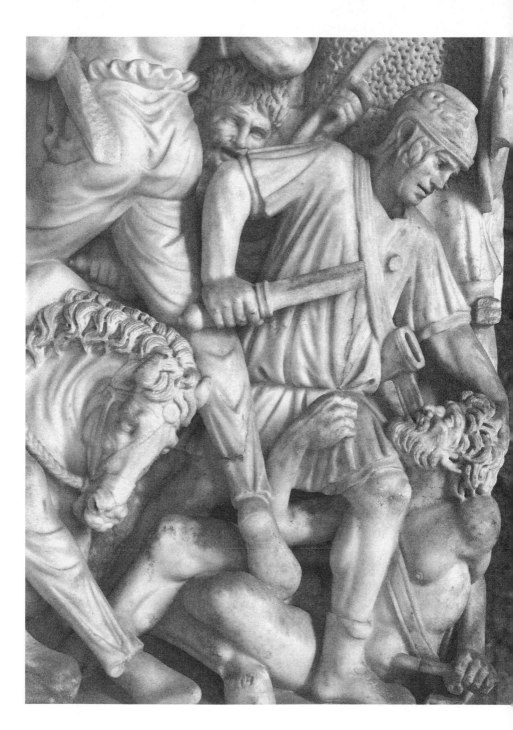

All surgically precise and clear, and sometimes it does happen like that: the weapons will generally (though not always) perform as predicted. But the men who wield them remain intensely human, and their behaviour on a battlefield, in Roman times or now, is complex and unpredictable. Like U.S. Marine corporal Anthony Swofford's first contact with the enemy in the Gulf War of 1991:

> Then we hear the voices of the Iraqi soldiers, and the idling diesel engines of their vehicles. Johnny and I low-crawl to the top of the rise while the rest of the team prepares to cover our right flank. . . . And then we hear the engine of their troop carrier move from idle to acceleration, and the slow, deep throaty drawl of the men's voices is gone, and we know that we've been just missed again. . . .
>
> I will never know why those men didn't attack us over the rise. Perhaps we shared an aura of mutual assured existence, allowing us to slowly approach one another and prepare to engage, but finally when the numbers were crunched, the numbers were bad for both sides, and the engagement thus sensibly aborted. If wars were only fought by the men on the ground, the men facing one another in real battle, most wars would end quickly and sensibly. Men are smart and men are animals, in that they don't want to die so simply for so little.[4]

It would be nice if it were as simple as that, but it isn't. A few days later the war is coming to a sudden end, and Corporal Swofford, one of two snipers in a perfect position overlooking an Iraqi airfield, is begging for permission on the radio to open fire. He is ordered not to by his captain, allegedly because that will deter the Iraqis from surrendering. Swofford doesn't believe it.

> I can't help but assume that certain commanders, at the company level, don't want to use us because they know that two snipers with two of the finest rifles in the world and a couple of hundred rounds between them will in a short time inflict severe and debilitating havoc on the enemy, causing the

entire airfield to surrender. The captains want some war, and they must know that the possibilities are dwindling. And also, same as us, the captains want no war, and here it is, but when you're a captain and you have a company to command and two snipers want to take a dozen easy shots and try to call it a day, of course you tell them no, because . . . what you need is some war ink spilled on your Service Record Book.[5]

So the whole company assaults the airfield, and people are killed and wounded on both sides, and the two snipers sit up on their ridge raging and forgotten—and Swofford is so frustrated that he spends half an hour aiming his sniper rifle at prisoners in the distance, "hopping from head to head with my crosshairs, yelling, *Bang, bang, you're a dead fucking Iraqi.*"

It isn't simple at all. The human complexities at the level of an infantry company do not get less complicated at the level of the generals. Indeed, they may be even more complex. War is a huge, multi-faceted, ancient human institution that is deeply entrenched in our societies, our history, and our psyches. No matter which angle we approach it from, we will initially be in the position of one of the blind men trying to describe the elephant. But the best place to begin, perhaps, is at the very heart of the matter: the nature of combat.

———

War is the province of uncertainty; three-fourths of the things on which action in war is based lie hidden in the fog of greater or less uncertainty.
Karl von Clausewitz

Their Majesties lunch with Doris and me, quite simply, at Government House. The King seemed anxious, but he did not . . . really comprehend the uncertainty of the result of all wars between great nations, no matter how well prepared one may think one is.
Gen. Douglas Haig, 11 August 1914[6]

11

The military is often criticized for its persistent—and persistently unsuccessful—attempts to reduce all action to routines, rules, and regulations. But all it amounts to, in practice, is a desperate and only partially successful attempt to reduce the immense number of variables with which the professional military officer must contend. To a limited extent the wild card represented by the unpredictable behaviour of his own people under stress can be brought under control by the imposition of uniform training and indoctrination, but there is no comparable way to confine the interplay of will, art, and chance between opponents on the battlefield to a predictable pattern.

Armies try, certainly—there are as many lists of "Principles of War" as there are general staffs, each consisting of ten or a dozen platitudes that are mostly either self-evident or useless to the man who has to take the decision under fire. Combat is an environment that cannot be mastered by set rules. Tactics and strategy must be learned and plans made, but the unpredictable and uncontrollable elements are so large that even the best plans, carried out by the most competent and daring officers, will often fail—and will always change.

Q. Can you tell me how a battle works?

A. Well, in my opinion a battle never works; it never works according to plan. . . . The plan is only a common base for changes. It's very important that everybody should know the plan, so you can change easily. But the modern battle is very fluid, and you have to make your decisions very fast—and mostly not according to plan.

Q. But at least everybody knows where you're coming from?

A. And where you're going to, more or less.

> *Gen. Dan Laner, Israeli Defense Forces*
> *commander, Golan Heights, 1973*

Combat at every level is an environment that requires officers to make decisions on inadequate information in a hurry and under great stress, and then inflicts the death penalty on many of those who make the wrong decision—and on some of those who have decided correctly as well. In such an environment, officers must rely on rules of thumb that are no more than rough calculations, distilled from much past experience, of the odds that a given action will succeed. On the whole, officers will cling to these rules even if the laws of chance occasionally betray them.

As we were going into the position, there was a large rice field we had to walk across, and I remember that I had to send somebody else across first. And you think, "Well, who do I send? Do I go myself?" But being the leader you can't afford that. You had to send somebody across. And if you sat back and thought about it you would say, "Am I sacrificing this individual? Am I sending him out there to draw fire?"

That may be part of it, but it's better to send an individual than walk out there with your entire force. And I remember pointing to an individual and telling him to go. Now there was one moment of hesitation, when he looked at me: "Do you mean me? Do you really mean it?" And the look I must have given him—he knew that I meant it, and he went across the field.

Everybody was watching that individual. I started sending them across in twos, and it was no problem. Then I took my entire force across. When we were about halfway across, they came up behind us, the VC [Viet Cong], and they were in spiderholes, and they caught most of my unit in the open.

Now tactically I had done everything the way it was supposed to be done, but we lost some soldiers. There was no other way. We could not go around that field; we had to go across it. So did I make a mistake? I don't know. Would I have done it differently [another time]? I don't think I would have, because that's the way I was trained. Did we lose less soldiers by my doing it that way? That's a question that'll never be answered.

Maj. Robert Ooley, U.S. Army

The battle drills in which Major Ooley was trained were worked out by experienced professional soldiers, with the aim of minimizing the chance of an unpleasant surprise and limiting the damage done if the surprise happens anyway. Tactical doctrines like these are constantly updated in the light of new experience, and the same process of analysis is applied to operations all the way up the chain of command. An enormous amount of effort now goes into the attempt to create rules that will give modern officers at least some general guidelines on how to combine all the resources under their command successfully on the battlefield; the tactical manuals of today's armies can run into hundreds of pages.

Yet in the end, the product of all this effort is the same, usually no more than programmed uncertainty and never a reliable guide to success. The official doctrines concentrate on manipulating what can be calculated and rationally planned in war, but the large incalculable elements are at best partly constrained by them—the rest is just hidden by the planning process. On the battlefield, the uncertainties cannot be hidden, and real combat is just as much a gamble for General Yossi Ben-Chanaan, who has fought in a number of short, victorious wars, as for Major Ooley, who fought a long, losing war.

Ben-Chanaan commanded a tank brigade on the Golan Heights during the 1973 war in the Middle East, and on the sixth day of the war, with only eight tanks left, he succeeded in penetrating the Syrian front line.

> . . . and once we arrived to the rear we took position, and all their positions were very exposed. We opened fire, and for about twenty minutes we destroyed whoever we could see, because we were in a great position there.
>
> I decided to charge and try to get that hill, but I had to leave a couple of tanks in cover; so I charged with six tanks. [The Syrians] opened fire from the flank with antitank missiles, and in a matter of seconds, three out of the six tanks were blown up. There was a big explosion in my tank. I blew out, and I was left there. . . . And also the whole attack was a mistake, I think.

General Ben-Chanaan is a very competent officer, but his attack failed and some of his men died. Yet if there had not been Syrian antitank missiles off on his flank (which he could not possibly have known), his attack would probably have succeeded, and a vital hill would have been taken by the Israelis at the critical time. Many Israelis who died in the subsequent fighting might now be alive, and the armistice line might be a good deal closer to Damascus. At the time, the gamble seemed worth it to Ben-Chanaan; he took a chance, and he was wrong. There are so many variables in combat that a commander cannot control, and so many things that he simply does not know.

———

Military officers, to be successful in combat, need a very high tolerance for uncertainty. This may seem one of the attributes least likely to be present in the armed forces, with their identical uniforms and rigid system of ranks, their bureaucratic standardizations of everything from "Swords, Ceremonial, Officers, for the Use of" to the format in which a commander must compose his operational orders, and their apparently generalized intolerance for deviations from the norm of any sort. Yet in fact these are two sides of the same coin.

It is not necessary for Acme Carpet Sales or the Department of Motor Vehicles to regiment their employees and rigidly routinize every aspect of their work, for they operate in an essentially secure and predictable environment. The mail will be delivered each morning, the sales representatives will not be ambushed and killed on the way to their afternoon appointments, and the accounts department will not be driven to mass panic and flight by mortar rounds landing in the parking lot. Armies in peacetime look preposterously over-organized, but peace is not their real working environment.

In battle, the apparent lunacies of orders given and acknowledged in standard forms, of rank formalized to an extent almost unknown elsewhere, of training that ensures that every officer will report his observations of enemy movements in *this* format rather

than some other when there seems no particular virtue in doing it one way rather than another, all find their justification by bringing some predictability and order to an essentially chaotic situation. Even the most bizarre aspect of military organization, the officer-enlisted man distinction, makes a kind of sense in this strange environment.

The rigid division of all military organizations into officers and enlisted men, two entirely separate hierarchies of people covering roughly the same span of age and often, at the more junior levels, doing much the same kind of job, is so universal that it is rarely considered remarkable. Yet armed forces have the most meticulously stratified system of rank to be found anywhere, and they positively flaunt it.

Among all the intricate distinctions of rank, it is the gulf between the officers and the other ranks that is most important. Army lieutenants at the age of twenty or twenty-one will normally be placed in charge of a body of enlisted men who are older and more experienced than themselves. The army will expect them to rely heavily on the judgment of their noncommissioned officers, but the final decision and the ultimate responsibility are theirs. Indeed, the twenty-year-old lieutenant is legally of a higher rank than the most experienced and trusted NCO in the army (though he would be wise not to exercise his authority without careful consideration). Moreover, in all armies it is deliberately made difficult to transfer from the enlisted ranks to the officer caste.

The historical origins of the officer/man distinction are political and social, but it is striking that even the most formally egalitarian states like revolutionary France or Bolshevik Russia never abolished it. The fundamental reason is that officers must use their men's lives up in order to accomplish the purposes of the state.

> You've got to keep distant from [your soldiers]. The officer-enlisted man distance helps. This is one of the most painful

You have to dress the part. General Hans von Seeckt, the embodiment of Prussian military professionalism, receiving birthday congratulations in 1936.

things, having to withhold sometimes your affection for them, because you know you're going to have to destroy them on occasion. And you do. You use them up: they're material. And part of being a good officer is knowing how much of them you can use up and still get the job done.

Paul Fussell, infantry officer,
World War II

Officers play a very large role in battles, and their casualties are usually higher proportionally than those of the enlisted men. The brief life expectancy of infantry lieutenants on the Western Front in World War I is legendary, but the figures were actually just as bad in World War II.

It occurred to me to count the number of officers who had served in the Battalion since D-Day. Up to March 27th, the end of the Rhine crossing [less than ten months] . . . I found that we had had 55 officers commanding the twelve rifle platoons, and that their average service with the Battalion was 38 days. . . . Of these 53% were wounded, 24% killed or died of wounds, 15% invalided, and 5% survived.

Col. M. Lindsay, 1st Gordon Highlanders[7]

In general, officer casualties in the British and American armies in World War II in the rifle battalions that did most of the fighting were twice as high proportionally as the casualties among enlisted men. Similar figures seem to apply for most other armies that have seen major combat in the past several centuries. (Suspiciously, the officer casualty rate for American forces in the Vietnam War was slightly *below* the enlisted rate.)[8] Nevertheless, there is a fundamental difference in the officer's experience of battle. He feels as much fear and is exposed to as much danger as his men, but except in the most extreme circumstances, he will not be using a weapon himself. His role is to direct those who do and make them go on doing it. The task officers must perform and the circumstances in which they must do it have instilled in them a very special view of the world and how it works.

The military ethic emphasizes the permanence of irrationality, weakness and evil in human affairs. It stresses the supremacy of society over the individual and the importance of order, hierarchy and division of function.

It accepts the nation state as the highest form of political organization and recognizes the continuing likelihood of war among nation states. . . . It exalts obedience as the highest virtue of military men. . . . It is, in brief, realistic and conservative.

Samuel Huntington[9]

Much of Huntington's classic definition of the "military mind" would have applied to long-serving military officers of the distant past, but there is an added dimension to it now, for it represents the outlook of a separate and specialized profession. Although there have always been full-time specialists in the military art at the lower levels of army command structures, it is only in the past few centuries that there has come into existence in every country an autonomous body of people—the professional military officers—whose sole task is to maintain the armed forces in peacetime and lead them in war.

Profession is the correct word for the calling of the career military officer today, in much the same sense that the word is applied to older professions like medicine or the law. The officer corps is a self-regulating body of men and women with expert knowledge of a complex intellectual discipline. It has a monopoly of the exercise of its function, and the exclusive right to select and train those new members who will be admitted to the discipline. Its client is society as a whole (through the mediation of the government, its sole employer), and it enjoys special privileges in compensation for its grave responsibilities. Like any other profession, it also has a wide range of corporate interests and views to defend and advance. But there is one key respect in which the military is very different from its civilian counterparts: what soldiers call the "unlimited liability" of their contract to serve. Few other contracts oblige the employee to lay down his life when the employer demands it.

Politicians may . . . pretend that the soldier is ethically in no different position than any other professional. He is. He serves under an unlimited liability, and it is the unlimited liability which lends dignity to the military profession. . . . There's also the fact that military action is group action, particularly in armies. . . . The success of armies depends to a very high degree on the coherence of the group, and the coherence of the group depends on the degree of trust and confidence of its members in each other.

Now what Arnold Toynbee used to call the military virtues—fortitude, endurance, loyalty, courage, and so on— these are good qualities in any collection of men and enrich the society in which they are prominent. But in the military society, they are functional necessities, which is something quite, quite different. I mean a man can be false, fleeting, perjured, in every way corrupt, and be a brilliant mathematician or one of the world's greatest painters. But there's one thing he can't be, and that is a good soldier, sailor or airman. Now it's this group coherence and the unlimited liability which, between them, set the military professional apart, and I think will continue to do so.

Gen. Sir John Hackett

There are bad officers, of course, of whom none of this is true, but General Hackett is right: the lack of those virtues is what makes them bad officers. In a way, he is simply offering a general and somewhat romanticized formulation of the state of grace amid evil that does prevail, by necessity, among front-line soldiers. It is the same phenomenon that a private soldier described in talking of "the friendly helpfulness and almost gaiety that increases until it is an almost unbelievably tangible and incongruous thing as you get nearer to the front. A cousin writing to me recently . . . said, 'Men are never so loving or so lovable as they are in action.' That is not only true, it is the beginning and end of the matter."[10]

But this, too, is not the whole of the truth.

I went where I was told to go and did what I was told to do,
but no more. I was scared shitless just about all the time.
                    James Jones, infantry private,
                    World War II

If blood was brown, we'd all have medals.
                    Canadian sergeant, northwest Europe,
                    1944−45

Fear is not just a state of mind; it is a physical thing. With its useful mania for questionnaires, the U.S. Army set out during World War II to find out just how much fear affected the ability of soldiers to perform on the battlefield. In one infantry division in France in August 1944, 65 percent of the soldiers admitted that they had been unable to do their jobs properly because of extreme fear on at least one occasion, and over two-fifths said it had happened repeatedly.

In another U.S. infantry division in the South Pacific, over two thousand soldiers were asked about the physical symptoms of fear: 84 percent said they had a violent pounding of the heart, and over three-fifths said they shook or trembled all over. Around half admitted to feeling faint, breaking out in a cold sweat, and feeling sick to their stomachs. Over a quarter said they had vomited, and 21 percent said they had lost control of their bowels.[11] These figures are based only on voluntary admissions, of course, and the true ones are probably higher in all categories, especially the more embarrassing ones. James Jones's remark about being "scared shit-less" was not just a colourful expression.

This is the raw material with which officers must conduct their battles: men whose training and self-respect and loyalty to their close friends around them are very nearly outweighed by extreme physical terror and a desperate desire not to die. Soldiers in battle, however steady they may appear, are always a potential mob capable of panic and flight, and armies must expend an enormous amount of effort to keep them in action, beginning in basic training and continuing on the battlefield.

The officer's task has grown even more difficult over time, for he no longer has all his men lined up in ranks under the eagle eyes of his NCOs in a situation in which, as long as they continue to go through the mechanical motions of loading and firing, they are being militarily effective. Modern ground forces fight in circumstances of extreme dispersion in which it is impossible for the officer to exercise direct supervision and control over his men's actions. Though the structure of command, compulsion, and punishment for poor performance remains in place, the officer must now rely much more on persuasion and manipulation of his men.

> You lead by example. I don't think it was unknown that I was afraid to be shot at. I didn't like it, I don't think anybody does; but I did what had to be done, given the situation at any given time, and I think that's a contagious-type thing. When the shooting starts and things start happening, you do what has to be done, and other people start doing what has to be done, and it's a team effort.
>
> *Lt. Col. Michael Petty, U.S. Army,*
> *Vietnam, 1969—71*

If too many soldiers in a unit fail to do their jobs, nobody is likely to survive. This approach to leadership, therefore, often produces acceptable results, especially in small wars like Vietnam, in which casualties are relatively low (only about one in fifty of the U.S. soldiers who served in Vietnam was killed), and episodes of intensive combat are generally brief and intermittent. It was the collapse of morale, not the attrition of combat, that destroyed the U.S. Army's fighting capability in Vietnam.

But in large-scale warfare between regular armies, things are different, and have been for at least the past two generations. In any big battle down to the latter part of the nineteenth century, the dead and wounded on a single day of fighting could amount to up to 40 or 50 percent of the men engaged, and the average figure was rarely less than 20 percent. Given a couple of battles a year, the infantryman stood an even chance of being killed or wounded for each year the war continued—a very discouraging prospect. But for 363 days of the year, it was merely a hypothetical prospect, for he was not in battle or even in close contact with the enemy on

...ory at some point you should get a

...elopment of forms of

ks along these

ortunately, not

e subject from

.so written for a

nor produced in

ury. It discusses

.s, battles, etc.--

l science,

itary history must

est to find them in

erested in some

the chapter on

ile I'd recommend

cip around without

that Dwyer makes some

story, but it will be

1.

those days. He might be cold, wet, tired, and hungry much of the time—if it was the campaigning season and the army was manoeuvring around the countryside—but for a good part of the year he was probably billeted somewhere indoors at night. In such circumstances the high probability that he would be dead or wounded within the year could be dealt with in the same sort of way that everybody deals with the eventual certainty of death.

The navies and air forces of today fight a kind of war that is still recognizably the same in its psychological effects. On a warship there is the constant psychological strain of being below deck knowing that a torpedo could hit at any time, but actual close contact with an enemy rarely averages more than a few hours a month. Even the bomber crews of World War II, whose life expectancy was measured in months, were still fighting that kind of war, although in an extreme form: in between the brief moments of stark terror when the flak or the fighters came too close, they slept between clean sheets and might even get to the pub some evenings. But for armies, things have changed irreversibly.

> There is no such thing as "getting used to combat." . . . Each moment of combat imposes a strain so great that men will break down in direct relation to the intensity and duration of their exposure.
>
> *U.S. Army psychological investigation*
> *into the effects of combat*[12]

The most striking visible sign of the change that has made ground warfare so much harder on the soldiers, paradoxically, is a steep drop in the casualty toll in a day of battle. Unlucky small units can still be virtually exterminated in an hour when something goes badly wrong, but the average daily loss for a division-sized force in intensive combat in World War II was about 2 percent of its personnel. For entire armies, the casualties even on the first day of a great offensive rarely amounted to 1 percent. The lethality of weapons has increased several thousandfold over the past two hundred years, but the extent to which the potential targets of those weapons have spread out is even greater, and it is certainly far safer to be a soldier on any given day of battle today than it was a hundred or a thousand years ago. The problem for the soldiers is that battles can now continue for weeks, with individual units being sent back in at frequent intervals, and the battles may follow each other in quick succession.

In terms of overall casualties per year, the loss rate in major wars is cumulatively about the same as it was in earlier times, with combat infantrymen facing at best an even chance of death or a serious wound within a year. But the psychological effect is very different. Being in contact with the enemy and exposed to the elements most of the time, being shelled every day, and living amid constant death gradually erode men's desperate faith in their own hope of survival and eventually destroy everybody's courage and will. Anyone can be brave once, but nobody can go on forever: "Your courage flows at its outset with the fullest force and thereafter diminishes; perhaps if you are very brave it diminishes imperceptibly; but it does diminish . . . and it can never behave otherwise," wrote a British soldier who had been through too much.[13]

The U.S. Army concluded during World War II that almost every soldier, if he escaped death or wounds, would break down after two hundred to two hundred and forty "combat days"; the British, who rotated their troops out of the front line more often, reckoned four hundred days, but they agreed that breakdown was inevitable. The reason that only about one-sixth of the casualties were psychiatric was that most combat troops did not survive long enough to go to pieces.

The pattern was universal, in all units of every nationality on all fronts. After the first few days of combat, in which the members of a fresh unit would show signs of constant fear and apprehension, they would learn to distinguish the truly dangerous phenomena of combat from the merely frightening, and their confidence and performance steadily improved. After three weeks they were at their peak—and then the long deterioration began. By the sixth week of continuous combat, two Army psychiatrists who accompanied a U.S. infantry battalion in 1944 reported, most soldiers had become convinced of the inevitability of their own death and had stopped believing that their own skill or courage could make any difference. They would continue to function with gradually diminishing effectiveness for some months, but in the end, if they were not killed, wounded, or withdrawn from battle, the result was the same: "As far as they were concerned the situation was one of absolute hopelessness. . . . The soldier was slow-witted. . . . Mental defects became so extreme that he could not be counted on to relay a verbal order. . . . He remained almost constantly in or near his slit trench, and during acute actions took little or no part, trembling constantly." At this point the "two-thousand-year stare" appeared (in Vietnam it was known as the "thousand-yard stare"), and the next stage was catatonia or total disorientation and breakdown.[14]

The amount of time it took soldiers to reach this point varied from individual to individual and could be greatly extended if they had some periods of relief from combat. The principal reason that relatively few entire units collapsed was that the same combat environment that produced these symptoms also caused so many casualties that there was a constant flow of replacements. (The Soviet army's casualties in 1943, for example, were 80 percent of the forces engaged, and the same in 1944.) Most units in prolonged combat in modern war, therefore, consist of an uneasy mixture of some utterly green and unsure replacements, some surviving veterans of many months of combat, most of whom are nearing collapse, and a proportion of soldiers—the larger the better, from the unit's point of view—who are still in transition from the former stage to the latter.

This is the reality that an officer must deal with (if he is not yet too far gone himself to cope with it). Except in the very first experiences of a unit in combat, he must reckon at best with the state of mind described by Colonel S. L. A. Marshall:

> Wherever one surveys the forces of the battlefield, it is to see that fear is general among men, but to observe further that men commonly are loath that their fear will be expressed in specific acts which their comrades will recognize as cowardice. The majority are unwilling to take extraordinary risks and do not aspire to a hero's role, but they are equally

unwilling that they should be considered the least worthy among those present. . . .

The seeds of panic are always present in troops so long as they are in the midst of physical danger. The retention of self-discipline . . . depends upon the maintaining of an appearance of discipline within the unit. . . . When other men flee, the social pressure is lifted and the average soldier will respond as if he had been given a release from duty, for he knows that his personal failure is made inconspicuous by the general dissolution.[15]

The experienced professional officer takes an unromantic view of men's behaviour under stress and believes that all his efforts in war amount to no more than trying to build shaky bridges across chaos with highly volatile human material. A young American infantry officer was strikingly frank about these realities to the survivors of his company in a post-combat debriefing that Marshall attended after the company had assaulted a small German fort outside Brest in 1944. The men had made a remarkable seven-hundred-yard charge across an open field, causing most of the German garrison to flee, and reached the cover of a hedgerow only fifteen yards from the fort. But they could not then be persuaded to get up and cross the scant remaining distance for seven hours, although only a handful of German defenders remained.

You have a plan. You have an objective. Your men get started with the objective in mind. But in the course of getting to the objective and taking up fire positions, disorganization sets in. The men look for cover and that scatters them. Fire comes against them and that scatters their thoughts. They no longer think as a group but as individuals. Each man wants to stay where he is. To get them going again as a group, an officer must expose himself to the point of suicide. The men are in a mental slump; they always get that way when they have taken a great risk. . . . It is harder to get men to mop up after a charge than to get them to charge.

Lt. Robert W. Rideout, Brest, 1944[16]

Marshall offers dozens of instances of the "lightning emotional changes" of men in combat, which will cause "the same group of soldiers [to] act like lions and then like scared hares within the passage of a few minutes." He is also acutely aware of how easily the apparent authority of officers can be undermined by the reluctance of the soldiers. They may, for example, seize upon the failure of some promised element of support for an attack (tanks, an artillery barrage, etc.) to arrive at the right time in the promised quantities: "The men squat in their foxholes and count. If they see a default anywhere they feel this gives them a moral excuse to default in their portion. They procrastinate and argue. . . ." In the end the attack goes off half-heartedly, without hope of success. "The rule for the soldier," Marshall concludes, "should be that given the Australian mounted infantryman when he asked the Sphinx for the wisdom of the ages: 'Don't expect too much!'"[17]

Everything army officers know about the nature of battle leads them toward the same conclusion: that it is an environment where nothing works reliably, and no plan or stratagem succeeds for very long. And everything that they know about human nature tells them that man is a frail and fallible creature who requires strong leadership and firm discipline in order to behave properly and function effectively in combat. This fundamental pessimism about the limits of heroism and idealism is central to the professional soldiers' world, and on the outermost margins of human experience, where they must operate in combat, their assumptions about human nature are absolutely right. So it is only understandable that they are quite ruthless in the ways that they manipulate the ideas and the behaviour of their soldiers.

2

Anybody's Son Will Do

You think about it and you know you're going to have to kill but you don't understand the implications of that, because in the society in which you've lived murder is the most heinous of crimes . . . and you are in a situation in which it's turned the other way round. . . . When you do actually kill someone the experience, my experience, was one of revulsion and disgust.

I was utterly terrified—petrified—but I knew there had to be a Japanese sniper in a small fishing shack near the shore. He was firing in the other direction at Marines in another battalion, but I knew as soon as he picked off the people there—there was a window on our side—that he would start picking us off. And there was nobody else to go . . . and so I ran towards the shack and broke in and found myself in an empty room.

There was a door which meant there was another room and the sniper was in that—and I just broke that down. I was just absolutely gripped by the fear that this man would expect me and would shoot me. But as it turned out he was in a sniper harness and he couldn't turn around fast enough. He was entangled in the harness so I shot him with a .45 and I felt remorse and shame. I can remember whispering foolishly, "I'm sorry" and then just throwing up. . . . I threw up all over myself. It was a betrayal of what I'd been taught since a child.

William Manchester

YET HE DID KILL THE JAPANESE SOLDIER, JUST AS HE HAD BEEN trained to—the revulsion only came afterwards. And even after Manchester knew what it was like to kill another human being, a young man like himself, he went on trying to kill his "enemies" until the war was over. Like all the other tens of millions of soldiers who had been taught from infancy that killing was wrong, and had then been sent off to kill for their countries, he was almost helpless to disobey, for he had fallen into the hands of an institution so powerful and so subtle that it could quickly reverse the moral training of a lifetime.

The whole vast edifice of the military institution rests on its ability to obtain obedience from its members even unto death—and the killing of others. It has enormous powers of compulsion at its command, of course, but all authority must be based ultimately on consent. The task of extracting that consent from its members has probably grown harder in recent times, as the gulf between the military and the civilian worlds has widened. Civilians no longer perceive the threat of violent death as an everyday hazard of existence, and the categories of people whom it is not morally permissible to kill have broadened to include, in peacetime, the entire human race. Yet the armed forces of every country can still take almost any young male civilian and in only a few weeks turn him into a soldier with all the right reflexes and attitudes. Their recruits usually have no more than twenty years' experience of the world, most of it as children, while the armies have had all of history to practise and perfect their techniques.

Just think of how the soldier is treated. While still a child he is shut up in the barracks. During his training he is always being knocked about. If he makes the least mistake he is beaten, a burning blow on his body, another on his eye, perhaps his head is laid open with a wound. He is battered and bruised with flogging. On the march . . . they hang heavy loads round his neck like that of an ass.

Egyptian, ca. 1500 BC[1]

The moment I talk to the new conscripts about the homeland I strike a land mine. So I keep quiet. Instead I try to make soldiers of them. I give them hell from morning to sunset. They begin to curse me, curse the army, curse the state. Then they begin to curse together; and become a truly cohesive group, a unit—a fighting unit.

Israeli, ca. AD 1970[2]

Human beings are fairly malleable, especially when they are young, and in every young man there are attitudes for any army to work with: the inherited values and postures, more or less dimly recalled, of the tribal warriors who were once the model for every young boy to emulate. The anarchic machismo of the primitive warrior is not what modern armies really need in their soldiers, but it does provide them with promising raw material for the transformation they must work in their recruits.

Just how this transformation is wrought varies from time to time and from country to country. In totally militarized societies—ancient Sparta, the samurai class of medieval Japan, the areas controlled by organizations like the Liberation Tigers of Tamil Eelam today—it begins at puberty or before, when the young boy is immersed in a disciplined society in which only the military values are allowed to penetrate. In large modern societies, the process is briefer and more concentrated, and the way it works is much more visible. It is, essentially, a conversion process in an almost religious sense—and as in all conversion phenomena, the emotions are far more important than the specific ideas.

When I was going to school, we used to have to recite the Pledge of Allegiance every day. They don't do that now. You know, we've got kids that come in here now, when they first get here, they don't know the Pledge of Allegiance to the flag. And that's something—that's like a cardinal sin. . . . My daughter will know that stuff by the time she's three; she's two now and she's working on it. . . . You know, you've got to have your basics, the groundwork where you can start to build a child's brain from. . . .

USMC drill instructor, Parris Island
recruit training depot, 1981

Many soldiers feel the need for some patriotic or ideological justification for what they do, but which nation, which ideology, does not matter: men will fight as well and die as bravely for the Khmer Rouge as for "God, King, and Country." And although the people who send the soldiers to war may have high national or moral purposes in mind, most of the men on the ground fight for more basic motives. The closer you get to the front line, the fewer abstract nouns you hear.

What really enables men to fight is their own self-respect, and a special kind of love that has nothing to do with sex or idealism. Very few men have died in battle, when the moment actually arrived, for the United States of America or for the cause of Communism, or even for their homes and families; if they had any choice in the matter at all, they chose to die for each other and for their own vision of themselves.

Once you get out there and you realize a guy is shooting at you, your first instinct, regardless of all your training, is to live. . . . But you can't turn around and run the other way. Peer pressure, you know? There's people here with you that have probably saved your life or will save your life in the future; you can't back down.

USMC Vietnam veteran

This is going to sound really strange, but there's a love relationship that is nurtured in combat because the man next to
you—you're depending on him for the most important thing
you have, your life, and if he lets you down you're either
maimed or killed. If you make a mistake the same thing happens to him, so the bond of trust has to be extremely close,
and I'd say this bond is stronger than almost anything, with
the exception of parent and child. It's a hell of a lot stronger
than man and wife—your life is in his hands, you trust that
person with the most valuable thing you have. And you'll
find that people who pursue the aphrodisiac of combat or
whatever you want to call it are there because they're friends;
the same people show up in the same wars time and again.

Capt. John Early, ex-U.S. Army,
Vietnam; ex-mercenary, Rhodesia

John Early is an intelligent and sensitive man who became a
combat junkie ("I'm a contradiction in terms, and I can't explain
it") and as such he is a rarity. For most men, the trust and intimacy
of a small unit in combat never compensate for the fear and revulsion. But the selfless identification of the soldier with the men in
his unit is what makes armies work in combat, and the foundations
must be laid in peacetime. "Fighting is a social art, based upon
collective activity, cooperation and mutual support," an Israeli soldier observed. "This utter reliance on others is an integral part of
the effort to meet the enemy irrespective of odds, and it largely
determines men's willingness to risk their lives in pressing the
attack. . . . In short, there is rarely brotherhood in facing death
when there is none in peace."[3]

The way armies produce this sense of brotherhood in peacetime is basic training, a feat of psychological manipulation on the
grand scale which has been so consistently successful and so universal that we fail to notice how remarkable it is. In countries
where the army must extract its recruits in their late teens,
whether voluntarily or by conscription, from a civilian environment that does not share the military values, basic training
involves a brief but intense indoctrination whose purpose is not

He's one of you. The bond of mutual trust in a small military unit that is "greater than that of man and wife." Japanese soldiers with a captured American gun, Philippines, 1942.

really to teach the recruits basic military skills but rather to change their values and their loyalties. "I guess you could say we brainwash them a little bit," admitted a U.S. Marine drill instructor, "but they're good people."

The duration and intensity of basic training depend on what kind of society the recruits are coming from, and on what sort of military organization they are going to. It is obviously quicker to train men from a martial culture than from one in which the dominant values are civilian and commercial, and easier to deal with volunteers than with reluctant conscripts. Conscripts are not always unwilling, however; there are many instances in which the army is popular for economic reasons.

In early modern Europe, for example, military service was always intensely unpopular with the mass of the population, and most soldiers were drawn from the most deprived and desperate groups on the margins of society. That changed suddenly in the nineteenth century, with conscription—and at the same time, surprisingly, military service became extremely popular. The fervent nationalism of the nineteenth century had something to do with it, but meat probably had even more.

In the army, the conscripts were fed meat every day and were issued two pairs of boots and a change of underwear—which was more than most of them had back on the farm or in the back streets of the cities. Most armies in the Third World still benefit from this kind of popularity today and have five or ten applicants for every available place (in some countries it is necessary to bribe the recruiter to get in). But even in the modern industrialized nations, where the average civilian's living standard has long since overtaken that of the private soldier and the white heat of nationalism has subsided somewhat, armies have no difficulty in turning recruits, whether conscripts or not, into soldiers.

A more complex question is what kind of soldier (or sailor, or airman) the recruit must now be turned into. This is usually seen mainly in relation to the increased requirement for technical knowledge brought about by modern weapons, but that is not really a problem of basic training. The real crux of the issue is the kind of social environment the recruit will eventually have to fight in.

For all of military history down to less than a century ago, the environment was invariably the same: an extremely crowded one, with his comrades all around him. In a Roman legion, on the gun deck of a seventeenth-century warship, or in a Napoleonic infantry battalion, the men fought close together, and the presence of so many others going through the same ordeal gave each individual enormous moral support—and exerted enormous moral pressure on him to play his full part. So long as you drilled the recruit to the point of boredom and beyond in the use of his sword, cannon, or musket; instilled in him a loyalty to his legion, ship, or regiment; and put him in mortal fear of his officers, he would probably perform all right on the day of the battle.

To a very large extent the crews of modern ships and aircraft (and even tanks)—all the men who fight together from inside machines—are still living in the same social environment, though the crowds have thinned out noticeably. And when men go into battle in the presence of their peers, the same principles of training will still produce the same results. But for the infantry, who fought shoulder to shoulder all through history, the world has been turned upside down.

Even in World War I, infantrymen could still usually see their whole company in an attack, but the dispersion forced on them by modern firepower has reduced the group who will actually be within sight or hearing of each other in a typical position to ten men or fewer—and even they will probably be spread out over a considerable area. For the foot soldier, the battlefield has become a desperately lonely place, deceptively empty in appearance but bristling with menace, where he can expect neither direct supervision by his officer or NCO in combat, nor the comforting presence of a group of other men beside him.

The more sophisticated forms of infantry basic training have now recognized that fact, and in the latter phases of the training they place far greater stress on "small-group dynamics": building the solidarity of the "primary group" of five to ten men who will be the individual's only source of succour and the only audience of his actions in combat. Far greater dependence must now be placed on the individual soldier's initiative and motivation than ever before, and so armies have to try harder. In the United States, where the contrast between the austerity, hierarchy, and discipline of military life and the prevailing civilian values is most extreme, basic training—the conversion of young civilians into soldiers—is given a greater emphasis than almost anywhere else. The U.S. Army, which reckons that all its members could, under some circumstances, find themselves in a combat zone, insists on seven weeks' basic training, followed by advanced individual training in a specific trade—and the U.S. Marine Corps gives twelve weeks of basic training to every man and woman who joins the Corps.

The Marines are a very old-fashioned organization (the last of the U.S. armed forces to get its hands on any desirable piece of new weapons technology) that clings to the belief that every Marine must be a qualified combat rifleman first, even if his subsequent specialty will be cooking or supply. The USMC is also an elite assault force, whose battle doctrine accepts the necessity, on occasion, of trading casualties for time. The entire orientation of the Marine Corps is toward the demands of combat: it informs everything the Corps does.

This makes the Marines atypical of contemporary armed forces in the United States or anywhere else, which generally consist of very large numbers of pseudo-military personnel doing technical, administrative, and even public relations jobs, surrounding a much smaller combat core. The Marines are almost all core. But for this very reason they are an ideal case study in how basic training works: they draw their recruits from the most extravagantly individualistic civilian society in the world and turn them into elite combat soldiers in twelve weeks.

―――

It's easier if you catch them young. You can train older men to be soldiers; it's done in every major war. But you can never get them to believe that they like it, which is the major reason armies try to get their recruits before they are twenty.

Young civilians who have volunteered and been accepted by the Marine Corps arrive at Parris Island, the Corps's East Coast facility for basic training, in a state of considerable excitement and apprehension. Most are aware that they are about to undergo an extraordinary and very difficult experience. But they do not make their own way to the base; rather they trickle into Charleston airport on various flights throughout the day on which their training platoon is due to form, and are held there in a state of suppressed but mounting nervous tension until late in the evening. When the buses finally come to carry them the seventy-six miles to Parris Island, it is often after midnight—and this is not an administrative

Recruits usually have less than twenty years' experience in the world, mostly as a child. Clockwise from top left: soldiers in Angola, the U.S. and Afghanistan.

oversight. The shock treatment they are about to receive will work most efficiently if they are worn out and somewhat disoriented when they arrive.

The basic training organization is a machine, processing several thousand young men every month, and every facet and gear of it has been designed with the sole purpose of turning civilians into Marines as efficiently as possible. Provided it can have total control over their bodies and their environment for approximately three months, it can practically guarantee converts. Parris Island provides that controlled environment, and the recruits do not set foot outside it again until they graduate as Marine privates twelve weeks later.

> They're allowed to call home, so long as it doesn't get out of hand—every three weeks or so they can call home and make sure everything's all right, if they haven't gotten a letter or there's a particular set of circumstances. If it's a case of an emergency call coming in, then they're allowed to accept that call; if not, one of my staff will take the message. . . .
>
> In some cases I'll get calls from parents who haven't quite gotten adjusted to the idea that their son had cut the strings— and in a lot of cases that's what they're doing. The military provides them with an opportunity to leave home but they're still in a rather secure environment.
>
> *Captain Brassington, USMC*

For the young recruits, basic training is the closest thing their society can offer to a formal rite of passage, and the institution probably stands in an unbroken line of descent from the lengthy ordeals by which young males in tribal societies were initiated into the adult community of warriors.

Basic training is not really about teaching people skills; it's about changing them so that they can do things they wouldn't have dreamt of otherwise. It works by applying enormous physical and mental pressure to men who have been isolated from their normal civilian environment and placed in one where the only right way to think and behave is the way the Marine Corps wants them to. The key word the men who run machine use to describe this process is *motivation*.

> I can motivate a recruit and in third phase, if I tell him to jump off the third deck, he'll jump off the third deck. Like I said before, it's a captive audience and I can train that guy; I can get him to do anything I want him to do. . . . They're good kids and they're out to do the right thing. We get some bad kids, but you know, we weed those out. But as far as motivation—here, we can motivate them to do anything you want, in recruit training.
>
> *USMC drill instructor, Parris Island*

The first three days the raw recruits spend at Parris Island are actually relatively easy, though they are hustled and shouted at continuously. It is during this time that they are documented and inoculated, receive uniforms, and learn the basic orders of drill that will enable young Americans (who are not very accustomed to this aspect of life) to do everything simultaneously in large groups. But the most important thing that happens in "forming" is the surrender of the recruits' own clothes, their hair—all the physical evidence of their individual civilian identities.

During a period of only seventy-two hours, in which they are allowed little sleep, the recruits lay aside their former lives in a series of hasty rituals (like being shaven to the scalp) whose symbolic significance is quite clear to them even though they are deliberately given no time for reflection, nor any hint that they might have the option of turning back from their commitment. The men in charge of them know how delicate a tightrope they are walking, though, because at this stage the recruits are still newly caught civilians who have not yet made their ultimate inner submission to the discipline of the Corps.

> Forming Day One makes me nervous. You've got a whole new mob of recruits, you know, sixty or seventy depending, and they don't know anything. You don't know what kind of

a reaction you're going to get from the stress you're going to lay on them, and it just worries me the first day.

Things could happen, I'm not going to lie to you. Something might happen. A recruit might decide he doesn't want any part of this stuff and maybe take a poke at you or something like that. In a situation like that it's going to be a spur-of-the-moment thing and that worries me.
USMC drill instructor

But it rarely happens. The frantic bustle of forming is designed to give the recruit no time to think about resisting what is happening to him. And so the recruits emerge from their initiation into the system, stripped of their civilian clothes, shorn of their hair, and deprived of whatever confidence in their own identity they may previously have had as eighteen-year-olds, like so many blanks ready to have the Marine identity impressed upon them.

The first stage in any conversion process is the destruction of an individual's former beliefs and confidence, and his reduction to a position of helplessness and need. Three days cannot cancel out eighteen years—the inner thoughts and the basic character are not erased—but the recruits have already learned that the only acceptable behaviour is to repress any unorthodox thoughts and to mimic the character the Marine Corps wants. Nor are they, on the whole, reluctant to do so, for they want to be Marines. From the moment they arrive at Parris Island, the vague notion that has been passed down for a thousand generations that masculinity means being a warrior becomes an explicit article of faith, relentlessly preached: to be a man means to be a Marine.

Most eighteen-year-old boys have highly romanticized ideas of what it means to be a man, so the Marine Corps has plenty of buttons to push. And it starts pushing them on the first day of real training: the officer in charge of the formation appears before them for the first time, in full dress uniform with medals, and tells them how to become men.

You have made the most important decision in your life . . . by signing your name, your life, your pledge to the

Government of the United States, and even more importantly, to the United States Marine Corps — a brotherhood, an elite unit. . . . You are going to become a member of that history, those traditions, this organization — if you have what it takes.

All of you want to do that by virtue of your signing your name as a man. The Marine Corps says that we build men. Well, I'll go a little bit further. We develop the tools that you have — and everybody has those tools to a certain extent right now. We're going to give you the blueprints, and we are going to show you how to build a Marine. You've got to build a Marine — you understand?

Captain Pingree, USMC

The recruits, gazing at him with awe and adoration, shout in unison, "Yes, sir!" just as they have been taught. They do it willingly, because they are volunteers — but even conscripts tend to have the romantic fervour of volunteers if they are only eighteen years old. Basic training, whatever its hardships, is a quick way to become a man among men with an undeniable status, and beyond the initial consent to undergo it, it doesn't even require any decisions.

I had just dropped out of high school and I wasn't doing much on the street except hanging out, as most teenagers would be doing. So they gave me an opportunity — a recruiter picked me up, gave me a good line, and said that I could make it in the Marines, that I have a future ahead of me. And since I was living with my parents, I figured that I could start my own life here and grow up a little.

USMC recruit

I like the hand-to-hand combat and . . . things like that. It's a little rough going on me, and since I have a small frame I would like to become deadly, as I would put it. I like to have them words, especially the way they've been teaching me here.

USMC recruit

"I have to work myself to death just to fit in" (The Who). Marine recruits get their hands on M16s for the first time, San Diego, 1984.

The training, when it starts, seems impossibly demanding for most of the recruits—and then it gets harder week by week. There is a constant barrage of abuse and insults aimed at the recruits, with the deliberate purpose of breaking down their pride and so destroying their ability to resist the transformation of values and attitudes that the Corps intends them to undergo. At the same time the demands for constant alertness and for instant obedience are continuously stepped up, and the standards by which the dress and behaviour of the recruits are judged become steadily more unforgiving. But it is all carefully calculated by the men who run the machine, who think and talk in terms of the stress they are placing on the recruits: "We take so many c.c.'s of stress and we administer it to each man—they should be a little bit scared and they should be unsure, but they're adjusting." The aim is to keep the training arduous but just within most of the recruits' capability to withstand. One of the most striking achievements of the drill instructors is to create and maintain the illusion that basic training is an extraordinary challenge, one that will set those who graduate apart from others, when in fact almost everyone can succeed.

There has been some preliminary weeding out of potential recruits even before they begin training, to eliminate the obviously unsuitable minority, and some people do "fail" basic training and get sent home, at least in peacetime. The standards of acceptable performance in the U.S. armed forces, as in most military organizations, tend to rise and fall in inverse proportion to the number and quality of recruits available to fill the forces to the authorized manpower levels. But there are very few young men who cannot be turned into passable soldiers if the forces are willing to invest enough effort in it. Not even physical violence is necessary to effect the transformation, though it has been used by most armies at most times.

> Our society changes as all societies do, and our society felt that through enlightened training methods we could still produce the same product—and when you examine it, they're right. . . . Our 100 c.c.'s of stress is really all we need, not two gallons of it, which is what it used to be. . . . In some cases with some of the younger drill instructors it was more an initiation than it was an acute test, and so we introduced extra officers and we select our drill instructors to "fine-tune" it.
>
> *Captain Brassington, USMC*

There is, indeed, a good deal of fine-tuning in the roles that the men in charge of training any specific group of recruits assume. At the simplest level, there is a sort of "good cop/bad cop" manipulation of the recruits' attitudes toward those applying the stress. The three younger drill instructors who accompany each "serial" through its time in Parris Island are quite close to the recruits in age and unremittingly harsh in their demands for ever higher performance, but the senior drill instructor, a man almost old enough to be their father, plays a more benevolent and understanding part and is available for individual counselling. And generally offstage, but always looming in the background, is the company commander, an impossibly austere and almost godlike personage.

At least these are the images conveyed to the recruits, although of course all these men cooperate closely with an identical goal in view. It works: in the end they become not just role models and authority figures, but the focus of the recruits' developing loyalty to the organization.

> I imagine there's some fear, especially in the beginning, because they don't know what to expect. . . . I think they hate you at first, at least for a week or two, but it turns to respect. . . . They're seeking discipline, they're seeking someone to take charge, 'cause at home they never got it. . . . They're looking to be told what to do and then someone is standing there enforcing what they tell them to do, and it's kind of like the father-and-son game, all the way through. They form a fatherly image of the DI whether they want to or not.
>
> *Sergeant Carrington, USMC*

Just the sheer physical exercise, administered in massive doses, soon has the recruits feeling stronger and more competent than ever before. Inspections, often several times daily, quickly build up their ability to wear the uniform and carry themselves like real Marines, which is a considerable source of pride. The inspections also help to set up the pattern in the recruits of unquestioning submission to military authority: standing stock-still, staring straight ahead, while somebody else examines you closely for faults is about as extreme a ritual act of submission as you can make with your clothes on.

But they are not submitting themselves merely to the abusive sergeant making unpleasant remarks about the hair in their nostrils. All around them are deliberate reminders—the flags and insignia displayed on parade, the military music, the marching formations and drill instructors' cadenced calls—of the idealized organization, the "brotherhood" to which they will be admitted as full members if they submit and conform. Nowhere in the armed forces are the military courtesies so elaborately observed, the staffs' uniforms so immaculate (some DIs change several times a day), and the ritual aspects of military life so highly visible as on a basic training establishment.

Even the seeming inanity of close-order drill has a practical role in the conversion process. It has been over a century since mass formations of men were of any use on the battlefield, but every army in the world still drills its troops, especially during basic training, because marching in formation, with every man moving his body in the same way at the same moment, is a direct physical

soldier must believe: that orders have
and instantly; and that you are no
art of a group.

ntification with the other members of
rtant lesson of all, and everything pos-
ey spend almost every waking moment
is an anomaly to be looked into at
of that time they are enduring shared
ergo collective punishments, often for
of a single individual (talking in the
ler during barracks inspection), which is
of suppressing any tendencies toward
urse, the DIs place relentless emphasis
her "serials" in training: there may be
etic to outsiders about a marching group
anting, "Lift your heads and hold them
" but it doesn't seem like that to the men

effective in building up a group's morale
as a steady diet of small triumphs. Quite
the recruits begin to do things that seem,
igerous: descend by ropes from fifty-foot
aps hand-over-hand on high wires (known
of course), and the like. The common
iese activities are daunting but not really
ill prevent anyone from falling to his death
er, and there is a pond of just the right
to cushion a falling man, but not deep
ly to drown—under the Slide for Life. The
iits, but to build up their confidence as indi-
p by allowing them to overcome apparently

You have an enemy here at Parris Island. The enemy that you're going to have at Parris Island is in every one of us. It's in the form of cowardice. The most rewarding experience you're going to have in recruit training is standing on line every evening, and you'll be able to look into each other's eyes, and you'll be able to say to each other with your eyes: "By God, we've made it one more day! We've defeated the coward."

Captain Pingree, USMC

Number on deck, sir, forty-five . . . highly motivated, truly dedicated, rompin,' stompin,' bloodthirsty, kill-crazy United States Marine Corps recruits, SIR!

Marine chant, Parris Island

If somebody does fail a particular test, he tends to be alone, for the hurdles are deliberately set low enough that most recruits can clear them if they try. In any large group of people there is usually a goat: someone whose intelligence or manner or lack of physical stamina marks him for failure and contempt. The competent drill instructor, without deliberately setting up this unfortunate individual for disgrace, will use his failure to strengthen the solidarity and confidence of the rest. When one hapless young man fell off the Slide for Life into the pond, for example, his drill instructor shouted the usual invective—"Well, get out of the water. Don't contaminate it all day"—and then delivered the payoff line: "Go back and change your clothes. You're useless to your unit now."

"Useless to your unit" is the key phrase, and all the recruits know that what it means is "useless *in battle*." The Marine drill instructors at Parris Island are not rear-echelon people filling comfortable jobs, but the most dedicated and intelligent NCOs the Marine Corps can find. The Corps has a clear-eyed understanding of precisely what it is training its recruits for—combat—and it ensures that those who do the training keep that objective constantly in sight.

The DIs "stress" the recruits, feed them their daily ration of synthetic triumphs over apparent obstacles, and bear in mind all the time that the goal is to instill the foundations for the instinctive, selfless reactions and the fierce group loyalty that is what the recruits will need if they ever see combat. They are arch-manipulators, fully conscious of it, and utterly unashamed. These kids have signed up as Marines, and they could well see combat; this is the way they have to think if they want to live.

> I've seen guys come to Vietnam from all over. They were all sorts of people that had been scared—some of them had been scared all their life and still scared—but when they got in combat they all reacted the same—99 percent of them reacted the same. . . . A lot of it is training here at Parris Island, but the other part of it is survival. They know if they don't conform—conform I call it, but if they don't react in the same way other people are reacting, they won't survive. That's just it. You know, if you don't react together, then nobody survives.
>
> USMC *drill instructor, Parris Island,* 1982

> When I went to boot camp and did individual combat train-ing they said if you walk into an ambush what you want to do is just do a right face—you just turn right or left, whichever way the fire is coming from, and assault. I said, "Man, that's crazy. I'd never do anything like that. It's stupid."
>
> The first time we came under fire, on Hill 1044 in Laos, we did it automatically. Just like you look at your watch to see what time it is. We done a right face, assaulted the hill—a for-tified position with concrete bunkers emplaced, machine guns, automatic weapons—and we took it. And we killed—I'd estimate probably thirty-five North Vietnamese soldiers in the assault, and we only lost three killed. I think it was about two or three, and about eight or ten wounded.
>
> But you know, what they teach you, it doesn't faze you until it comes down to the time to use it, but it's in the back of your head, like, What do you do when you come to a stop sign? It's in the back of your head, and you react automatically.
>
> USMC *sergeant,* 1982

For those destined to see ground combat, the key question is whether basic training actually prepares them for battle—to which the answer is an unequivocal yes and no. No, because *nothing* can prepare a man for the reality of combat: killing is still very hard.

> I think that if the recruits who leave here now were to go into combat, it would take somebody with combat experience, somebody who had . . . been in combat and had actually had to kill, to motivate them to the point where they would do it. And once the first one went down, then it would be a lot easier.
>
> *USMC drill instructor, Parris Island,*
> *1982*

But also yes, because the training at Parris Island has given the recruits everything they could hope to possess before they have seen combat: the skills and reactions that will help them to survive personally, the attitudes that will quickly transform any combat unit into a closed circle of mutual loyalty, and an almost laughably high confidence in themselves that will carry them as far as the battlefield.

> I'd like to be the first on the beach. I'm not scared at all, because when I came here I never thought I'd jump off a fifty-foot tower or throw a grenade. The drill instructors build your confidence up. Right now I feel I can do anything.
>
> *Graduating recruit, Parris Island, 1982*

He felt that way even though he had been told repeatedly that doing this job might require that he die. The knowledge may not really have struck home—eighteen-year-olds will not truly believe in the possibility of their own deaths until and unless they see combat and live long enough to understand what is going on—but the Marine Corps does not avoid the question. On the contrary, it puts a considerable effort into telling the recruits why they must, under certain circumstances, throw their lives away. It happens in the latter part of their training, when the emphasis is shifting increasingly to how Marines should behave in combat, and though they may not understand the logic that makes the individual's self-sacrifice good for the organization, they are by then more than ready to understand it emotionally.

> A Marine is lying out in the middle of a paddy and he's wounded. He's not crying for Mom! He's wounded. He might be moaning a little bit; he might be cussin,' because he's mad. Another Marine that's in safety because he got behind a dike—he's real safe, but he crawls out into that paddy, and he pulls that wounded Marine to safety, risking his own life, when probably the Marine's going to bite the bullet! He's going to die! And probably the one that goes out and tries to save him is going to die!
>
> Why is that done? You ask yourself that question. And you don't check out the Marine's name; you don't check out where he came from. . . . All you care about is—he's a Marine, and he's in your unit. He's one of you.
>
> *Captain Pingree, USMC, 1982*

Not always, but very often, people do behave that way in combat. It is certainly the way the Marine Corps wants its men to behave in combat, for the severely practical reason that men will be more willing to risk their lives if they are confident that the others in their unit will take equally great risks to save them if they get in trouble. But the practical necessities and the romantic vision of soldiering are inextricably mixed. In battle the unit will become the only important thing in the infantryman's universe; nothing outside it matters, and no sacrifice for the other men in it is too great.

> I remember one occasion in which two army officers from another unit came up on the line. They were rather bossy and arrogant, and they wanted to know where the front was, and the sergeant said to them, "You go right down there," and they did and they were instantly cut to pieces [by Japanese machine guns]. Civilians have a great deal of trouble

handling that, but the veteran understands it perfectly. You don't love anybody who is not yours.

You're dealing with excesses of love and hate, and among men who fight together there is an intense love. You are closer to those men than to anyone except your immediate family when you were young. . . . I was not a brave young man [but after I was wounded] I went back because I learned that my regiment was going to . . . land behind the Japanese lines, and I felt that if I were there I might save men who had saved my life many times, and the thought of not being there was just intolerable. I missed them, I yearned for them—it was, as I say, a variety of love, and I was joyful to be reunited with them. It didn't last long—two days later I was hit much harder and I was out of the war for good.

William Manchester

Only the experience of combat itself will produce such devotion and selflessness in men, but basic training is the indispensable foundation for it. Despite the ways in which it has been altered to take into account the changes in the battlefields soldiers now inhabit and the societies they serve, basic training has remained essentially the same, because it works with the same raw material that's always there in teenage boys: a fair amount of aggression, a strong tendency to hang around in groups, and an absolutely desperate desire to fit in. Soldiering takes up a much bigger part of your life than most jobs, but it doesn't take a special kind of person: anybody's son will do.

Moreover, the men like Captain Pingree who teach the recruits how to kill and how to die are not cynical in their manipulation of the minds of impressionable teenagers; they believe every word they say. If you accept the necessity of armed force in the world as it is—as Captain Pingree does—then he is absolutely right. More than that, he is admirable, for he asks nothing of the recruits that he is not willing to do himself. Soldiers are not criminals; they are mostly honourable men doing the difficult and sometimes terrifying job the rest of us have asked them to do. But we do repeatedly ask them to kill on our behalf, and they remain willing to do it—which seems to be saying something about all of us; even about the nature of human nature. What is it, exactly?

———

There is such a thing as a "natural soldier": the kind of man who derives his greatest satisfaction from male companionship, from excitement, and from the conquering of physical and psychological obstacles. He doesn't necessarily want to kill people as such, but he will have no objections if it occurs within a moral framework that gives him a justification—like war—and if it is the price of gaining admission to the kind of environment he craves. Whether such men are born or made, I do not know, but most of them end up in armies (and many move on again to become mercenaries, because regular army life in peacetime is too routine and boring).

> Most mercenaries are there because of their friends . . . and they're there because they feel important, and it makes them feel good to win, because they're playing a game. . . . It's a very exuberant feeling, combat.
>
> There's a euphoric effect whenever you make contact with an enemy unit or you're ambushed and you can feel the volume of fire start to build up, and you know that the decisions you make have to be absolutely correct because if they're not somebody's going to be killed or maimed, and that's a tremendous responsibility.
>
> You stay scared, all the time. When you're on patrol you never ever know what's going to happen, and that heightens your senses. You're extremely aware; it's almost like you can feel the texture of the air around you, and it just makes you feel extremely alive, and a lot of people like that. . . .
> *Capt. John Early*

But men like John Early are so rare that they form only a modest fraction even of small professional armies, mostly congregating in the commando-type special forces. In large conscript armies they virtually disappear beneath the weight of numbers of more ordinary men. And it is these ordinary men, who do not like combat at all, that the armies must persuade to kill. Until only a generation ago, they did not even realize that persuasion was needed.

Armies had always assumed that, given the proper weapons training, the average man would kill in combat with no further incentive than the knowledge that it was the only way to defend his own life. After all, there are no historical records of Roman legionnaires refusing to use their swords, or Marlborough's infantrymen refusing to fire their muskets against the enemy. But then dispersion hit the battlefield, removing each rifleman from the direct observation of his companions—and when U.S. Army Colonel S. L. A. Marshall finally took the trouble to inquire into what American infantrymen were actually doing on the battlefield in 1943—45, he found that on average only 15 percent of trained combat riflemen fired their weapons at all in battle. The rest did not flee, but they would not kill—even when their own position was under attack and their lives were in immediate danger.

> The thing is simply this, that out of an average one hundred men along the line of fire during the period of an encounter, only fifteen men on average would take any part with the weapons. This was true whether the action was spread over a day, or two days or three. . . . In the most aggressive infantry companies, under the most intense local pressure, the figure rarely rose above 25 percent of total strength from the opening to the close of an action.
>
> *Col. S. L. A. Marshall*[4]

Marshall conducted both individual interviews and group interviews with over four hundred infantry companies, both in Europe and in the Central Pacific, immediately after they had been in close combat with German or Japanese troops, and the results were the same each time. They were, moreover, as astonishing to the company officers and the soldiers themselves as they were to Marshall; each man who hadn't fired his rifle thought he had been alone in his defection from duty.

Even more indicative of what was going on was the fact that almost all the crew-served weapons had been fired. Every man had been trained to kill and knew it was his duty to kill, and so long as he was in the presence of other soldiers who could see his actions, he went ahead and did it. But the great majority of the riflemen, each unobserved by the others in his individual foxhole, had chosen not to kill, even though it increased the likelihood of his own death.

It is therefore reasonable to believe that the average and healthy individual—the man who can endure the mental and physical stresses of combat—still has such an inner and usually unrealized resistance towards killing a fellow man that he will not of his own volition take life if it is possible to turn away from that responsibility. . . . At the vital point he becomes a conscientious objector, unknowing. . . .

I well recall that in World War I the great sense of relief that came to troops when they were passed to a quiet sector such as the old Toul front was due not so much to the realization that things were safer there as to the blessed knowledge that for a time they were not under the compulsion to take life. "Let 'em go; we'll get 'em some other time," was the remark frequently made when the enemy grew careless and offered himself as a target.

Col. S. L. A. Marshall[5]

Marshall initially believed that this fundamental disinclination to kill, while it may always have existed in human beings, had only recently become a major factor in war because of the increasing dispersion of infantrymen on the battlefield and their escape from direct observation by their comrades. Surely it would have been impossible for soldiers in the days of mass formations and black-powder muskets to shirk their duty to fire, for they had to go through a complex sequence of actions to load their muskets, which produced a visible kick and a cloud of black-powder smoke when fired. Subsequent research, however, suggests that a very high proportion of soldiers did not fire even in these circumstances:

of 27,574 abandoned muskets picked up after the battle of Gettysburg in 1863, over 90 percent were loaded, although the nineteen-to-one ratio between loading time and firing time would logically argue that only about 5 percent of the muskets should have been loaded and ready to fire when their owners dropped them. Indeed, almost half of them—twelve thousand—were loaded more than once, and six thousand of them had between three and ten rounds loaded in the barrel. The only rational conclusion is that huge numbers of soldiers at Gettysburg, both Union and Confederate, were refusing to fire their weapons even in stand-up, face-to-face combat at short range, and were presumably going through the act of loading and perhaps even mimicking the act of firing when somebody nearby actually did fire in order to hide their internal defection from the killing process. And very many of those who did fire were probably deliberately aiming high.[6]

This conclusion, counterintuitive though it is, applies even to the shoulder-to-shoulder formations of eighteenth-century infantry that blasted volleys at each other from close range: the "kill-rate" was far lower than it logically ought to have been, given the accuracy of those weapons at those distances.[7] And there is no reason to believe that the phenomenon Marshall found in the American army in World War II was any different in the German or Soviet or Japanese armies; there were no comparable studies made, but if a higher proportion of Japanese or Germans had been willing to kill, then the volume of fire they actually managed to produce would have been three, four, or five times greater than a similar number of Americans—and it wasn't.

Hein Severloh was a twenty-year-old Wehrmacht private manning a machine gun overlooking Omaha Beach in Normandy when American troops came ashore on D-Day, June 6, 1944. His bunker, WN62, was one of the few not destroyed by Allied bombing and naval gunfire, and his machine gun accounted for at least half of the 4,184 Americans who died in front of that bunker on Private Severloh's first and last day of combat. He fired it for nine hours, pausing only to change gun-barrels as they overheated, mowing down American soldiers as they exited their landing craft in the shallow water 600 yards away. "At that distance they looked like ants," said Severloh, and he felt no reluctance about what he was doing. But then one young American who had escaped the slaughter came running up the beach during a lull in the fighting, and Severloh picked up his rifle. The round smashed into the GI's forehead, sending his helmet spinning, and he slumped dead in the sand. At that range, Severloh could see the contorted expression on his face. "It was only then I realized I had been killing people all the time," he said. "I still dream of that soldier now [in 2004]. I feel sick when I think about it."

Men will kill under compulsion—men will do almost anything if they know it is expected of them and they are under strong social pressure to comply—but the vast majority of men are not born killers. It may be significant, in this regard, that the U.S. Air Force discovered during World War II that less than 1 percent of its fighter pilots became "aces"—five kills in aerial combat— and that these men accounted for roughly 30 to 40 percent of all enemy aircraft destroyed in the air, while the majority of fighter pilots never shot anybody down. Fighter pilots almost all flew in single-seat aircraft where nobody else could observe closely what they were doing, and as late as World War II they could often see that inside the enemy aircraft was another human being. It may be that the same inhibition that stopped most individual infantrymen from killing their enemies also operated in the air.[8] On the whole, however, distance is a sufficient buffer: gunners fire at grid references they cannot see; submarine crews fire torpedoes at "ships" (and not, somehow, at the people in the ships); nowadays pilots launch their missiles from much farther away at "targets."

> I would draw one distinction between being a combat aviator and being someone who is fighting the enemy face-to-face on the ground. In the air environment, it's very clinical, very clean, and it's not so personalized. You see an aircraft; you see a target on the ground—you're not eyeball to eyeball with the sweat and the emotions of combat, and so it doesn't become so emotional for you and so personalized. And I think it's easier to do in that sense—you're not so affected.
>
> *Col. Barry Bridger, U.S. Air Force*

But for the infantry, the problem of persuading soldiers to kill is now recognized as a centrally important part of the training process. That an infantry company in World War II could wreak such havoc with only about one-seventh of the soldiers willing to use their weapons is a testimony to the lethal effects of modern firepower, but once armies realized what was actually going on, they at once set about to raise the average. Part of the job can be done by weapons training that actually lays down reflex pathways that bypass the moral censor. The long, grassy fields with bull's-eyes propped up at the end give way to combat simulators with pop-up human silhouettes that stay in sight only briefly: fire instantly and accurately and they drop; hesitate and they disappear in a couple of seconds anyway. But conditioning the reflexes only does half the job; it is also necessary to address the psychological reluctance to kill directly. These days soldiers are taught, very specifically, to kill.

Almost all this work is done in basic training. The re-shaping of the recruits' attitudes toward actual violence begins quite early in the training, with an exercise known as "pugil-sticks." Recruits are matched up in pairs, helmeted and gloved, given heavily padded sticks, and made to fight each other in a style that would certainly cause numerous deaths if not for all the padding. And the rhetoric of the instructor makes it clear what is required of them.

> You have got to be very aggressive! Once you've got your opponent on the run, that means you go on and strike with that first killing blow. Recruit, you don't stop there! Just because you made contact that don't mean you stop. You don't cut him no slack! Don't give him room to breathe, stay on top of him . . . keep pumping that stick. That means there should be nothin' out here today but a lot of groanin,' moanin,' a lot of eyeballs fallin' — a lot of heads rollin' all over the place.

Later, the recruits spend much of their time practising with the weapons that will really be the tools of their trade: rifles, bayonets ("cut on the dotted line"), grenades, and the like. With those weapons, of course, there is no dividing recruits into teams and letting them behave as they would in real combat. But if you can't actually blow your enemy up in basic training, you can certainly be encouraged to relish the prospect of his demise, and even the gory manner of it.

> Well, first off, what is a mine? A mine is nothing more, privates, than an explosive or chemical substance made to destroy and kill the enemy. . . . You want to rip his eyeballs out, you want to tear apart his love machine, you want to destroy him, privates, you don't want to have nothing left of him. You want to send him home in a Glad Bag to his mommy!
>
> Hey, show no mercy to the enemy, they are not going to show it on you. Marines are born and trained killers; you've got to prove that every day. Do you understand?
>
> *Lecture on the use of mines, Parris Island, 1982*

And the recruits grunt loudly with enthusiasm, as they have been taught, although most of them would vomit or faint if they were suddenly confronted with someone whose genitals had been blown off by a mine. Most of the language used in Parris Island to describe the joys of killing people is bloodthirsty but meaningless hyperbole, and the recruits realize that even as they enjoy it. Nevertheless, it does help to desensitize them to the suffering of an "enemy," and at the same time they are being indoctrinated in the most explicit fashion (as previous generations of soldiers were not) with the notion that their purpose is not just to be brave or to fight well; it is to kill people.

> The Vietnam era was, of course, then at its peak, you know, and everybody was motivated more or less towards, you know, the kill thing. We'd run PT in the morning and every time your left foot hit the deck you'd have to chant "Kill, kill, kill, kill." It was drilled into your mind so much that it seemed like when it actually came down to it, it didn't

bother you, you know? Of course the first one always does, but it seems to get easier—not easier, because it still bothers you with every one that, you know, that you actually kill and you know you've killed.

USMC sergeant (Vietnam veteran),
1982

Most of the recruits have never seen anybody dead (except laid out in a coffin, perhaps) before they arrive at Parris Island, and they still haven't when they leave. But by then they also half-inhabit a dream world in which they have not just seen dead

"Cut on the dotted line." USMC 2nd Lt. Garrick Sevilla shows 1st Lt. John Black how to slit a throat. Balikatan 2002 exercise, Philippines.

people, but killed them themselves, again and again. And it's all right to do it, because they've been told again and again, by everyone they respect, that the enemy, whoever he may be, is not really a full human being like themselves; it is permissible and praiseworthy to kill him.

> The idea of me killing a person when I first came down here just . . . you know, it was unheard of, you didn't do that. It was like squirrel hunting without a licence—you didn't do things like that. But once you came here and they motivated you and just kept you every day constantly thinking about it, and by the time you left here—it's something you still don't want to do, but you've got it in your mind that you want to do it so bad that you actually go out and do it when you have to. It seemed like it was a lot easier because of the motivation here.
>
> *Parris Island graduate, 1968*

> Sometimes the drill instructors make you feel like you're going to like it. Like the war—goin' out and killing people. They psych your mind out for you. . . . I haven't done it. I can't say whether I'd like it or not because I never killed anybody, you know? I'd go out there if I had to, though.
>
> *Parris Island graduate, 1982*

The training works. "We are reluctant to admit that essentially war is the business of killing," Marshall wrote in 1947, but it is readily enough admitted now. When Marshall was sent back to make the same kind of investigation during the Korean War in the early 1950s, he found that, with the new training, 50 percent of infantrymen were firing their weapons—and in some perimeter defence crises, almost everybody did.[9] By the Vietnam War, with further modifications to the training, around 80 percent of American soldiers were shooting to kill. Indeed, one of the main reasons for the continuing superiority of Western armies when confronting other military forces is not the technological gap in their weaponry (which is sometimes not that great), but the fact that most Western armies now explicitly train their soldiers to be killers and most other armies still do not. This effect is often masked by the fact that Western armies generally fight with over-whelming air and artillery superiority, so that most of the enemy casualties are caused by long-range weapons, but in circum-stances like the Falklands War where these factors were much less prominent, the huge disparity in casualties between the British and Argentine forces was presumably due almost entirely to the fact that the British troops were trained by the new methods and the Argentines were not. The most extreme case is the commando units of the Rhodesian army in the 1970s, operating against brave but poorly trained guerrilla forces: they had little by way of artillery or air cover, and they were using basically the same types of personal weapons as the guerrillas but the commandos consistently achieved kill ratios of between thirty-five and fifty to one.[10]

So what are we to make of the fact that men can so easily be turned into killers? There is the consoling fact that most men are so daunted by the enormity of killing another human being that they avoid it if they possibly can. If armies succeed in tricking them into doing it by modern training methods, moreover, a huge subsequent burden of guilt is laid on those soldiers who did what they were asked: it is now widely suspected that the high rate of combat participation in Vietnam was directly responsible for the extremely high rate of "post-traumatic stress disorder" among American veterans of that war.[11]

Nevertheless, if the inhibition against killing can be removed in most people by a little routine psychological conditioning, then we still have a lot to worry about. War has been chronic for most of the time since we moved into the mass civilizations around ten thousand years ago. Is it an inevitable part of civilization? And does it, perhaps, go even deeper than that?

3

The Roots of War: Rousseau, Darwin and Hobbes

Walbiri society did not emphasise militarism—there was no class of permanent or professional warriors; there was no hierarchy of military command; and groups rarely engaged in wars of conquest. . . . There was in any case little reason for all-out warfare between communities. Slavery was unknown; portable goods were few; and territory seized in a battle was virtually an embarrassment to the victors, whose spiritual ties were with other localities.

From *Desert People*, an anthropological study published in 1960[1]

. . . we were unexpectedly intruded upon by a very numerous tribe, about three hundred. Their appearance coming across the plain, occasioned great alarm. . . . On the hostile tribe coming near, I saw they were all men. . . . In a very short time, the fight began. . . . Men and women were fighting furiously and indiscriminately covered with blood . . . [Two members of Buckley's group were killed in the clash, but they counterattacked that night] and finding most of them asleep, laying about in groups, our party rushed upon them, killing three on the spot, and wounding several others. The enemy fled . . . leaving their war implements in the hands of their assailants and their wounded to be beaten to death by boomerangs.

William Buckley, ca. 1835[2]

ALL SERIOUS DISCUSSIONS ABOUT THE ROLE OF WAR IN HUMAN societies, and especially about its inevitability or otherwise, quickly bring us back to the question of origins. We know that organized war has been the constant companion of civilization from the start of recorded history, but that is not much more than five thousand years ago. If war is just another artifact of civilisation, then we can deal with it as easily as we have dealt with slavery and the oppression of women, which is to say, only with very great difficulty and over a long period of time, but it can theoretically be done. However, if it should turn out that warfare of a less formal but no less brutal sort extends far back into the pre-civilized and even the pre-human past, then the worrisome possibility arises that war may be an inescapable part of our genetic heritage. That would be a truly discouraging thought, but we do have to consider it.

When I wrote the first edition of this book twenty years ago, I used only the first quote that opens this chapter, describing an aboriginal group in Australia that was studied in the first half of the twentieth century. Every word of it is true, at least for the time when the study was done, and I used it as evidence that "real" warfare did not exist before the rise of civilization. In fact, I wrote: "Only a generation ago the Walbiri aborigines of Australia still lived in small bands in a hunting-and-gathering economy, as the entire human race did for at least 98 percent of its history, and although every male Walbiri was a warrior, their way of fighting did not resemble what we call 'war.' Very few people got killed; there were no leaders, no strategy, and no tactics; and only the kinship group affected by the issue at stake—most often revenge for a killing or a ritual offence committed by another group, and hardly ever territory—would take part in the fighting." This was how anthropologists invariably talked about warfare among hunter-gatherers at the time, and the only factual amendments I would make to the passage even today would be to point out that very few people got killed *at any one time*, and that the "kinship group" was actually the whole band—the entire tiny society in which people lived their lives.

But contrast the second quotation, taken from a book written by William Buckley, who escaped from a penal colony on the southern coast of Australia in 1803 and lived for thirty-two years as a fugitive among the Aborigines. Writing for a European audience in the mid-nineteenth century, Buckley was not going to display the sensitivities of a late twentieth-century anthropologist, and there may be some element of exaggeration in his account: three hundred is an astonishingly high total for any hunter-gatherer group, even if we allow for the fact that this encounter was taking place in relatively fertile country before encroaching settlement made it impossible for Aborigines to follow their traditional life in the more hospitable parts of Australia. But unless he was a total fantasist, the encounter he describes was bloody, merciless, and not in the least ritualistic—and it was not the only one. If I had been a member of that band of Aborigines, I would have thought that war was a very big problem. So why is it that descriptions of the first sort, and not of the second, have shaped our perceptions of the hunter-gatherer past?

In the twenty-first century we still live amid the echoes of a great debate about the nature of human nature that broke out in Europe in early modern times. The opening shot in the intellectual battle was fired by Thomas Hobbes in 1651 when he published *Leviathan*, an exaltation of the powerful centralized state as mankind's only hope of safety in a world of violence and chance. He was writing just after the Thirty Years War had wrecked much of Europe and the English Civil War had devastated his own country; his purpose was to construct a defence of constituted authority, and his method was to emphasize the chaos and misery of life without it. He had no knowledge and little interest in how people really lived in the "state of nature," but their place in his argument was to serve as a horrible example of what life would be like without the state, so he had no hesitation in describing the lot of pre-civilized man as follows: "No arts; no letters; no society; and which is worst of all, continual fear, and danger of violent death; and the life of man, solitary, poor, nasty, brutish and short."

The man who ultimately got the upper hand in the argument, however, was Jean-Jacques Rousseau. Writing a century later, in a generation when revolutionary ideas about equality and democracy were sweeping through the European world (he died two years after the American Revolution began, and eleven years before the outbreak of the French Revolution), Rousseau chose to make the "Noble Savage" his model of how human beings had lived before kings and priests had subjugated them to an unjust and unequal order. He knew very little about real hunter-gatherers other than that they lived in freedom and equality, but those were the values he cared about. By pointing out that people who lived in little pre-state societies still possessed these virtues, he was able to argue (in his *Discourse on the Origin of Inequality* in 1755) that freedom and equality were the original heritage of all mankind. Rousseau wasn't particularly concerned about what kind of wars his Noble Savages did or didn't fight, but his idealized picture of how people lived pre-"civilization" was hugely influential with a broad audience still living under absolute monarchies. It came to be assumed that free and equal people unburdened by the corrupt institutions of the state would also be able to avoid the brutal wars that tormented the civilized lands. The French revolutionaries believed it, the Marxists believed it, and in the late twentieth century most Western anthropologists still believed it despite all the evidence to the contrary.

This debate about the hunter-gatherers was and remains a centrally important argument because the best evidence for the true nature of human nature will surely be found among those who are still living as everybody lived for all but the last ten thousand years. Before mass societies, farming, commerce, religion, and the state changed us in so many ways, what were human beings really like? Were we warlike or peaceful? Tyrants or democrats? Selfish or sharing? Ecologically conscious guardians of the natural environment or rapacious destroyers? So anthropology (and archaeology) have always been politically charged disciplines—and to make matters worse, there weren't actually many hunter-gatherers left even when Hobbes and Rousseau were writing. By the time professional anthropologists appeared on the scene in the early twentieth century, there were virtually no surviving hunter-gatherer societies that had not been in contact with more complex societies for decades or generations, and none at all that still lived in the well-watered, desirable lands that had once been home to the vast majority of hunter-gatherers: all those had been lost to the farmers long before.

The evidence we do have for the way human beings used to live, therefore, is the archaeological data gathered about long-ago hunter-gatherer bands (mostly tools, weapons, and bones), written accounts of first contacts with aboriginal groups during the centuries of European expansion, and oral histories of hunter-gatherer groups taken down by early anthropologists a generation or two after contact began to change their lives, plus contemporary observations of the few groups living in very marginal lands who still preserve many elements of the original lifestyle. It could be better, but it's vastly more than we knew about hunter-gatherers (and therefore about ourselves) a hundred years ago—and it's mostly pretty encouraging. Rousseau beats Hobbes by about three to one.

Little hunter-gatherer bands, generally around twenty to fifty strong, operated on the basis of rough equality among the adult members, with no designated leaders and no hierarchy. When collective decisions were necessary, which was not all that often, they were usually made by discussion and consensus—and if anybody didn't like the decision, they were free to leave and join some other band. There were almost always other bands in the vicinity who spoke the same language, more or less, and since these little groups had to marry out to avoid genetic problems, there would probably be some relative in a neighbouring group who could help you settle in to the new band if you had to move. There was a sharp division of labour between the sexes, and men had a political advantage when group decisions had to be made because they were likelier to be related to one another (it tended to be women who moved to a different group on marriage), but there was a fair degree of equality between the sexes too. So all of our pre-history—thirty thousand generations of hunter-gatherers—tells us that we are egalitarian by nature, and democratic too.

Good news, but not really surprising: even after thousands of years in the belly of Leviathan, subordinated to the autocracy and hierarchy of the great civilized states, ordinary people have continued to behave in just this way among the small circle of family and friends that is their real social environment. Whatever we may do to foreigners at state level, at the level of individual relations we generally treat one another quite well. There remains the question of *why* the mass societies were so different politically, at least until very recently—but let us leave that for the moment and drop the other shoe. How did Hobbes do in the amateur anthropologist stakes?

He was dead wrong about "no society": life in the hunter-gatherer world was not solitary, but rather total immersion in a society of a few dozen people whom you had known since childhood. It has been variously compared to a non-stop encounter group and to living your entire life on the top deck of a London bus. Hobbes was technically right about the lives of hunter-gatherers being short—most modern women cannot conceive past their mid-forties because too few of their ancestors survived that long, and so there was no evolutionary selection for fertility past that age—but while they lived they were quite impressive specimens: closer to modern Europeans or North Americans in stature, thanks to their high-protein diet, than to the undernourished and stunted Europeans of Hobbes's time. In one big thing, however, he was right: they did live in "continual fear and danger of violent death" at the hands of their fellow men.

————

One year later, a gang from Kasekela found their third victim. This time the target was Goliath, now well past his prime, with a bald head, very worn teeth, protruding ribs and spine. . . . He had been a well-integrated member of the Kasekela community only five years before, and now (though he had since joined the Kahama group) he was little threat to anyone. But none of that mattered to the aggressors.

It began as a border patrol. At one point . . . they spotted Goliath, apparently hiding only 25 metres away. The raiders rushed madly down the slope to their target. While Goliath screamed and the patrol hooted and displayed, he was held and beaten and kicked and lifted and dropped and bitten and jumped on. At first he tried to protect his head, but soon he gave up and lay stretched out and still. . . . They kept up the attack for 18 minutes, then turned for home. . . . Bleeding freely from his head, gashed on his back, Goliath tried to sit up but fell back shivering. He too was never seen again.

The end of a Gombe chimpanzee [3]

Jane Goodall's discovery in 1973 that the chimpanzee troop she was observing in Gombe National Park in Tanzania actually waged a kind of war against neighbouring bands came as a great surprise at the time, but subsequent studies by a number of anthropologists—some chimpanzee bands have been observed for almost forty years now, with each member named and his or her behaviour recorded over lengthy periods of time—confirmed that fighting between rival groups of chimps is widespread, chronic, and very serious. There are never pitched battles involving large numbers of individuals on each side—most of the raids that end in actual fighting are distinctly one-sided ambushes—but individuals (mostly males) are frequently killed, and on occasion entire bands are wiped out one at a time. How relevant is this to human beings?

Our line of descent separated from that of the chimpanzees five or six million years ago, but about 98 percent of our genetic material is still common to the two species. Until ten or twelve thousand years ago, all of our human ancestors made their living in essentially the same way as chimps, by foraging for food in small bands of about the same size. Both humans and chimps were hunters as well as gatherers—chimps hunt monkeys regularly, and do so in coordinated groups using clearly conscious strategies—although human weapons, and perhaps human language as well, enabled us to tackle bigger game and to incorporate much more meat in our diet.

On the other hand, apart from our greater size and intelligence, there are sharp social differences between humans and chimps. Chimpanzee society is defined by acute rivalry for dominance among the males, whereas human hunter-gatherers and their proto-human ancestors have probably lived in relatively egalitarian societies with semi-permanent bonds between individual males and females and their children—families, in other words—for several million years. Hunting big game provides large amounts of meat that must be eaten before it spoils, and so human hunter-gatherers shared food, and especially meat, as a matter of course; chimpanzees also share meat, but with much greater reluctance. And of course, we have been much more successful than chimps in evolutionary terms: we now outnumber them about twenty-five thousand to one and live in every climatic zone of the planet, while they inhabit a rapidly diminishing range in Central Africa. Nevertheless, they are our closest relatives, and how they behave is relevant to our understanding of ourselves.

Chimpanzee "warfare" is hampered by the fact that they lack weapons, and it is very difficult for chimpanzees to kill each other with their bare hands. As a result, most successful raids involve a number of male chimps from one band attacking a lone chimp from another, with some holding him down while others pummel and bite him—and even then the victim is often still alive when the attackers leave, though he generally dies afterwards. But it *is* warfare, in the sense that it is purposeful and calculated. According to primatologist Richard Wrangel, who did his earliest work with Goodall's team in Gombe in the early 1970s, they conduct deliberate raids and make considerable use of surprise. Nor is it just blind aggression, triggered by the proximity of a chimp from another band: these raiding parties listen and count the calls of other troops to see if they are outnumbered. In fact, they almost always withdraw rather than attack unless they can catch a single victim from a rival band on his own. Moreover, although the great majority of killings involve the ambush of single chimps separated from their group, a campaign may be waged over a period of months or years until all the males of the rival band have been annihilated. Once that is done, the territory of the defeated group may be taken over, and the surviving females may be incorporated into the victorious group—but the infants will be killed.

Two more things, both of them with worrisome echoes in human behaviour. One of them is that chimpanzee bands typically have a territory of about fourteen square miles, but spend almost all their time in only the six central square miles. The rest is equally rich in resources but they treat it as a "no-man's land," presumably because of the danger of ambush and death at the hands of a neighbouring troop. The other is that this endemic chimpanzee warfare, according to long-term studies of several troops, eventually causes the death of about 30 percent of males and a much lower but still significant proportion of females.[4]

> My old friend . . . had a spear sent right through his body, and
> then they hunted out his wife and killed her dead upon the
> spot. The savages then came back to where I was supporting
> my wounded friend; who seeing them approaching, sprung
> up, even in the last agonies of death, and speared the nearest
> assailant in the arm. My friend was, of course, dispatched
> immediately, with spears and boomerangs, as was a son of his.
> *William Buckley*[5]

Similar studies of human hunter-gatherers who still lived in intact societies were almost never made by direct observation; William Buckley's account of life among Australian aborigines in the early nineteenth century is a rare exception. In the early twentieth century, however, ethnographer Lloyd Warner conducted extensive interviews among the Murngin people of Arnhem Land in northern Australia, who lived in a resource-rich territory where human population density was relatively high, and who had only recently come into regular contact with Europeans. Relying on the strong oral history tradition among preliterate peoples, he reconstructed as best he could from the interviews the scale of warfare among the Murngin of the late 1800s. The Murngin numbered around three thousand people and lived in many separate bands of the classic hunter-gatherer type. Out of a fighting-age population of about eight hundred adult males, Warner estimated that around two hundred had died in warfare over a two-decade period at the end of the nineteenth century. Twenty years is roughly the length of time that any individual male would have been regarded as an active warrior, so these figures translate into a cumulative 25 percent death rate from warfare among males.[6]

So how could anybody believe, as most anthropologists have done throughout the twentieth century, that warfare among hunter-gatherers was a mostly harmless ritual activity? It was possible partly because of the continuing influence of Rousseau, and partly because among the Murngin and their brethren elsewhere there were relatively few pitched battles that resembled the kind of war that dominated the anthropologists' own societies. They did occasionally have a formal battle (including two recorded by Warner in which over a dozen men were killed), but the great majority of clashes followed the usual hunter-gatherer pattern of raids on sleeping camps or ambushes of severely outnumbered opponents. In most of these events, only a few individuals, or one, or most frequently none at all, were killed, but the clashes were so constant that over a lifetime Murngin men stood as great a chance of dying in war as the conscript soldiers of Napoleon's France or Hitler's Germany.

Exactly half a world away from the Murngin, anthropologist Ernest Burch launched a very similar investigation of warfare among the Eskimos of northwestern Alaska in the 1960s. Since warfare had largely ceased once contact with Europeans and Americans was established ninety years before, he drew his information from contemporary historical records, oral history, and the memories of older Eskimo men. The picture that emerged was of the war of "all against all," as Hobbes put it: the bands under investigation fought one another; they fought Eskimo groups from further away in Alaska and Siberia; and they fought the Athabaskan

Indians to the east in what is now the Yukon. Warriors typically wore body armour consisting of plates cut from bone or ivory and strung together like chain mail under their outer garments. There was at least one war a year somewhere in the region, and attacking parties might travel for many days and could be as big as fifty men, though fifteen or twenty was more usual. Alliances between bands were constantly forming and shifting as rival groups tried to gain numerical superiority, and there were occasional pitched battles in which lines of men would face each other. Much more common, however, were dawn raids on villages, which were frequently located in places with difficult access. It was not even uncommon to dig escape tunnels between the dwellings.

The ultimate goal of pre-twentieth century warfare among the native people of Alaska, according to the older Eskimo men interviewed by Burch, was nothing less than the annihilation of the opposing group: prisoners were taken only if they were to be kept for later torture and killing, and women and children were not normally spared. Burch was unable to estimate the proportion of the total population that ultimately died from this kind of warfare, but there is physical evidence (including mass graves) that massacres did occur.[7]

And that, unfortunately, just about brings us to the end of the direct or oral evidence about warfare among hunter-gatherers, because the Arctic (where farming was impossible) and Australia (where agriculture never developed despite forty thousand years of human settlement) were the only large parts of the world where there were still significant populations of hunter-gatherers by the time Europe and North America developed anthropologists. (It is estimated that 99 percent of the indigenous population of North America were already farmers at the time of Columbus's voyages.)

There is one final group, the !Kung Bushmen, much studied and certainly not warlike in the present, who are frequently held out as a model of the hunter-gatherer as peaceful Noble Savage, but numerous historical accounts attest that in the seventeenth, eighteenth, and even nineteenth centuries Bushmen bands were very warlike, fighting one another and even successfully fending off for considerable periods of time Bantu and European farmers seeking to settle on their lands.

One way to expand the database, so to speak, is to consider also what are generally known as horticulturalists or tribal farmers. These are groups that continue to get a good deal of their food from hunting but who also practise a simple form of slash-and-burn agriculture. This lets them stay in one place for some years rather than the mere weeks that pure hunter-gatherers can manage. Their villages are more elaborate than hunter-gatherer camps, and their material possessions are more bulky and varied because they don't have to be able to carry everything they own. In the most important ways, however, they remain on the far side of the gulf that divides prehistoric groups from agricultural mass societies. They are egalitarian cultures in which every man is both a hunter and a warrior, and their numbers are small. Individual villages are not much bigger than hunter-gatherer bands, because otherwise they would hunt out the nearby game too fast. And the ethno-linguistic groups (tribes) to which they belong rarely exceed a few tens of thousands. They marry out, and as with hunter-gatherers it is generally women who move to their husband's group. Whereas hunter-gatherer groups will often come together for a few weeks each year in some place where resources are seasonally plentiful to party and matchmake, horticulturalist villages tend to invite one another to feasts for the same purpose. They have no formal leaders (though obviously some individuals will be more persuasive or influential than others), and they make their decisions by discussion and consensus. In a sense, they are just less mobile hunter-gatherers.

There aren't many horticulturalists left on the planet either: in most places, the transition to full-scale farming and much bigger societies was quite rapid and happened thousands of years ago. Those who survived into modern times were found mostly in isolated and resource-poor places like the Amazonian jungle and the New Guinea highlands—and wherever they were found, they were continually at war.

> Suddenly I heard shouts: the enemy, the enemy. . . . The
> men had gone running to meet the enemy . . . [the men of

the group are defeated and flee, and the women and children scatter to escape capture] . . . we could not flee any more; the Karawetari [the enemy] were by now quite close [the speaker's group of women and children are surrounded and captured]. . . . Then the men began to kill the children; little ones, bigger ones, they killed many of them. They tried to run away, but they caught them, and threw them on the ground, and stuck them with arrows which went through their bodies and rooted them to the ground. Taking the smallest by the feet, they beat them against the trees and rocks. The children's eyes trembled. . . . They killed so many.

A captive of the Yanomamo, 1930s[8]

The Karawetari and their victims were all members of the Yanomamo tribe, some twenty thousand horticulturalists who live in the Amazonian rain forest along the upper reaches of the Orinoco River in Venezuela and Brazil. Wars between their villages (average population around ninety people) were endemic until quite recently—the account of a raid above is from a white girl who was kidnapped at the age of twelve and lived among them in the 1930s—but as with all hunter-gatherer and horticulturalist warfare, the level of organization was low and discipline poor. Raiding parties often broke up before reaching their destinations, and clashes might result in only a minor injury or two. To the casual observer, the whole phenomenon of Yanomamo warfare could seem unserious—but when they got it right, with both surprise and numbers on their side, attackers could eliminate whole villages, killing or driving off their men, absorbing the women into the victorious village, and killing the younger children.

Was Yanomamo warfare serious? Why else were villages routinely fortified by building the houses in a closed circle opening onto a central courtyard? Why else were buffer zones averaging thirty miles maintained between villages for safety's sake? Why else were the Yanomamo (just like chimps and hunter-gatherers) reluctant to venture too far into the buffer zone when not in large groups, even though it meant that much of their territory was unusable? And despite all these precautions, warfare took just the same cumulative toll that it did among the Murngin: anthropologist Napoleon Chagnon, who studied the Yanomamo in the 1960s, estimated that the death rate due to warfare was 24 percent of the men and 7 percent of the women.[9]

Chagnon's findings have been bitterly disputed by rival anthropologists, who even accused him of instigating the warfare he observed among the Yanomamo, but the dissent seems driven largely by excessive loyalty to Rousseau's hallowed vision of the Noble Savage. In any case, there is another, less controversial group of tribal farmers halfway around the world who displayed exactly the same behaviour.

The people of the New Guinea highlands are not, strictly speaking, horticulturalists, since the isolated mountain valleys where they live filled up with farmers long ago. Groups like the Mae Enga live at a population density of around a hundred people per square kilometre (compared to less than one person per square kilometre for Yanomamo tribal farmers, for hunter-gatherers, and for chimpanzees). As a result, there is little left to hunt: they grow yams and raise pigs for a living. But in most social and cultural respects they belong with the tribal farmers, not with the peasants of mass civilization. Their dispersed clan settlements, the equivalent of the Yanomamo villages, are only a couple of hundred people strong, and each is a separate political entity with sole responsibility for its own survival. The settlements are stable enough for complex alliance systems to form, however, and when prospectors first crossed the mountain barrier and discovered the New Guinea highlanders in the 1930s, warfare among them was constant. Indeed, people had become so tightly squeezed into their confined world that buffer zones between villages were down to something like half a mile, not the thirty miles of the Yanomamo.

Battles among the Mae Enga were often so tentative and indecisive that to the anthropologists who first studied them they seemed almost like play—the serious soldiers of civilized states don't call off a battle just because it starts to rain heavily. Each party to a dispute showed up at a designated "battlefield" with all its allies, sometimes amounting to several hundred male warriors

Dani formal battle, highland New Guinea. The men must dodge the arrows and thrown spears; no shields are used. Keep your eyes open, never turn your back, and you'll probably be all right.

plus women to cheer them on, and they proceeded to form rough lines and run at one another. But it was by no means a battle to the death, and indeed the whole day's "war" was usually called off if somebody was seriously injured or killed. So the initial conclusion of anthropologists who went to study them was that this was a ritual activity, not real war.

Later, anthropologists began working out genealogies and asking how each person died, and it turned out that 25 percent of the men and about 5 percent of the women in Mae Enga groups died from warfare. The highly choreographed "battles" look relatively harmless, but if you fight a dozen such battles a year, you still lose a lot of people in the long run. Moreover, it turned out that these staged confrontations were mainly a way to measure the strength of the opposing alliance. If the rival alliance looks about as numerous as your own, then everybody goes home again and forgets about it—but once in a while one side is severely diminished by defections, and it's clear that the other has a decisive numerical advantage. At that point, it gets serious, and choreographed daytime battles give way to the nighttime or dawn raids aimed at exterminating the entire rival group. Nor was the warfare really indecisive. About 30 percent of independent social groups—villages, in other words—became extinct each century, either because they were massacred to the last man (and the women taken by the victors), or more commonly because attrition wore them down to the point where they lost a battle decisively and the survivors fled to take refuge with distant relatives, abandoning their territory.

It's a pity that more hunter-gatherer and tribal farmer societies did not survive into the present or at least the recent past, so that we had a statistical sample of such societies and could be certain about our conclusions, but the available evidence argues strongly that our ancestors have been fighting wars since long before the rise of civilization. Indeed, the question arises: have we always done it? Does warfare among humans and proto-humans extend all the way back to the 5 or 6 million years ago when our lineage diverged from that of modern chimpanzees?

We cannot answer that question about the deep past from the archaeological evidence we now have, and it is unlikely that we ever will. But some of the fossilized remains of *Homo erectus* found in Europe show signs of violence that might well have been inflicted by human-style weapons 750,000 years ago, particularly depression fractures in skulls that could be the result of blows from clubs. There are also numerous cut marks on *Homo erectus* bones that suggest de-fleshing and cannibalism, which on evidence from later, fully human groups is likely to be associated with killing. Human awe in the presence of death, presumably a consequence of the fact that we, unlike our primate relatives, live with the certain knowledge that we ourselves must die, led us from very early times not only to bury our dead but to surround the killing of human beings with ritual. Complex purification rituals for warriors who kill are a common feature of pre-civilized groups like the Yanomamo, and cannibalism, as a way of assimilating and/or propitiating the victim's spirit, seems to have been equally widespread. Evidence for cannibalism among our proto-human ancestors does not automatically mean they were acting from the same motives and in the same context of constant warfare, but it is suggestive.

By the time of the Neanderthals, the evidence gets stronger. Fossils found on several continents and dating back between forty thousand and one hundred thousand years seem to suggest death from injuries inflicted by human weapons—spear wounds, a stone blade lodged between the ribs—and there has even been a mass burial found in France. Indeed, more than 5 percent of Neanderthal burials show violence of one form or another, and since many violent deaths do not leave marks on the skeletons, that could be taken to mean that warfare bulked as large in the lives of Neanderthals as it did in the lives of relatively recent hunter-gatherers. We can have our suspicions, therefore, but we cannot really know for certain until we reach *Homo sapiens*—and then the evidence is overwhelming.[10]

How did we miss it for so long? How could Quincy Wright, who studied data from 633 primitive cultures for his monumental work *A Study of War*, conclude that "the collectors, lower hunters and lower agriculturalists are the least warlike. The higher hunters and higher agriculturalists are more warlike, while the highest agriculturalists and the [pastoral peoples] are the most warlike of all"?[11]

Rousseau has a role in it, certainly: we want to believe in the Noble Savage because it would mean that human nature is peaceful and war is just an invention of civilization. The contempt of people who know "real" war in the modern style for warriors who would rather run away than stand and die plays a part in it as well. But mainly we just didn't do the arithmetic; we didn't count up the cumulative death toll of the battles and raids.

So why did they do it? It would be arrogant and ignorant to assume that "primitive" people everywhere habitually threw their lives away in purely ritual activities—as if hunter-gatherers didn't love their lives as much as we do, or were too stupid to understand the consequences of their actions. There must be logical reasons why they have waged this sort of warfare across the millennia on every continent. It would help if we knew what the reasons were, because it's clear that modern human beings did not invent warfare. We inherited it.

———

[Yanomamo] villages are situated in the forest among neighbouring villages they do not, and cannot, fully trust. Most of the Yanomamo people regard their perpetual intervillage warfare as dangerous and ultimately reprehensible, and if there were a magic way to end it perfectly and certainly, undoubtedly they would choose that magic. But they know there is no such thing. They know that their neighbours are, or can soon turn into, the bad guys: treacherous and committed enemies. In the absence of full trust, Yanomamo villages deal with one another through trading, inter-marriage, the formal creation of imperfect political treaties—and by inspiring terror through an implacable readiness for revenge.[12]

Just change the names, and that would serve equally well as a description of the relationship of the great powers in the years leading up to the outbreak of World War I in 1914. Remove the details about trading and political alliances and the introspective bits about how the Yanomamo *feel* about their predicament, and it's equally good as a description of the relations between the Kasekela and Kahama bands of chimpanzees in the early 1970s before the latter band was destroyed, and of relations between chimpanzee bands in general. In fact, it's also a reasonably good depiction of the relationship between neighbouring packs of wolves, prides of lions, and packs of hyenas. This is a seriously disturbing thought, but we might as well face it: territory is important, and predators play for keeps.

The "predator" distinction is important: this phenomenon of raiding and waging "war" against other members of the same species occurs only among predators. Moralists will start looking for the mark of Cain, but pragmatists would simply observe that if you are not equipped in some way to kill members of other species, you probably cannot easily kill members of your own either. Thus, for example, only two species among the great apes, humans and chimpanzees, routinely hunt, and they are also the only two primate species that regularly engage in intra-species killing. *Why* these predators (and some others) make a kind of war is a difficult and contentious question, but the *how* is simple: they can do it because both their physiology and their group-living habits make it easy for them to do so.

Lethal claws or teeth are not the sole issue. Tigers, hawks, weasels, and other predators that live alone or in single-family groups rarely experience fights to the death among adults. It is simply too risky: equally well-armed individuals are equally likely to die as a result of the fight, and no advantage that could come from winning the fight is worth a 50 percent risk of death. Dominance struggles among predators that live in groups do not usually lead to deaths, either; this would obviously not be to the advantage of the group, so evolution has generally equipped such species with very recognizable submissive behaviours that enable the loser in a dominance contest to switch off the winner's aggression and escape with his life. But these gestures of submission do not have the same power to defuse aggression in confrontations between members of different groups, packs, bands, prides, etc., nor are such confrontations about any individual's place in the dominance hierarchy (which is internal to each group). So when do killings happen between groups, and why?

The only large animals that regularly and deliberately kill adult members of their own species are predators who live in loosely related groups *of variable size*. When the whole group is together, no rival group would dream of running the risks involved in attacking it. Often, however, they have to spread out in search of food, and individuals get separated from their home group for a time. They then run the risk of encountering a party of several adults from a neighbouring group.

> The lions [of northern Botswana's Chobe National Park] live
> in prides that defend their territory against neighbours. The

prides are parties of female kin. . . . During a zebra hunt one night, two lion prides converge near the boundary and a fight ensues. In the chaos, an old female of the Maome pride becomes isolated by intruders behind the battle lines. We see her surrounded and held captive at first by three hostile lionesses, eventually by as many as seven. And her death is particularly distressing because it looks so deliberate. She starts alert, erect, snarling, though already bleeding from the shoulder. Naturally she can face only one way at a time. She turns repeatedly to check behind her. She is wise to check, for lions can die from a single bite to the spine, but whenever her head is turned, someone swipes at her. The attempt to stop one antagonist merely opens the door for another. Like some hideous children's game, everyone takes a turn striking or biting, while the surrounded victim hopelessly spins and writhes and rears and twists. She is prevented from escaping, constantly herded back to the center. Motsumi, the leader of the Maomi pride, approaches once in an apparent effort to rescue her pride-mate, but she is quickly chased off. And the victim is tormented in this fashion for several hours before she weakens and finally collapses, exhausted, finished. The female killers leave, and then the corpse is eaten by hyenas. With minimal risk to themselves, the pride has relentlessly caused a rival's death.

The killing of a lioness in the 1992
nature film Eternal Enemies[13]

Lions do not normally eat lion: the confrontation was not about food, and the corpse of the old female was left for hyenas to eat. Similar killings occur among hyenas (whose packs, like lion prides, are groups of related females) and among wolves (whose packs are built around male kinship groups). They also occur between bands of chimpanzees and of human hunter-gatherers (both founded on groups of male relatives). In all of these cases, the main enabling factor is that an isolated individual from one group can on occasion be caught and killed without much risk by a gang of individuals from the rival group. However, only the two great ape species carry out deliberate raids and only the humans sometimes go beyond many-on-one ambushes and engage in many-against-many fights. What drives all this behaviour? A lot of the answer comes from Darwin and his modern successors.

> A tribe including many members who, from possessing in a high degree the spirit of patriotism, fidelity, obedience, courage and sympathy, were always ready to aid one another, and to sacrifice themselves for the common good, would be victorious over most other tribes, and this would be natural selection.
>
> *Charles Darwin,* The Descent of Man
> (1871)[4]

Modern evolutionary theorists, building on the foundations laid by Darwin, emphasize that while evolution shapes an entire species, the multitudes of decisions that go into defining the future of a species are all made by individuals. This has an important consequence: these billions of individual decisions are each made with the goal of perpetuating not the species but the genes of the particular individual making the decision. This approach to evolutionary theory, vividly summarized for the general public in Richard Dawkins's *The Selfish Gene*, immediately explains why infanticide, so apparently counter to survival for a species and yet so widespread, can make evolutionary sense. For the individual male lion or gorilla who takes over a dead rival's harem, killing all the former proprietor's offspring is perfectly sensible, since the females he has inherited will then stop wasting energy on raising the dead male's offspring and become fertile again, allowing him to get started on ensuring his own genetic future.

Does the same genetic logic explain why it makes sense for predators belonging to one band, pack, or pride to kill a member of a neighbouring band when they can do so safely and economically? What is in it, with regard to perpetuating their genes, for the individuals in the group that does the killing? They do not directly gain access to better reproductive opportunities, obviously, but the killer's group does gain a potential advantage over the neighbour group by making it one adult member weaker in a world of almost constant scarcity and competition for resources. And since the adults who do the killing are probably related to one another, if their group does well, so do their genes.

It's important to note that this sort of group is just a temporary coalition of individuals, one sex of whom are related (males among primates and wolves, females among lions and hyenas). The group may persist for several generations, grow to the point where it splits into two separate groups (which may rapidly become rivals), break up, or die out, but it has no permanent genetic existence in the sense that a species does. Nevertheless, it is a stable enough social grouping that its collective fortunes will play a large role in deciding the fate of the individual member's genes, so it pays to weaken rival groups by killing their members when the opportunity arises and the risk is low.

Among group-living predators, therefore, there has been selection for individuals who engage in this sort of behaviour, which is much more common than anybody realized even a few decades ago. It is most extreme among the primate predators, chimpanzees and humans, who carry out deliberate raids against rival groups, perhaps because they are also the most intelligent of the predators. But what underlies all these arguments about competition and evolutionary advantage is the assumption that resources will be scarce at least part of the time, and that some groups will lose out when times are bad.

The world was never empty, and food was always limited. The fact that human hunter-gatherers, like other predators, lived at very low population densities compared to the tightly packed farmers of a later time does not mean that there was ample space for all the bands to spread out and avoid competition over resources. Once in a while there would have been a few generations who had that happy experience, just after human beings had moved into previously inaccessible territory for the first time, but it never lasted long. The territory would soon fill up with people living at the maximum density that could be sustained by the available game resources, and then the old reality returned.

This is not to say that our early ancestors waged a kind of war against one another because they knew that population pressure would ultimately bring them into conflict with neighbouring groups (so we might as well start killing them now whenever we get the chance). In fact, even the hunter-gatherer groups that we know something about rarely explained their wars in terms of resources, generally blaming them instead on insults, quarrels over women, and the like. Most of the time, people probably just went on doing what their ancestors had done since long before we were human, driven by an evolutionary logic that had shaped their social structures as well as their emotional reflexes. But as the millennia passed and people's ability to articulate how their world worked grew, at least some of the wars among human groups would gradually have become more considered and more consciously related to current or anticipated conflicts over food supplies.

To account for how these conflicts become chronic wherever humans lived, we do not even need to prove that they have links with the pre-human past or with the behaviour of other predator populations. We merely need to establish three propositions. The first is that human beings have the physical and psychological ability to kill members of their own species. The second is that human populations will always grow up to the carrying capacity of the environment and beyond. The third is that human beings are no better at conserving their environment and preserving their long-term food supply than any other animal. If these three things are true, then prehistory *will* have been filled with conflicts between human groups over resources, and many of those conflicts will have been violent.

Well, we know that human beings can kill each other. The second proposition, that human populations prior to modern times always tended to grow unless checked by some outside force like famine or violence, cannot be absolutely proved one way or the other, but it has the ring of truth. We certainly do not know of any pre-modern human group that succeeded in halting population growth over the long term by voluntary measures, nor do we have many examples of such restraint among other animal species, many of which go through regular cycles of population boom followed by population crash.

The population would have grown much more slowly among prehistoric hunter-gatherers than it did at the peak of the twentieth-century population boom, when the human race tripled from two billion to six billion in only fifty years. Hunter-gatherer mothers, who found it hard to deal with more than one toddler who had to be carried, spaced the birth of their children as much as four years apart by nursing for a very long time: the average woman might have as few as four or five children in a lifetime. Almost all human societies practised infanticide until recently—cross-cultural surveys suggest that an average of about 15 percent of babies (always many more girls than boys) have died in this way in societies ranging from hunter-gatherers to nineteenth-century England[15]—but infanticide among humans is a decision that relates to family rather than group welfare, not a deliberate means of population control. Even allowing for infanticide, child mortality rates were well below 50 percent among hunter-gatherers who were not exposed to the epidemic diseases of mass civilization. So populations usually grew slowly but steadily—and given the magic of compound interest, it would not have taken many generations for hunter-gatherers to reach the carrying capacity of any given territory.[16]

The mere fact that humans and proto-humans did not remain in their original home territories in Africa, but instead spread into every environment on the planet that could support the hunter-gatherer way of life, however inhospitable, is proof in itself that populations grew. Why else would some bands have moved on? Where else would the extra people to fill up the new territories have come from? But if populations grew and resources did not (since hunter-gatherers had no technologies to increase the productivity of their territories), then problems lay ahead. Their numbers would eventually be contained either by starvation or by violence.

There is a powerful mythology that insists that "native peoples," whether hunter-gatherers, horticulturalists, or early farmers, were in tune with nature and the guardians of their environment.

Unfortunately, there is no empirical evidence that early humans were any more conscious of the moral imperative to preserve the environment than the other animals that they shared the environment with. Hunter-gatherers were limited in the ways in which they could damage their environments, but within those constraints they were even more ruthless than modern human beings. The most striking examples are the "New World blitzkriegs"—the mass extinctions of large game animals—that followed the arrival of the first modern humans in all the continents and islands outside the old hunting grounds of proto-human groups in Africa and Eurasia. In the world-island where successive versions of our ancestors and very close relatives evolved and spread over millions of years, from *Homo australopithecus* and *Homo erectus* to Neanderthal and Cro-Magnon, most prey animals had time to adapt to the gradually improving skills of human-like hunters (though there may have been occasional extinctions in which human hunters were a significant factor). But when modern human beings arrived in parts of the world that had never been accessible to earlier human groups, mostly by boat, the carnage was astonishing. The local animals had no knowledge or fear of human hunters, *and the hunters showed no restraint whatever.*

When the first human beings arrived in Australia over fifty thousand years ago, in the Americas about fourteen thousand years ago, in the large Caribbean islands four or five thousand years ago, on the great island of Madagascar about two thousand years ago, in the Hawaiian islands around AD 300, and in New Zealand about AD 700, the result was invariably the same: the extinction of many or most of the larger animal species. It took as little as five centuries in smaller environments like New Zealand, where all the giant moas vanished, and Madagascar, where some two dozen species including giant lemurs, giant tortoises, and a local variety of hippo became extinct. In the Americas, two entire continents, it took over a millennium before the giant ground sloths, mastodons, camels, woolly bison, and even the horses were all hunted out, but that is still just the blink of an eye in the normal lifespan of a species. Surrounded by plenty on the hoof, the hunter-gatherers' numbers grew almost exponentially—the frontier of human occupation was probably moving forward by several miles a year—and the numbers of the more vulnerable animals dwindled toward extinction. Some people try to dismiss the evidence of the blitzkriegs with talk of climate change and disease, but such arguments do not really hold water: the coincidences of human arrival and mass extinctions in so many places admit of no other explanation.[17] Besides, recent ethnological investigations of surviving hunter-gatherer groups like the Hadza of Tanzania show that the same behaviours persist today.

> [T]he Hadza give little attention to conservation of their food resources. When women dig up roots, they do not attempt to replace any portion of the plant to grow again. When they gather berries, heavily laden branches are often torn from the trees and carried back to camp. . . . When a nest of wild bees is found and raided for its honey, no portion of the comb is left to encourage the bees to stay on. . . . In hunting, no attempt is made at systematic cropping. . . . There are no inhibitions about shooting females (even pregnant females) or immature animals. . . . If two animals are killed on the same day, the more distant one may be abandoned.
>
> *An anthropological investigation of*
> *Hadza attitudes to the environment,*
> *1960*[18]

Why would anybody expect anything different? Human beings are animals before they are anything else, and animals are not ecologically conscious. Animals do not live "in harmony with nature"; they live in a Darwinian dialectic with the other species around them, permanently threatened by predation and/or hunger, and many species ride the roller coaster of large population booms followed by big die-offs. They often alter their environments, too, sometimes so drastically that they suffer for it, but often with beneficial results for themselves. Prehistoric human hunters, for example, used their mastery of fire to burn down immense tracts of woodland in order to create the more open terrain preferred by the big grazing animals that were their favourite prey. But it is fantasy to imagine that they actively "managed" their total environment, or understood the full implications of their impacts on it, or indeed gave the matter much thought at all. They probably did worship nature, but that does not mean that they understood it.

Even in newly inhabited areas, therefore, human populations would grow and the available resources, both game and other food, would come under increasing pressure. They would already be engaging in low-level warfare of the traditional sort with their neighbours, making sporadic raids and restricting their hunting to the central parts of their territory for safety. The steady toll from warfare plus a fair amount of infanticide might keep their populations sufficiently in check to avoid serious hunger so long as times remained good. But even a brief interruption in normal food supply due to changing weather patterns, alterations in animal migration routes, or other unpredictable factors would create an instant crisis, since most of the foods people eat cannot be stored. In a matter of weeks or months everybody is hungry all the time, and since human beings are gifted with foresight, they *know* what lies ahead for most of the group if this goes on. They also know that other groups in the vicinity are facing the same problems. It is probably at this point that warfare became for the first time a fully rational (and utterly ruthless) activity. Almost everybody will fight rather than watch their children starve.

How will fighting help? Those universal no-man's lands between the groups will account for over half the available territory, and that is exactly where the surviving game will congregate in a heavily hunted region. The only safe way to exploit that game is to eliminate or drive away the band on the far side of the buffer zone, and that is the course that must have been chosen by tens of thousands of desperate bands over the past million years. If they were competent and lucky, it ended with one surprise attack, a massacre, and total victory. If not, it became a long attritional struggle, perhaps with both sides drawing allies into the conflict— and the fact that this may not happen often is less important than the fact that it happens repeatedly, and that one day your neighbours might do the same thing to you. Soon the suspicion, the alliance-making, and the warlike demonstrations are a routine part of life, and serious warfare is a permanent possibility.

———

Primatologists have no reluctance about explaining the warlike behaviour of chimpanzees in terms of evolutionary advantage— that is, that members of a troop that is good at aggression will probably have better resources for raising their young and passing on their genes—even though nobody imagines that chimpanzees are making conscious calculations of this subtlety in their heads. Neither are they puzzled when they encounter chimpanzee bands that are attacking their neighbours at a time when resources are not particularly scarce: whether this behaviour is just a deeply entrenched cultural pattern or partly a genetically driven one, it's certainly not something that chimps would be able to turn on and off like a tap.

Traditional anthropologists, by contrast, were hugely reluctant to accept that prehistoric human groups might have had a deeply entrenched cultural tradition of waging war with neighbouring bands that rewarded groups who were good at it with a better prospect of surviving hard times and perpetuating their genes. Captivated by the notion of the Noble Savage, they insisted that the people they were able to study directly, while they did wage something that looked like war against one another, were actually engaging in a ritual activity—part art form, part healthy outdoor exercise for underemployed hunters—that had nothing to do with achieving economic or political aims. "The idea of conquest never arose in aboriginal North America, and this made it possible for almost all these Indian tribes to do a very extreme thing: to separate war from the state," wrote anthropologist Ruth Benedict. " . . . Any man who could attract a following led a war party when and where he could, and in some tribes he was in complete control for the duration of the expedition. But this lasted only until the return of the war party. The state . . . had no conceivable interest in these ventures, which were only highly desirable demonstrations of rugged individualism."[19]

The "state" did not really exist in most American Indian tribes, but the point of emphasizing the total separation of warfare and the state was to prove that whatever the Indians were doing, it was not the terrible phenomenon that we know as war. Two other early anthropologists, Ernest Wallace and E. Adamson Hoebel, were making essentially the same point by explaining that the highest honour a warrior could gain among the Indians of the Great Plains was not to kill the enemy but to "count coup"—to approach the enemy without weapons and touch him with a stick or his hand. The purpose of inter-tribal warfare, in other words, was to give warriors an opportunity to demonstrate their courage. Thus the most famous and respected Comanche warrior of his time was a man who acquired a blanket made by the Utes, his tribal enemies, and used it to walk in among them unarmed.

> After dark, he drew his blanket over his head and sauntered into the Ute encampment. From within one of the lodges he heard the sound of a hand game in progress. Protected by his disguise, he walked right through the door to join the spectators. Nobody paid any attention to him. Casually and slowly moving about he touched one after another all the Utes in the lodge. When he had touched them all, he strolled out and rejoined his friend. He had counted coup on twenty enemies at once. It was a great deed.[20]

Well, of course. Cultures where warrior values dominate are bound to include various customs and institutions that appeal to the warrior mentality, from counting coup to jousting to duelling, even though these activities are not strictly functional with respect to winning a war. That does not mean that the wars these cultures wage are meaningless rituals. The battles they fight may be badly organized and indecisive by the standards of more disciplined cultures, and the warriors may be more inclined (or just freer) to run away when things look bad in order to fight another day. But people die in significant numbers, and in the end real things get decided: some bands or tribes expand and prosper, while others shrink or disappear.

———

The fact that the bands and tribes caught up in conflict generally explain their wars by recounting insults exchanged, women stolen, or ancestral enmity does not mean that the wars lack deeper and more serious causes. At one level, World War I was just caused by Gavrilo Princip assassinating Archduke Franz Ferdinand, but we all know that there was also another level of causation. There almost always is.

The kind of war that was waged by our early ancestors and by our more distant evolutionary cousins seems almost childlike to the modern mind. Either they didn't understand what their wars were really about (foolish of them), or they actually were just fighting over stolen women and/or some insult to the group's honour, as they generally said they were (even sillier). Nor did they ever fight "properly," veering between formal battles in which everybody was careful not to get too close to the enemy, raids in which a group of hunters ambush and murder a single opponent, and occasional sneak attacks, often on sleeping people, that ended in massacre. There was little strategy, less discipline, and not even much of the kind of courage that we expect in the soldiers of civilization. To generations of military historians raised on the doctrines of Clausewitz, this cannot be "true" war.

On the other hand, there are those appalling statistics: 24 percent of Yanomamo males and 7 percent of females killed in war—taking the two sexes together, a fatal casualty rate of 15 percent per generation. Among the Murngin of Australia, 25 percent of men killed in battle. Twenty-five percent of men and 5 percent of women killed in warfare among New Guinea highlanders, and one-third of all existing independent groups destroyed by war each century. (Not to mention an estimated 30 percent fatal casualty rate from warfare among male chimpanzees.) If this is not "true" war, it is nevertheless a very bad kind of war.

Besides, the differences between us and our ancestors are smaller than they seem. The primitives may have been unclear on the underlying causes of the wars they fought, but the spectacular diversity of opinion among Americans about their own government's motives in invading Iraq in 2003 suggests that this is not solely a problem of the ancients. Standing your ground under fire until you are killed is certainly a modern behaviour, but not necessarily a clever one. And on the fundamental issue of casualties, prehistoric warriors leave the soldiers of civilization standing: few modern societies have ever sustained a 15 percent death rate from war in a single generation, let alone in every generation.

For a country the size of the United States today, 15 percent fatal casualties per generation would work out at about a million deaths from war per year, every year, forever. In fact, the United States has not lost a million people killed in war in its entire independent existence, now more than two and a quarter centuries. Even countries that have borne the brunt of heavy bombing and major land warfare on their own territory in recent wars rarely approach this level of losses—although most of the countries of central and eastern Europe from Germany to Russia came close during World War II—and *no* modern society has experienced this level of violent deaths over an extended period of time. The lives of our prehistoric ancestors were utterly immersed in war—intermittent, low-level war for the most part, but the deaths were real enough—and fear would have been their constant companion.

We have long been taught to believe that the rise of civilization led to an intensification of warfare (nasty moderns vs. noble savages), but the evidence actually suggests the opposite: that the creation of mass societies sharply reduced the casualty rate from war. Civilized societies fight with armies, which include a far smaller proportion of the adult male population than the all-in scrum of the warrior band, and for most of history those armies fought only one or two major battles a year. Casualties were high on the actual day of battle, but much lower than those suffered by hunter-gatherers in the long run. In fact, there have not been many generations of human beings since the rise of civilization in which the direct loss of life from war has exceeded 2 or 3 percent of the population. (The principal pre-twentieth century exceptions were during the recurrent nomad invasions.)

There is also a less obvious, almost mechanistic explanation for the steep fall in the death toll from war. Tiny hunter-gatherer

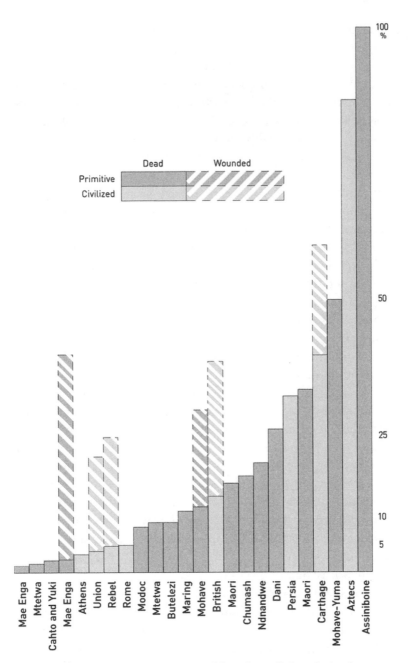

Casualties (percentage killed and wounded) in various tribal, ancient and modern battles.

societies of thirty or forty people—a couple of hundred at most, in the case of horticulturalists—had absolutely no strategic depth: everybody lived on the front line, so to speak. In a settled agricultural society of a million people, by contrast, as few as 5 percent of the population would live within a day's walk of borders with potentially hostile neighbours. Such societies simply could not get at each other as a totality; at least at the beginning of a war, they could fight only at the edges of their territories, with armies. The only recent conflicts in which a huge casualty toll occurred without much resort to heavy weapons have been in countries where rival populations were intertwined in ways that left everybody close to a potential enemy: for example, Yugoslavia's civil war during World War II (which killed an estimated two million people although there was not a single major battle fought on Yugoslav soil), or the Rwanda genocide of 1994 (in which 10 percent of the population was murdered by their neighbours in only a few months). Most of the time, bigger countries with more homogeneous cultures were a lot safer.

Until recently. Over the past century, we have seen industrial countries develop the ability to mobilize their vast resources and deliver armies of millions to the battle fronts and then develop the technologies to deliver the battle to the enemy's "home front" from the skies. Suddenly, advanced societies are back in the position of their earliest ancestors, with every part of their population equally exposed to the possibility of an instant and horrible death in war. After ten thousand years we have come full circle, and everybody is once again in somebody else's sights all the time. Even the very largest countries must live with the constant possibility of extermination. It's a tiny risk in any one year, just as it was for hunter-gatherer bands, but cumulatively it is serious and deeply worrisome.

So are we doomed, then? Not necessarily. We *have* learned and changed during the thousands of years we have spent in the mass societies, and we are not trapped in the Malthusian dilemma of the hunter-gatherers: we do not actually have to fight to survive. War clearly has deep roots in our human lineage, but that no more condemns us to perpetual war than a long tradition of infanticide condemns us to a future of baby-killing. So much of our mental-ity and so many of our institutions are built on the assumption that war is a constant that it's very hard to break out of the old pattern, but self-interest and perhaps even empathy push us away from war and toward more cooperative behaviour. The little tribes of high-land New Guinea went on fighting their vicious little wars in the early 1940s even as the larger war raged around them, recounts Peter Richter, an expert in cultural evolution at the University of California at Davis, "but when, after World War II, the Australian police patrols went around and told people they couldn't fight any more, the New Guineans thought that was wonderful. They were glad to have an excuse."[21]

4

The Rise of Battle

Man, supposing you and I, escaping this battle, would be able to live on forever, ageless, immortal, so neither would I myself go on fighting in the foremost nor would I urge you into the fighting where men win glory. But now, seeing that the spirits of death stand close around us in their thousands, no man can turn aside or escape them, let us go on and win glory for ourselves, or yield it to others.

Sarpedon of the Lykians, ca. 1200 BC[1]

Come on, you sons of bitches! Do you want to live forever?

Gunnery Sergeant Dan Daly, USMC, Belleau Wood, 6 June 1918

THE ILLUSION THAT CIVILIZED WAR IS MORE DREADFUL THAN "primitive" war may be statistically wrong, but it is enormously powerful because the centrepiece of civilized war is battle, a huge event that overwhelms both the senses and the emotions. It cannot be proved, but it is a safe assumption that the first time five thousand male human beings were ever gathered together in one place, they belonged to armies that had come together for a battle—and it is an equally safe bet that the first truly large-scale slaughter of people in human history happened soon afterwards.

It probably happened between five and six thousand years ago, and although an army from that time would have looked to our eyes like an undisciplined rabble, it was a miracle of discipline and coordination by all earlier standards of human behaviour. Its soldiers carried weapons no different from those that hunters and warriors had been using on animals and each other for thousands of years previously—spears, knives, axes, bows and arrows—but they actually stood and fought, at least for a few minutes. It was a truly new thing in the world: a multitude of men obeying a single commander and killing his enemies to achieve his goals.

It was, in fact, the most awesome concentration of power that the world had ever seen, and nothing except another army could hope to resist it.

By the time battles had grown into their full classic form between three and four thousand years ago, they were an extraordinary combination of mechanical killing and mass psychodrama far removed from the tentative battles of pre-civilized warfare. The soldiers were pressed forward by the ranks behind them against the anonymous strangers in that part of the enemy line facing them, and though in the end it was pairs of individuals who thrust at each other with spears for a moment before one went down, there was nothing personal in the exchange. "Their shields locked, they pushed, fought, killed and died. There was no shouting, and yet not silence either, but rather such a noise as might be made by the angry clash of armed men."

The result of such a merciless struggle in a confined space was killing on an unprecedented scale. Hundreds or thousands of men would die in half an hour, in an area no bigger than a couple of football fields.

> The battle over, one could see on the site of the struggle the ground covered with blood, friend and foe lying dead on one another, shields broken, spears shattered and unsheathed swords, some on the ground, some fixed in corpses, some still held in the hands of the dead. It was now getting late, so they dragged the enemy corpses inside their lines, had a meal, and went to rest.[2]

And the question we rarely ask, because our history is replete with such scenes, is: how could men do this? After all, in the hunter-gatherer cultures we all come from, they could not have done it. Being a warrior and taking part in a carefully limited battle with a small but invigorating element of risk is one thing; the mechanistic and impersonal mass slaughter of civilized warfare is quite another, and any traditional warrior would do the sensible thing and leave instantly. Yet men of three thousand years ago or of today will stay at such scenes of horror even in the knowledge that they will probably die within the next few minutes. The invention of armies required more than just working out ways of drilling large numbers of people to act together, although that was certainly part of the formula. A formation of drilled men has a different psychology—a controlled form of mob psychology—that tends to overpower the personal identity and fears of the individuals who make it up.

Of course, by the time it has become clear to an individual soldier seeing civilized war for the first time that a battle is no place for a sane man to be, there is often physically no way to leave—and in all armies the penalty for trying to leave is death at the hands of your own side. But even experienced soldiers who know what to expect submit themselves to the ordeal of battle again and again, more or less willingly, because to do otherwise is to disgrace themselves in front of the people whose respect is the foundation of their own self-respect: their fellow soldiers. Men will kill and die rather than lose face, but the face that is being saved, the image that is being preserved, is that of the tribal warrior of the pre-civilized past, who fought for personal glory and stood a very good chance of surviving the fight.

> You're dealing here with complicated psychological states. No man in battle is really sane. The mindset of the soldier on the battlefield is a highly disturbed mind, and this is an epidemic of insanity which affects everybody there—and those not afflicted by it die very quickly.
> *William Manchester,*
> *World War II veteran*

Aggression is certainly part of our genetic makeup, and necessarily so, but the normal human being's quota of aggression will not even cause him to kill acquaintances, let alone wage war against strangers from a different country. We live among millions of people who have killed fellow human beings with pitiless efficiency—machine-gunning them, using flame-throwers on them, dropping high explosive bombs on them from twenty thousand feet up—yet we do not fear these people. The overwhelming majority of those who have killed, now or at any time in the past five thousand years, have done so as soldiers in war, and we recognize that that has practically nothing to do with the kind of personal aggressiveness that would endanger us as their fellow citizens.

So how were these people persuaded to submit themselves more or less voluntarily to an institution that will compel them to kill and perhaps to die? Patriotism, religion, the belief that you are defending your home and family are powerful reasons for men to fight, but mercenary troops with none of those motives to sustain them have often fought to the death too. The most important factor that makes it possible for men to fight in the terrible battles of civilized states is that all armies everywhere have always exploited the ancient and ingrained warrior ethic that is the cultural heritage of every young human male.

It is not that soldiers delude themselves about the possibility of dying in battle or about the terrible things that weapons do to living flesh; on the contrary, they are all too aware of it. Even the earliest surviving accounts of battle dwell in almost obsessive anatomical detail on how death comes to soldiers: "Ideomeneus stabbed Erymas in the mouth with the pitiless bronze, so that the brazen spear smashed its way clean through below the brain in an upward stroke, and the white bones splintered, and the teeth were shaken out with the stroke and both eyes filled up with blood, and gaping he blew a spray of blood through the nostrils and through his mouth, and death in a dark mist closed over him."[3]

Soldiers know about violent death in all its forms, and though they have their preferences among the forms—there was, for example, an irrational but understandable preference in the trenches of World War I for death by bullets rather than by artillery fire, because a close shell explosion would distort and rend the victim's body into scarcely human fragments—nevertheless they accept the chance of death. But what they require in return is the assurance (or the illusion) that their death will not be wasted or unnoticed or meaningless. Yet most soldiers' deaths in civilized warfare are all of those things. The tribe will not mourn the fallen warrior's death or sing songs about his prowess, and the purposes of the war have little to do with his personal life, even in the unlikely event that his death affects its outcome. So to make the bleak realities of war more acceptable to the regimented soldiers of civilization there is a universal conspiracy to pretend that they still dwell in a moral and psychological landscape of a more bearably human scale: that of the distant warrior past.

From the earliest recorded history, the language that civilized armies consistently use to describe their slaughterhouse battles employs the old vocabulary of the primitive warrior. Soldiers are heroes doing deeds of valour, not number fifty-four in the second rank of the fifth cohort. Battles are decided by such deeds of valour, not by numbers or better weapons or sheer chance. Every man counts. And of course the victims of these falsehoods generally collaborate in the deceit, even if they are veterans who have seen battle before, because to question them would be to undermine the value of their own courage and professionalism. But it is important to recognize that there is a trick being played here: it must have taken much massaging and manipulation of the old warrior values to reshape them into the far sterner disciplines required on a civilized battlefield. That may explain why it took some thousands of years after the rise of the very first agricultural societies before battles evolved into the savagely efficient affairs of high classical times.

———

As soon as the people heard the sound of the trumpets, they raised a great shout, and the wall [of Jericho] fell down flat; so the people charged straight ahead into the city and captured it. Then they devoted to destruction by the edge of the sword all in the city, both men and women, young and old, oxen, sheep and donkeys.[4]

The ruthless extermination of the entire population, even down to babies and animals, of the city of Jericho after the Israelites captured it was presumably an act of calculated frightfulness meant to ease the conquest of the "promised land" by terrifying the rest of the original inhabitants into submission or flight. Joshua's policy was extreme even for the twelfth century BC, when sieges and massacres had become commonplace, but it took a long time for human beings whose heritage was low-level attritional warfare to work their way up to the point where they had an army capable of taking a walled town and slaughtering ten or twenty thousand people in a single day. In fact, counting from the earliest beginnings of agriculture, it probably took around five thousand years—but right at the start there was a harbinger of all that was to come. Ironically, it was at the very same place: Jericho.

Archaeologists were astonished when they discovered in the 1950s that Jericho had become the first walled town in the world over ten thousand years ago, between 8500 and 8000 BC. Nobody had realized that organized war went back that far, but there it was: a fully fortified town dating from the very beginning of settled agricultural life in the Middle East. The town wall was at least twelve feet high and six feet thick, with a rock-cut moat ten feet deep and thirty feet wide at its base, and it encircled an area of ten acres. Estimates of the population who lived behind it range from two thousand to thirty-five hundred. Including the twenty-five-foot-high tower inside the walls that probably served as a final refuge or keep, the total weight of the fortifications was around thirteen thousand tons of limestone, all of which had to be moved by hand. Clearly, the people of Jericho ten thousand years ago had something that other people wanted.

Jericho's walls appeared at the end of a period of some two thousand years when local "Natufian" hunter-gatherers in the Fertile Crescent, while continuing to hunt wild game, had begun to devote more and more of their time to harvesting wild plants. Their technology included grinding stones, mortars and pestles, and small sharp flakes of stone that were used as blades on sickles. Their semi-permanent settlements, which included grain-storage pits, were substantial enough to leave a trace in the archaeological record: indeed, their average size was three times bigger than those of previous cultures in the region, suggesting a rapid growth in population. The town of Jericho was much bigger than any of the other settlements, perhaps simply because it was an extraordinarily fertile location. Although it is six hundred feet below sea level in the arid valley of the river Jordan, it is located at the point where a very rich aquifer pours water down over a fan-like series of natural terraces, so its crop-growing potential was enormous and its reserves of stored food may have been huge by contemporary standards. There have been suggestions that the town also grew wealthy by trading in asphalt, sulphur, and salt from the nearby Dead Sea, but in a world without money or any easy means of transporting bulk goods that was unlikely to be the main attraction.[5]

The ideal climatic conditions that encouraged this first foray into the new world of agriculture in the Fertile Crescent did not last, however. Toward the end of the Natufian period, around 8500 BC, a shift to much drier climatic conditions caused the number of settlements to shrink dramatically. This crisis in the food supply may have been what triggered the shift by the surviving Natufians from merely reaping wild grains to deliberately sowing them: the start of true agriculture. It may also have led to one or more attempts by hungry tribes to seize control of the Jericho aquifer, one of the few reliable agricultural sites amid general desiccation. That would explain the walls.

We do not know if these ten-thousand-year-old walls were ever attacked, but they would have done the job if they were. There were not yet any real armies in the world when the citizens of Jericho built their town's defences, and it's unlikely that anybody had even thought in terms of fixed defences before, but once the need became clear, so did the solution. Human beings are rarely more than six feet tall and cannot normally jump higher than about three feet, so a twelve-foot wall will thwart attackers without ladders. The moat would further complicate their task. And just in case the walls were taken, there was a keep to which important people could retreat in the hope of outlasting the attackers' patience.

Jericho's walls are an early example of how large a role physics and common sense play in military affairs, and how limited the options in warfare are. There are not ten possible ways to fortify a town; the basic design used at Jericho was still standard less than one thousand years ago.

In the end, however, the first walls around Jericho were just a flash in the pan, a local response to a transient crisis. They demonstrate that any human community can work out the rules of organized warfare with no prior knowledge, but that crisis passed and there is no evidence of other city walls in the Fertile Crescent for another three thousand years. Real war crept up on us quite slowly. Meanwhile, two larger questions demand an answer: why did agriculture start around ten thousand years ago, and why is it in the Middle East, rather than in northern China, the valley of

Mexico, or western Europe, that civilized warfare first assumes its characteristic forms?

> [Why did] the transition to food production in the Fertile Crescent [begin] around 8500 B.C., not around 18,500 or 28,500 B.C.? At the latter two dates hunting-gathering was still much more rewarding than incipient food production, because wild mammals were still abundant; wild cereals were not yet abundant; people had not yet developed the inventions necessary for collecting, processing and storing cereals efficiently; and human population densities were not yet high enough for a large premium to be placed on extracting more calories per acre.[6]

The last couple of decades have seen an unprecedented subtlety and sophistication transform the explanations for why and how civilization arose. It is no longer assumed that hunter-gatherers were eager to settle down and become farmers, or even that they deliberately domesticated plants at some point—at least, no more than the plants domesticated them. The implicit racism in the traditional Eurocentric view of history has been rightly condemned and yet any serious history of human civilization, including any history of war, still has to concentrate on the doings of the Middle Eastern dawn civilizations and their Mediterranean, European, and "Western" heirs. There is a single dominant military tradition on this planet. It is overwhelmingly Western in technology and in historical origins and cultural style, and there are rational, non-racist reasons why that should be so.

If an interstellar guidebook publisher sent a writer to prepare an Earth edition, one of the first things he, she, or it would notice is the fact that about two-thirds of human beings, the dominant land species, follow religions that arose in the Middle East. Moses, Jesus, and Mohammed were all born within a long day's drive of one another. The once-Fertile Crescent is now a denuded, ravaged region that shows all too clearly what ten thousand years of farmers and goats can do to even the most bountiful environment, but it retains a central importance for anyone interested in understanding why things are as they are. Perhaps the best place to start is with Jared Diamond's remarkably persuasive explanation for why agriculture, pastoralism, and civilization itself all first arose in the Middle East.

Diamond is a professor of physiology at the UCLA School of Medicine whose influential book, *Guns, Germs and Steel*, is in part an attempt to answer exactly those questions. He begins with the premise that no sane hunter-gatherer would voluntarily trade his life of freedom, equality, and ample animal protein for the cramped, unhealthy existence of a peasant farmer in the early civilizations. By ten thousand years ago, however, human population densities were pushing up against the sustainable limits for hunter-gatherers even in the richest environments, and in one region in particular there was a readily available alternative. The region was the Fertile Crescent, and the alternative was agriculture.

There are some two hundred thousand plant species that human beings might consider for domestication if they were thinking of an agricultural future, Diamond points out, but the vast majority are inappropriate because they put most of their energy into creating inedible woody trunks or fibrous stems. The most promising plants for domestication are annuals—those that die each year in the dry season, and so put most of their energy into generating seeds that will survive until the next wet season—because it is the seeds that are edible. Annuals flourish in Mediterranean climates, where a mild, wet winter is followed by a hot, dry summer, and of the five regions in the world with Mediterranean climates, southwestern Eurasia (also known as the Fertile Crescent) is the biggest and most diverse.

The Fertile Crescent's extraordinary range of altitudes, from far below sea level to high mountains, gives it a huge range of microclimates where different plants flourish, or where the same plants ripen at different times. It is as big in area as the other four "Mediterranean" regions combined (southwestern Australia, southwestern South Africa, central Chile, and southern California). It also has greater climatic variation from season to season and year to year than any of the other Mediterranean zones, which further increases the diversity of its annual plants. As a result, according to geographer Mark Blumler's studies of wild grass distributions, thirty-two out of the fifty-six species with the largest seeds (ten times heavier than the median grass seed) are found in the Fertile Crescent. Only six are found in East Asia, only four in sub-Saharan Africa, only four in North America, and only two in South America.[7] If you are planning to found a mass civilization based mainly on eating cultivated grains, then the Middle East would be the right place to start.

Nobody ever had such a plan, of course. What actually happened was a good deal subtler. Hunter-gatherers would learn to show up when large stands of particularly big-seeded annual grasses like barley and emmer wheat were ripe and about to shed their seeds. By selectively harvesting those plants with the biggest seeds and scattering some of the seeds in the process, they would effectively turn themselves into a new dispersal agent for the plants' seeds. It was far more efficient than the wind, and in best Darwinian fashion the plant species in question would respond to this new opportunity by producing bigger seeds to attract this new agent.

We talk about people domesticating plants, but the reality is that plants also domesticated people, for hunter-gatherers began to spend more of their time in one place, harvesting the new grain, replanting for next year, and living off the stored proceeds. Why move if you don't have to? They continued to hunt, of course, but as time passed the local game got scarcer, and meanwhile their own population was growing thanks to the steady supply of plant food. Almost imperceptibly, a time arrived when they were bound to the plants for their very survival: they had been domesticated. It did them little good as individuals. They worked much longer hours than hunter-gatherers, their stature and their health were significantly worse because of their relatively limited diet, and they therefore tended to die a good deal younger—but their population soared because the same piece of ground, intensively cultivated, will support a hundred times as many farmers as it will hunter-gatherers. The farmers always win in the end because there are just so many of them.

It's not just big-seeded grains that lured people in the Fertile Crescent into what historian Robert L. O'Connell calls the "plant trap." Wheat and barley were the carbohydrate base for the new civilized diet, but the wheats also contained 8 to 14 percent protein, and easily domesticated pulses like lentils, peas, and chickpeas that contained 20 to 25 percent protein were also available to Middle Eastern proto-farmers, as was flax for fibre and oil. Nobody would have abandoned the free and easy hunter-gatherer life for dependence on just one or two of these plants, but in the Fertile Crescent there was a whole package of easily domesticated crops available to tempt people into the new way of life. And for reasons that still remain relatively obscure, the same was true for large animals that could be domesticated.

Of the world's five most important domesticated mammals, the wild ancestors of four—sheep, goats, pigs, and cattle—lived in the Middle East, and they were all domesticated quite early: the first three by 8000 BC, and cattle by 6000 BC. Pigs may have been independently domesticated in China, genetic studies show that Indian cattle were separately domesticated from a different wild strain than the Middle Eastern aurochs, and the horse was domesticated only about 4000 BC in what is now the Ukraine, but nowhere except the Fertile Crescent had such a rich suite of domesticable animals to start with. Indeed, nowhere except Eurasia and its North African annex had *any* of the Major Five. There were bighorn sheep in North America, but unlike their Eurasian cousins they were impossible to domesticate because of their social habits. There were zebras in Africa, but their extremely bad tempers meant that they could never be domesticated as horses were. Even counting relatively minor domesticated species like yaks, camels, and reindeer, thirteen of the fourteen large mammals domesticated in ancient times came from ancestral stock that inhabited Eurasia.[8]

It is hard to account for the extraordinary advantages that Eurasia enjoyed in the crucial matter of domesticable animals. The mass extinctions of large game animals that occurred shortly after human hunters first arrived in the Americas and Australia may partially explain the scarcity of good candidates for domestication there, but it's not obvious why none of the big African fauna south of the tsetse-fly belt were suitable candidates either. The fact remains that Africa, Australia, and the Americas were far poorer than Eurasia in both animal and plant species that could be easily and profitably domesticated, and that the speed with which civilizations emerged and developed on these other continents was therefore far slower than in Eurasia. To load the dice further in favour of Eurasia, the other continents are oriented on a north-south axis, which means that they contain bands of radically different climate that act as barriers to the rapid diffusion of domesticated plants and animals. Eurasia, by contrast, has an east-west orientation, allowing newly domesticated species of plants and animals to spread easily from one end of the super-continent to the other without ever changing latitude or encountering a radically different climate.[9] The game was fixed in Eurasia's favour from the start, and the Fertile Crescent in particular got a head start on civilization that it and its daughter cultures never really lost.

This was the crucible in which the old primate and hunter-gatherer custom of sporadic low-level ambushes and raids on neighbouring groups was gradually transformed into the civilized institution of "real war." And we know almost nothing about it. During the five thousand years between Jericho's first wall and the appearance of the first phalanxes in Sumeria, conscious calculations about strategy, tactics, and political goals would gradually have shifted what was happening from mere customary behaviour to deliberate policy, and warrior bands would have started to look more and more like mini-armies. Unfortunately, writing had not yet been invented, so the record is almost blank.

———

The next large proto-urban settlement we know about, two thousand years after the walled town of Jericho and at least twice as big, is Çatal Hüyük, a community of around a thousand houses and five to six thousand people that thrived in what is now southern Turkey between about 6250 and 5400 BC. The inhabitants had pottery, jewellery, and all sorts of religious or cult objects. (This was the period when the diffuse animism of hunter-gatherers and tribal farmers started turning into religious cults and shamans started turning into priests, although at this point it was still female fertility figures, not male sky-gods, who dominated the emerging supernatural landscape of the Fertile Crescent.) There may have been a dozen other centres like Çatal Hüyük scattered around the region at the same time, but this is the only one that has been found, and it reflects a relatively relaxed approach to the danger of attack. The houses are built in such a way that they present a continuous outside wall to the world, rather like a Yanomamo village but on a far larger scale. There are, however, no fortifications that would withstand a serious army even for a day.

The pressure on scarce fertile land that presumably caused the walling of Jericho two thousand years before seems to have been low in this period. The full array of food crops and domesticated animals was now available to the agricultural pioneers of Çatal Hüyük, among the first to abandon the hunting-gathering way of life and commit themselves wholly to farming. The climate was benevolent, and the world was full of empty land that was being scandalously under-utilized by primitive hunter-gatherers. It has been estimated that the frontier of farming was advancing both eastward and westward from its Middle Eastern point of origin at as much as a mile per year in this era, displacing or destroying the hunter-gatherer cultures that had previously occupied the land. Farming would reach both Britain and the highlands of north and northwest China by 4000 BC. But there was still plenty of fertile potential farmland left in the Middle East, so nobody was desperate for land.

There were plenty of weapons in Çatal Hüyük—mainly flint knives and spearheads, baked clay sling balls, and stone maces— and some of the weapons were clearly intended for killing people. (There is not much demand for maces in hunting.) The people of Çatal Hüyük would have been seen as incredibly wealthy by any surviving hunter-gatherer groups in the vicinity—they had more physical possessions than any human beings had ever had before, and they also had stored food and flocks of domesticated animals. It would be very surprising if they didn't have to deal with thieves and even organized raids, and that is what the defences of Çatal Hüyük, such as they were, seem designed to deal with: individual robbers and opportunistic bands of raiders, not armies.

Çatal Hüyük may also have been involved in occasional clashes with other farming communities, if there were any within reach, and it's possible that there were also inter-clan struggles within Çatal Hüyük. We have no way of knowing how big or frequent clashes with other towns might have been, but at worst they were probably similar to the "battles" fought between rival groups of tribal farmers in the New Guinea highlands. The groups may have been bigger and better coordinated than in New Guinea (and of course massacre was always possible if one side turned out to be decisively stronger than the other), but at this stage the confrontations would probably still have been seriously limited by ritual and custom. It is almost certainly still too early to talk about real armies.

It may not be too early to talk of slavery, however, for settled farming societies have a use for extra labour, and a successful raid can yield captives. Probably only female ones would be spared at first, since they are less dangerous than males, especially once they have been raped and have given birth to children who are hostages for their good behaviour. At first, therefore, slavery is just a variant of the old chimpanzee and human habit of killing the males of a rival band and appropriating the females—but now the captive women never attain the status of full members of the group. They and their children, female and male, will be slaves for good. By the time we have written records that tell us about the social structure of the new civilized societies, around the start of the third millennium BC, slavery is already a well-established institution.

Drawing on analogies with other human communities that reach this size, we can also conclude that the old egalitarianism of the hunter-gatherer band was being severely eroded in these bigger settlements. The town, including the surrounding farming communities that were attached to it, was of a size to fit the chiefdom model, where a "big man" depending on clan ties and on naked force sets himself up as boss, others are reduced to dumb obedience, and social inequalities start to multiply. (Çatal Hüyük burials show sharp variations in the material wealth of the dead, unlike hunter-gatherer burials.) The status of women has not yet collapsed to the nadir it reached in the early mass civilizations, and it's still a long time before the era when god-kings bestride the human world, but the old freedoms and equality are going fast. There is a boss, he's not interested in your opinion, and it's getting very hard to avail yourself of the old solution of moving on to another group if you have a run-in with him.[10]

Although there is no evidence for it in the archaeological record, there was probably something else going on at Çatal Hüyük in the sixth millennium BC as well: the gradual separation and alienation of a significant portion of the animal herders from the rest of the community. The initial job of domesticating large animals was doubtless done by people who were committed to the new agricultural lifestyle, and the settled farming communities will always continue to keep "farm animals," but the mere act of domesticating those animals has created the possibility of an entirely new way of life: pastoralism. People could conceivably live neither by hunting nor by farming, but by herding these newly domesticated animals and using their meat, hide, wool, milk, and blood to support an entirely independent lifestyle.

Why would they want to leave? Because the new agricultural lifestyle, even in this early and relatively non-toxic version, was fundamentally at odds with the values and traditions of free men and women. Our evolutionary heritage as human beings may include war and massacre, but it also includes the presumption of equality between adults of the same sex, and even between the sexes; freedom of speech; and the right to leave. Now our ancestors were trapped in societies that were becoming steadily more arbitrary and authoritarian, and their future was thousands of years of tyranny and outright slavery. Most people had to accept the new system, but the people who looked after the animals had a choice. They lived their lives on the fringes of the farming community anyway, since it was important to keep the animals from eating or trampling the crops everybody depended on, and they would regularly disappear off into the uplands in spring to find the animals fresh pasture. At some point, it would have occurred to the herders that they didn't need to come back.

Pastoralism is as radical a departure from the traditional hunter-gatherer lifestyle as farming. Pastoralists, or nomads, as they are often called, are just as much involved in the conscious production of food as farmers; they just have "fields on the hoof." It is a harsh way of life, without a roof over your head or much in the way of material possessions, but it would have been attractive to those who were unwilling to submit to what was happening in the settled communities: hierarchy, subordination, and a general impoverishment that was hardly compensated for by the fact that there were now more people. (Between 10,000 and 3,000 BC, the human population of the world grew from the steady-state five or ten million of the hunter-gatherer past to about a hundred million, with almost all of the increase occurring in Eurasia.)

Faced with the end of the hunter-gatherer way of life, the pastoralists chose the alternative that still left them some freedom and some dignity. It meant material poverty and endless hardship, but they willingly paid the price and despised those who would not pay it. At various points between the sixth and the third millennia BC, whole pastoral societies were breaking away from the nascent farming communities throughout the Middle East. They would never remotely rival the farming societies in numbers—pastoralism cannot support millions of people—and they would always depend on the settled societies for their higher technologies, including their metal weapons. But they were a culturally credible alternative to the cramped farming lifestyle, and from the beginning they were imbued with a deep contempt for the settled folk. In fact, they quickly came to see the farmers not just as enemies but as prey.

It was the beginning of a confrontation that lasted for several hundred generations, down to the final defeat of the nomads only a few centuries ago. Over the millennia millions died in the unceasing (but always ephemeral) incursions of the pastoralists into the settled lands, and in the course of it the farming peoples of Eurasia were forced to militarize themselves and learn a way of war as ruthless as that of the herders.

Around 5500 BC, walls start appearing around communities throughout the Fertile Crescent and the average size of settlements goes up considerably, as though people were concentrating for protection. Although there is no direct evidence about where the threat came from, the prime suspects are the new pastoral groups, for they had both the motive and the capability to attack the settled peoples. Their primary resource was the most mobile of all forms of wealth, animals on the hoof, and it would be astonishing if they did not start raiding each other's herds soon after they came into existence. An even more attractive option, however, would be to steal the farmers' animals—and while they were at it, all the other valuable things that the farmers had and the herders didn't. It was tempting, and it was easy.

The pastoralists still lacked horses at this stage, but even on foot they were far more mobile than any agricultural society could be. They were also far fewer in numbers than the farmers, of course, but they could concentrate all their fighting strength against a chosen target at short notice, a feat that no society of settled farmers could match. They might be greatly outnumbered in general, but they were rarely outnumbered at the right place on the right day. Unless they were completely different from all the pastoralists we know from subsequent history, their pattern would have been the surprise raid followed by a rapid retreat into the highlands with the spoils—but since you can't retreat very fast on foot with all your animals, they would probably have taken steps to minimize the likelihood of pursuit. The obvious steps are terror, atrocity, and massacre.

In both anthropological and historical studies, it is often observed that fighting between groups that recognize their common humanity ("intraspecific" fighting) has generally been constrained by custom and ritual, while the same groups approach hunting wild animals in a very different and more pragmatic spirit: deceive the animal, and then kill it. But the psychological relationship between nomads and farmers, from the point of view of the former, is the relationship between predator and prey: the settled peoples are seen as lesser beings who have sold out and are no longer fully human. So they can be killed without compunction, and the whole history of attacks by pastoralists on farming peoples is a tale of remorseless cruelty and contempt by the former toward the latter. If this was also true before history began to be recorded, then the early pastoralists would often have covered their retreat by deliberate shock tactics, killing and destroying everybody and everything they could not carry away.

It wouldn't take too many attacks like that to cause a general panic and a wave of wall-building among the agricultural communities—and a wave of militarization as well. Indeed, nomad attacks may have been the main driver behind the increasing intensity of warfare in this and later periods, as the settled communities gradually imported nomad ruthlessness into their own conflicts.[11] The strongest evidence for this is the startling contrast between the style of warfare in societies that did not face conflicts with the nomads and those that did. Egypt, for example, was sheltered by geography from virtually all contact with nomads for over fifteen hundred years after the Nile valley was first united under a single ruler in about 3100 BC. Beyond the narrow river valley and the densely populated delta were only open deserts wide enough to bar passage to nomads who emerged in other parts of the region—and Egyptian warfare remained remarkably old-fashioned by comparison with war in other parts of the Middle East.

> The defending archers could direct their arrows from three different angles downwards onto the attackers in the ditch, and level onto targets coming over the counterscarp. Some conception of the immense strength of these defences is apparent when standing at the bottom of the ditch, we realise that an attacking force must first storm the glacis, destroying any outposts concealed in the covered way, while under fire from sling-shots and arrows from the main wall above. They would then have to descend the steep counterscarp to the bottom of the ditch, under an intense cross-fire from the loopholed ramparts and bastions, behind which the defenders would be completely concealed. Should they survive this ordeal, they would then have to storm the scarp and rampart above it, only to find themselves in a narrow corridor at the foot of the main walls, from the top of which would come a shower of stones and other missiles.[12]

The Egyptian paradox: sophisticated architecture, unsophisticated weapons. The four-thousand-year-old fortress of Buhen, now submerged behind the Aswan High Dam.

Far beneath the waters of Lake Nasser, which now stretch a hundred miles southwards from the Aswan Dam, twenty giant mud-brick fortresses are gradually dissolving along the submerged banks of what used to be the Second Cataract of the Nile. They were built to guard the southern approaches of Egypt about four thousand years ago, and they show just how good Egyptian architects and civil engineers were. In their complexity and sophistication, the elaborate defences of the fortresses guarding Egypt's southern frontier, from Buhen in the north to Semna and Kumma in the south, compare favourably with the medieval castles of only eight centuries ago. The forts were at a distance from one another that allowed visual communications; they had grain stores and tunnels dug to the river so that they would have food and water to withstand even a long siege; and their purpose, according to an inscription, was "to prevent any Nubian from passing . . . when faring northward, whether on foot or by boat, as well as any cattle of the Nubians. An exception is a Nubian who shall come to barter at Iken, or one with an official message." The Egyptians even maintained a corps of locally recruited Nubians to patrol the desert region beyond the forts.

It was a classic imperial "military frontier," the first example of a model that would be duplicated dozens of times from Roman England and China's Great Wall down to the British defences on India's North-West Frontier—even the use of "native troops" to patrol the forward zone would become standard. The only thing that doesn't fit is the weapons technology: these forts started going up in the 1990s BC, at a time when armies to the north and east of Egypt in the Fertile Crescent had already been wearing metal armour and using bronze spearheads and composite bows for half a millennium. Yet the Egyptians were still using clubs, simple bows with stone arrow-points, and short flint-tipped spears, and they did not wear armour either. They had no need of advanced military technology to hold the Nubians at bay—and there are indications that their own internal battles, which mostly involved disputed successions to the throne, were curiously formal and ritualized affairs in which there was little close combat (though there is ample evidence that captives were slaughtered afterwards).

The concentration of human population in the valley of the Nile and the commitment to farming in Egypt began comparatively late, around 5500 BC, as a drying climate pushed people down from the previously savannah-like uplands of the Red Sea Hills and the Sahara to the east and west. But then things moved fast: in less than a thousand years the tablelands became mostly true desert, incapable of supporting even pastoralists, except for an area around the great eastward bow of the upper Nile (near today's Luxor and ancient Thebes) where some herders could survive for another thousand years or so. Everybody else was already down in the valley, farming—and the style of farming that grew up beside this river in a desert was unique, for it did not require a lot of work and it did not drive the animal-herders away. Late each summer, usually in mid-August, the rains that had fallen on the Ethiopian highlands during that year's monsoon would reach upper (southern) Egypt as the Nile flood, a normally gentle rise in the river's level that would inundate most of the flood plain and then recede, leaving a richly fertile deposit of fresh silt behind. For the next three or four months the crops would grow lushly on the land. Then it would be available for the next eight months as grazing land for the animals, since no further crops could be grown that year without irrigation (which did not start in the Nile valley until about 2000 BC).

Unlike some parts of the Fertile Crescent, where crops could be grown year-round, Egypt's agriculture did not require the permanent expulsion of the animals and their herders to the outskirts of the community. Besides, where else could they go when the open desert generally began less than five miles from the river's edge? As a result, the new settled communities did not generate new pastoral groups that split away and became their enemies, a happy chance that was reflected in the fact that the farming communities lining the Nile were for the most part quite dispersed settlements that did not have walls.

They began, presumably, as tribal farming villages like those of the Yanomamo or the New Guinea highlanders, although in vastly more bountiful natural circumstances. They were gradually consolidated into chiefdoms with some tens of thousands of people and an administrative and ceremonial centre. The process doubtless involved some violence: the archaeology suggests that these chiefdoms, with the typical buffer zones of unfarmed land between them, were the basis for the forty-two nomes that remained the administrative provinces of pharaonic Egypt for two thousand years after unification. But as late as 3500 BC there were few walls except in the bow of the Nile, where some desperate pastoralists from the old Saharan populations were still trying to eke out a living on the rapidly drying uplands and raiding into the valley. There, in the chiefdoms or mini-kingdoms of Nagada and This and Hierakonopolis ("Falconville"), the farmers had walled towns or forts to protect themselves from the incursions of the nomads, and lived in much more militarized societies. So it was from there, naturally, that the unification of Egypt commenced.

The details of the process are unknown, but it began with the establishment of Hierakonopolis's power over the whole bow of the Nile, and then over the entire upper reach of the river down to the delta. It involved a good deal of fighting to subdue the other chiefdoms and it took several hundred years at least. But by 3100 BC all of upper Egypt was ruled by one man who then conquered his remaining rival, the ruler of at least part of the delta, in a victory that is commemorated in the Narmer palette, a large slate bas-relief dating from about 3050 BC. It shows a pharaoh in the dress of upper Egypt dispatching a man, probably another pharaoh, dressed in the style of lower Egypt. In another scene on the same palette, the pharaoh is shown viewing the bodies of dead enemies, all of whom have been decapitated: the creation of the first large state on earth, extending 625 miles from south to north and containing perhaps half a million people at that time, was not accomplished by sweet reason. But once it was unified, it was a very reasonable place.[13]

In fact, Egypt was as close to Eden as an early agricultural society could hope to get. Once unified, it could largely demilitarize, since there were no powerful neighbours who could reach it and hurt it. What need there was for military force to repel the surviving nomads and protect the southern border, to guard grain storage sites during famines when the Nile flood was too much or too little, and to settle occasional dynastic disputes could be supplied by relatively untrained and lightly armed militias raised on a temporary basis from the peasantry. Levies of temporary labour also supplied the workforce that built the enormous public works typical of early Egypt, most notably the pyramids. Given that farmers were basically idle eight months of the year, this may have been a useful way to channel surplus energy rather than an intolerable imposition. In fact, the general attractiveness of Egyptian society for the first fifteen hundred years after unification seems closely connected to its very low degree of militarization. The status of women, for example, seems to have been far higher than in contemporary societies in the Fertile Crescent, which was almost certainly related to the fact that men's status was not inflated by their monopoly of war-making.

Egypt was not really Eden, because no early agricultural society could approach that happy state. Its population rose in good times—probably to well over a million by the time that the great pyramids of Giza were built in the twenty-third century BC—but it was repeatedly knocked back by terrible famines when abnormally high or low floods persisted long enough to empty the grain stores maintained by the pharaoh's government. It was an absolute monarchy ruled by a god-king: for ninety-nine people out of a hundred, the class they were born into was the class they would die in, and most of the old social freedoms enjoyed by ten thousand generations of hunter-gatherers were gone for everyone. Nevertheless, the art of Old Kingdom Egypt, less prudish and more naturalistic than that of other early civilizations, does suggest a more relaxed attitude to life and even a joie de vivre that seems to have been largely absent elsewhere in the ancient Middle East, and one is tempted to speculate that this was somehow connected with a low level of militarization and the absence of the nomad threat. One should resist that temptation, and consider the Aztecs.

If we want examples of how traditional hunter-gatherer warfare might have evolved in a civilization that was not under regular attack by pastoralists, our best example is not Egypt but the pre-Columbian mass societies of Mesoamerica and South America. There were never any pastoralists in the Americas before Columbus, because there was no suite of domesticated animals there from which pastoral groups could make an independent living. Does the absence of constant nomad raiding explain why battles among the Mayans, the Incas, and the various ruling peoples of the Valley of Mexico, from our limited knowledge of them, involved much more ritualized behaviour and much less purposeful ruthlessness than was the norm in the Fertile Crescent even five thousand years ago? Might it even explain why they didn't develop metal weapons?

It's not that Mayan, Inca, or Aztec battles decided nothing, for many of these societies ended up as empires. But perhaps without the attacks of the nomads to clarify their minds and show them what can be done if you treat your opponents as prey, they just could not conceive of battles as contests to be decided simply by who could kill the most enemies most quickly. Instead, most battles in the pre-Columbian Americas seem to have been closer in spirit to the sort of battles that the Mae Enga of New Guinea might fight: on a far larger scale, of course, and with much greater likelihood of a decisive result, but still with many of the limitations typical of "intraspecific" war.

An Aztec army five hundred years ago was quite similar in broad outline to an army of the Fertile Crescent dating from between three and four thousand years ago, with massed archers and other projectile-throwers backing an elite corps of warriors armed and armoured (with quilted cotton armour) for close combat. The main aim of these warriors, however, was not to destroy the enemy's army by killing as many of his soldiers as possible. On the contrary, it was to capture opponents in one-on-one combat — bringing them down with a blow to the hamstring or knee, and then grappling them into submission so that minions could bind and remove them to the rear. Battles did include other types of fighting (projectiles, particularly arrows, must have taken a considerable toll), and hostilities proceeded in a familiar enough sequence, beginning at long range and intensifying as armies drew together. There was clearly a pursuit of victory through breaking the other side's formations. But the core and essence of everything was still capture: this is why elite weapons were designed to bleed and weaken, not to kill, and why the rules of engagement were carefully defined to promote individualized fighting and unambiguous outcomes with regard to who captured whom.

The outcome of battles mattered politically for the rulers, and could even mean subjugation for an entire society, but the motives and actions of the individual warriors were divorced from those of the state in a way that looks very strange to those who have inherited the Eurasian military tradition. In Aztec society a man's prisoner, captured in battle, was his future, the key to rank and privileges at home, not to mention a major source of protein for him and his family, so he fought to capture, not to kill.[14] The Aztec obsession with human sacrifice and eating the victims afterwards does distort the picture compared to, say, an Inca army, but there was only room on the battlefield for such a massive distortion of conventional Eurasian military logic because the Aztecs had not been exposed to the concept of efficiency in battle. For all the pre-Columbian mass societies, battle remained primarily a social event with political consequences. What allowed Hernando Cortés's three hundred Spaniards to defeat an Aztec army at least a hundred times larger and conquer the entire Aztec empire in 1521, far more than firearms or even horses, was the single-minded Spanish focus on military victory. And even though Incas were not equally obsessed with the necessity of taking captives for human sacrifice, the same advantage of sheer pragmatic ruthlessness enabled Francisco Pizarro's even smaller force to overthrow and destroy the entire Inca empire two years later. In the end, every other military tradition was buried by the Eurasian bulldozer.

———

Meriones pursued and overtaking [Pheraklos]
struck in the right buttock and the spearhead drove straight
on and passing under the bone went into the bladder.
He dropped, screaming, to his knees, and death was a mist
    about him.

Meges . . . killed Pedaios . . .
Struck him the sharp spear behind the head at the tendon
and straight on through the teeth and under the tongue cut

> the bronze blade
> and he dropped in the dust gripping in his teeth the
>   cold bronze.
>
> Euryplos . . . killed brilliant Hypsenor . . .
> Running in chase as he fled before him struck in the shoulder
> with a blow swept from the sword and cut the arm's weight
>   from him,
> so that the arm dropped bleeding to the ground,
>   and the red death
> and destiny the powerful took hold of both eyes.
>
> So they went at their work all about the mighty encounter.
>   *Homer*, The Iliad[15]

A real battle is an astonishing and terrible event. The one under the walls of Troy that is described in the *Iliad* actually took place around 1200 BC, but the poem about it wasn't written down until about 800 BC and probably more closely describes the warfare of that period. It also follows the conventions of the "Heroic Age" and describes the battle as epic encounters between individual heroes, but that does not do justice to what is actually happening on the ground. This is the war of infantry phalanxes — of the first real armies — and it is indeed a mighty encounter.

To fight in an infantry phalanx requires a level of discipline and coordination that has never before been asked of people. Holding spears and shields, they have to form in straight lines hundreds of men long, or even thousands: not just one line, but three, five, or even more, one behind the other. They have to move over often bumpy ground without losing their formation until they make contact with the enemy, who is arrayed in an equally unwieldy formation — and once they collide with the enemy phalanx, they can neither hear their commander's orders over the noise nor obey them if by chance they do hear. What really matters is what happens at the line of contact where the two disciplined mobs of soldiery crunch together. And there it is push and stab and shove and stumble in a sweating frenzy, with the leading edge of the two formations eroding moment by moment as men go down, until one side starts to panic and tries to break contact. But it cannot break contact, of course, for there are other lines of men behind who have not yet caught the panic and continue to press forward. So the cohesion of the losing formation breaks, and once that happens it is doomed. The men seeking to flee find themselves trapped in their own crowd and are cut down from behind.

It is that last and ugliest phase of the battle that is described in the lines above, with "heroes" being cut down from behind as they try to flee. The language is elevated warrior's prose to provide the required epic tone; the reality is frightened young men away from home for the first time, running for their lives and not making it, left to bleed to death amid the wreckage of a broken phalanx. It is ruthless, deliberate slaughter on a scale that the "primitives" could never match or even imagine, and it began not in 1200 or 800 BC, but in the time of the very first true urban civilization, over five thousand years ago. The first phalanxes belonged to the rival city-states of Mesopotamia.

You can see one on the Stele of the Vultures, the first representation of a Mesopotamian army, dating from around 2500 BC. Eannatum, the ruler of Lagash, is leading his army out to battle, and behind him are the soldiers of the city—but they are neither a jumbled mass nor the single ragged line of "tribal" war. They are shoulder to shoulder with their shields overlapping, several rows deep, and with the spears of all the rows bristling ahead of the formation in the classic phalanx style. Almost certainly, they were marching in step. And when they met the enemy formation, from the neighbouring city of Umma, the experience of the soldiers would have been as shocking as that of the heroes under the walls of Troy over a thousand years later: a brief but savage face-to-face struggle followed by the slaughter of the phalanx that broke first. The Stele of the Vultures claims that three thousand men of the army of Umma died on the battlefield—and then those who were taken captive were marched to the foot of their own city's walls and slaughtered.

This was violence pushed to the limit with an almost Clausewitzian determination, and it was there right at the start of

The Vulture Stele of King Eannatum of Lagash, ca. 2500 BC. The Phalanx is above,
the slaughter of the prisoner below.

civilization. Maybe the cumulative losses in the hunter-gatherer
and tribal style of warfare were still proportionately greater over a
generation than those suffered by Mesopotamian city-states in
war—there were many tens of thousands of men in the city-state
of Umma, after all, and this did not happen all that often—but the
intensity of the fighting, the willingness of large numbers of men
to stand their ground and fight even given the high probability that
they would die there in the next five minutes, had no precedent in

the long human, primate, or even mammalian past. To find anything comparable, you must go to the battles fought between ant colonies, but at least the ants have the excuse of a shared genetic heritage as a reason for their acts of sacrifice on behalf of the community. The population of the Mesopotamian city-states was probably reaching the level where they could each be largely endogamous (marrying within the community), but the men of the phalanx did not have enough genetic material in common to make their sacrifice sensible in terms of the "selfish gene" theory, or indeed in any other context of purely rational self-interest. It was culture that made their sacrifice possible.

> The military makes demands which few if any other callings do, and of course emotionally disturbed people talk about being trained to kill. . . . The whole essence of being a soldier is not to slay but to be slain. You offer yourself up to be slain, rather than setting yourself up as a slayer. Now one can get into very deep water here, but there's food for thought in it.
> *Gen. Sir John Hackett*

You can get into very deep water indeed, but that is where we need to go, for there is an enduring puzzle about what has been called the Western way of war. The lethal phalanx style of head-on, close-quarters warfare, whether conducted with bronze spears, Roman short swords, Renaissance pikes, or Brown Bess muskets, will dominate the battlefields of the Fertile Crescent, the classical Mediterranean world, and all the successor civilizations down to the modern West for the next five thousand years. Even now, though modern battlefields look relatively empty, it is with us in spirit. There have been long intervals when more limited forms of warfare took its place even in the West, and in other parts of the world highly ritualized forms of combat have often been the norm, but in the West the spirit of the phalanx always came back in the end. To wage battle in this ruthless, all-or-nothing style demands a high degree of commitment by the opposing sides: two phalanxes cannot collide at all, any more than two line infantry battalions of the eighteenth century could successfully open fire on each other, unless the two sides tacitly cooperate by arraying their forces just so on an agreed battlefield. Why did the people of this particular cultural continuum repeatedly choose to fight this way, when other cultures couldn't or at least didn't?

It is undoubtedly a more fearsome way of fighting, and that has practical consequences. If an army that is used to standing and fighting within lethal range of the other side's short-range weapons encounters an army whose traditions tell it never to fight a major battle without the advantages of numbers or surprise, the former is likely to win. Like bad money driving out good, the style of un-bridled, headlong violence (one is even tempted to say the style that is more in love with glorious death) will drive out the saner, more measured style. In the end, Western armies that combined new technology with their ancient tradition of extreme violence overran the entire planet for a while. But we know of whole civilizations where that extreme form of warfare never became dominant. Chinese civilization, for example, had an approach to war infused with the Confucian ideal that the superior man should be able to attain his ends without violence. As Sun Tzu put it in *The Art of War* (490 BC): "To fight and conquer in all your battles is not supreme excellence; supreme excellence consists in breaking the enemy's resistance without fighting." Yet Chinese history was not exactly a picnic: there were endless wars involved in the process of unifying China, many civil wars thereafter, and the constant and grave threat of barbarian invasion. So once again, why did the ultra-violent style of war triumph in the ancient Fertile Crescent and its successor cultures?

Maybe it's because this really is the oldest civilization, and it has arrived at the present by the longest, hardest route. The ancient Middle East had a lead of at least a thousand to fifteen hundred years over every other region of the world, even over rival parts of Eurasia like the Indus Valley and China, in the creation of city-states and the first agricultural or "hydraulic" empires. It is possible that doing everything first—inventing cities, inventing the state, inventing armies and money and writing—had social and psychological consequences. The first cultures to go through this series of transformations had to do it one step at a time, missing no steps out, whereas others following them down the same path a millennium later, even at the far end of Eurasia, may have been able to skip or abridge some of the more painful steps. In particular, they may have bypassed some of the steps by which the old warrior band was transformed in Mesopotamia into the more or less disciplined militia of an agricultural chiefdom, and then cajoled and tricked into behaving with the almost kamikaze bravery of a city-state's phalanx.

The transformation began with the move into towns and other walled places in the Fertile Crescent after 5500 BC, a shift probably driven at this early stage not so much by rising population density as by the growing menace from pastoral peoples who have broken free from the farming communities. Already there is a big difference from Egypt in the ferocity of the battles and the level of discipline of the warriors of civilization, because if you are fighting nomads the battles are never just ritual occasions to measure the relative strength of the two sides, as they often were in the old days. Against nomads, it is always for keeps, and the penalty for losing is pretty close to total. This is happening in societies where change is starting to move fast enough to be visible, tradition is losing its veto, and the deliberate use of innovation to solve real-world problems is becoming more acceptable — so, of course, innovation is applied to warfare, too. We can imagine a gradual rise in the discipline demanded of the individual warrior and the control exercised by the chieftain or commander, because these changes bring more success in battle. Against nomadic raiders, these new, efficient ways of fighting are indispensable. And once the settled people know how to do that, will they revert to their old, inefficient ways in the chronic confrontations with neighbouring farming communities? Of course not. And so the lethality of battle starts to rise.

It rises most rapidly in the land of the two rivers, Mesopotamia, because of that place's unique geography. Mesopotamia, corresponding to central and southern Iraq of today, is a flat, almost featureless plain created by the two rivers, the Tigris and Euphrates, that drain most of the upland part of the Fertile Crescent. Virtually rainless and treeless, this barren, sun-baked land was not colonized by the early farmers of the region, who preferred higher places with rain, trees, and lots of wild game. But the two rivers meandering across Mesopotamia—many braided rivers, in practice, since they repeatedly split and re-unite as they cross the flat plain, and arbitrarily change their course entirely every thousand years or so—provide virtually year-round water to anyone willing to invest in a little irrigation, and the soil is amazingly fertile because it is pure silt laid down by past floods. You can easily get two crops a year off this land; with more effort, you might even get three. So around 5000 BC the first farmers from the surrounding highlands (today's Kurdistan and Iran) ventured down into the plain and put the enterprise of civilization into high gear.

The settlers of Sumer, as they called it, had struck the agricultural mother lode. Their populations soared, doubling every half-century or less, because the irrigated land would feed hundreds of people per square mile. (Their health declined, on the other hand, because their low-protein diet stunted their growth, and also because their populations were getting dense enough to support deadly epidemic diseases.) Their enormous wealth in food was a constant attraction to the hill peoples who overlooked them—and the scarcity of wood, of metal, and even of stone down in the alluvial plain meant that they needed things from the hill peoples, too. It was an ideal opportunity for mutually profitable trade, if the people on both sides were reasonable and the means of transportation had been a bit better, but not necessarily a recipe for happy coexistence in the circumstances of the time. So down in the Sumerian plain, a kind of cultural pressure cooker emerged.

The evidence is buried too deeply under the later cities to be very helpful, but the various tribes of Sumer almost certainly went through the usual business of withdrawing into walled villages as the pastoral groups separated out and began raiding during the fifth millennium BC. With their populations growing so fast, the villages would have quickly become towns—and the need to link the irrigation ditches to ensure a regular supply of water would have encouraged consolidation among the towns, perhaps by agreement, perhaps by force. But in the quite different terrain of Mesopotamia, this did not culminate in a single nation-state like Egypt, even though the earliest settlers of Sumeria, like the Egyptians, all spoke essentially the same language. Instead, about a dozen city-states emerged, each with a population that was probably nearing six figures by the early third millennium BC. No evidence exists for large-scale warfare during this long period of consolidation, which doesn't mean that it did not occur—but it may not have been all that severe, either, for the Sumerians very early hit upon the device of using religion to provide a non-military source of authority and adjudicate disputes. It was temple priests and the gods they served, not secular rulers backed by military power, who dominated the life of the early Sumerian cities, collecting and recording the tithes of grain and distributing it when necessary (and in the process inventing mathematics and writing).

Human societies are not doomed to wage war always and everywhere: intelligent leadership and good institutions can make a great deal of difference. The priests of the various cities would have cooperated to preserve their own authority by ensuring that inter-city disputes over land and water rights were settled in ways that left no party utterly dissatisfied. Too unbalanced an outcome would have created an opening for the leading warriors of each city, who would always have been seeking an opportunity to usurp the power of the priests by offering to produce a more satisfactory outcome by violence. The best proof of the long-term success of the temples is the fact that while there were probably always some sort of walls to discourage raiding, really massive ramparts able to withstand major sieges did not start going up around the Sumerian cities until after the beginning of the third millennium BC. The priests had bought Sumer five, maybe even ten centuries of relative peace. When it finally broke down, it was probably because the growth of population and the ensuing scarcity of arable land made it impossible to produce satisfactory compromise solutions to the inter-city disputes any more.

In the end, the escalating inter-city wars enabled the warriors to take over and make themselves kings as absolute as the pharaohs of Egypt, but as in the case of many city-states in classical Greece two thousand years later, it took some centuries before the old, more or less egalitarian institutions of the traditional Sumerian city-states were utterly erased by the new tyrants. It is in this period, with war on the rise and tyrants on the make, but with the old proto-democratic city assemblies that may have been a direct heritage from hunter-gatherer times still in existence, that we see the first evidence for phalanxes in warfare.

The saga of Gilgamesh, ruler of the city-state of Uruk about 2700 BC, may be showing us some of the process, for it was by exploiting a quarrel with the neighbouring city of Kish that he gained power in Uruk—and, according to legend, built Uruk's walls, which extended for five miles around the city. This is the very first period of written history, giving us at last some names, some dates, and some (heavily mythologized) stories. Centre stage at once is the hero Gilgamesh, a warrior who became the big man ("lugal") or proto-king of Uruk. The epic is the usual quest story (Gilgamesh seeks eternal life), combined with some heavily disguised renderings of local politics in twenty-seventh-century BC Uruk but, reading between the lines, it seems likely that he was the man who finally subverted all the old institutions of Uruk and diverted them to his own purposes. It is at least safe to say that alongside the temple authorities, an assembly of Uruk's tribal elders (a kind of senate) and a general assembly of all the adult men had both survived down to Gilgamesh's time, and that Gilgamesh used a combination of rhetoric and threats to persuade these assemblies to accept his ascendancy over the city. Even then, he did not become an absolute monarch: he had to keep the people on his side, and most of them probably continued to see themselves not as mere subjects of his will but as full citizens. Uruk and the other Sumerian cities were rapidly moving toward authoritarian models as the difficulties of running large and complex societies overwhelmed the old egalitarian institutions, but they were not all the way there yet—and that precarious survival of egalitarian values was what made phalanxes possible.

Bear in mind who these people are. They are the heirs of ten or twenty thousand generations of free men and women who lived in tiny societies, made their own choices, and lived or died by the results. They have pride, they have intelligence, and they are not going to surrender their independence to the first fast-talking thug who comes along. The logic of the kind of society they are moving into, as the dependence on agriculture becomes total and the number of people soars, is that a few people must give orders and everybody else must obey. In the absence of effective means of mass communications, a society of ten or a hundred thousand people can only be run from the top down, by force. The old system of endless discussion leading to an eventual consensus, time-consuming even for a hunter-gatherer band of a couple of dozen adults, simply will not work once the numbers go over ten thousand or so. Yet everything that makes them human rejects an ant-like existence of dumb obedience, and they do not go willingly into bondage.

They live in an increasingly stratified society where property and social class are setting some people above others, but there is still a fair amount of social mobility. The status of women has fallen catastrophically (as it did everywhere with the rise of civilization), and there is no remedy in sight for that. But the myth of social equality lives on in the assembly of elders—probably heads of clans by origin—and even more significantly in the assembly of all free adult males. Allowing for two thousand years of technological and cultural differences, the cities of Ur and Lagash and Shuruppak and Kish *are* the Greek city-states of classical times. The rich and well-born generally get their way in the end, but at this stage the proprieties of public consultation and consensus in assemblies of all the citizens (or at least all citizens capable of bearing arms) must still be observed.[16] This would have been a nuisance for aspiring oligarchs and tyrants, but it did have one advantage: if the whole adult male population felt involved in the decision to go to war, then you could legitimately demand that they follow through by putting their lives on the line. That is why the cities of Sumer, in the early days, could actually send their men out to battle in phalanxes.

The attractiveness of the phalanx is not just that it is an awesomely effective military tool; it is also cheap. In one free afternoon a week, the soldiers in the ranks can be trained to use their simple shields and spears effectively and to move in tight formations. Bronze spearheads are the only significant expense in equipping them (bronze is replacing stone in weapons at this time, though it is still relatively expensive), and the better-off members of the community will certainly invest in bronze helmets and shin protection as well. You may even find that the assembly demands that you subsidize the cost of basic bronze armour for the poorer men in the community, but it's still quite a bargain: a truly effective military force, practically unstoppable except by another phalanx, for little more than a song. No need to hire expensive and unreliable mercenaries (they existed even then), or to withdraw productive members of the community from the workforce for lengthy training in the use of more complicated and demanding weapons like the bow or the sword (then just coming into use), let alone the horse. Indeed, the real question is why phalanxes ever went out of fashion.

The answer is that it requires an extraordinarily high level of commitment from the men who take their places in the phalanx, especially if they are coming from an older and less disciplined fighting tradition. What made it possible for the citizen-soldiers of the early Sumerian cities to fight in phalanxes was precisely their sense of commitment and belonging to the cities they fought for. All their kin were in the city and many were right around them in the phalanx, which undoubtedly helped, but they also felt a deep involvement in the city's fate because their decisions in the assembly shaped (or seemed to shape) its policies. So they turned up unpaid for the weekly drills, they adapted to a style of fighting that was utterly alien to the old tradition, and when necessary they risked their lives, unpaid, in war in the ranks of the phalanx.

As the centuries passed and the tyrannies deepened in the Sumerian cities, the phalanx style of warfare would gradually erode and vanish, for absolute monarchs would not be willing to allow the sense of popular participation that made these earliest of mass armies possible. Increasingly, they preferred to fight battles where only the new military elites and their standing armies of hired soldiers took part, leaving the mass of the citizenry unarmed, untrained, and politically inert. By the latter part of the third millennium, phalanxes had virtually disappeared from Mesopotamian battlefields. But before they did, they probably played a big part in shaping the pattern of chronic, indecisive war that arose among the cities of Sumer, for the thing about a military system that could quickly and cheaply mobilize the whole adult male population for war was that it gave each player limited offensive strength, but immense defensive strength.

For many centuries the thirteen city-states of classic Sumer co-existed in a state of rapidly shifting alliances and recurrent wars that rarely changed anything. They had not chosen it, but circumstances had delivered them into a balance-of-power system. If a losing player could just hang on long enough, various other players would start to fear the growing strength of the recent big winners and shift alliances to counterbalance their power. The pattern was not new to humanity—it would actually be recognizable to most New Guinea highlanders, once they made the adjustment for scale, and even the chimpanzees of Gombe might understand the underlying logic of the system. But this was the first time that a balance-of-power system had appeared among the society of states, for no such society had previously existed, and it would never really go away again for long.

It is a system that guaranteed fairly frequent wars, but it has lasted, with only rare interruptions, for five thousand years, as dominant a factor in the global rivalries of the early twentieth-century great powers as it was in the local squabbles of the Mesopotamian city-states. Within the past couple of centuries Britain and France, France and the United States, and the United States and Britain have all been both enemies and allies; Italy has gone from alliance to enmity with Germany and back again five times since 1914. Kish, Shuruppak, Ur, Nippur, and E-Ninmar would doubtless be able to match that record if we knew enough about the details of their local game. The alliances shift but the wars continue—and although each war seems to have some specific cause that people can cling to in order to make sense of the carnage, it is the system itself that produces the wars.

It did it then, and it does it now. Modern nation-states have gone to war, on average, about once per generation in the period

1800 to 1945, and were at war for about one year in five during that entire period. That is exactly what you would expect from a system that makes every state exclusively responsible for its own survival. It can ensure this only by having sufficient military force, either on its own or in alliance with others. Since you can never have enough of the right forces, available at the right place and time, to meet every contingency, at least 90 percent of the states that ever existed have been destroyed by war: the balance-of-power game merely postpones the inevitable, though if you are clever and lucky it can postpone it for a very long time.

That is not good enough in a world where weapons of mass destruction now threaten to destroy entire populations, so there has been a concerted international attempt to break out of the balance-of-power system since World War II. None of the major players, the great powers, has fought any of the others for almost sixty years now, which is a moderately hopeful sign. But this is a very old pattern, and we have not been free from it long enough yet to be confident that the Great Escape will really succeed.

Meanwhile, what about the war between Lagash and Umma that started around 2500 BC with a clash of phalanxes that left three thousand men from Umma dead on the battlefield? It went on, at intervals, for 150 years, like the long duel for superiority between Britain and France in the eighteenth and early nineteenth centuries. The two city-states were not just trying to overthrow each other but to establish their hegemony over all of Sumer—which is what often happens in balance-of-power systems—and as the advantage in war swayed back and forth and allies changed sides over the generations they seized each other's lands, imposed huge grain indemnities, and slaughtered or enslaved each other's citizens. It must have seemed as important to the people of those two cities as the Cold War felt to Americans and Russians, but it's all over now. In the end the army of Umma won a decisive victory, sacked the city of Lagash, and looted its

Naram-Sin, grandson of the first would-be world conqueror, Sargon of Akkad, after putting down a revolt. The captives are being forced to commit suicide in his presence.

temple — just in time to be subjugated by a new phenomenon: the world's first military empire.

———

Sargon, the mighty king, king of Akkad, am I.
He Who Keeps Travelling the Four
Lands (as Sargon called himself)

By the mid-2300s BC, newcomers speaking Semitic languages were muscling their way down onto the fertile Mesopotamian plains and setting up their own cities, but Sargon, though of Semitic origin, grew up in the old Sumerian city of Kish. He rose to become cup-bearer to King Ur-Zababa before seizing power himself in a coup whose details remain unknown, although it may have involved support from the Akkadian semi-nomads, also Semitic, who lived on the fringes of Kish's territory. At any rate, he was not content to stop with being king of Kish. His first conquest was Uruk, from which he brought back King Lugalzagezi in a dog collar and displayed him outside the city gate. He destroyed Uruk's walls, then did the same to Ur, Lagash, Umma and all the cities of Sumer. Then his armies moved farther afield to the upland kingdoms of Elam, Mari, Ebla, and the Hittites, in what is today western Iran, eastern Syria, and eastern Turkey. Governors were appointed, garrisons were put in place, tax lists were drawn up in each new conquered province, and the whole of it was administered by a centralized imperial bureaucracy. It was the first multinational empire ever, and to celebrate it Sargon built a new capital, Akkad.

His army was also different. It was no longer a phalanx of volunteers sharing loyalty to a single city and its gods, but a professional, multi-ethnic force that was history's first regular army: one of Sargon's inscriptions boasts that fifty-four hundred men daily took their meals in his presence. It could campaign far from home, unlike any previous army, as it had some form of logistical train. It knew how to build fortifications, and how to breach walls by undermining them or cross them with scaling ladders. The soldiers were very well armed and armoured by comparison with previous armies (Sargon's workshops may even have turned out standardized weapons). But it is very unlikely that they ever fought in a pure phalanx: that is both a lot to ask of mere mercenaries and a waste of their special talents. These were men who had the time and the skill to master not only the spear and the sword but also the composite bow, a recent innovation that remained the best projectile weapon for thousands of years to come. Such an army would have fought a very methodical battle, but it would have won almost every time against the enthusiastic amateurs it was up against. Sargon fought thirty-four campaigns in his fifty-five years on the throne, all of them successful.

Sargon of Akkad was the prototype of Alexander, Napoleon, and Hitler: a man who set out to conquer the world (or at least those parts of it that he knew). The chronicles boasted that his empire ran "from the Lower Sea to the Upper Sea" (from the Gulf to the Mediterranean), but it rested on nothing but military power and his army could not be everywhere at once. Sargon and his successors spent their entire reigns dealing with the endless revolts that broke out in all quarters as soon as any sign of Akkadian weakness was detected. When his grandson Naram-Sin came to the throne in 2260 BC, he faced simultaneous revolts in the Mesopotamian cities of Kish, Kutha, Kazallu, Marad, Umma, Nippur, Uruk, and Sippar, and in eight other provinces of his empire. In spite of all the cities shorn of their walls or destroyed outright for daring to rebel, the Akkadians were eventually worn down by the ceaseless effort to control the empire they had inherited from Sargon. By 2159 BC the empire was gone and the city of Akkad itself had been destroyed—but other empires followed in endless succession.

————

Aramu the Urartian, being struck with fear by the terror of my mighty army . . . withdrew from his city and went up into the mountains of Adduri. Then I went up after him and fought a mighty battle in the mountains. With my army I overthrew

3,400 warriors; like Adad I brought a great rain-cloud down upon them; with the blood of the enemy I dyed the mountain as if it had been wool, and I captured their camp. Then Aramu, to save his life, fled to an inaccessible mountain. In my mighty strength I trampled on his land like a wild bull, and his cities I reduced to ruins and consumed with fire.

Shalmaneser III of Assyria, on the
campaign against Urartu[17]

Tell me one operation of war which is moral. . . . Sticking a bayonet into a man's belly, is that moral? Then they say, well, of course strategic bombing involved civilians. Civilians are always involved in major wars.

After all, previous wars ended up in the besieging of major cities, and in besieging a city what was the idea? To cut off all supplies, and the city held out if it could until they'd eaten the last cat, dog and sewer rat and were all starving, and meanwhile the besieging forces lobbed every missile they could lay their hands on into the city, more or less regardless of where those missiles landed, as an added incentive to surrender. . . .

Sir Arthur Harris, head of RAF Bomber
Command, 1942—45

When Shalmaneser took Arzashku, the royal capital of Urartu (near Lake Van in eastern Turkey), he impaled the defenders on sharpened stakes and then piled their severed heads against the city walls. We know this because he boasted of his deed on bronze gates he had erected in the city of Imgur-Enlil, near his capital of Nineveh. The Assyrians had the reputation of being particularly ruthless even by contemporary standards, but Shalmaneser's behaviour was by no means unusual.

Frightfulness as policy. A pile of severed heads (the curled hair says they are Babylonians) being counted by an Assyrian scribe whose arm appears at the right. Scribes recording the booty of the Babylonian campaign; Nineveh, Southwest Palace.

When Air Marshal Harris's Lancaster and Halifax bombers devastated the cities of Germany night after night just over half a century ago, children suffocated in air-raid shelters and young women burned in the street. Very few of the young Britons and Canadians who made up his bomber crews would have been willing to strangle a child or burn a young woman with a blowtorch even if he had ordered them to do it personally, so maybe there is such a thing as moral progress—but given the emotional insulation of altitude, they acted without hesitation in ways that led to the same result, and their behaviour was by no means unusual. Neither was their willingness to go on doing it even though they knew that the odds against them surviving more than a few months themselves were very long. Warriors always understood that the business comes down to killing in the end, whether they enjoyed the act or not, and the soldiers of civilization have added an extraordinary stoicism to the mix: at least in big wars where they believe great issues are at stake, there is a sense in which they really do offer themselves up to be slain.

But we should not let ourselves get carried away by all this, as if civilized war represented a quantum leap in human behaviour. It is a much more impressive event than primitive war because of the sheer numbers involved, and later also because of the spectacular technology, but neither the cruelty nor the courage are new. Warfare has mutated from a chronic low-level activity to a sporadic but much more intense phenomenon, but it was generally less lethal (in relative terms) in its civilized version. What really changed with the rise of civilization was practically everything else.

By 2000 BC or thereabouts, all the main institutions, values, and behaviours of civilization were in place, and they would not change drastically for another three millennia. By then, at least 90 percent of the human race was making its living from agriculture, and the vast majority of these people lived in states that were social pyramids with semi-divine kings at the top. The old egalitarian values survived only in a few small city-states, and among the relatively small number of people who made their living as pastoralists or as tribal farmers and hunter-gatherers. The multinational empires built on sheer force rose and fell, growing even larger as time passed, and tyranny and slavery had become normal. Were there really no other viable options for how to run a mass society?

Probably not. The basic problem was numbers: human beings and all their near primate relatives had always lived in very small groups, and their new style of life suddenly required them to live in relatively huge groups. They quickly came up with innovative social technologies that made it possible to organize and control these large new societies—writing and money and bureaucracy but they failed utterly to come up with any mechanism that would allow traditional human politics to continue. Decision-making based on endless discussion among equals and the gradual generation of consensus works in a society of thirty or forty people; it cannot work well for a society of even three or four thousand people, and it ceases to be workable at all long before the numbers reach three or four million. Until and unless you can come up with some technology that lets very huge numbers of people communicate with one another, or at least hold more or less simultaneous discussions on the same agenda and then pool their results, the old political system is dead. And so it died.

Equality died with it, because the only system that did work was a crude social pyramid in which orders were passed down from the top and slavishly obeyed at the bottom. As the numbers went up, so did the degree of inequality and compulsion in the society, regardless of the previous values and traditions of the culture in question. Tyranny became universal in large agricultural societies simply because no other system worked at that scale. It lasted for unbroken thousands of years: the social structure of the average ancient empire was closer to the anthill than to our own hunter-gatherer past. Yet the empires were never very stable, because human beings had not actually *become* ants; behind the bitten tongues and the bowed heads, they remained the same people they had always been. That was why most large societies became heavily militarized: physical force, or at least the permanent threat of force, was needed to keep all these newly tamed heirs of the hunter-gatherers in line, and there is some truth in the argument that the elites fought wars because that justified the armies that kept them in power at home. It was not the war that was new, but the militarization and the tyranny.

Looking back from our vantage point, we can tell ourselves that the experiment of civilization would eventually pay off for at least some of its children, but from the standpoint of 2000 BC there were few compensations, nor were many due to appear for a long time to come. Even physically, most of the people of the agricultural mass societies were stunted and bent by poor diet and endless labour. Women were the biggest losers, reduced to social inferiority and confined to narrow lives of endless child-bearing, but for men the life of a peasant farmer was little better. The number of people had gone up hugely, but the quality of life had fallen drastically: Rousseau's noble savages had become overworked slaves, divided by class and gender and insulted and oppressed by tyranny. The human race had dug itself a very deep pit, and we would be living in it for a very long time.

5

The Middle Passage

How can we take this pass which is so narrow? It is reported that the enemy are at the exit in great numbers. Will not the horses have to go single file, and the soldiers likewise? Won't our vanguard already be fighting (at the far end of the pass) while the rear stands here at Aruna and does not fight?

Advice of Tuthmose III's officers on the eve
of the battle of Armageddon[1]

IT IS TEMPTING TO SEE THE WHOLE OF HISTORY FROM THE middle of the second millennium BC to the beginning of the present era four or five centuries ago as a sort of middle passage in a long ocean voyage. The shores of the tribal past, on which we built the ship of civilization, have long since dropped astern, and the opposite shore, the new world of rapid change and expanding possibilities, is not yet in sight. The crew is turbulent, but the ship and the horizons do not seem to change. This is particularly true for the history of war: during the three thousand years between 1500 BC and AD 1500, for which historical records are far more ample— and most of the history recorded is military—there was scarcely any change in the pattern of warfare that would seem important to a non-specialist. Indeed, most military historians would agree that competent professional armies chosen at random from anywhere between 500 BC and AD 1500 would stand a roughly equal chance in battle against each other—and that span could probably be pushed all the way back to 1500 BC if the earlier armies were allowed to exchange their bronze weapons for iron ones.

This godlike perspective does involve an optical illusion, of course. Things seem so slow to change in this more recent period mainly because we know much more about it than we do about the really distant past. So little information has survived from 3000 BC or 5000 BC that the history of those times seems to move quite quickly. If archaeologists know only a dozen facts about a whole century in the history of an ancient empire, then the centuries of its life flash by rapidly, whereas the reality is that change was generally slow. Once we reach a period when facts are more plentiful and the years seem crowded with incident, the centuries take on something closer to their real length in our imagination, and we grow impatient with the actual slowness of change. War was more or less a "steady state" phenomenon during this middle passage, and we are not obliged to trudge chronologically through hundreds of forgotten wars and thousands of obscure battles fought over three millennia in order to understand the evolution of the institution of warfare. We can afford to be selective—and at least we can now hear individual human voices and get a feel for what is actually going on.

> You determine to go forward, though you don't know the way. Shuddering seizes you, the hair of your head stands on end, your soul lies in your hand. Your path is full of boulders and shingle, there is no passable track, for it is all overgrown with thorns, neh-plants and wolf's-pad. The ravine is on one side of you, the mountain rises on the other. On you go, and guide your chariot beside you, and fear that the horse will fall. . . . The sky is open, and you imagine that the enemy is behind you.
>
> *Letter from Hori, an Egyptian scribe*
> *and veteran, to a young officer*[2]

The first battle for which we actually have details happened almost three thousand years ago, in the same place where the very last battle will allegedly be fought: Armageddon. It was fought because the cities of Syria and Palestine, which had been vassals to Egypt for several generations past, rebelled in 1463 BC. The king of Kadesh, a rich and strategically important city at the top end of the Bekaa valley in southern Syria, declared his independence, and most of the cities in the region promptly acknowledged his rule, for the Egyptian army had not left the valley of the Nile in twenty-two years. By early the following spring, however, there was a new pharaoh on the throne, and the army moved north.

The Egyptian army that the twenty-two-year-old pharaoh Tuthmose III led into his first campaign was a much more serious organization than the lightly armed and unarmoured armies of the Old and Middle Kingdoms. Some twenty thousand strong, it consisted mainly of infantrymen carrying spears, swords, and axes, but it also included archers equipped with powerful composite bows. It was divided into divisions of about five thousand men (which were given the names of the gods—the Division of Re, the Division of Amun, etc.) and so had the ability to perform at least moderately complicated manoeuvres on the battlefield. The army, like others of this period, also had hundreds of chariots that could manoeuvre in mass formations. The chariots were attached to each division and were very useful to harass unbroken formations of enemy infantry from a distance, darting in, launching weapons, and swiftly withdrawing again. They charged home, however, only against troops already showing signs of flight; infantry massed shoulder to shoulder could usually stare them down, as horses will simply refuse to charge into an unbroken hedge of spears.

Tuthmose's army took three weeks to march from the Egyptian frontier fortress at Tjel (near today's Suez Canal) to a place called Yehem in northern Palestine, just the other side of the mountains from the city of Megiddo, also known as Armageddon. There the army of Kadesh was drawn up to meet him. There were three passes through the mountains, two of them long and circuitous but wide enough for an army to preserve some sort of formation while passing through; the other, through the village of Aruna, shorter but dangerously narrow.

Emerging from any of the passes into the plain of Armageddon would be a risky business, for the enemy army might be waiting at the exits and attack Tuthmose before his forces had time to deploy into battle formation. At the staff conference on the evening before the final advance, the pharaoh rejected the advice of his officers (quoted above) and decided to chance taking the Aruna road. He might have had up-to-date intelligence about the enemy's positions on the other side of the mountains, but he was probably just gambling that the Kadesh forces, unwilling to spread themselves too thin by covering all three passes, would reckon that nobody in his right mind would take the Aruna road and so would leave that pass unguarded.

The Egyptian army began marching up the narrow pass soon after dawn with great trepidation, for this was enemy territory, and even a small force in the hills could cause great difficulty to the strung-out Egyptians. But the head of the Egyptian column emerged from the defile some hours later to discover that the young pharaoh's gamble had worked: the forces of Kadesh had been divided between the exits from the other two passes, and the Egyptian vanguard began to deploy on the plain unhindered.

There is a hint in the account on the temple walls at Karnak that Tuthmose may have rashly proposed to push his luck by attacking the nearer fraction of the divided Kadesh army before all his own troops had got clear of the pass, for at this time his officers addressed him again: "Behold, His Majesty has come forth together with his victorious army and they have filled the valley; let our victorious lord hearken to us this once, and let our lord await the rear of his army. When the rear of the army has come right out to us, then we shall fight against these Asiatics [as the Egyptians contemptuously called all the Levantine peoples]." This time the pharaoh heeded his officers and waited until all his army was through the pass, around noon, before advancing toward Megiddo. There was no contact with the enemy that day, and around seven in the evening the Egyptian army camped south of Megiddo by the side of the stream.

The mood of an army on the eve of a great battle is always the same: the veterans tense because they know what will happen, the younger soldiers nervous because they don't know, and all of them talking confidently to smother their fear or busying themselves with their equipment to hide it. "Command was given to the whole army, saying 'Equip yourselves! Prepare your weapons! For we shall advance to fight the wretched foe in the morning!' Therefore the pharaoh rested in the royal tent . . . and the watch of the army went about saying 'Steady of heart! Steady of heart! Watchful! Watchful!' . . . One came to say to His Majesty 'The land is well, and the infantry of the South and of the North (of Egypt) likewise. . . .'"

In the morning, the Egyptian army marched out with all the panoply and splendour it could muster: "His Majesty went forward in a chariot of electrum [an alloy of gold and silver] arrayed in his weapons of war, like Horus, the Smiter, lord of power; like Montu of Thebes, while his father, Amun, strengthened his arms." The army of Kadesh marched out from its own camp—and then, just when they were going to give us our first detailed glimpse of an ancient battle waged in full costume dress, the Kadesh army took a good look at how long the Egyptian line was, filling the valley from one side to the other, did a quick mental calculation of the odds, and decided that saving their lives took precedence over saving their honour. "They fled to Megiddo in fear, abandoning their horses and their chariots of gold and silver."[3] The Egyptian army was ordered to give chase, but its soldiers could not be prevented from stopping to plunder the enemy's abandoned camp: fewer than five hundred soldiers of Kadesh's army were killed or captured.

The citizens of Megiddo slammed their gates shut to keep the pursuing Egyptians out, but many of the fleeing soldiers made it over the walls on ropes thrown down by the inhabitants. The siege lasted seven months, the Egyptians even going to the trouble of building a great wooden wall around their siege lines to thwart possible attempts by Kadesh to drive away their besieging army, but eventually the city negotiated its surrender. The pharaoh went on to capture and plunder a number of other cities in Lebanon, and the rich loot that he gathered from them, carefully itemized in the inscription, was more than enough to repay the cost of the expedition. Tuthmose III was so favourably impressed by this return on investment that he waged fifteen more campaigns in Lebanon and Syria during his reign, all of them successful (if you believe the inscriptions that he paid for). Pity about the lack of an actual head-on clash between the two armies to show us exactly how battles were fought in 1462 BC, but the soldiers probably didn't mind. And there ends the story—except for a few unanswered questions. When did Egypt start raising armies that left the Nile valley and fought with modern weapons? What happened to the missing five hundred years between 2000 and 1500 BC? And where did all those chariots come from?

———

Happiness lies in conquering your enemies, in driving them
in front of you, in taking their property, in savouring their
despair, in raping their wives and daughters.

Genghis Khan[4]

The missing years were the first Dark Age, when pastoral
peoples driving chariots swept in and overwhelmed almost all the
centres of civilization in Eurasia. The history of civilization cannot
be explained only in terms of wars, any more than it can be seen
solely in terms of climate change or monetary policy or even the
spread of infectious diseases (though all these have been
attempted), but if we sometimes wonder why the middle passage
took so long, it is because we overlook how vulnerable earlier civilizations were. They did quite enough damage to themselves with
their incessant wars, but they faced a greater peril from outside.

By now we have forgotten the terror, and nomads are pic-
turesque, dying cultures to be preserved and patronized. But for
most of recorded history, the civilized societies of the Old World
were relatively small areas of intense cultivation—in China,
northern India, the Middle East, and Europe—fringing the vast
five-thousand-mile sweep of open grasslands from southern
Russia to Manchuria that nurtured the horse nomads.
Periodically the nomads erupted outwards from the Eurasian
heartland to smash those civilizations or drive them back to a
lower level. They also guaranteed that all the survivors would be
thoroughly militarized states.

The first pastoral peoples did not live out on the open
steppes, of course; they arose among, and then separated from,
the early farming communities of the Fertile Crescent. What
allowed them to colonize first the fringes of the grasslands, and
much later the whole million and a half square miles of the sea of
grass, was the horse. Horses were first domesticated in the southern Ukraine before 4000 BC, and while they may have been used
primarily as a food animal at first, there is evidence that people in
that area were soon beginning to ride them. They were far smaller

and weaker in the back than modern horses, which are the product of six thousand years of selective breeding, but as they spread among the pastoral peoples they probably led to more wide-ranging raids against the farming settlements. Nobody would have tried to fight from the back of a horse of that time, but they would have been an excellent getaway vehicle. The remains of domesticated horses in various agricultural settlements in the Fertile Crescent dating to well before 3000 BC show that nomads from the north were at least bringing them in to trade by then; it would be very surprising if they were not raiding on horseback too.[5]

Meanwhile, back home, horses were already enabling the pastoral peoples to move their herds deeper into the grasslands, but it was the invention of the wheel around 3300 BC that let them load their belongings into wagons and cut loose from the whole notion of a settled existence. The unique nomadic culture that was to spawn Hittite, Aryan, Hun, Magyar, Mongol, and Manchu conquerors from the steppes over the next three thousand years may have sprung into being practically fully formed in only a couple of centuries. And once they had filled up the grasslands to their carrying capacity for pastoralists (probably only three to five million people), the nomads came calling back in the civilized lands.

Their vehicle was the chariot, and it gave them a huge military advantage over the civilized armies of the period. The chariot had been invented in the civilized lands as early as 2300 BC, by the simple process of taking two of the four wheels off the traditional cart or war-wagon (already a thousand years old) drawn by oxen or donkeys, and using the lightest and most flexible construction materials available to produce a vehicle that even the small horses of the day could pull at high speed (two-man chariots could weigh as little as a hundred pounds). It probably began as an elite toy, a vehicle in which wealthy and powerful people who owned horses could race across the landscape at twice the speed of even the fastest runner, hunting gazelles and other fast-moving prey. There is no evidence that civilized empires were incorporating it into their armies in the late third millennium BC. But out on the fringes of civilization, especially on the northern part of the Iranian

plateau where large areas of fertile farmlands were interspersed
with grasslands suitable only for pastoralists, some of the herders
got their hands on chariots and found them ideal for rounding up
flocks and chasing off predators. They undoubtedly also found
them useful for raiding other people's stock—and the new composite bow, longer-range, faster-shooting, and above all smaller
(and therefore perfect for use from a chariot) was just coming into
use at around this time.[6]

So the pastoral peoples of Iran, the northern Caucasus, and
the Balkans-Ukraine borderlands honed their skills with this lethal
new combination of chariot and composite bow and discovered
that they could even beat civilized armies with it. Until now,
nomad raids on farming communities had depended on surprise
and a temporary local superiority in numbers, but the pastoralists
had no particular edge in combat except, perhaps, for their greater
personal experience with the weapons of the time. The chariot
changed all that: now they had the ultimate weapon, and they
were no longer coming to raid, but to conquer.

An ideal vehicle for managing herds and conquering farmers. Scythian
war-chariot modelled in gold.

Military historian Sir John Keegan has pointed out that the charioteers' advantage was not just the speed and manoeuvrability that let them swoop into range, launch volleys of lethal arrows at packed formations of infantry, and then race out of range again before the latter could retaliate. It was the very fact that they were herdsmen, accustomed to controlling flocks of animals and inured to the business of efficient, unemotional one-shot killing: it was part of their daily job to select older animals, sick or injured animals, and many of the annual crop of new animals for killing on a rotational basis, and to dispatch them without ruining their hides or frightening the other animals. Moreover, they had a cultural predisposition to regard farmers as inferior beings, less than human and almost prey, so their attitudes toward stock management easily transferred to war against civilized armies. And the armies of the civilized empires, now that the highly motivated volunteer phalanxes of the early city-states were long gone, were perfect targets for such tactics.

> It was flock management, as much as slaughter and butchery, which made the pastoralists so cold-bloodedly adept at confronting the sedentary agriculturalists of the civilised lands in battle. . . . [Civilised] battle formations were likely to have been loose, discipline weak and battlefield behaviour crowd- or herd-like. Working a herd, however, was the pastoralists' stock in trade. They knew how to break a flock up into manageable sections, how to cut off a line of retreat by circling to a flank, how to compress scattered beasts into a compact mass, how to isolate flock-leaders, how to dominate superior numbers by threat and menace, how to kill the chosen few while leaving the mass inert and subject to control.
>
> *Sir John Keegan*, A History of Warfare[7]

The nomad style of fighting in later invasions by mounted horsemen for which we have detailed accounts—and presumably this would be true for the chariot invaders of the early second millennium as well—was to approach in a loose crescent formation whose horns would soon extend around the flank of the civilized army. They would harass the defenders with showers of arrows, not committing themselves to a decisive attack unless the enemy began to flee. "Circling at a distance of 100 or 200 yards from the herds of unarmoured foot soldiers," Keegan writes, "a chariot crew—one to drive, one to shoot—might have transfixed six men a minute. Ten minutes work by ten chariots would cause 500 casualties or more, a Battle of the Somme–like toll among the small armies of the period."[8] And if the enemy still resisted strongly, then the charioteers would withdraw, hoping to draw the civilized army into a pursuit that would break its ranks—and then turn back and close with them while they were in disarray.

"In battle they swoop upon the enemy, uttering frightful yells," wrote Ammianus Marcellinus about the Huns in the fourth century AD. "When opposed they disperse, only to return with the same speed, smashing and overturning everything in their path. . . . There is nothing to equal the skill with which—from prodigious distances—they discharge their arrows, which are tipped with sharpened bones as hard and murderous as iron."[9] By the time of the late Roman empire, of course, the nomads were actually riding and fighting on horseback, something that could not be done with the still puny horses of 2000 BC, but the chariots must have been just as daunting to the foot soldiers who were trying to defend civilization fifty generations earlier.

The first wave of nomad invaders to overwhelm civilization did not come from all that far away, in most cases—invaders coming directly from the deep steppes would not arrive for a long time—but they were almost impossible for the armies of the early empires to deal with. The remnants of Sargon's empire in Mesopotamia had already been picked over by the Gutians and the Elamites, formerly pastoral peoples who had taken up farming in the northern hills leading to the Iranian plateau, but Mesopotamian unity was then re-established by Hammurabi, a local man who ruled from a new capital at Babylon. However, his Amorite empire, still dependent on a mainly infantry army, was no match for the Kassite and Hurrian charioteers who in the seventeenth century BC flooded in from the highland area that is now Kurdistan: it went under, and the charioteers divided Mesopotamia between them.

Nobody knows what language the Kassites spoke, but the Hurrians spoke an Indo-European language, as did the Hittite charioteers who conquered most of central Anatolia (today's Turkey) to the west. Still farther to the west, the Mycenaeans who swept down the Balkans into Greece had the same chariots and spoke another Indo-European language. Their warlike descendants would eventually take over the mercantile and non-militaristic Minoan civilization of Crete, helped along by the enormous volcanic explosion of 1470 BC on the island of Thera that destroyed the cities and coastal villages of northern Crete.

The list of catastrophes rolls on, with the Hyksos, chariot-driving pastoralists from northwestern Arabia who spoke a Semitic language, successfully invading the relatively non-militarized Egyptian kingdom for the first time. Far to the east the Aryans, an Indo-European people originating on the Iranian plateau, utterly destroyed the huge (and so far as we know largely peaceful) civilization of the Indus valley and established their rule over most of northern India. The origins of the Shang dynasty in northern China around 1700 BC remain in dispute, but the sudden appearance of chariots in a part of the world where there was previously no wheeled transport of any kind, plus rock drawings of chariots in six different sites from northern Iran to the upper Yangtse valley, suggest that the founders of the Shang state may also have been barbarian conquerors, quite possibly other Indo-European pastoralists who had begun their eastward trek centuries before in northern Iran.[10]

In many places the nomadic charioteers lasted only a century or so as rulers, for they would have been tiny minorities ruling over resentful populations with the help of slave administrators drawn from the subject peoples; they themselves had neither writing nor bureaucracy. The Egyptians drove the Hyksos out in 1567 BC. The native Mesopotamians revolted under the leadership of Ashuruballit to overthrow their Hurrian overlords in 1365 BC and recreate a united kingdom with about the same boundaries as Sargon's empire. The founders of the Shang dynasty, if they were originally outsiders, were quickly absorbed by the more sophisticated Chinese culture and presented themselves to the world as a native Chinese dynasty. Even where the nomad conquerors remained as overlords for a long time and their own language and culture eventually prevailed, as in Greece, in Hittite Anatolia, and in Aryan-ruled northern India, they were soon not really pastoralists any more; just a highly militaristic ruling class with a taste for hunting wild animals from chariots. But whether their culture survived or not, their impact was enormous; after this first wave of nomad conquerors, almost everybody was militarized, and slavery was a major institution almost everywhere.

The Hittites and the Mycenaean Greeks were famously aggressive, and the Egyptian New Kingdom that expelled the Hyksos was now a militarized state like all the rest: the soldiers that Tuthmose III led up to Megiddo in 1462 BC were no longer the charmingly old-fashioned, largely ritual force typical of the Middle Kingdom, but a full-service, state-of-the-art Bronze Age army. Minoan Crete, a civilization that had avoided large-scale militarization (perhaps because as an island it had never suffered raids by pastoralists), was gone almost without a trace, as was the civilization of the Indus valley. The Aryan overlords of northern India stayed in power forever, in a sense; the modern Indian caste system is widely thought to be an echo of the system of slavery and serfdom that the Aryans used to secure their hold on power.

China escaped the worst cultural consequences of the nomad invasions, perhaps because its early farming cultures, dating from only a thousand years or so after those of the Fertile Crescent, did not spin off their own nemesis, pastoralists. Domesticated sheep, goats, and cattle were present in northern China in small numbers for a long time, but for reasons that are not clear they never became numerous enough to support true pastoralism, and in most of China in Neolithic times the only domesticated animals were the pig and the dog. This may explain why walls started going up around Chinese settlements only in about 3000 BC, two and a half thousand years after they went up in the Fertile Crescent, and even then they appeared only in the north. It seems likely that almost all the pastoralists who were to plague China for the rest of its history had their origins in the Middle East; they just took that long to spread along the edge of the grasslands to China."

In the end China would be conquered by barbarians many times, but its own culture had been granted the time to mature to the point where it would never simply surrender to barbarian values. This may also explain the "Chinese way in war," which combines a strong preference for nomad-style tactics (surprise, deceit, and the avoidance of pitched battles) with an underlying distaste for the whole business of warfare. But no major culture west of China was given that crucial breathing space, and the results were most regrettable. The saddest case was Mesopotamia, which emerged from its first interlude of subjugation by barbarians under the rule of a northern Mesopotamian kingdom—in the foothills, not the plains—called Assyria. It was a society almost gone mad with militarism, and for the next twelve centuries it waged endless war against its subject peoples and its neighbours.

> The commander-in-chief of the king of Elam, together with his nobles . . . I cut their throats like sheep. . . . My prancing steeds, trained to harness, plunged into their welling blood as into a river; the wheels of my battle chariots were bespattered with blood and filth. I filled the plain with the corpses of their warriors. . . . As to the sheikhs of the Chaldeans, panic from my onslaught overwhelmed them like a demon. They abandoned their tents and fled for their lives, crushing the corpses of their troops as they went. . . . [In their terror] they passed scalding urine and voided their excrement in their chariots.
>
> *Sennacherib, King of Assyria,*
> *691 BC*[12]

The prototype for Assyria was the Akkadian empire, which had the same core area (some Assyrian kings even took Sargon's name), but this was a state built almost entirely for war. The Assyrians were wedded to the chariot from the beginning to the end of their empire, but around it they built an army that was almost modern in its structure, with military engineers, supply depots, transport columns, and bridging equipment. On the royal highways that were maintained throughout the empire, it could move as fast as any army until the invention of the internal combustion engine, and it could campaign as far as three hundred miles away from its base. It was the first army to incorporate really effective siege machinery, to equip its soldiers with iron armour and weapons—archaeologists found 160 tons of iron in the palace arsenal of Sargon II (721–705 BC)—and to supplement its chariots with a force of actual horse-riding cavalry. And it was on campaign almost all the time: it has been calculated that during the last 250 years of its existence, the Assyrian empire was at war for 180 years.

Assyria waxed and waned repeatedly over the centuries, as any empire with no natural geographical, historical, or ethnic borders is likely to do. Under Shalmaneser I and his son Tukulti-Ninurta I (1274—1208 BC), the empire spread in every direction and reached the Persian Gulf in the south, only to collapse back to the core area after their deaths. A century later, under Tiglath-Pileser I, it expanded again, this time reaching all the way to the Mediterranean—but by the end of the 900s it was at its lowest ebb, controlling an area barely a hundred miles long and fifty miles wide. And then, in the last three hundred years of its history, "Neo-Assyria" (as some archaeologists call it) became a one-dimensional monster, constantly at war and terrorizing the whole Middle East in order to ensure a constant flow of booty and tribute to its treasury. There is even speculation that it deliberately held its provinces in a loose grip in order to encourage revolts that would give it an excuse to conquer and loot them again. Whole populations were deported amid appalling massacres and resettled far from home in punishment for rebellions, but perhaps also in fulfilment of the empire's need to repopulate some other devastated province: the Israelites were by no means the only people to suffer this fate. Assyria's army rose to the astonishing total (for the times) of 120,000 men, able to carry on several campaigns at once, and its kings and commanders deliberately cultivated a reputation for extreme cruelty as a means of cowing their opponents in advance. Indeed, we know of the Assyrians' addiction to sadism (the phrase is not too strong) mainly from their own inscriptions; they boasted about it.

In the end, the Assyrian empire was consumed by war. "The King knows that all lands hate us," wrote an imperial official to

Esarhaddon early in the seventh century BC, and no wonder: Assyrian armies sacked Babylon in Mesopotamia in 689 BC, Sidon in Lebanon in 677, Memphis in lower Egypt in 671, Thebes in upper Egypt in 663, Babylon again in 648, and Susa in Iran in 646. When new nomad invaders drove into the Middle East in the seventh century BC—genuine cavalry this time, not charioteers, for selective breeding had finally produced horses strong enough to carry a rider in the forward "control" position—Assyria's civilized enemies combined with them to bring the hated empire down: in 612 BC the Assyrian capital, Nineveh, fell to an alliance of Babylonians and Medes (recently settled pastoralists from Iran). The city was destroyed so comprehensively that two centuries later nobody knew where its site had been.[13]

By now the last pieces of the jigsaw puzzle that was civilization during the middle passage had fallen into place. Human settlement of the great grasslands had reached its final stage, with the pastoralists and their herds so close to the carrying capacity of that harsh and variable environment that any major climatic downturn, even a brief one, would set off a struggle for scarce resources that would drive some losing groups right off the grasslands and into the civilized world, where their huge military advantages would cause enormous disruption. And meanwhile, in that civilized world, states dedicated almost exclusively to war had made their first appearance. They would not go away again. In fact, by now organized force dominated everything.

From piracy on the seas and organized banditry in the hills, to enslavement, looting, and destruction as the natural fate of captured cities, organized violence didn't just make the rules; it *was* the rule, and those who ruled were those who were good at it. In the circumstances, it is hardly surprising that most civilized peoples until modern times saw the basic trend of history not as progress toward a better future but as decline from a lost golden age. Surely, they felt, things couldn't always have been this bad— but they always were. The triumphs and tragedies dwindled into meaninglessness with the passage of a few generations, the battles and sieges came and went, the empires rose and fell, and the only constants were oppression and cruelty. Things might get better for a time—they might even stay that way for whole generations, in some fortunate intervals of peace and prosperity—but in the long run, it was three steps forward, three steps back. Violence was the only way to survive, and the quickest way to get rich.

———

As the light faded, the Flavian army arrived in full strength [outside the city of Cremona]. Once they began to march over the heaps of dead and the fresh traces of bloodshed, they thought that the fighting was over and clamoured to press on towards Cremona to receive, or enforce, the surrender of the beaten enemy. This at any rate was what they said openly, and it sounded well. But what each man thought in his heart was something different. A city on flat ground could be rushed, and an army which forced an entrance during the hours of darkness would . . . enjoy greater license to plunder. But if they waited for dawn, it would be too late; there would be peace terms, and appeals for mercy. . . . When a city was stormed, its booty fell to the troops, when surrendered, to the commanders.

Cornelius Tacitus, The Histories[14]

The city did in fact surrender, but this did not prevent the Roman troops from sacking it. Nor did the fact that this was civil war and the citizens of Cremona were fellow countrymen.

Forty thousand armed men forced their way into the city. . . . Neither rank nor years saved the victims from an indiscriminate orgy in which rape alternated with murder and murder with rape. Greybeards and frail old women, who had no value as loot, were dragged off to raise a laugh, but any full-grown girl or good-looking lad who crossed their path was pulled this way and that in a violent tug-of-war between the would-be captors. . . . A single looter trailing a hoard of money or temple-offerings of massive gold was often cut to pieces by others who were stronger. . . . In their hands they held firebrands, which, once they had got their spoil away, they wantonly flung into empty houses and rifled temples. ... There was a diversity of wild desires, differing conceptions of what was lawful, and nothing barred. Cremona lasted them four days.

Tacitus[15]

The destruction of Cremona in AD 69 caused a scandal throughout Italy—an undefended Roman city sacked by Roman legions—and the soldiers who had done it found their captives valueless because of a concerted refusal to buy them as slaves. Although many were then murdered by their captors, some were ransomed by relatives, and other Italian cities contributed to the rebuilding of Cremona. In the vast majority of cases, there was no such help for a slaughtered city or a devastated province. Yet provided there was a generation or two of relative peace, the city would usually be restored, the fields repopulated—in time for the same thing to happen again.

There is far too much history, but it lacks variety. Languages and religions changed, borders fluctuated or disappeared, populations rose or fell—and almost fifteen hundred years after Cremona fell, practically the identical scene was being re-enacted a few hundred miles to the south, in Rome. Sebastian Schertlin, commander of the Spanish Imperial troops, recalled: "In the year 1527, on 6 May, we took Rome by storm, put over 6,000 men to the sword, seized all that we could find in the churches and elsewhere, burned down a great part of the city, tearing and destroying all copyists' work, all registers, letters and documents."[16]

After leading a charmed life in the first thousand years of its history, Rome had been sacked half a dozen times in its second millennium and had shrunk to a tenth of its former population, but the events of AD 1527 were probably the most brutal since the Visigoths under Alaric had ravaged the city for the first time in AD 410. The conquerors were greedy, they were imaginative, and they had plenty of time to deal with the citizens at leisure. According to Luigi Guicciardini, "Many were suspended for hours by the arms; many were cruelly bound by the private parts; many were suspended by the feet high above the road, or over water, while their tormentors threatened to cut the cord. Some were half buried in the cellars, others nailed up in casks, while many were villainously beaten and wounded; not few were cut all over their persons by red-hot irons. Some were tortured by extreme thirst, others by insupportable noise, and many were cruelly tortured by having their own good teeth drawn. Others again were forced to eat their own ears, or nose, or their roasted testicles. . . ."

> I am a prisoner of the Spaniards. They have fixed my ransom at 1,000 ducats on the pretext I am an official. They have tortured me twice, and finished by lighting a fire under the soles of my feet. . . . Dear brother, do not let me perish thus miserably. . . . For the love of God and the Blessed Virgin, help me."
>
> *Giovanni Barozzi*[17]

Such a stable pattern of cruelty over so long a time is more than a little disturbing: all the wars, all the wrecked cities, all the greed and the delight in causing pain. So what are we to make of all this? Was civilization an unmitigated curse?

———

Nobody would argue that civilization was an unalloyed blessing, but there is a babies-and-bath-water issue here. We have no reliable statistics for a comparison, but it seems probable that the proportion of people who died each century as a result of war in civilized societies during the millennia of the middle passage was still less than the average losses from violence suffered by hunter-gatherer groups over a similar span of time. This does not mean that it *felt* better to live in Babylon when the Assyrians arrived, or in Cremona when the Roman legions entered, than to live as a hunter-gatherer. It almost certainly felt a great deal worse, because "civilized" war was mass horror right before your eyes, whereas "savage" warfare was a slow, cumulative, half-invisible drain of lives that never even submitted an invoice for the total cost. The sheer scale makes a difference, too: people were dying in thousands now, not in ones and twos. But the question remains: what does all this tell us about the interplay of human heredity, human intellect, and mass civilization? Or to put it more simply: are we doomed?

The pro argument is deeply worrisome. We belong to an evolutionary line that has a heritage of strong dominance hierarchies, especially among males. Our closest primate relative, the only other ape species that regularly hunts and eats meat, also has a pattern of intraspecific aggression that approximates to what we would call "war," so this is a deeply entrenched behaviour. Many people—perhaps even most people, if the circumstances are right—are capable of ignoring the pain that they inflict on others, or even taking pleasure in it, and this is not merely some perversion of "civilization": the ritual tortures that used to be inflicted on captives by many Native American tribes were in every way, other than the sheer number of victims, as cruel as the behaviour of victorious Assyrian and Spanish armies.

It gets worse. Even when the human line broke away from the strict dominance hierarchies and turned egalitarian at the start of our independent career as hunter-gatherers, we went on killing one another with great enthusiasm. Then we hit civilization, re-erected the old dominance hierarchies in an even more vicious form, and turned war from a social custom into a gigantic, unchallengeable institution. It is embedded in our genes, our psychology, and our institutions, and sooner or later we will blow ourselves away in a nuclear war.

But there is another argument, less strident and less certain of its interpretations, which leaves the question wide open. It observes that human beings broke decisively with the old primate dominance hierarchies at the very start of our independent trajectory, and that we did so because the whole human evolutionary strategy involves big brains and a lot of non-instinctive, culturally transmitted learning. That meant that human babies were hopelessly dependent for a long time, which in turn meant that the babies with two supportive parents were the ones likeliest to survive—which meant that we had to call a truce in the war of the sexes. And we did: human males and females form bonds so strong that they even take precedence over the old single-sex dominance hierarchies for most people. The basic human social institution is the family, not the pecking order.

This matters because the equality of the sexes, or more precisely the millions of alliances between individual men and women in the interest of raising their children to adulthood, is probably the primary reason for our remarkable commitment as a species—particularly remarkable for a primate species—to egalitarianism. It was families that broke the old monkey-king game of dominance among human beings, or at least reduced it to mere background noise most of the time. For at least a million years the equality of all adult males—of all adults regardless of sex in some societies—has been the default-mode human value system. We all still had the old primate dominance reflexes buried somewhere back there in our evolutionary repertoire, and every generation produced ambitious individuals who wanted to play monkey-king, but in practice equality won almost every time because the majority in the band always preferred it. This did not stop us from fighting wars with neighbouring bands, of course, but it is relevant to our future.

Fast-forward to the early civilizations: equality disappears and the old primate dominance hierarchies take over instead. Why? Because those older primate values were still accessible to human beings, and because they had become functionally desirable: the objective requirements of living in a pre-modern mass society without mass communications demanded authoritarian rule. The real question is whether we are now permanently trapped in a new and lethal paradigm. History says no, and its strongest argument is the rise of the new religions.

By 2,500 years ago, most of the human race had been living in the new mass societies for so many generations that all memory of the egalitarian past was long gone. All the visible evidence in these societies argued that tyranny, hierarchy, and privilege were the natural order of things for human beings (although individual social relations stubbornly continued to operate in the old way, for the most part). And then, between about 600 BC and AD 600, in almost all the areas that had seen the rise of the first civilizations, something extraordinary happened. The wars continued and the tyrannies did not fall, but new religions arose—Buddhism in India, and Judaism and its twin descendants, Christianity and Islam, in the Middle East—that were founded on the principle that all human beings are fundamentally of equal worth. People had learned to keep their heads down, but they had not forgotten who they really were.

In the same way, people had long accepted the need to defend themselves and the duty of killing that comes with it, but apart from a few psychopathic individuals, they did not actually like it: the tribes of the New Guinea highlands were glad when they were told they could stop, and the people of civilization would have been happy to do so too if they could really have believed that it was safe. From the beginning of recorded history the monarchs' crude boasts of conquest and carnage have been accompanied by a minor-key counterpoint of lamentation at the waste and cruelty of war, and there were actually societies in the early days of civilization—in Egypt, in Crete, in the Indus valley, and in China—that managed to avoid militarization and even became less violent as they developed (though not less hierarchical, for somebody had to run them). In the end, the nomads did for all the gentler civilizations, and the world was inherited by militarized states that were fully adapted to the circumstances of the middle passage. Nevertheless, we have some evidence, if we want it, that civilized human beings are not simply condemned by their ancestry and their genes to create societies of warrior ants.

However, so long as civilized people were compelled by the cruel logic of numbers to live in rigid hierarchies of power and privilege, their own preferences would remain always subordinate to the whims of their rulers—and the whole system was set up to bring the most ruthless contenders to the top of the heap. Not all of them would be aggressively expansionist in foreign policy, but the principle of the Bad Apple applies with full rigour to the state system as it emerged in the first millennia of civilization: only a few highly militarized and aggressive states would be enough to force every other state to militarize as well, and if the civilized states themselves did not produce enough candidates for that role, then the nomads would be glad to oblige. This is the system that we have inherited from the long past, and it's hard to see how it could have evolved any other way given the realities of numbers and of nomads.

On the other hand, it also seems clear that there is no direct and inevitable connection between the nature of human nature and the way that warfare evolved in civilized societies. Different circumstances could produce a different social order, different kinds of thinking, and ultimately a different result. It certainly wouldn't be easy to break out of the grooves that civilization has travelled in for so many thousands of years, but if one could imagine a hypothetical future in which the nomads are no longer a threat and the people of the mass societies have found a way to escape from tyranny, then just maybe. . . .

A sweet dream, but not one that would have swayed many opinions back in the twelfth century BC.

———

An ancient city was falling and the long years of her empire were at an end. Everywhere the dead lay motionless about the streets, in the houses, and on these temple stairs which our tread had reverenced so long. . . . The Greeks were dashing to the [palace], and thronging round the entrance with their shields locked together over their backs: ladders were already firmly in place against the walls, and the attackers even now putting their weight on the rungs near the door-lintels. Holding shields on their left arms thrust forward for protection, with their right hands they grasped the roof. To oppose them the Trojans, on the brink of death and knowing their plight was desperate, sought to defend themselves by tearing up tiles from the roof-tops of houses . . . to use as missiles. . . . Inside the palace there was sobbing and a confused and pitiful uproar. The building rang from end to end with the anguished cries of women.

Virgil, The Aeneid[18]

The traditional date for the fall of Troy is 1183 BC, a time when history was rapidly transformed into legend. The story of the Trojan Horse, for example, may well be a garbled account of the siege machinery with which the city's walls were finally breached. The semi-barbaric Achaean Greeks besieging Troy lacked such advanced technology, but they could easily have hired military engineers from one of the more civilized countries to the east: around this time the fall of the Hittite empire (under the onslaught of a new wave of nomadic invaders) would have left a lot of unemployed professional soldiers on the loose in Asia Minor. If Hittite mercenaries had built a proper siege tower for the attackers—a wooden structure several stories high, mounted on wheels, with a hide-covered roof to protect the men inside and a metal-tipped battering ram slung in the interior—the Achaeans might well have

Assyrians assaulting the city of Dabigu. Note the scaling ladders on the left of the city, a siege tower that somewhat resembles Homer's "Trojan horse" battering the walls on the right, and the slaughter and impaling of captives after the city fell (bottom and top right). The campaigns of Tiglath-Pileser III, from the bronze gates of Balawat.

dubbed it a wooden horse, leaving subsequent generations to embellish the story. (A siege tower pictured in a roughly contemporary Assyrian bas-relief does look somewhat like a giant horse.)

Troy was actually destroyed after a long siege — the excavated ruins show evidence of huge fires and destruction among the great stone buildings of the city and the refugee hovels packed tightly between them — but the *Iliad* was not written down until four centuries later. It was about eight centuries after that when Virgil wrote his vivid account of the sack of Troy, in a personalized style that would never have been used by those who lived through the event. What he writes is almost all fiction, but it is also as true to the essence of the disaster as if he had been there himself. He lived in a world where some unfortunate city had met its end like this every few years for as long as memory ran, and he had no more freedom to distort the events and emotions of such a siege than a modern European writer would have to misrepresent the experience of an air raid: too many people knew what it was really like.

Carthage, for example, was stormed by Roman troops in 146 BC after a three-year siege at the end of the Third Punic War, and there is an eyewitness account of how the despairing, half-starved Carthaginians held out inside the city through six more days of street fighting: "Three streets leading from the market place to the citadel were lined on both sides with six-story houses, from which the Romans were pelted. They seized the first houses and from their roofs they made bridges of planks and beams to cross over to the next. While one battle was in progress on the roofs, another was fought, against all comers, in the street below. Everywhere there was groaning and wailing and shouting and agony of every description. Some were killed out of hand, some flung down alive from the roofs to the pavement, and of those some were caught on upright spears. . . ."[19]

And when the tangle of debris and civilian bodies in the streets threatened to impede the advance of solid ranks of Roman infantry, auxiliary troops were sent forward to clear it away: "Those told to remove the debris . . . shoved the dead and those still living in pits in the ground, using their axes and crow-bars and shoving and turning them with their tools like blocks of wood or stone.

Human beings filled up the gullies. Some were thrown in head down, and their legs protruding from the ground writhed for some little while. Some fell feet down and their heads were above the surface. Their faces and skulls were trampled by the galloping horses. . . ."[20]

Those familiar with the activities of SS Sonderkommandos in Russia in 1941 at places like Babi Yar will recognize the scene. And the final solution enforced at Carthage (and at Troy) was in no way less ambitious than Hitler's: the relatively few Carthaginians who survived the siege and sack of their city (out of a population of about three hundred thousand) were sold into slavery, and the devastated site was formally cursed and sprinkled with salt by the victorious Roman general. It remained uninhabited until a Roman colony was founded on the ruins over a century later. It all leaves an impression of berserk violence and insane vindictiveness, but that is just the impression that the victorious Romans wanted to leave. In fact, the violence and the vindictiveness were both carefully calculated, as they usually are. Effective brutality requires forethought, calm preparation, and a command of both physics and psychology.

————

In the battle line each man requires a lateral space of three feet, while the distance between ranks is six feet. Thus, 10,000 men can be placed in a rectangle about 1,500 yards by twelve yards.

Vegetius on Roman tactics[21]

Battles determined the course of our ancestors' lives, and they were no less clever than we are. If for several thousand years they could think of no better way to fight than massed in shoulder-to-shoulder formations, there had to be a very good reason. Soldiers are notoriously conservative about experimenting with new weapons and tactics—often with very good reason, for if the innovations fail to perform as advertised, then soldiers will die—but there have been, on the countless battlefields of the past, enough desperate men with nothing left to lose that practically everything got tried sooner or later. And nothing, until well after the introduction of firearms, worked better than the organization and tactics that were already more or less standard before the time of Alexander the Great.

In a world that possessed no force superior to that of arms, a body of armed men that attacked an enemy's territory could do pretty much whatever it wanted—rob and kill anybody it met, destroy the crops, burn the houses—unless the enemy produced a similar body of armed men. The defenders could not just sit behind their walls (they'd eventually starve to death), so they usually came out to fight if they had any chance whatever of success. War almost always involved a real battle, and by the middle of the first millennium BC, battle was probably going to involve a phalanx again. Disciplined and drilled close-combat infantry formations of that kind had gone out of fashion with the rise of the multinational empires whose paid soldiery lacked the cohesion and commitment needed for fighting in phalanxes. (Besides, phalanxes weren't a great deal of use against nomadic invaders.) But as the centres of wealth and power moved west from the Fertile Crescent to the rising city-states of Greece and Rome, large numbers of men with civic patriotism and high motivation were becoming available again for the first time since the early Sumerian city-states. And against the troops of another civilized state who would stand and fight, a phalanx was still the most effective way to deploy infantry in battle.

A battle, for almost all of human history, has been an event as stylized and limited in its movements as a classical ballet, and for much the same reasons: the inherent capabilities and limitations of the human body. When two large groups of men fight, using hand-held weapons or missiles that can be hurled or propelled at most a few hundred yards, the possibilities are very restricted. This is all the more true because the highest priority for both sides is to keep their men disciplined and organized. A few hundred armed men acting in concert, moving in the same direction and with a common purpose, will always be more powerful than a mob ten times their number. In the battle of Mantinea, in

418 BC, "the Spartans came on slowly and to the music of many flute-players in their ranks. This custom of theirs has nothing to do with religion; it is designed to make them keep in step and move forward steadily without breaking their ranks, as large armies often do when they are just about to join battle."[22] Indeed, the basic forms of military drill are among the most pervasive and unchanging elements of human civilization: the Twelfth Dynasty Egyptian armies of 1900 BC stepped off "by the left," and so has every army down to the present day.

Modern armies talk of winning or losing ground, and for them it has some relevance, but for all the armies of earlier times the ground is merely the stage across which the formations move. It is the formations themselves that count, and the ground matters only if it includes obstacles that disrupt those carefully aligned and articulated ranks of thousands of well-drilled troops. The strength of the formation vanishes if gaps open up in the line, for the army can only face and fight to its front and will meet disaster if the enemy can attack it from the side or rear. It will also be helpless if the terrain (or panic) causes the men in the formation to crowd together so closely that they do not have the space necessary to swing or hurl or jab with their weapons: a great deal of the endless drill goes into training the soldiers to maintain that vital three-foot interval at all costs. But if they are well trained, these soldiers are a formidable fighting machine.

A Greek phalanx of the fifth century BC consisted of thousands of hoplites (heavy infantry) in serried ranks, almost fully protected in front by large shields and bronze greaves on their shins, with glittering spear-points extending forward beyond the shield wall. It took a great deal of time and effort to array such huge formations on a battlefield facing the enemy. (It would be even better to attack the enemy's flank or rear, obviously, but the difficulties of complicated movements with these unwieldy masses of men meant that that almost never happened.) Battle could not normally be joined at all unless the commander of the opposing phalanx cooperated, but both sides usually wanted a prompt and decisive outcome. The hoplites were property-owning citizens (who paid for their own weapons and armour), and 80 percent of them were farmers whose crops might be ravaged by the enemy if their army retreated or left to rot unharvested in the fields if the two armies wasted too much time on manoeuvre. They wanted a decision now, and generally they got it. But committing his phalanx to battle was about the last meaningful decision that the commander could make on the battlefield.

There were tactical choices to be made beforehand: should we make the phalanx as deep as possible to achieve a breakthrough (at Leuctra in 371 BC, the Thebans used a formation fifty men deep on the left of their line), or make it shallower but longer so as to extend past the ends of the enemy's phalanx and outflank it? Even the latter tactic would often prove irrelevant, however, for

Why phalanxes drift to the right: each man tucks in behind his neighbour's shield. The figures on the left represent a skirmish line of light infantry (their bronze bows have disappeared). The Battle of Gods and the Giants from the north frieze of the Siphnian Treasure-House at Delphi.

when phalanxes advanced they tended to drift to the right; the shields were carried in the left hand, and so each man tried to protect his exposed right side by tucking in behind the shield of the man to his right. Despite the hundreds of hours spent on the parade ground, therefore, the two opposing lines would often overlap each other on the right by the time they collided. And once they did come together, there was virtually nothing more that the commanders could do.

The men in the front ranks fought each other for a time, being replaced from behind as they fell, until one side or the other thought it was getting the upper hand. At that point, all the ranks united their efforts in a gigantic shove to break the enemy's line decisively, and if they succeeded, then they had won. The enemy's formation would crumble, men would turn to flee, and the massacre would begin. The losers could suffer casualties of half their force or more if the winners pushed their advantage to the limit, but typically the pursuit would relent after a short while (armoured hoplites were not good long-distance runners), and deaths on the losing side would be held to around 15 percent of the total force.

> The Athenian troops weakened their centre by the effort to extend the line sufficiently to cover the whole Persian front: the two wings were strong, but the line in the centre was only a few ranks deep. . . . The word was given to move, and the Athenians advanced at a run towards the enemy, not less than a mile away . . . the first Greeks, as far as I know, to charge at a run. . . . In the centre . . . the foreigners breached the Greek line . . . but the Athenians on one wing and the Plataeans on the other were both victorious. . . . Then . . . they turned their attention to the Persians who had broken through in the centre. Here again they were triumphant, chasing the routed enemy, and cutting them down until they came to the sea, and men were calling for fire and taking hold of the [Persian] ships. . . . Cynegirus [the brother of Aeschylus the playwright] had his hand cut off with an axe as he was getting hold of a ship's stern, and so lost his

life. . . . The Athenians secured in this way seven ships, but
the rest got off. . . .

Thucydides, History of The
Peloponnesian Wars [23]

The only real formula for success was "more hoplites, or better hoplites, or more and better hoplites,"[24] and these clumsy and
bloody shoving matches like gigantic, regimented caricatures of an
American football game or a rugby scrum, fought over a couple of
hours on a rectangular patch of ground perhaps a hundred acres
in area, could determine the future of whole peoples.

There were also lightly armed infantry on the typical Greek
battlefield, mostly men who could not afford to buy hoplite arms
and armour, who would advance in skirmish lines ahead of the
main formations and attack the other side with missile weapons,
but they were rarely decisive. "First the stone-throwers, slingers
and archers on both sides engaged each other in front of the main
lines of battle, with now one party and now another having the
advantage, as is normal with these light troops," said Thucydides
dismissively about their role in one battle. They could be an infernal nuisance to a phalanx of heavy infantry, which could not deal
with them even by charging them. "In a short distance no infantryman, however fast he runs, can catch up with another who has a
bow-shot's start of him," Xenophon sourly remarked, but they
could not hope to defeat the phalanx unless it ventured onto
ground so broken that its formation dissolved.

And there were cavalry (for mounted horsemen had now
replaced chariots on the battlefield everywhere except in a few
militarily conservative places like Persia and downright backward
places like Celtic Britain). The cavalry could move rapidly round
to the flank or rear of the other side's phalanx and cause considerable disruption by throwing javelins and firing arrows, if they
were not first intercepted by that side's own cavalry. They might
even charge the infantry if they caught them off guard—but they
would almost never try to charge well-trained infantry who were
prepared to receive them. A mass of horsemen thundering down
on a formation of mere pedestrians looks irresistible, but horses,

whatever their riders' views on the matter may be, are much too sensible to run straight into an unwavering line of spear-points. They will stop or turn aside at the last moment, and as long as the infantry could keep that thought firmly in mind and hold their formation, they were relatively safe from charges. The cavalry's main purposes were scouting, skirmishing, and above all, riding down and killing the refugees of the defeated side once they had turned to flee.

Heavy infantry dominated the battlefields almost everywhere by classical times (say, 550 BC to AD 350), and within fairly wide limits even their numbers were less important than their discipline and morale. When Alexander the Great fought the Persian army of Darius at Issus in 333 BC, he had only forty thousand men (including light infantry and cavalry) against one hundred thousand; Alexander's army fully deployed extended for considerably less than a mile, while the Persian army's front was about two miles. But once the preliminaries to the battle were past, his veteran hoplites charged straight across the field at the Persian centre. The effect can best be understood in terms of sheer physics: a disciplined mass of, say, thirty thousand heavily armed and armoured men running in tight formation would have hit the Persian line with a force equivalent to twenty-five hundred tons moving at six or seven miles an hour, building up over just a few seconds, and at its leading edge was a hedge of spear-points. There were probably not many men in the first two ranks of Alexander's phalanx who survived the impact (which is why the more experienced veterans would find themselves places a little farther back in the phalanx), but the sheer momentum of this force smashed through the centre of Darius's army in only a few minutes, long before the troops on either end of the longer Persian line could curl round to take Alexander's men in the flank and rear. With its cohesion gone, the Persian army was efficiently exterminated by Alexander's troops; probably half the Persian force was killed within two hours.

As time went on, various military leaders tinkered with this basic formula for military success in order to make it more flexible. The Romans were best at it. In over two centuries of almost constant war in which they first subjugated all the other city-states of Italy and then conquered the other great power of the time, Carthage, they evolved a far more sophisticated version of the phalanx. The unwieldy mass of the phalanx gave way to the more open battle formation of the legion, in which the troops were broken up into mini-phalanxes ("maniples" or handfuls) of about 150 men in three ranks, the maniples being arrayed checkerboard fashion in three overlapping lines. It gave them far more manoeuvrability, especially on broken ground. At the battle of Zama (202 BC) during the Second Punic War, when the Carthaginians tried to rout the Roman legions by a massive elephant charge, Scipio Africanus was even able to move the maniples of his middle line sideways in order to create straight corridors through all three lines of his formation, down which Hannibal's elephants were herded quite harmlessly.

The weapons changed, too. In the Roman legions the long spear gave way to two shorter throwing spears, one lighter and of longer range than the other, which the legionaries threw in succession as they advanced, plus a short sword for close-in work when they had made physical contact with the enemy. Why a short sword? Because it compelled the Roman soldier to get in close and do the killing in a highly personal way, which is what really terrifies the enemy. It was the "Western way of war" again, and it was as much about the psychology of the highly militarized societies that chose this sort of approach as it was about the presumed psychological effects on the enemy.

By high Roman times, battles had become much less of a shoving match and all manner of tactical stratagems flourished, but the basic logic of the battlefield was unchanged. Masses of armed men in highly disciplined formations, equipped only with edged weapons powered by their own muscles, have very limited

The tortoise beats the hare every time. The "testudo" (tortoise), a standard Roman army drill in which soldiers locked their shields over their backs to ward off the shower of missiles from above as they approached the walls of a besieged town, was typical of the methodical, relentless Roman style of warfare. Column of Marcus Aurelius.

alternatives for effective fighting, and infantry ruled the battlefields of the third century AD as confidently as it had the battlefields of the twenty-third century BC.

———

> Straightaway a ship struck its bronze beak against a[nother] ship. A Greek began the ramming and smashed off the entire stern of a Phoenician ship; each captain steered his ship against another. At first the flood of the Persian force put up a resistance; but when the mass of their ships was crowded together in a narrow strait, and they could not bring any assistance to one another, they struck each other with their bronze-mouthed beaks and shattered all the [oars]; the Greek ships judiciously encircled them and made their strike, and ships' hulls were turned upside down, and it was no longer possible to glimpse the sea, which was brimming with wrecked ships and dead men.
>
> *Persian messenger*[25]

Navies have always been far more dependent on technology than armies: a ship is a kind of machine, even if it is a galley whose oars are powered by human muscles. The sea is an alien environment for human beings, and it was never possible for them to survive there without technology. Nor did significant numbers of people have any need to be able to operate in this environment until civilization was well established.

Armies were part of civilization from the start, growing directly out of the warrior bands of pre-civilized societies, but navies only became possible and necessary considerably later in the process. Pre-civilized people used small boats for fishing and for crossing narrow waters, but the extensive use of the sea for trade had to await the emergence of civilizations that produced a variety of specialized goods, such as grain, wine, minerals, and timber, that were worth trading in bulk. Once trade of this sort did become desirable, however, it was inevitable that most of it would be conducted by sea. Ships are by far the most economical means of transporting large volumes of goods over long distances even today, and they were virtually the only means until the invention of railways less than two centuries ago.

Attacking the maritime commerce of states that derived much of their wealth from trade was an obvious (and highly profitable) tactic in war, and undoubtedly the first specialized warships were developed for this purpose. Moreover, the transport by ships of whole armies was an especially attractive military option in the Mediterranean, where the sea was more often than not the quickest route between any two points. Given such valuable targets, naval warfare in the Mediterranean soon grew into an affair of large fleets of warships whose first purpose was to destroy the other side's navy, after which the enemy's merchant shipping could be destroyed with impunity. Given the primacy of technology in naval warfare, however, what is truly remarkable is that Mediterranean warships rapidly matured into a standard design whose technology, complex though it was by the standards of the time, then scarcely changed at all for several thousand years.

There was extensive maritime commerce more than four thousand years ago on the inland seas like the Mediterranean, and it was already beginning to expand outwards up the Atlantic coast of Europe at one extreme and east across the Arabian Sea to India at the other. Then, and for three and a half millennia afterwards, the merchant ships employed a combination of sail and oars, but the warships, which needed to move rapidly in any direction regardless of wind, depended mainly on muscle power: up to several hundred rowers to pull the naval vessels through the water at high speed. The need for discipline and coordination was as great as in the phalanx, whether the crew were free or slaves.

Moreover, large-scale naval warfare has always called for techniques of organization and production that resemble those of industrial societies. When Greece was faced with the great Persian invasion early in the fifth century BC, the Athenian shipyards adopted mass production methods and produced between six and eight triremes (galleys with three banks of oars) each month for over two years. By 480 BC some 250 galleys had been

built, requiring over forty thousand men to crew them. All the
military manpower of Athens went into the fleet, leaving the other
Greek city-states to provide the land forces for the peninsula's
defence. But this diversion of effort proved its worth when the
Greek fleet, predominantly Athenian, destroyed the Persian fleet
at Salamis and forced the emperor Xerxes to retreat from Greece.

> Now, as for the battle, if I can help it I shall not fight it in the
> gulf, nor shall I sail into the gulf. I fully realise that a lack of
> sea room is a disadvantage for a small, experienced and fast
> squadron [like our own], fighting against a lot of badly man-
> aged ships. One cannot sail up in the proper way to make an
> attack by ramming unless one has a good long view of the
> enemy ahead, nor can one back away at the right moment if
> one is hard pressed oneself; it is impossible also to sail
> through the enemy's line and then wheel back on him which
> are the right tactics for the fleet which has the superior sea-
> manship. Instead of all this, one would be compelled to fight
> a naval action as though it were a battle on land, and under
> those circumstances the side with the greater number of
> ships has the advantage. So you can be sure that I shall be
> watching out for all this as far as I can.
>
> *Phormio addressing the Athenian fleet*
> *before the battle of Naupactus, 429 BC*[26]

Naval warfare in classical and medieval times was a simple
affair, sometimes virtually the aquatic version of a land battle.
The two opposing forces of galleys, often numbering in the hundreds, would line up facing each other off some stretch of
coastline (galleys hugged the coasts whenever possible; such
ships were not very seaworthy nor were their captains capable of
accurate navigation out of sight of land), and charge at each
other. The ships would endeavour to hole each other head-on
with their bronze rams, or at least shear off the oars on one side
of the enemy galley (crushing most of the rowers on that side in
the process) and then turn back and ram the disabled enemy
from astern. As often as not, however, they would end up lying

alongside each other, with the soldiers that each galley carried fighting it out along the decks of one ship or the other, as in the battle in Syracuse harbour in 413 BC, where almost two hundred ships fought one another in a very confined space:

> Many ships crowded in upon each other in a small area. Consequently there were not many attacks made with the rams amidships. . . . Once the ships met, the soldiers fought hand to hand, each trying to board the enemy. Because of the narrowness of the space, it often happened that . . . three, or sometimes more ships found themselves jammed together, so that the steersmen had to think of defence on one side and attack on the other . . . and the great din of all these ships crashing together was not only frightening in itself, but also made it impossible to hear the orders given by the boat swains.
> *Thucydides*[27]

The greatest naval battles of classical times were fought between Rome, essentially a land power at the beginning of the Punic wars in 264 BC, and Carthage, a maritime power with allies or possessions in Spain, Sardinia, Sicily, and southern Italy. The naval harbour of Carthage (near modern Tunis) was an entirely

State-of-the-art for almost two thousand years. Roman war galleys were not much different from Athenian ones five hundred years before, or Venetian ones fifteen hundred years later. Decorative fresco from the Room of the Vettii, Pompeii.

man-made construction approached through the commercial port, which was itself protected by a series of heavy iron chains across the entrance. Inside the naval harbour, a circular space over a thousand yards across with a central island, there were sheds for working on two hundred galleys at once. A standard Carthaginian quinquireme (with more than one rower per oar) bore a crew of 270 rowers, 30 officers, and 120 marines for fighting—and Carthage's shipyards were able to build as many as sixty galleys a month.

In the generations of war that convulsed the western Mediterranean from 264 to 146 BC before Rome finally defeated Carthage, the Romans learned to build and fight a navy too. Once again, the rate of production was remarkable: soon after the outbreak of the war, realizing they would need a navy, the Romans adapted a Carthaginian design and produced a fleet of a hundred quinquiremes and twenty triremes in less than two months. In the naval battles that followed, and even more in the sudden storms that sometimes overtook the fleets of flimsy galleys in open waters, the losses of life were tremendously heavy.

In 256 BC, at Ecnomus off the coast of North Africa, a Roman fleet of 330 galleys routed a Carthaginian fleet of equal size, sinking thirty and capturing sixty-four, a loss to the Carthaginians of between thirty and forty thousand men. And on its return to Italy, the Roman fleet was caught in a great storm off the west coast of Sicily and 270 of its ships were sunk or driven ashore, drowning well over fifty thousand men. There has not been a comparable loss in naval warfare since.

The nature and scale of naval warfare two thousand years ago compel two observations. One is the obvious, by now repetitive remark about the "steady state" character of warfare during the middle passage. Eighteen hundred years after Ecnomus, in AD 1571, the allied naval forces of western Europe fought the Turkish navy at Lepanto. There were over two hundred galleys on each side, built from designs that would not have caused any surprise in the shipyards of ancient Carthage, and the tactics would not have surprised them either: ram if you can, board if you can't. And close to thirty thousand men drowned in an afternoon.

The other observation is that the conflict between Rome and Carthage was as close as classical civilization ever got to the concept of total war.

Carthago delenda est. (Carthage must be destroyed.)
Cato the Elder

The Mediterranean was big enough for both Carthage and Rome, just as it is big enough to contain both Tunisia and Italy today. There was no deep-rooted historical or racial hatred between the two peoples before the Punic wars began (though there certainly was by the end, over a century later). The basic cause of the wars was no more (and no less) than the anxiety of two rising imperial powers over the mere existence of a rival that had enough power to pose a serious threat. The potential for war became the reason for war and, once begun, the conflict escalated rapidly to a war of annihilation, because neither side was willing to back down.

The classical civilizations of the second century BC were capable of feats of organization and production equal to those of sixteenth-century Europe: a society that can send over a hundred thousand men to sea would be a formidable contender in the great-power stakes even today. Moreover, the classical Mediterranean world seems in almost every respect, not just the naval, to be as competent in the tasks and trades of civilization as was the world of the sixteenth century.

Rome and Carthage were not just building huge fleets of warships to fight each other; at times they were also maintaining armies on three or four fronts simultaneously, spread all over the western Mediterranean. The drain on manpower was huge: it has been calculated that at the height of the Second Punic War in 213 BC, 29 percent of Rome's male citizens were under arms,[28] a level that was rarely exceeded even in the great wars of the past century. Although Rome was ultimately victorious, 10 percent of its entire male population was killed in battle during the final two decades of the war.[29] As for the Carthaginians, their casualties were virtually total: by the end of the Third Punic War in 146 BC, not only was their empire gone, but Carthage itself was razed, and those Carthaginians left alive were sold into slavery. Not even their language survived. A nuclear strike on Carthage would have ended their agony more quickly, but the result would not have differed much.

The Punic wars are the outstanding case, or at least the best documented case, of an approach to total war between civilized states before modern times. Out of the three elements that make our kind of total war possible today—the ability to mobilize the entire population for war, the resources that make that degree of mobilization possible, and the technology of mass destruction—only the technology was obviously missing in the Punic wars. All that meant, in the end, was that it took longer to destroy Carthage utterly than total destruction would take these days. (And, of course, it happened to only one side.)

But although the example is apt enough in terms of how wars sometimes escalate to the furthest extremes of violence that available resources permit, regardless of the original cause, the Punic wars were not really comparable in scale to the wars of the past century.

Rome was a complex and sophisticated civilization, but it was fundamentally different in certain key respects from our own. Its organizational ability was great, as was its aptitude for large-scale civil engineering projects, but its interest in technological innovation was very low. The tradition of rational and dispassionate analysis that the Romans inherited from Greece was consistently applied to political, legal, military, and cultural topics but very rarely to the economic or scientific subjects that were the key to changing the age-old terms of the argument and setting rapid technological change loose in the world. Throughout its history the Roman empire remained a mostly illiterate peasant society in which the availability of a huge and growing slave population made any departures from existing political and economic relations unattractive to the few million people who had a say in things. Rome lived and died in the mould of classical civilization, without ever showing any sign of being able to get off the tread-mill: its natural habitat was the middle passage.

Classical civilizations also lacked the wealth necessary for real total war. The city-states of Rome and Carthage, each containing fewer than a million full citizens, both controlled large empires whose resources they could draw on. Three-quarters of the Roman state's revenues came from abroad by 200 BC so it was able to mobilize a very high proportion of its own citizens for war and pay for large numbers of allied troops (and mercenaries, in Carthage's case) as well. But the basic military equation of pre-modern times held true: societies whose economic base is subsistence agriculture cannot afford to withdraw more than a very small fraction of their population from production to be sent off to war.

Rome and Carthage were able to draw on the resources of the entire western Mediterranean in their war, and yet the total number of men they had under arms probably never exceeded three-quarters of a million, around 3 percent of the total population of the region. That was probably close to the upper limit that any pre-modern civilized society could afford to devote to war, even though the armed forces did not then make huge demands on the civilian economy for supplies. The soldiers had to be fed and paid, but the only other major calls the war made on resources were iron for weapons, and wood and labour for ship-building. The Punic wars were total for the cities of Rome and Carthage in a quite modern sense, but for the western Mediterranean as a whole they were nothing of the sort.

The actual size of the Roman army a few centuries later, when Rome ruled the entire Mediterranean and had legions guarding borders as far away as Scotland and Sudan, is a more accurate measure of the size of military forces a pre-modern agrarian society could sustain over the long run. At the turn of the millennium, AD 1 or thereabouts, the population of the Mediterranean region was about sixty million, and the total size of the army, including not only legionary troops but all the cavalry and auxiliary forces, was not much above three hundred thousand. Even in the late third century AD, when the population had risen to one hundred million and the barbarian pressure on the frontiers was getting serious, the Roman army never exceeded three-quarters of a million troops.[30]

It was a very good army, and quite modern in many respects. The troops were reasonably well paid, they were well trained, and they could even expect a decent pension if they lived long enough to retire. In the centurions, it had the first professional officer corps that has ever existed. It occasionally lost a battle, but against other civilized armies it was almost guaranteed to win in the long run. It hadn't really had to fight against the horse nomads, because after the incursions of the Cimmerians and the Scythians in the seventh century BC just as Rome was getting started, the civilized world of Europe and the Middle East had not had to contend with any major barbarian invasions for almost a thousand years. But then some change in climate or population out in the heart of the Central Asian steppes set the nomads moving again, and a few generations later the ripple effect began to hit the borders of the Roman empire. In the end, the empire went under, and most of Europe's civilization with it. It was almost a thousand years before it regained its former level.

———

In AD 378 the combined forces of the Visigoths and the Ostrogoths, having spent decades wandering along the Vistula and Dniester rivers, crossed the frontier into the Roman empire with over a hundred thousand men. As usual they were accompanied by their families, and the wagons formed a vast encampment eight miles from the city of Adrianople while the bulk of the riders raided through central Thrace. The Roman emperor Valens marched out from Constantinople with sixty thousand soldiers, two-thirds of them infantry, and reached Adrianople on 9 August.

Just as the Roman army began to rush the camp, tens of thousands of Visigothic horsemen swept down from the flank, swamped the Roman cavalry, and swarmed around the unprotected sides and rear of the Roman legions. Forty thousand of them were slaughtered in a couple of hours, including the emperor himself. The barbarians had destroyed a Roman army for the first time since Varus had led three legions too far into the forests of Germany over three and a half centuries previously, and this time it was not an isolated incident. The Dark Ages (or rather, the latest dark age) had arrived.

The classical world took a long time dying: western and southern Europe went down before the Germanic invasions in

Roman high tide. Dacians attacking a small Roman fort during Trajan's conquest of Dacia (Romania), 1st century AD. Trajan's column.

the fourth and fifth centuries, but virtually the whole of the eastern Roman empire (Byzantium, as it later came to be called) survived intact for more than two hundred years. North Africa and the Fertile Crescent were overrun by Arab nomads fired by the new faith of Islam in the seventh and eighth centuries, but a Greek-speaking and Christianized version of Roman civilization was preserved in the Balkans and Asia Minor until the destruction of the main Byzantine army by incoming Turkish nomads at Manzikert in AD 1071. Thereafter it was reduced to a small area around Constantinople in little more than a century, but civilization never collapsed in the eastern Mediterranean. What emerged there instead, under Arab and Turkish rule, was an Islamized version of classical civilization that preserved and even refined the urban, literate, and commercial character of that culture. Indeed, it is only thanks to them that substantial knowledge of that classical tradition survived.

The Dark Age that Europe remembers, when successive waves of invaders—Goths, Vandals, Huns, Magyars, and Norsemen—overran the western Roman world in the fifth century and kept coming until the tenth, was at least the third such upheaval since 2000 BC to devastate and disrupt the civilizations whose deepest roots lay in the Fertile Crescent. Each time it took centuries to put the pieces back together, especially since it was often the victorious nomads who had to do the job of reconstruction. Of all the areas where civilization emerged in the Old World, only China still speaks more or less the language it started out with; elsewhere, the Indo-European, Turkic, and Semitic languages of the various waves of nomad conquerors have blotted out the old tongues.

Although China's language and culture survived the nomads, its people often didn't: the Great Wall was not a lasting military success. The Huns overran northern China in AD 304 (some seventy years before Fritigern destroyed the Roman legions at Adrianople), initiating an era of complete chaos that lasted four centuries. The Mongols in the thirteenth century were even worse: an estimated forty million Chinese were systematically slaughtered by Genghis Khan's soldiers to depopulate the northern areas of the country and free them for nomadic herding. And

Iraq, which was visited by the Mongols for only two years, from 1258 to 1260, was so thoroughly devastated that its population did not recover to the pre-Mongol level until the twentieth century.

The delays, setbacks, and lost chances suffered by civilization through most of its history because of these sporadic but overwhelming catastrophes go a long way toward explaining why "progress" is a relatively recent concept. It is, after all, only seven centuries since Mongol horsemen were operating a day's ride from Vienna. If they had overrun western Europe at that time even for a few years—as genuine horse nomads straight off the steppes they could not have stayed long, for they could not have found adequate pasture for all their horses while still keeping their army together in the very different terrain of western Europe—it is hard to believe that the process of cumulative and accelerating change that arose in Europe over the following centuries to produce the modern world would ever have begun at all. But when Hungary and Poland were already in the Mongols' grasp, Genghis Khan died, and they turned back to deal with the succession struggle within the new Mongol Empire. Europe got its chance, and the style of civilization it produced has now pushed the nomads to the utmost borders of irrelevance. It has also delivered us to the brink of the abyss.

———

The history of warfare is inevitably Eurocentric, because it was the Europeans who eventually conquered most of the world, and the weapons and modes of warfare devised by European civilization still dominate the planet. But for a period of almost a thousand years, in the latter part of the middle passage, Europe fell out of the military mainstream and adopted a rather eccentric style of warfare. The barbarians had taken over, and they brought their military customs with them. In fact, they brought a great deal of baggage with them.

The Dark Ages were not dark at all in those areas that were overrun by the Islamic cultures. In the Muslim states, what eventually emerged was a politically fragmented variant of the old classical civilizations in an Islamic idiom. The Arab and later Turkish conquerors arrived as victorious but tiny minorities—the steppe and semi-desert areas they came from had far smaller populations than the agricultural areas they had conquered— and despite enthusiastic immigration into the conquered lands they never became majorities. It has been estimated that no more than one hundred thousand genuine Central Asian Turks ever made it to Anatolia throughout the period of the "Turkish invasions" (which is why today's Turks look Mediterranean, not Central Asian), and most Egyptians are descended from the people who were already living there in the time of the pharaohs, not from Bedouin newcomers. The invaders were therefore almost obliged to take over the existing systems for running such large societies. The cultural prestige of Islam ensured that the majority of the conquered populations would end up converting to Islam and speaking the Arab or Turkish languages of the conquerors—about half the population of what had been the Christian world in late Roman days had been conquered by Muslims by AD 800—but the institutions of the new Muslim empires (and the bureaucrats who ran them) were largely taken over from the late Roman—Byzantine model. They were only doing what the best pastoral conquerors have always done— keeping the old traditions of civilization going—but it may have put Muslims at a grave disadvantage later on, for things happened very differently in Europe.

In western Europe, the invaders were genuine barbarians. They shared few of the assumptions and values of civilized societies, and they were pagan in their religious beliefs. The destruction they wrought was far greater and they came in very large numbers. They were, in fact, whole nations on the move: nations of subsistence farmers from central and eastern Europe beyond the borders of the Roman empire, partly pushed by population pressure and drawn by the prospect of loot, partly fleeing before the incursions of genuine horse nomads like the Huns from the steppes. They came with an elite of mounted warriors and battered down the defences of the empire, but when they arrived in present-day France or Spain or Italy they mostly settled down to farm again. They probably never outnumbered the surviving Roman citizens in the western parts of the empire, and the fact that they were soon Christianized helped to ensure that it was the language of the conquered, not their own Germanic tongues, that ended up as the common language. (Of all the parts of western Europe formerly ruled by Rome, only the southern parts of the German-speaking lands, the Low Countries, and England do not still speak some dialect of late Latin, and even English is a half-French pidgin with strong Latin influences.) But there were enough of the newcomers to ensure that it was their way of running things, not the old ways evolved during three thousand years of imperial rule in the Middle Eastern—Mediterranean world, that prevailed.

There were several centuries of almost total breakdown in western Europe, and when a stable social structure re-emerged, it was based on an extreme dispersal of political and military power. The real power base in feudal times was not the state (which scarcely existed), but the few dozens or hundreds of square miles that had been granted to some local warrior or just seized by him. And the only military tool available to what passed for a central administration of the kingdom was an assembly of such warriors— if they decided to show up, for as long as they were willing to stay. The mould of classical civilization had been decisively broken, which guaranteed Europe a millennium of constant internal strife and external weakness. But it may also be what eventually set it free to change.

In the military sphere, the nomad and barbarian conquests meant that cavalry came to dominate the battlefield everywhere in the European—Mediterranean region, and continued to do so even many centuries after the new order was thoroughly established. In the Muslim east, the main method of warfare remained fully in the nomad tradition: fast, lightly armed and armoured clouds of horsemen who used composite bows for harassing attacks from a safe distance, and the sword and light lance for the much rarer occasions when they closed with their opponents. In the west, cavalry warfare took a quite different course, eventually evolving into the unique form of riders with armour covering their entire bodies astride lumbering horses bred for their ability to bear weight, depending for their effect on the sheer physical impact of their charge—a mounted (and distinctly less organized) version of the phalanx.

Horses had been growing bigger and better as weapons platforms throughout the classical period, and as the threat on the Roman empire's borders mounted, the proportion of cavalry to infantry in Roman armies rose steadily. However valuable infantry may be on the battlefield, men on foot move more slowly than men on horseback, and infantry are of no use if they can't be there when you need them. For the Arab and Turkish tribesmen who finally burst through the borders of the eastern Roman empire, horses were practically a way of life, so their subsequent domination of warfare in the Muslim lands is understandable. Horses were not a way of life for most of the barbarians who overran the western Roman empire (although their elite warriors certainly rode them), so the subsequent dominance of cavalry in western European warfare needs more explanation. After all, the conquerors were soon in charge of large settled populations able to provide trained and disciplined infantry armies in the old style.

Partly it was a question of money: the conquerors lacked the ability or even the desire to recreate states that could collect taxes on a regular basis, so how could you train and pay a Roman-style infantry army? But to an even greater extent it was a question of cultural style. Horses, as the upper class everywhere in Europe remembers to this day (and as every former infantryman would readily agree), are much more fun. They also offered far more scope for the individual feats of glory that were the whole reason for being of the Germanic tribal warriors and their heirs, the European nobility, than being stuck somewhere in the middle rank of a phalanx. If nobody spoiled the game by raising a serious force of infantry, then cavalry would settle all the battles.

Warfare is a serious business, and it may seem incredible that anything as frivolous as one kind of fighting being more fun and more "honourable" than another could influence the dominant military style of an entire era, but there is a precedent. When chariots were first introduced into warfare early in the second millennium BC they were genuinely frightening weapons systems, but as time passed their real military value must have degraded rapidly. Infantry would learn anti-chariot tactics soon enough: if you ground your spears and don't panic when the charioteers charge, their horses will veer away at the last moment, and a company of good archers with the infantry will stop their harassing tactics of driving up to a couple of hundred yards away and firing off a bunch of arrows. In the *Iliad*, set in the twelfth century BC, chariots have been reduced to the role of mere "battlefield taxis" delivering the heroes to single combat (though that may more accurately reflect their role in the eighth century BC, when the oral tradition was finally written down.)

Nevertheless, it is clear that for a long time—much longer than makes tactical sense—chariots remained the highest-status weapon on the battlefield. But it makes political and social sense if you recall that the chariot was the hereditary fighting vehicle of the pastoral conquerors who were running the civilized world after the first Dark Age. It was much more exciting (and probably safer) to dash around the battlefield in a chariot than to be an infantryman, and as long as everybody cooperated they could keep the old game alive. The suspicion lingers that the total dominance of cavalry in western Europe in the centuries between the fall of Rome and late medieval times owes much to a similar sentiment.

The other factor militating against a revival of infantry was explicitly political: it would have meant handing over military power from the rulers to the ruled. The average subject in a medieval peasant society could not take part in cavalry warfare because only wealthy feudal landowners could afford the horses and armour that were required, but given proper training he could certainly have been turned into an effective infantryman. However, infantry means large numbers, and that means placing military power in the hands of ordinary citizens. That would have had revolutionary implications (and eventually did have) for the rigidly stratified feudal societies that grew out of the barbarian invasions in western Europe.

It is striking, too, how strongly the cultural tradition of close combat carried through even in the seemingly inhospitable context of cavalry warfare. Everywhere else, horse-mounted troops exploited their mobility and the extremely effective composite bow to wage an arm's-length, hit-and-run, harassing style of war, at least until they had reduced the ranks of the enemy to confusion. In the West, the cavalry went in for headlong, death-or-glory charges that actually depended to a significant extent on the sheer inertial momentum of big horses and armoured riders. The full unfolding of this trend had to wait for the stirrup (which had arrived in Europe, probably from China, by the eighth century), much more elaborate saddles, and ever bigger horses, but by the time of the Crusades in the twelfth century the chivalry of Christendom were actually fighting like a mounted phalanx—a heavily armoured phalanx eight feet tall and moving at twenty-five miles an hour. If it hit you, that was the end of it, but it was pretty easy to evade if you were not culturally committed to fighting that way, which (among other things) is why the Crusaders had to go home to Europe in the end. And by late Middle Ages, when the population, prosperity, and organizational competence of western Europe were again approaching the level of Roman times, infantry re-emerged as the dominant force on the battlefield, even though there had been no significant change in the technology of weapons.

———

The first signs of the shift back to infantry weapons came during the Hundred Years' War (fourteenth to fifteenth centuries), when English longbowmen protected themselves from cavalry charges by patterns of holes dug in front of their lines to break the legs of charging horses or by pointed stakes dug into the ground (the equivalent of the phalanx's hedge of spears), and repeatedly decimated French formations of heavily armoured cavalry.

In an attempt to deal with the threat posed by longbows (and crossbows), which could penetrate chain mail at a considerable distance, the mounted knights were first driven to the use of plate armour: the classic iron pyjamas worn by the last few generations of European chivalry. Their plate armour was carefully designed with ridges and oblique facets that would deflect arrows. To pierce plate armour effectively, an arrow had to strike at an angle of nearly ninety degrees within a distance of two hundred yards. But similar plate armour to protect their horses was prohibitively heavy and expensive, and the last battles of the Hundred Years' War, like Agincourt in 1415, saw the pathetic spectacle of dismounted knights, wearing about sixty pounds of plate armour each, attempting to charge on foot. Chivalry, in the most literal sense, was dead.

The lesson was taken: if infantry is really the most effective element on the battlefield, then it ought to be really infantry, and not dismounted horsemen in metal clothing. By the sixteenth century, despite the advent of gunpowder weapons on the battlefields of western Europe, combat once again centred on clashes of heavy infantry fighting in a style that would have been entirely familiar to Alexander the Great. For example, toward the end of the Italian wars, a conflict between France and the "Imperial" forces (Spain and most of Germany and Austria) that was fought mostly in northern Italy between 1464 and 1559, two well-matched armies met each other at Ceresole, not far from Turin.

They were smaller than most of the armies at the great battles of classical times, only about fifteen thousand on each side, and the year was AD 1544, not 332 BC. But over the previous century the Europeans had reinvented the principles of a serious body of infantry: uniforms, numbered units, flags to identify them and keep them together, drill, rigid discipline, marching in step, the lot. And when the two sides lined up one pleasant April morning on two facing ridges with a gentle dip between them, Alexander could have taken command of either side with no more preparation than a crash course in a new language (four languages, actually, as there were Spaniards on one side, French on the other, and Italians and German or Swiss-German mercenaries on both sides).

There were a few tactical variations, caused by the innovation of firearms: the infantry phalanxes were essentially the same, carrying pikes that were no more than glorified spears, but the French had thought it might be useful to place a rank of arquebusiers (men armed with heavy matchlock muskets that fired a half-ounce bullet) behind the first rank of pikemen. As Captain Blaise de Montluc explained, "In this way we should kill all their captains in the front rank. But we found they were as ingenious as ourselves, for behind their first line of pikes they had put pistoleers. Neither side fired till we were touching and then there was wholesale slaughter. Every shot told: the front rank on each side went down. The second and third ranks met over the corpses of their comrades in front, the rear ranks pushing them forward. And as we pushed harder, the enemy tumbled over."[31]

In the end, it came to the same old shoving match that the hoplites knew: "the push of pike," as men of the sixteenth century called it. The French and their Swiss mercenary allies had the advantage of pushing downhill. The Landsknechte, their German mercenary opponents in the centre of the Imperial line, had rashly advanced beyond the bottom of the dip and onwards, uphill toward the French. When a small force of French heavy cavalry hit the Germans in the flank, their formation folded up, and they were herded into a tightly packed mob where they had no space to use their pikes. Out of seven thousand Landsknechte, nearly five thousand were slaughtered. The Italian infantry on the left wing of the Imperial line had already marched off the field to save itself, but when the Spanish and German veterans on the Imperial right tried to retreat through a small wood in their rear, they were quickly cut off by the French cavalry, with the French infantry close behind.

> And when they descried us only 400 paces away, and with our cavalry ready to charge, they threw down their pikes and surrendered to the horsemen. You might see fifteen or twenty of

Infantry resurgent: the sixteenth-century "push of pike." Cavalry are dashing around in the foreground of this Bruegel painting, but the real business is being settled by the Spanish-style *tercios* of pikemen in the centre of the picture. Detail from *The Suicide of Saul*, Pieter Bruegel the Elder.

them around a man at arms, pressing about him and asking for quarter, for fear of us of the infantry who were wanting to cut all their throats. A great many, perhaps half, got killed, the rest were accepted as prisoners.[32]

Presumably the battle of Ceresole settled something, though nobody remembers exactly what it was. But it was full circle: the Dark Ages and their cavalry interlude were long past, and what happened at Ceresole was indistinguishable, except in minor details, from what had happened under the walls of Umma four thousand years before, or at Issus halfway between the two.

6

The Road to Mass Warfare

Blessed be those happy ages that were strangers to the dreadful fury of these devilish instruments of artillery, whose inventor I am satisfied is now in hell, receiving the reward of his cursed invention, which is the cause that very often a cowardly base hand takes away the life of the bravest gentleman.

Cervantes, *Don Quixote*

AT THE TIME OF CERESOLE, THE MOST POWERFUL WEAPONS IN the world, the great siege cannons, were capable of killing perhaps half a dozen people (if they stood close together) at a range of a few hundred yards. Today, less than five centuries later, the modern counterparts of those weapons, the intercontinental ballistic missiles, can kill several million people at a range of seven or eight thousand miles. The process that has delivered us from there to here has not been a simple one but in retrospect it seems almost inevitable.

"Modern" Europe, whose style of warfare has become the model for most of the world, emerged from its feudal cocoon five or six centuries ago, but only in the last 150 years or so have its weapons been anything special. From the start, however, it was evolving an approach to war distinguished by the rational and disciplined application of existing technology to battle. Even more importantly, it was becoming a society whose wealth and political beliefs would eventually allow it to make the leap into mass warfare on an unprecedented scale—and mass warfare was the only foundation on which, with the aid of technology, the absurd and lethal phenomenon of total war could ever have been built.

We now tend to identify the invention of gunpowder as the point of departure for the drastic changes that ultimately produced total war. But new technology was only peripheral to the early phases of change, in which mercenaries replaced feudal armies, regular armies supplanted the mercenaries, and the regular armies of professional soldiers were finally expanded into mass armies. It was not really firearms that demoted the mounted knight from the leading actor on the battlefield to the position of ornate irrelevance that he occupied by the time *Don Quixote* was written.

The explosive results of mixing saltpetre, sulphur, and charcoal were first discovered in China (probably by accident, as the soil near Beijing is heavily impregnated with saltpetre). The Sung dynasty was a period of remarkable technological innovation in China, and as early as 1232 Chinese troops defending the city of Loyang against the Mongols used a "thunder bomb," an iron vessel filled with gunpowder and hurled among the besiegers by catapult. The explosion blew those nearby to pieces, and splinters from the casing pierced metal armour.

Within twenty-five years Chinese technicians had developed the "fire-lance," a primitive gun consisting of a bamboo tube stuffed with gunpowder that, when ignited, would fire a cluster of pellets about 250 yards. Their Mongol enemies also adopted the new weapon and probably transmitted it to Europe, where Mongol armies were also active. By the 1320s, the first real metal guns were being cast in Europe.[1]

From that point on, the lead in developing firearms passed entirely to Europe, a region of rapidly growing wealth and population that was straining against the confines of its medieval straitjacket—and also a continent divided into dozens of separate states and torn by constant wars. Indeed, Jared Diamond has theorized that Europe rapidly overtook China in the application of new technologies precisely because it was divided into so many rival states, a consequence of its geography. The numerous peninsulas, offshore islands, and mountain ranges of western Europe were as likely to produce many different states as China's smooth coastline, big rivers, and interior plains were to produce a single big state— and indeed, while China was first united under one ruler more than two thousand years ago and has remained united most of the time since, Europe has never been successfully united by force.[2]

With rival European states perpetually preparing for the next war, any new technology that offered an advantage was likely to be seized on, and weapons technologies most of all. There were the usual conservatives who feared (often correctly) that the new technologies would undermine their social position and therefore rejected them, but if European innovators were rejected by one ruler, they had only to go to the neighbouring kingdom with their idea or device to find a warm welcome. (In China, by contrast, a single emperor's order could permanently shut down a promising new technology—and sometimes did, as in the famous 1421 ban on ocean-going ships that cheated China out of its share of the new worlds of the Americas and Australasia that were about to be "discovered," conquered, and colonized solely by Europeans.)[3] So China never independently went beyond "fire-lances," while in Europe within two centuries firearms had been elaborated at one extreme into giant cannons able to hurl an iron shot weighing 1,125 pounds at city walls, and at the other extreme into arquebuses (early muskets) that fired half-ounce bullets to an effective range of one hundred yards.

Our latter-day obsession with technology is so great that it was even common at one time for historians to give a specific date for the end of the Middle Ages: 1453. That was when the massed cannons of the Turkish army under the young Sultan Mehmet II finally breached the fourteen miles of massive walls surrounding the city of Constantinople, for most of the previous thousand years the world's greatest metropolis, and so brought to an end the Byzantine Empire, the last surviving remnant of the Roman Empire.

But those nineteenth-century historians were using Constantinople only as a symbolic turning point; what really interested them was the end of feudalism in Europe, and they thought they had a perfectly obvious chain of cause and effect. Cannon could knock over castle walls; therefore the independent power of the feudal nobility was destroyed; and therefore gunpowder began the long march of progress that has culminated in the peace, prosperity and enlightenment of our very own nineteenth century.

The military reality of the time was quite different. The old-style medieval castles and town walls were hopelessly vulnerable to cannon-fire, which brought the walls tumbling down of their own weight by simply banging away at the base until they dug a deep enough groove. But by the seventeenth century a new kind of fortification based on deep ditches, sloping walls, and angular bastions was winning the technological race against the cannons of the time. It was at sea that massed cannon-fire had its most profound impact, for the broad-beamed, ocean-going sailing ships of western Europe were ideal artillery platforms. By the mid-1500s western European men-of-war were mounting broadside-firing cannon and fighting it out at close range—and these extraordinary artillery duels, modified only by the addition of more and better cannon ranged on two or even three decks, would decide most battles at sea for the next three hundred years. On the battlefield, however, firearms took longer to come into their own.

Primitive muskets gradually took over from longbows or crossbows as the principal missile-firing weapon—in 1476 one-fifth of the infantry of Milan was already equipped with them, and by a century later archers had disappeared from European armies—but weapons like arquebuses made very little real change in the way battles were fought.[4] They would produce about the same effect as a crossbow and took no more training to use, and they made a very satisfactory bang (which was undoubtedly one of the reasons for preferring them), but the arquebusiers remained essentially a secondary element in battle right down to the seventeenth century. The core of the army was the massed ranks of disciplined pikemen who could defend themselves (and the arquebusiers) from cavalry charges, and whose clashes with the other side's similarly equipped phalanxes of pikemen generally decided the battle.

What the Europeans were really doing during the fifteenth and sixteenth centuries was reinventing the infantry armies of classical antiquity—which required the overthrow of the power of the old feudal aristocracy, who had gained a stranglehold on the military profession. There was much popular support for this, of course, and the first places where pikemen established their dominance were Switzerland and Flanders, where the aristocracies were weakest. But the same change had great appeal for the aspiring absolute monarchs of the bigger European powers, who wanted to expand the power of the central government at the expense of the feudal class, so they soon began to foster the new infantry armies too.

The last bit of the Roman Empire goes under. The siege of Constantinople, 1453.

Ideally the monarch would have conscripted his new model army from his own population, and there were numerous attempts to create national militias under the control of the central government. In practice, however, these attempts usually foundered because of the reluctance of the peasantry to serve, so it became instead the golden age of the mercenaries, who would fight under contract for any government able to pay them: the export of companies of trained mercenary soldiers became practically a national industry in the poorer parts of Europe like Switzerland and Scotland.[5] And because mercenaries cost so much, armies stayed small—on average only about ten thousand men per side in a sixteenth-century battle.

Feudalism was not destroyed by firearms. The whole basis for the economic and political power of the feudal nobility was being undermined by the shift from agriculture to commerce as the main source of wealth, and by the growing centralization of political power in the monarch. Even on the battlefield, what destroyed the military predominance of the mounted knight in armour was the re-emergence of disciplined infantry armies, with or without guns. But it was understandable that the old chivalry of Europe, increasingly desperate as its power in the state inexorably declined, should have identified firearms as the root of the problem. With a few weeks' training a peasant with a musket could kill a knight who had spent his entire life training for battle, a monstrous reversal of the natural order of things. In Europe the feudal aristocracy could not do anything about it because there were too many other factors working against them—but on the other side of the world, where the warrior nobility faced only the threat of firearms and not a wholesale upheaval in the organization of society, they actually managed to buck the trend.

———

They have not more than five hundred matchlock-men, and if you reckon on them all hitting at the first volley, and also at the second, for after that men shoot wildly, we shall not

lose more than a thousand killed and wounded, and that is
nothing much.

> Gen. Atobe Oinosuke's advice to his
> lord, Takeda Katsuyori, before the battle
> of Nagashino, 1575[6]

Modern European firearms had reached Japan in Portuguese
ships in 1542, and within a generation the Japanese were manufacturing cannons and arquebuses that were fully comparable to the
contemporary European weapons. Moreover, the Japanese were
soon using their new firearms more effectively than the Europeans,
for in the sixteenth century the entire country was caught up in a
long civil war and military efficiency was at a premium. In 1567
Lord Takeda Shingen instructed his officers: "Hereafter, guns will
be the most important arms. Therefore decrease the number of
spears [per unit] and have your most capable men carry guns." He
was killed by a bullet himself six years later.

It was his successor, Takeda Katsuyori, who was reassured
by his general in 1575 that he faced only five hundred musketeers at the crucial battle of Nagashino (recreated in Akiro
Kurosawa's superb 1980 film *Kagemusha*). But General Atobe's
advice to his master was disastrously wrong, for his enemies,
Tokugawa Ieyasu and Oda Nobunaga, had not five hundred but
ten thousand arquebusiers. They were drawn up in three ranks
and trained to fire in volleys, one rank at a time, so that there
was no long pause in the firing during reloading—a practice
that did not appear on European battlefields for another half-
century. But Takeda took his general's advice and committed all
his men in a series of frontal assaults. The defenders stood
their ground and fired methodically, mowing down sixteen
thousand of Takeda's men. The Takeda clan never recovered
from its losses.

> Nobunaga and I were superior in numbers, and yet though
> we had a triple stockade in front of us he must come charg-
> ing down on it. Naturally he got beaten. But if he had taken
> up a position behind the Takigawa river he could have held

us for ten days anyhow and we should have had to retire. . . .
It is a pity he was such a fool.

Tokugawa Ieyasu[7]

In 1575, Japanese musketry was already the best in the world, and by the time of the great invasion of Korea in 1590, when three hundred thousand Japanese troops were bogged down by Korean resistance and facing a massive Chinese intervention, no practical Japanese soldier wanted to hear about edged weapons. One Japanese lord wrote home saying: "Please arrange to send us guns and ammunition. There is absolutely no need for spears." Another ordered that his reinforcements should "bring as many guns as possible. . . . Give strict orders that all the men, even samurai, carry guns."

And yet by 1675 there was hardly a gun of any kind to be found in Japan, and they had altogether disappeared from war. It is one of the most extraordinary about-faces in history: the Japanese looked down the road on which firearms were taking them, decided that they did not like the destination, and simply turned back. When Commodore Perry's "black ships" finally forced Japan to re-establish contact with the rest of the world in 1854, they found a perfectly preserved medieval society in which the weapons of war were swords, spears, and bows and arrows.

It is true that by 1615 the "Age of the Country at War" was over. Tokugawa's long struggle against his rivals ended in complete victory and inaugurated a period of over two centuries during which Japan had a relatively stable feudal system of government: the urgent pressure for efficiency in war had diminished. But that is not enough to explain the deliberate abandonment of firearms by the Japanese; what really worried the elite was the social implications of muzzle-loading muskets.

It is not doing too much violence to history to compare the warrior class of samurai in Japan with the feudal nobility of Europe. Both were groups who owed their wealth, power, and social position to their proficiency with arms and derived their own self-respect from it. But proficiency with arms is an important distinguishing mark only if it takes long and arduous training to

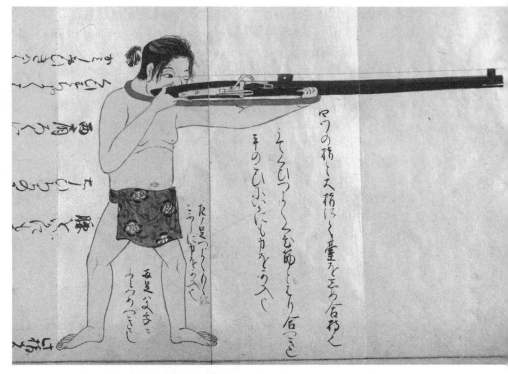

How to use a musket: the *Inatomi Gun Manual of 1607.* In this year, Tokugawa Ieyasu began the process of eliminating guns from Japan.

achieve and has a direct relationship to a man's chances of success and survival in battle, as it does with the sword, the spear, or the bow. Firearms take much less time to master and are much more democratic in their effects: samurai and commoners died with equal speed and equal futility in the Takeda clan's desperate charges at Nagashino.

From the very beginning, the introduction of guns to battle roused resistance in Japan, because they practically abolished the single combats in which samurai could win personal glory. The samurai distaste for guns was so great that the majority of Oda's matchlockmen at Nagashino were peasant farmers. That just increased the offensiveness of the new weapon to the samurai: they were being killed by their social inferiors. The professional warrior class in Japan was huge—between 7 and 10 percent of the population, compared to

213

less than 1 percent for the feudal nobility in Europe—so once the civil wars and the Korean adventure were over, the pressure to abandon these ignoble weapons became irresistible.

In 1607 Tokugawa Ieyasu centralized firearms production at only two centres and created a commissioner of guns to license all orders. In practice, only government orders were licensed, and those dwindled away to nothing in the course of the seventeenth century; as their craft was slowly strangled, the best Japanese gun-smiths gradually turned to making swords. Technological change is not irreversible: the ruling military caste in Japan gave up the gun because they feared that its socially levelling implications would ultimately undermine the military equation that kept them at the top of the social order.

———

There was a similar concern over the social effects of firearms among the professional military class in Europe. At the end of the fifteenth century, Gian Paolo Vitelli, one of the leading Italian *condottieri*, took to plucking out the eyes and cutting off the hands of all the arquebusiers he could capture, considering it disgraceful that noble men-at-arms should be killed from a distance by low-born infantrymen.[8] But this was no more than had been done to captured crossbow-men and longbow-men by zealous defenders of the old social order for several hundred years already, and it was not going to turn back the tide of change.

Europe was not Japan. It was undergoing not just a military revolution, but far-reaching transformations in the whole structure of political authority and economic productivity that could not be stopped by mere military Luddism. By the mid-1500s Brescia and surrounding Val Trompia, the main arms-producing area in Italy, were making twenty-five thousand muskets a year even in peace-time—and managed to quadruple that output during the war against the Turks in 1570—73.

Nevertheless, armies in Europe remained founded on the model perfected by the Spaniards, the most successful military power of the age: solid *tercios* (phalanxes) of pikemen sixteen, twenty, or even thirty ranks deep with musketeers posted in the corners of the formation and the extremely heavy, barely mobile field artillery of the time stationed across the front of the line. Cavalry were still present, posted in the wings, but their role continued to shrink even after they, too, acquired firearms. Frequently they did no more than trot up to an infantry formation, fire their pistols, retreat, reload, and repeat. But this unwieldy, slowed-down version of classical warfare was to change (along with much else) in the cataclysm known as the Thirty Years War.

From the mid-sixteenth century, Europe was increasingly torn by wars of religion arising out of the Protestant Reformation — notably the Huguenot wars in France from 1562 to 1593 and the eighty-year Dutch revolt against Spanish rule that began in 1567. In the years after 1618 all the particular quarrels coalesced into the first war in which all the European powers became involved. By the time the Thirty Years War ended in 1648, the international system based on the absolute sovereignty of the state that now covers the whole world was firmly in place, battles had taken on the form they were to retain until little more than a century ago — and eight million people were dead.

There was a genuine element of religious fervour in the war, which made victors even more brutal and intolerant toward losers, but it was governments, not churches, that fought the war. The beginnings of modern nationalism were also stirring in some of the peoples involved — especially the French, English, Dutch, and Swedish — and governments were quick to enlist both nationalist and religious sentiments in support of their policies. But the monarchs and their advisers mainly calculated in terms of power and security; religion had rather the same role in their thinking that ideology has in that of governments today.

Most Catholic and Protestant rulers really believed in their particular version of the truth, of course, and used it to justify their actions. They genuinely saw other like-minded rulers as their natural allies in the endless, merciless struggle for position, and even sheer survival, among the states of Europe. Most of them could not have separated the ideological component in their decisions from their reflexive concern for the state's power; it was all part of the same calculation. But what was actually emerging in the course of the Thirty Years War was a unified system of European states that all saw themselves as being in the same game: a zero-sum game in which every increase in power for one state was automatically a loss of security for all the others. Even countries as far apart as Sweden and Spain, with little by way of concrete reasons for fighting each other, ended up killing each other's troops on the battlefields of Germany—and in the end, religious ideology was less important than the game of power. Just as the fear of Soviet power drove Communist China into a loose association with the capitalist states in the 1970s, so the fear of triumphant Catholic "Imperial" (Hapsburg) power drove Catholic France to ally itself with the weakening Protestant powers and prolong the war until the "balance of power" was restored (i.e., the war ended in a draw).

It was the Germans, on whose territory most of the battles of the Thirty Years War were fought, who paid the price for this policy.

> Drunk with victory, the troops defied all efforts to control them. . . . Towards midday flames suddenly shot up at almost the same moment at twenty different places. There was no time for Tilly and Pappenheim to ask whence came the fire; staring in consternation, they rallied the drunken, disorderly, exhausted men to fight it. The wind was too strong, and in a few minutes the city was a furnace, the wooden houses crashing to their foundations in columns of smoke and flame. The cry was now to save the army and the imperialist officers struggled in vain to drive their men into the open. Rapidly whole quarters were cut off by walls of smoke so that those who lingered for booty or lost their way, or lay in a drunken stupor in the cellars, alike perished.[9]

The sack and destruction by fire of Magdeburg, with the death of some forty thousand inhabitants, came in 1631, when the worst phase of the war was just beginning. As ruthless armies of mercenaries marched across Germany season after season, taking whatever they wanted and spreading disease in their wake, the increasingly desperate and starving peasants were repeatedly driven to revolt, only to be ferociously repressed by all sides. The supply arrangements of the armies steadily deteriorated over the long years of the war, and the hungry soldiers' depredations on an already impoverished and denuded countryside grew even greater. Social order among the civilians and military discipline among the soldiers completely broke down over wider and wider areas of the country; the landscape was filled with desperate bands of refugees and marauding groups of deserters whose behaviour was virtually indistinguishable. Murder for a loaf of bread was commonplace, and there were cases of cannibalism. By the time the Treaty of Westphalia brought a peace of exhaustion to Europe in 1648, the population of Germany had fallen from twenty-one million to only thirteen million; the thirty-five thousand villages of Bohemia had been reduced to only six thousand.

It was a century and a half before there was another war in Europe that caused deaths on anything like the same scale, and fully three centuries before civilian losses again outnumbered the military casualties. But the caution that restrained the rulers of Europe from engaging in another such bloodbath for so long had little to do with the horrors inflicted on the victims (of whom the overwhelming majority had been German peasants—only 350,000 soldiers were killed). It had a great deal to do with the rulers' vivid recollection that if wars get too badly out of hand, whole states and dynasties can disappear, as so many petty kingdoms did in Germany during the Thirty Years War.

The primary goal of any state, any dynasty, is survival. The vivid demonstration of what happens when wars go too far probably explains why the monarchs, even as they consolidated their newly won positions as the absolute rulers of sovereign states, simultaneously behaved as though they were all members of the same club. They would fight wars against each other, seize each other's border provinces or overseas territories, try to undermine each other's power in a hundred ruthless ways, but behind all that was the tacit agreement that no member of the rulers' club—or at least no important member—would ever lose so badly as to disappear from the game entirely. (The one significant exception, Poland, was a weak state partitioned by the unanimous agreement of all its powerful neighbours.) The aims of wars remained remarkably limited in the next 150 years, and the main source of the limitation was the overriding interest of each dynasty in survival.

That is not to say that battles became less violent, for this was the period in which firearms finally became the dominant weapon on the battlefield. The man most responsible for the change, King Gustavus Adolphus of Sweden, ruled a kingdom whose small population (less than one-and-a-half million) left it in permanent difficulties against the stronger countries that surrounded it: Russia, Poland, and Denmark. Lacking the numbers he needed to fight his neighbours on an equal basis in the standard "push of pike," he set out in 1611 to remedy Sweden's military problems by tactical innovation—and created the first army that Alexander the Great would not have known how to command.

Gustavus Adolphus realized that the solid formations of pikemen modelled on the Spanish *tercios*, which then dominated European battlefields, were ideal targets for gunfire, if only he could get enough of it. So he had the standard Swedish musket redesigned until it was light enough to be used without a wooden rest propping up the front and replaced the old matchlock with the so-called 'Baltic snaplock' (an early version of the flintlock) to make it fire more reliably. He then converted two-thirds of his infantry into musketeers operating in ranks only six deep, and took almost all their armour away to make them more mobile. He wrought the same transformation in artillery, abandoning the usual heavy field pieces drawn by twenty-four horses for light, quick-firing guns using a prepared cartridge that could be pulled by only one or two horses—and so could be moved around on the battlefield, even under fire.

The result of these changes was to make firepower highly effective on the battlefield for the first time. The musket volleys and cannon fire of Gustavus Adolphus's army could shatter a formation of pikemen from a hundred yards away, without any need for physical contact. And once the enemy formations were disordered by gunfire, his cavalry was trained to charge home with the sword and turn disorder into rout.

In addition to all this, his army was made up not of mercenaries but mostly of Swedes animated by genuine religious and national fervour. Thanks to the military reforms of his father, each district of Sweden was required to furnish a fixed number of men to Gustavus Adolphus's standing army. When this army arrived in Germany to rescue the failing Protestant cause in 1630, it demolished the old-style mercenary armies of its imperial (Spanish and Austrian) opponents with convincing efficiency. Gustavus Adolphus himself was killed in battle in 1632, and the Swedish intervention was in the end only one more episode in a seemingly endless war, but every other army in Europe rapidly adopted the revolutionary tactics originated by the Swedish king.

———

Firearms and not cold steel now decide battles.
J. F. Puysegur, 1748[10]

The proportion of cavalry in European armies fell from almost a half to only a quarter in the century after the Thirty Years War. Infantry had become the "Queen of Battles." The proportion of pikemen to musketeers also dwindled rapidly, as musketeers were now issued with "plug bayonets" that they could insert into their muskets to serve as makeshift pikes if they were faced with a cavalry charge. This did, however, leave them with an unhappy choice as the cavalry neared: whether to try for one last volley and risk not having enough time to fix bayonets if it did not break the charge, or to plug the bayonets into their muskets early and abandon their firepower. The invention of the socket bayonet, which ended this dilemma by leaving the musket free to fire, eliminated the pike's role entirely; and by 1700 all infantrymen carried muskets.

Moreover, the muskets they carried were now flintlocks, much improved weapons that misfired only twice in every ten shots and, in the hands of a well-trained soldier, could be loaded and fired twice a minute. They were highly inaccurate except at very close range, but that scarcely mattered, since they were not used against individual targets. The infantry battalion's job was to deliver volleys of fire; it could almost be described as a human machine gun with several hundred moving parts (the soldiers), capable of delivering a single burst of fire every thirty seconds.

Toward the end of the eighteenth century the Prussian army even conducted experiments with their muskets, setting up a canvas target one hundred feet wide and six feet high to simulate an enemy unit and having a battalion of Prussian infantry fire volleys at it from various ranges. At 225 yards only 25 percent of the bullets struck this huge target, but at 150 yards 40 percent hit, and at 75 yards, 60 percent of the shots told—which simply confirmed what every practical soldier already knew: fighting had to be done at as close a range as possible.[11]

During the battle of Fontenoy in 1745, for example, the British Guards Brigade, emerging from a sunken road, caught sight of the French infantry. The French officers called out to the British commander, Lord Charles Hay, inviting him to open fire, to which he replied with impeccable courtesy: "No, sir, we never fire first. After you." The British continued to advance (a guardsman in the ranks called out, "For what we are about to receive, may the Lord make us truly thankful") until the French finally let off their volley. And then while they were reloading, the surviving British troops marched to a distance of only thirty paces and fired an answering volley that killed or wounded nineteen officers and six hundred men of the French regiment in a single second— whereupon the rest understandably broke and fled. The famous command given to the American revolutionary troops at Bunker Hill—"Hold your fire until you see the whites of their eyes"—was not bravado, but the standard tactical doctrine of the time.

The discipline required for soldiers to stand up to this sort of battle was of a new order: the soldier had to go through the several dozen complicated movements necessary to load and aim his musket while facing what amounted to a firing squad only a hundred yards away, without even the emotional release of violent exertion and physical contact with the enemy. Standing in the ranks for hours under steady fire from artillery only five or six hundred yards away must have been even worse. This was often the lot of battalions not directly engaged in the fighting. To keep men in the lines under such conditions took the most severe discipline: Prussian army regulations stated that "if a soldier during an action looks as if about to flee, or so much as sets foot outside the line, the non-commissioned officer standing behind him will run him through with his bayonet and kill him on the spot."[12]

The casualties in eighteenth-century battle rivalled anything in ancient warfare, and now they were more evenly shared by the two sides than in the battles of earlier times. Most killing was now done at a distance, so there was less chance of a massacre when the losers turned to retreat. Over two-fifths of the casualties in a typical battle now came from musket fire, and another two-fifths from field artillery; under a fifth were caused by swords and bayonets used at close range. But the overall scale of the carnage was undiminished: at Blenheim in 1704, for example, the victors lost 12,500 men (24 percent of their force), and the losers suffered 20,000 killed and wounded (40 percent of their force) in five hours of fighting on a single day. During the Seven Years War (1756—63) the Prussian army lost 180,000 dead, three times the number of men it started the war with.[13] Its commander, King Frederick the Great, complained that "recruits can replace the numbers lost but not their quality. . . . One commands in the end nothing more than a band of badly drilled and badly disciplined rustics."[14]

And yet the century and a half between the Thirty Years War and the French Revolution (1648—1789) truly was an era of limited war. The battles were terrible, but they didn't happen very often. The armies grew larger—the average number of soldiers present on each side of the battlefield rose from ten thousand to thirty thousand during the Thirty Years War, and it jumped again to hover around the hundred thousand mark in the biggest battles of the eighteenth century—but they also grew steadily more isolated from civilian society both in their social composition and in their operations. Mostly they fought each other and left the civilians alone.

Wars were almost constant, but their political consequences were curiously small, at least in Europe: a province or a few fortresses would change hands here, some overseas colonies there, and a different candidate might gain a throne somewhere, but there was little disturbance to the steady growth of population, prosperity, and industry across most of the continent. At the height of the Seven Years War, Laurence Sterne left London for Paris without getting the necessary passport to travel in an enemy country ("It never entered my mind that we were at war with France"), but nobody stopped him at the French coast, and the French foreign minister courteously sent him a passport after he had arrived at Versailles.[15]

It could almost be said that the monarchies of eighteenth-century Europe were deliberately excluding the great mass of their subjects from anything to do with war, just as they denied them any role in domestic affairs of state. It was an age of absolutism, and an absolute ruler wants his servants to be obedient instruments of his will, not independent citizens with interests and opinions of their own. The France of Louis XIV was already far wealthier and more populous than the Roman Empire during the Punic Wars and could easily have created larger, cheaper armies based on the same principle of a universal obligation for military service—but that Roman army had served a republic, which was not at all what Louis XIV had in mind. The kind of army he and his fellow monarchs chose to create instead imposed severe limitations on the style of warfare, but they were limitations that they were willing to accept.

By the end of the seventeenth century, all the kingdoms of Europe had created standing armies controlled and paid directly by their own governments. Regular troops had to be paid even in peacetime, but they were more reliable than mercenaries, and they freed the newly absolute monarchs from the necessity of relying on any particular section of the civil population for military help in a crisis. The monarchs wanted to avoid the obligations and restraints on their power that that would imply. Moreover, it was an age intensely conscious of the need to build and safeguard the wealth of the national economy, and the last thing the monarchs wanted was to undermine it by putting several hundred thousand productive citizens into military service.

So the armies of Europe ended up being composed of "nobles and vagabonds." The numerous and still martially inclined nobility of Europe, many of whom were now verging on genteel poverty, were subsidized and politically neutralized by being granted a near-monopoly on officers' jobs in the new regular armies. In this capacity they no longer posed a threat to the central government's power, as they were now salaried servants of the state and no longer the independent commanders of troops they had raised themselves. The officer corps of the European armies became a vast system of outdoor relief for the titled classes (who proceeded to haggle and lobby to preserve and extend their near-monopoly over the officer ranks with a narrow determination worthy of a craft trade union).

The soldiers commanded by these officers came from the other extreme of the social spectrum: the best were landless peasants, penniless adventurers, and political refugees, but at least as many were drunks, chronic ne'er-do-wells, and outright criminals for whom the army was the last refuge from starvation or from justice. Up to a third of the troops in the typical European army were foreigners. Discipline in armies composed of such men could be maintained only by liberal use of the lash, the hangman's noose, and the firing squad: "In general, the common soldier must fear his officers more than the enemy," said Frederick the Great,[16] and Wellington remarked of his troops: "I don't know if they frighten the enemy; but by God they frighten me!"

What had happened, in essence, was that the groups in late seventeenth- and eighteenth-century society whose power and wealth were on the rise—the central government and the urban bourgeoisie—had hired the declining nobility and the down-and-outs of society to fight their wars for them. But the armies were still not cheap, at least in proportion to the resources available to the governments of the day, because they had to be kept up to full war strength even in peacetime. Basically, you fought a war mainly with the troops you had available at the start, since it took several years of training to turn a recruit into a useful soldier.

Conditioning, almost in the Pavlovian sense, is probably a better word than training. What was required of the ordinary soldier was not thought, far less enthusiasm—French soldiers were forbidden to speak or shout even in the charge—but obedience, endurance, and the ability to perform extremely complicated manoeuvres in large formations and to load and fire his musket automatically under the stress of combat. This was accomplished by thousands of hours of repetitive drilling, accompanied by the ever-present incentive of physical violence as the penalty for failure to perform correctly. The trained soldier, however despised as an individual, was an expensive commodity, irreplaceable in the short term, whose life the state was reluctant to squander in battle. As Marshal Saxe remarked in 1732, displaying an almost Chinese sensibility: "I do not favour pitched battles, especially at the beginning of a war, and I am convinced that a skilful general could make war all his life without being forced into one."[17]

Desertion in such armies was a chronic problem. The miserable living conditions, the brutal discipline, and the stupefying boredom of the training were unappealing enough in peacetime, but when soldiers devoid of patriotic feelings were also faced with the imminent prospect of a battle, their natural instinct was to desert. Despite the most stringent precautions against it, eighty thousand men managed to desert from the Russian army during the Seven Years War, and seventy thousand from the French.[18] And the extreme precautions armies had to take to prevent desertion imposed severe limitations on how they could operate in the field.

It was practically impossible for an army to live off the land because if the soldiers were allowed to forage for themselves, the army would simply melt away. Eighteenth-century armies were therefore unable to cut loose from their supply lines for more than a short time, and their supply arrangements were extremely cumbersome. There had to be some central magazine near the area of operations, prepared long beforehand, which stored huge amounts of food for the troops. (During the Seven Years War, bread was baked from flour forty years old.) The field ovens could advance up to sixty miles from the magazine in order to bake, and the bread wagons could deliver it another forty miles to the army, but that was the limit. In theory, at least, no army could advance more than a hundred miles into enemy territory without setting up an intermediate magazine.

Even this elaborate supply organization could not possibly bring up the fodder for the forty thousand animals that typically accompanied an army of a hundred thousand men. In practice, the army would spend much of its time just moving to new grazing grounds, as forty thousand animals went through eight hundred acres of grass a day.[19] This also obliged armies to restrict their campaigning to the months of May through October, when there was grass in the fields, except on the rarest of occasions.

So wars tended to be fought in certain well-defined border areas that were full of fortresses, and warfare was a slow and cumbersome business consisting mainly of sieges. In 1708 Marlborough's siege train of eighteen heavy guns and twenty siege mortars required three thousand wagons and sixteen thousand horses to move it and took thirty miles of road. Armies manoeuvred to threaten each other's supply lines and force a withdrawal. Actual battles were relatively rare because soldiers were too expensive to waste if an opponent could be forced to withdraw by manoeuvre, and the armies moved so slowly (except in the most skilled hands) that if either side was reluctant to fight, then the other would have great difficulty in forcing a battle.

All these limitations were reinforced by the limited goals of the wars, which were hardly ever life-and-death issues for the regimes that waged them. The unwritten understanding was that wars must not be pursued to the point where one power achieved total domination over the others or extinguished its rival utterly. This understanding was enforced by the device rather misleadingly known as the "balance of power": misleading, because it did not then (and does not now) mean that peace is to be ensured through establishing a permanent equality of power between states or alliances. Rather it meant that any country or alliance whose military power grew so great that it threatened the security of the other European states would automatically be confronted with an alliance big enough to curb its ambitions—and the mechanism that made the system work was war.

There is a sense, therefore, in which Europe has been a unified political space for over 350 years, ever since the Thirty Years War. Almost all its major wars, whatever their specific origin, have rapidly spread to involve all the great powers of the time—one definition of a world war. By the eighteenth century, they were also

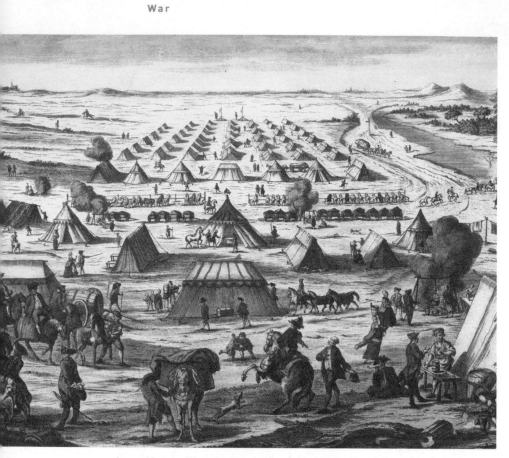

A very big travelling circus, or perhaps an eighteenth-century army on campaign. *The Encampment of the Austrian Army*, Georg Balthasar Probst.

world wars geographically: during the Seven Years War, for example, there was fighting in every continent except Australia. In the peace settlement Britain, the biggest winner, gained Canada, Senegal, and some West Indian islands. It also retained most of the fruits of Clive's military victories in India, but had to return Cuba, the Philippines, and Argentina to Spain. The only respects in which it didn't match the modern definition of a world war were the lethality of the killing systems and the scale of the casualties.

———

It was the development of ocean-going sailing ships, the biggest and most complex machines men had ever built, that enabled the Europeans to establish their control over the peoples of the Americas during the first period of colonial expansion, in the sixteenth and seventeenth centuries, but the conquest of the western hemisphere did not require technology and organization of a very high order. The array of epidemic diseases spawned in the crowded towns and cities of Eurasia over ten thousand years devastated the native populations even before a shot was fired, the Europeans' horses overawed them, and the methodical Eurasian ruthlessness of the invaders shocked them into passivity. But any other civilized domain—the Ottoman Empire in the Middle East, the Mogul Empire in India, or the Chinese Empire—would have had as little difficulty in subjugating the people of the Americas if they had possessed the ships and the commercial drive to take them there. As late as 1683, indeed, the military technology and organization of the Muslim world was still roughly comparable to that of Christian Europe, and an Ottoman army was able to besiege Vienna, more than halfway from Istanbul to Paris.

At that point, it was also still true that European power in other parts of Eurasia rarely extended inland beyond the range of a cannon shot: their ships were unbeatable, but their armies were less so. Nor did the technology of weapons change appreciably in the following century and a quarter. The flintlock muskets used at the battle of Blenheim in 1704 differed hardly at all from those employed by European armies of the 1830s, and the same applied to field artillery, warships, and almost every other category of weapon. But the rigid discipline and ruthlessly efficient organization that the Europeans brought to the use of these weapons, backed by their rapidly growing wealth, could not be matched by their opponents elsewhere. By the eighteenth century other parts of the civilized world were beginning to fall under European rule: the British conquered most of India, and the Ottoman borders began to contract under Austrian and Russian pressure.

To a European of the last generation before the French Revolution, therefore, war would have seemed a bearable evil—and perhaps even a beneficial phenomenon, on balance, since

Europe's proficiency in the modern art of war was rapidly giving it the mastery of the whole world at a relatively low cost in money and lives. The incessant wars within Europe itself could not be seen in the same cheerful light, but at least they were well contained. A few areas that had the misfortune to constitute some sort of military crossroads took a severe beating from time to time (the province of Pomerania suffered seventy thousand civilian deaths, one-fifth of the population, during the Seven Years War),[20] but usually the suffering caused by war fell mainly on the soldiers, who lived a life apart from civil society. Cities were not sacked, civilians did not face intolerable demands for their taxes and their sons in order to fight wars, and whole countries did not disappear or dissolve into chaos as a result of war. The institution of war had been brought under control, limited, and rationalized (as that extremely rational age might have put it).

What the eighteenth century did not realize was how fragile all the limitations on war were.

———

The balance of power will continue to fluctuate, and the prosperity of our own or the neighbouring kingdoms may be alternately exalted and depressed; but these partial events cannot essentially injure our general state of happiness, the system of arts, and laws, and manners, which so advantageously distinguish, above the rest of mankind, the Europeans and their colonies. In peace, the progress of knowledge and industry is accelerated by the emulation of so many active rivals: in war, the European forces are exercised by temperate and undecisive contests.

Edward Gibbon, 1782[21]

From this moment until that in which our enemies shall have been driven from the territory of the Republic, all Frenchmen are permanently requisitioned for service in the armies. The young men shall fight; the married men shall forge weapons and transport supplies; the women will make

tents and clothes and serve in hospitals. . . . The public buildings shall be turned into barracks, the public squares into
munition factories. . . . All firearms of suitable calibre shall
be turned over to the troops: the interior will be policed with
shotguns and cold steel. All saddle horses shall be seized for
the cavalry; all draft horses not employed in cultivation will
draw the artillery and supply wagons.

Decree of the National Convention,
Paris, 1793[22]

The idyllic world so complacently described by Gibbon had
less than a decade to run when he wrote, for it rested on highly
unstable foundations. In particular, its restraint in the conduct of
war was a highly artificial behaviour that depended on the conviction of Europe's absolute monarchs that their common interest
in the survival of their dynasties outweighed any disputes that
divided them, and that to exploit the military resources of their
kingdoms to the full in war would unleash social and political
forces that would threaten their thrones. But ideas about equality
and democracy, which were fundamentally hostile to the existing
order, were the common currency of late eighteenth century
thought, and even as Gibbon wrote, the first revolution based on
those ideas was triumphing in the United States.

In 1789 the revolution arrived in France. The impact of that
upheaval can only be compared to what would be the effect today
if Maoists seized power in the United States, for France was then
the intellectual and cultural centre of Western civilization and by
far the biggest country in Europe. Even Russia did not overtake
France in population until the mid-nineteenth century. Almost all
the monarchies of Europe launched their armies against France to
stamp out the sacrilegious revolutionaries. When what was left of
the old royal army, aided by volunteers, proved unable to stem the
attacks, the National Convention decided on conscription.

The first levy, in February 1793, demanded a quota of men
from each district, each local battalion to be united under a ban-
ner bearing the inscription "The French people risen against
tyranny." As the military situation continued to worsen, however,

the convention issued the call for a levee en masse—mass conscription—in August. By New Year's Day 1794, the French armies numbered about 770,000 men,[23] and the wars of mass armies that ensued ravaged Europe for the next two decades.

Conscription was not an entirely new idea—as early as 1506 the Ordinanza in Florence had decreed obligatory military service for all fit males between eighteen and thirty—but it had never really amounted to more than compulsory selection of an unfortunate minority, nor had it lasted long or been extended to an entire country. The French Revolution, with its principles of liberty and equality, first stimulated and then exploited a fervent nationalism that made conscription acceptable. It also made French troops behave differently.

The Attack on the Tuileries, 1792. Six months later, the National Convention introduced conscription in France. Painting by Jean Duplessis-Bertaux.

The "nation in arms" produced soldiers who had the loyalty and the initiative to fight in more open and mobile formations, with clouds of skirmishers out front. With their revolutionary enthusiasm and their numbers, they often simply overwhelmed the stolid regular troops of the old regimes that opposed them, who had been trained in a style of discipline that the Prussian army jokingly called *kadavergehorsam* (corpse-obedient). Since the new French armies were also less likely to desert—and were so numerous that a few desertions mattered less—they didn't always have to be kept together and could live off the land at least part of the time: if there was no bread they could dig in the fields for potatoes, recently introduced from the Americas. That in turn meant that they could cut loose from the magazines and supply trains of former days and move much faster and farther: a hundred miles was no longer their maximum practical range.

Battles rarely ended in draws any more, either, because French troops could now be turned loose to pursue and destroy a defeated enemy without fear that they would all desert. Carnot of the Committee of Public Safety instructed the French armies in 1794 "to act in mass formations and take the offensive. . . . Give battle on a large scale and pursue the enemy till he is utterly destroyed." Karl von Clausewitz, a Prussian officer who first saw action against the revolutionary forces in 1793 at the age of twelve, memorably said, "The colossal weight of the whole French people, unhinged by political fanaticism, came crashing down on us."[24]

Not much was said about the democratic ideals of the revolution after Napoleon made himself emperor in 1804: the war's aim was simply to establish French domination over all of Europe (and thus, in effect, to create a world empire). And yet, by adroit and cynical exploitation of the French appetite for national "glory," together with all the means of compulsion available to a dictatorial government, Napoleon managed to keep going for another ten years of constant war. Between 1804 and 1813 he drafted 2.4 million men, few of whom were ever released again so long as they were still physically fit (and fewer than half of whom returned home at the end of the empire). "Troops are made to get killed," he once said, though as time went on the conscripts became less willing. By 1810, 80 percent of the annual quota of conscripts failed to appear voluntarily.[25]

If troops had become much cheaper in France, the weapons they used had not. Still, the revolutionary regime quickly discovered how easy it was for a truly centralized government with dictatorial powers to get more out of the economy than the old monarchy had ever dared to demand. State-owned arms factories multiplied in which prices and wages were strictly controlled. Equipment, food, and horses could simply be requisitioned, with payment made later at government-set prices, or never. And after the conquests began to accumulate, there was so much money coming in from abroad that for a time the wars actually paid for themselves.

It was far more difficult for the opponents of the French. They had to match the size of the revolutionary armies but did not dare to introduce universal conscription for fear that it would destroy the precarious structure that underpinned the monarchies in their countries. That meant that troops had to be paid for, which imposed an awesome burden on their treasuries. Britain, the richest of the allies, which had to subsidize most of the others, introduced the world's first income tax in 1799 to meet its commitments. Yet the other countries of Europe had to do whatever was necessary to stop the French, for the rules of war had been changed drastically; the revolutionary armies spread republicanism wherever they went, and Napoleon simply annexed entire kingdoms or turned them into satellites and placed his own relatives or marshals of his armies on the thrones. For the governments that fought the French, it was a war for sheer survival, and they would take almost any risk in order to survive—even to the extent of arming their people.

Arming the people became much safer after Napoleon declared himself Emperor of the French and the remaining revolutionary credibility drained away from the French cause. Now the French armies were simply foreigners attacking the motherland, and the monarchs could exploit the nascent national feeling of their own people to mobilize resistance against them. Even Austria, a multinational empire, experimented with a popular militia in 1807 as being the only way "to remedy . . . the paucity of our resources" (though it was considered very dangerous politically by Austrian conservatives, and eventually withered away).[26] In Spain, which was under French occupation for half a decade, nationalist guerrillas fighting in the name of the exiled king, backed by a regular British army based in Portugal, inflicted as many casualties on the French over the years as the disastrous Russian campaign did. (The word *guerrilla* was coined in that struggle.)

And when Napoleon, having temporarily managed to subdue every other country on the continent, finally invaded Russia in 1812 with 440,000 men, the Russian response was similar. The campaign is known in Russian history as the "Great Patriotic War," a term revived by the Soviets to describe the struggle against Hitler, and the fighting was made more pitiless by a national antagonism that had simply not existed back in the time of limited wars and professional armies. At the battle of Borodino, the Russians' last stand before Moscow, described in the two eyewitness accounts below, they lost thirty-five thousand men, and the French, thirty thousand.

> When we reached the crest of the ravine, we were riddled with grapeshot from the battery and several others flanking it, but nothing stopped us. Despite my wounded leg I did as well as my [men] in jumping out of the way of roundshot which ricocheted into our ranks. Whole files, half platoons even, went down under the enemy's fire, and left huge gaps. . . . A Russian line tried to stop us, but at thirty yards range we fired a volley and passed through. Then we dashed towards the redoubt and clambered through the embrasures. I went in just after a piece had been discharged. The Russian gunners received us with handspikes and rammers, and we fought them hand to hand. They were redoubtable opponents. A great many Frenchmen fell into rifle pits, jumbled up with the Russians already occupying them.
>
> *Capt. Charles François,*
> *30th Regiment*[27]

It was horrible to see that enormous mass of riddled soldiers. French and Russians were cast together; and there were many wounded men who were incapable of moving and lay in that wild chaos intermingled with the bodies of horses and the wreckage of shattered cannon.

Barclay de Tolly[28]

Napoleon won all the battles, including the crucial battle of Borodino, and even occupied Moscow, but the Russians refused to acknowledge that they were beaten, and he was eventually forced to retreat in the dead of winter through lack of supplies. The Russians had destroyed their own crops and food stocks rather than leave them to the French. Only a few thousand of the French made it out of Russia alive.

The end of Napoleon's Grand Army: the retreat from Moscow.

By calling up the class of 1814 a year early and drafting all those who had previously had exemptions, Napoleon managed to assemble another large army in the spring of 1813, when he rightly expected all the powers of Europe to attack him in an attempt to exploit his Russian disaster. But he was scraping the bottom of the barrel for manpower by then, and some of the new recruits got as little as a week's training before being thrown into battle. Even more seriously, the Prussians had finally decided to bring in conscription too. There was no kingdom in Europe more autocratic, more riddled with class privileges and inequalities, than Prussia, but by the law of 1813 all male Prussians were made liable for three years' service in the regular army upon reaching twenty, followed by two years in the active reserve and fourteen years in the inactive reserve of the Landwehr (territorial army).[29]

The Prussian army reformers gambled that a combination of patriotism and compulsion would make conscription work even without the revolutionary ideal of the equality of all citizens, that men would be seduced by the promise of an equality in battle that they were denied in their ordinary lives. In token of that, they founded the Order of the Iron Cross at the opening of the new war against Napoleon—a decoration for bravery that broke all the rules of Prussian society by being open equally to peasants, bourgeoisie, and nobles. Its decree stated, "In the present great catastrophe in which everything is at stake for the Nation, the vigorous spirit which elevates the Nation so high deserves to be honoured and perpetuated by some quite peculiar monuments. That the perseverance by which the Nation endured the irresistible evils of an iron age did not shrink to timidity is proved by the high courage which now animates every breast and which could survive only because it was based on religion and true loyalty to King and Country."[30]

"Get me a national army," Marshal Blücher had begged the Prussian reformers, and in 1813 he had one: the conscripts tripled the size of his army and played a major part in the two decisive defeats of Napoleon at Leipzig in 1813 and at Waterloo in 1815. "The Landwehr battalions were so-so at first," Blucher said, "but after they had tasted plenty of powder, they did as well as the battalions of the Line."[31]

_____

The battles of the Revolutionary and Napoleonic wars were fiercer than those of the eighteenth century and somewhat larger on average—on one or two occasions Napoleon may have had close to two hundred thousand troops on or near the battlefield, though he had great difficulty controlling so many—but they were fundamentally the same sort of battle. The weapons were virtually identical, and the tactics not very much changed. Indeed, a typical Napoleonic battle was still not all that different from one of Alexander the Great's battles, except that firearms had replaced edged weapons for most purposes: about the same number of men arrayed themselves in roughly comparable formations in approximately the same compact space, fought for a similar length of time (perhaps a few hours more, by the nineteenth century), and left about the same proportion dead on the field.

The great change in war was in the number of battles. In classical times or in the Thirty Years War, there might be three or four battles in a year, and one or two in the whole war where the opposing armies exceeded a hundred thousand men in total. During the period 1792—1814 there were forty-nine such battles, and smaller but still major battles occurred on average more than once a week on one or another of the several fronts where campaigns were in progress.[32] The mobilization of whole populations for war had given the generals resources on a previously unheard of scale, and they used them: at least four million people died.

True, that is only half the death toll of the Thirty Years War, but it is a different phenomenon. The overwhelming majority of those who died in the Thirty Years War were civilians who fell victim to famine, plague, or murder when a long period of bitter fighting in Central Europe caused social and economic breakdown in a basically poor country. The overwhelming majority of the four million who died in the Revolutionary and Napoleonic wars were soldiers—a figure quite unprecedented in history. Yet European society did not break down under the strain. There was hardship, but no starvation, and the warring powers were able to keep at it—and keep their people at it—year after year with no end in sight. The European states had developed the wealth, the organizational techniques, and the methods of motivation needed to fight mass wars with a degree of popular participation that no other civilized society had ever even approached.

The other great change was political, not military: for the first time ever, mass societies had found a way to dispense with their autocratic rulers and revive the old human principle of equality. In less than fifteen years, popular revolutions overthrew the monarchs first in the British colonies in America (population three million), and then in France, the biggest state in Europe (population thirty million). These were the first large states whose official values were closer to those of our hunter-gatherer ancestors than to those of the anthill, and it is significant that they emerged just as the earliest form of mass communication was spreading through those societies: printing plus mass literacy. Once mass societies cracked the problem of numbers and regained the ability to discuss their affairs and make decisions collectively, the pyramidal structure of power and privilege in civilized states, never popular with most people, was no longer a practical necessity. Societies could become self-directing—democratic, in other words—and as soon as that became possible, people remembered that they had always preferred it.

That did not automatically make them peaceful, as the example of revolutionary France clearly demonstrates—but then, our hunter-gatherer ancestors were not exactly peaceful either. It definitely did open up some new possibilities if democracy ever became the dominant political form on the planet, but that lay far in the future. For the moment, unfortunately, the main effect of popular revolution was to show even the non-democratic majority of European states how to use the pseudo-egalitarian tool of nationalism to motivate their whole populations to participate in

OVERLEAF: The climax of an era: French Cuirassiers charging a British square (Highlanders), Waterloo, 1815. *Charging the British Square, The Battle of Waterloo*, Henri-Félix Emmanuel Philippoteaux.

238

the war effort. All that was lacking to transform mass warfare into total war was the technology—but the Industrial Revolution was already almost a generation old in 1815, and soon it would begin to fill that last remaining gap.

7

Reductio ad Absurdum: Total War

Restricted warfare was one of the loftiest achievements of the eighteenth century. It belongs to a class of hot-house plants which can only thrive in an aristocratic and qualitative civilisation. We are no longer capable of it. It is one of the fine things we have lost as a result of the French Revolution.

Guglielmo Ferrero, 1933[1]

He who uses force unsparingly, without reference against the bloodshed involved, must obtain a superiority if his adversary uses less vigour in its application. . . . To introduce into a philosophy of war a principle of moderation would be an absurdity. War is an act of violence pushed to its utmost bounds.

Karl von Clausewitz, 1819[2]

FERRERO'S REFINED NOSTALGIA FOR THE LIMITED WARFARE OF
the eighteenth century contains an elementary truth. Such limitations were part and parcel of an autocratic and hierarchical
social order, and could not survive in the new mass societies
infected with nationalism. The true military spokesman of the
nineteenth century was Karl von Clausewitz, a Prussian veteran of
the Napoleonic wars, whose writings on the theory of war became
gospel for succeeding generations of soldiers. But one form of
restriction from the old way of warfare did survive in an attenuated
form for over a century thereafter: by and large, civilians were
spared the worst horrors of war.

Once conscripted and put into uniform, of course, citizen-
soldiers were fair targets for any weapon the imagination of man
could devise, but those who remained at home—and even those
who lived in the battle zone—were largely left in peace. There were
three reasons for this: the still relatively minor importance of industrial production of weapons and equipment compared to the
all-important role of the masses of soldiers themselves; the absence
of weapons able to strike at the enemy's centres of production in any
case; and a genuine reluctance on the part of soldiers to turn their
weapons against civilians. Unfortunately, the last of these proved to
be no obstacle when the other two conditions were altered.

———

For forty years after the defeat of Napoleon in 1815, there was peace
between the major European states. It may have been a peace of

exhaustion; it was certainly everywhere a peace of conservative reaction to the excesses of the French Revolution. Among the dangerous innovations that were generally discarded was the mass army based on conscription; most of Europe went back to small, professional armies. But in Prussia, the smallest of the great powers in population, conscription was not abandoned, and elsewhere the knowledge of how to create mass armies was never forgotten. By the time the spate of mid-century wars arrived in 1854–70, every major power in Europe except Britain, protected by its navy, had reintroduced conscription—and by this time new technology was beginning to filter into war.

The greatest of the mid-century wars was not fought in Europe at all, however. It was the American Civil War, in which 622,000 American soldiers died—more than in both world wars,

More Americans died in the Civil War than in all the wars of the twentieth century. Collecting the remains long after the battle, Cold Harbor, Virginia, April 1865.

Korea, and Vietnam—out of a population only one-tenth as big as it is now. Both sides soon resorted to conscription—the Confederacy in 1862 and the Union a year later—and the resulting armies were huge. The U.S. Army enlisted almost two million men during the four years of the war, and the Confederates, almost a million, at a time when the entire population of both sides was only thirty million. And one-fifth of those who enlisted died.

The war, coming at a time of transition, was a curious combination of the old and the new. Both sides began the war using straight Napoleonic tactics, but within months defending infantry were taking shelter behind natural obstacles whenever possible. Exactly what drove them to ground remains controversial. During the previous decade, new rifled muskets had come into general use that effectively quintupled the range at which the average infantryman could hit his opponent—but in practice the range at which infantry opened fire didn't change much from the days of the smoothbore musket. Accuracy would certainly have improved, though. Most soldiers were taking aimed shots, and at an average opening range of engagement of 127 yards a great many of them would have hit their targets.[3]

At any rate, the results of the infantry's habit of taking cover whenever possible were clearly visible at battles like Second Manassas in August 1862, when Stonewall Jackson's eighteen thousand Virginians lined up behind the shelter of a railway cutting to receive the attack of some fifty thousand Northern infantry: "The Federals [of the first division] sprang forward with a long drawn 'huzzah' ringing from their 10,000 throats. On they went until half the distance to the cut, and then the smoke, flash and roar of 4,000 well-aimed guns burst from the Confederate entrenchments, and a wild, reckless and terrifying Southern yell echoed and re-echoed through the woodlands. . . . This last charge met the same disastrous fate that had befallen those preceding."[4]

Gen. A. P. Hill, author of the above passage, wrote in the high romantic style about war, and many of the ordinary soldiers on both sides still clung to the same antique values. At the height of the attack, a Northern officer rode forward through the black powder smoke, well ahead of his troops, and reached the lip of the railway cutting miraculously untouched. For a few seconds he paused there, sword in hand, as useless as he was brave. Some of the Southern soldiers just below him began to yell out, "Don't kill him! Don't kill him!" But within seconds both he and his horse were shot down by less romantic men.

The cry that had gone up was an echo from the eighteenth century, when it had been thought unsporting to aim at individual enemies, especially officers; everybody took his chance equally in the hail of unaimed volley fire. But it was out of place at Second Manassas, where the Confederate troops were aiming and firing individually, not in volleys. It did not matter that the Union troops had rifles too, because it is impossible to deliver carefully aimed rifle fire while running across broken ground. What was being demonstrated in battles like this was the new fact that troops behind cover equipped with rifles could stop much larger numbers of infantry attacking across open ground.

> I had taken part in two great battles, and heard the bullets whistle both days, and yet I had scarcely seen a Rebel save killed, wounded or prisoners. I remember even line officers, who were at the battle of Chancellorsville, said: "Why, we never saw any Rebels where we were; only smoke and bushes, and lots of our men tumbling about," and now I appreciate this most fully. The great art is to conceal men. . . . Put a man in a hole, and a good battery on a hill behind him, and he will beat off three times his number, even if he is not a very good soldier.
>
> *Col. Theodore Lyman, 1869*[5]

Not just the muzzle-loading single-shot rifles that produced such havoc at Second Manassas, but forerunners of practically every modem weapon were used in the American Civil War: breech-loading magazine-fed rifles like the fifteen-shot Henry repeater (the Confederates called it "that damn Yankee gun that can be loaded on Sunday and fired all week"), early hand-cranked machine guns like the Gatling gun, rifled

breech-loading cannons, land mines, armoured trains, submarines, ironclad warships, and even a primitive form of aerial
reconnaissance by means of hot-air balloons. (A young Prussian
lieutenant called Ferdinand von Zeppelin was among the
European observers who watched the demonstrations of military
balloons from the White House lawn.) The troops were moved
quickly over long distances on the extensive American railway
network—Civil War battles were the first in history in which the
infantry did not get there entirely on foot—and the telegraph
gave generals a new ability to coordinate the movement of large
forces spread out over a wide area.

In a sense, the Civil War happened just in time. Had it been
delayed another ten or fifteen years, most of those new weapons
would have been available in large numbers and reliable models,
and it would have taken on the character of World War I. As it was,

Another twenty years, and it would have been like World War I. Trenches,
dugouts and wire entanglements, Fort Malone ("Fort Damnation"), Petersburg,
Virginia, 1865.

they were mostly either rare or unreliable. The great majority of the artillery used, for example, was little improved on that of fifty years previously, so that it actually had not much greater range than the rifled muskets in use. The gunners had to be positioned well behind the front line to protect them from enemy rifle fire, and long-range bombardment was not possible. Out of 144,000 American soldiers for whom the cause of death is known, 108,000 were killed by rifle bullets, and only 12,500 by shell fragments and 7,000 by swords and bayonets. (Twenty years later, when field artillery could fire accurately for over a mile and shell bursts produced thousands of lethal fragments of shrapnel, the figures would have been very different.) Even without modern artillery, Civil War battlefields had taken on an ominously modern aspect by the end: in the lines around Petersburg in 1865 the field entrenchments grew so elaborate—complete with dugouts, wire entanglements, and listening posts—that they foreshadowed the trenches of World War I.

But European military observers dismissed these developments as due to uniquely North American circumstances. Neither did they appreciate how hard it would be in future to gain a decisive victory even against a relatively weak opponent. The North effectively outnumbered the South four to one in potential military manpower (since the Confederacy did not draw on its large black slave population for soldiers), and at least six to one in industrial resources. In the year before the Southern states seceded, the North produced 94 percent of the united country's steel, 97 percent of its coal, and 97 percent of its firearms. Yet it took four years of high-intensity war plus ruthless economic warfare to bring the South to its knees.[6]

From the beginning of the struggle, the North clamped a tight blockade on the South to strangle its overseas trade, and by the end General Sherman was deliberately devastating huge areas of the deep South. "We are not only fighting hostile armies but a hostile people," Sherman said, "and must make old and young, rich and poor, feel the hard hand of war."[7]

To those who protested, Sherman simply replied: "If the people raise a howl against my barbarity and cruelty, I will answer that war is war. . . . If they want peace they and their relatives must stop the war."[8] European soldiers ignored the worrisome aspects of the American Civil War and went on believing that they could still deliver quick and decisive victories by defeating the enemy's army in the field, but one man knew they were wrong—though he died a dozen years before the First World War came along to prove him right.

———

At first there will be increased slaughter—increased slaughter on so terrible a scale as to render it impossible to get troops to push the battle to a decisive issue. They will try to, thinking that they are fighting under the old conditions, and they will learn such a lesson that they will abandon the attempt forever. Then . . . we shall have . . . a long period of continually increasing strain upon the resources of the combatants. . . . Everybody will be entrenched in the next war.

J. S. Bloch, 1897[9]

We listen for an eternity to the iron sledgehammers beating on our trench. Percussion and time fuses, 105's, 150's, 210's — all the calibers. Amid this tempest of ruin we instantly recognize the shell that is coming to bury us. As soon as we pick out its dismal howl we look at each other in agony. All curled and shriveled up we crouch under the very weight of its breath, helmets clang together; we stagger about like drunks. The beams tremble, a cloud of choking smoke fills the dugout, the candles go out.

Verdun, 1916[10]

The predictions about the next great war published in Russian in 1897 by Jan Bloch, a Warsaw banker and ardent pacifist, were logically unassailable. Given the millions of soldiers that each power would call up and rush to the frontiers by rail when war came, and given the firepower now available to each man, stalemate was inevitable. Offensive warfare could not succeed.

But no professional soldiers took Bloch's work seriously, and every army went on the offensive simultaneously in 1914, convinced that a quick series of decisive battles in the Napoleonic style (though with far greater numbers of soldiers) would settle the war within six months at the outside.

The mobilization of the new mass armies went exactly according to plan: the German army, for example, grew sixfold in size in the first two weeks of August 1914 as all the reservists joined their regiments, and the trains then delivered them swiftly and efficiently to the various fronts. By the middle of the month there were 1,485,000 German soldiers on the borders with France and Belgium, ready to march and fight as soon as they got off the trains, and the French, the Austrians, and even the Russians performed similar miracles of organization. But then everything went wrong.

Within two months, the armies had ground to a halt. Industrial weapons—quick-firing artillery and machine guns spewing out six hundred bullets a minute—filled the air with a lethal steel sleet, and anybody trying to move above ground was almost certain to be hit. The act of killing had been mechanized, and men had become the prisoners of machines, trapped below ground level in the proliferating trenches. But just once, before they were completely swallowed up by the war, they remembered that they were more than just their tribal identities.

By Christmas of 1914, only six months into the war, there were already over a million dead, and the men in the trenches had seen them die—had killed them, in fact. But a couple of days before Christmas, soldiers from a Saxon regiment lobbed a carefully packaged chocolate cake across no-man's land to the British trenches with a note requesting a one-hour ceasefire that evening so they could celebrate their captain's birthday. At the appointed hour a German band struck up "Happy Birthday," the British stood up on their trench parapets and applauded—and saw that the whole of the front opposite was illuminated in a soft glow by Christmas trees lit with candles and stood on the German parapets. The German authorities had delivered the trees to the troops, but they hadn't planned what happened next.

The spirit of Christmas 1914. A wounded Canadian soldier lights his wounded German enemy's cigarette in the mud of Passchendaele, November 1917. The photograph was staged, of course, but what was in their minds as they staged it?

From both sides men began to climb out of the trenches without weapons and mingle in no-man's land. It started in front of that one Saxon regiment but it spread at the speed of (candle)light up and down the front until tens of thousands of men were standing together above ground, swapping German cigars and cake for British cigarettes and Christmas pudding, singing the familiar carols in two languages, even playing football with improvised balls and goalposts." These were not professional soldiers, after all; six months before they had been farmers or bank clerks or students, and for all the naive enthusiasm with which they had greeted the war they had never really wanted to kill anybody, let alone to die. In its inarticulate way, it was the first peace demonstration of modern times. No wonder the high commands on both sides panicked—but despite the strictest orders against "fraternization," it took them days to get everybody back in their trenches and start the killing again.

By the beginning of 1915, the military authorities were also starting to realize that the trenches were not just a tactical obstacle to the old way of doing battle; as they spread and linked up with each other, they had created a completely new strategic problem: the continuous front. Nobody had planned it, nobody expected it—and nobody had a solution to it.

General Foch, later commander of the entire French army, was one of the first to notice it. Sent to the western end of the front line in September 1914 after the armies had fought each other to a standstill north and east of Paris, he complained, "They have sent me here to manoeuvre, but things are not going very brightly; This eternal stretching out in a line is getting on my nerves."[12] Within a few more weeks, as the Allies and the Germans repeatedly tried to get around the remaining open flank of the trenches, only to collide, halt, and end up digging new stretches of trench, the front reached the sea. Suddenly there were no more enemy flanks that you could hope to get around, just an endless front line. It was theoretically possible to walk 475 miles from the English Channel to the border of neutral Switzerland along either of two parallel lines of trench, sometimes as close as ten or twenty yards apart (more usually several hundred), without ever setting a foot on the surface.

The mathematics that created the continuous front were quite straightforward. For almost all of history the weapons in use had forced soldiers to crowd together practically shoulder to shoulder in order to be able to control the space immediately in front of them—only ten feet in front of them in the case of a phalanx of pikemen, but no more than a hundred yards or so even in the case of an eighteenth-century infantry battalion using smoothbore muskets. Battles were therefore extremely congested events occurring in a small space, and relatively compact armies spent most of the rest of their time marching through open country manoeuvring to gain an advantageous position for the critical few hours when they would meet on the battlefield.

But as firepower grew by leaps and bounds in the latter half of the nineteenth century—rifles able to deliver ten shots a minute at a thousand yards, followed by machine guns and modern artillery—dispersion became the key to success. In the American Civil War, attacking troops were already spontaneously abandoning the vulnerable Napoleonic mass formations for a more open order, and the defenders were discovering that it took fewer men with rifles to hold a given frontage than it had with the old muskets. By the time of the South African War in 1899, the Boers were finding, at battles like Colenso, that they could stop British frontal attacks with only one rifleman every three yards.[13]

All the European armies had professional general staffs long before 1914, and they devoted their time to making elaborate plans for how the next war should be fought. (Indeed, their plans were a major factor in making it likely that war would come.) They all understood the effects of new weapons like the machine gun, which had seen use in small wars and "colonial wars." Even civilians like Hilaire Belloc knew that European troops always beat "natives" because

Whatever happens, we have got
The Maxim gun, and they have not.

But the generals had not done the crucial calculation, which was to multiply the width of the front an individual infantryman could now hold by the millions of men who would be available in a European war. The answer, of course, was that armies could now spread out to fill all the space available in a continuous front.

And so they did. Not only in France, but across the vast distances of Russia, and later across northern Italy, northern Greece, northeastern Turkey, and even Mesopotamia and Palestine. For the men in the trenches, it was a kind of war such as few soldiers had experienced before. Instead of fighting a battle on one or two days of the year, they were in the field, within shouting distance of the enemy, all the time. Each day they faced the risk of being killed, and each day they endured the misery of living in a ditch.

It's such hell when you're in the front line, especially in the wintertime. It was terrible in the winter. The summertime was

not so bad, but you know it was bad enough; but wintertime was awful. It was no place for a human being to be, really.
Canadian veteran

Constantly having your feet in this gruel-like muck caused a complaint which became known as "trench foot." There were dozens of amputation cases in the regiment.
British veteran

Rats bother you; rats eat you if you get wounded and nobody can look after you. It was a dirty lousy place to live with all the corruption that is known to mankind.
British veteran

The essence of the general's art had always been to manoeuvre his forces, but now no movement at all was possible until he had broken through the trench facing him—and the continuous front meant that *every* attack had to be a frontal attack. Since infantrymen could not hope to survive the hail of fire that would greet them if they tried to advance unaided—that was why they had dug the trenches in the first place—the only way to break through was to eliminate the sources of that fire by shelling the enemy's trenches and gun positions into ruin before the attack. At least that was the theory.

So the trench war became a war of artillery, and over half the casualties were now caused by shellfire. The greatest problem of 1915 for every country was not at the front but at home, where shell production could not keep up with demand. Pre-war French planning had allowed for the expenditure of 10,000 75-mm shells a day; by 1915 France was producing 200,000 shells a day and still not keeping up with demand. (Napoleon's artillery fired only about 25,000 rounds on the day of Waterloo in June 1815, and fought only on one other day that month.) Russia increased shell production tenfold between 1915 and 1916, to 4.5 million shells per month, and couldn't keep up either. Even

"Funk holes" in a Canadian trench.

"It was no place for a human being to be, really." A flooded dugout in a British front-line trench, January 1917.

in Britain, the world's most industrialized country, there was a critical shell shortage in 1915, and the demands went on mounting. At the Third Battle of Ypres in 1917, the nineteen-day British bombardment used 4.3 million shells weighing 107,000 tons, a year's production for 55,000 workers.[14]

And still the infantry could not break through, although they died in their millions trying. For though the shells could destroy most of the enemy's machine guns in the first-line trenches, and even the enemy's guns behind the lines, enough defenders always survived to make the advance a slow and costly business, and the bombardments turned the ground into a wilderness of shell holes across which any movement was very difficult. Eventually the attackers might take the enemy's first-line trenches—and by the middle of the war these alone could be a belt up to three thousand yards deep—but by that time the enemy's reserves would have arrived and manned a whole new trench system just to the rear.

There was simply no way around the trenches. The one attempt at a strategic flanking move, the attack that was meant to force the Dardanelles, capture Istanbul, drive the Ottoman Empire out of the war, and open up direct sea links between the Anglo-French forces and their Russian ally, was decisively defeated by mines in the Straits and Turkish infantry behind the beaches of Gallipoli. The British and German fleets of giant Dreadnought battleships on which enormous sums had been lavished before the war in the first real arms race just glowered at each other across the North Sea except for one day's battle at Jutland in 1916; the Germans won on points, but since they didn't break the British blockade, they really lost. And for over three years, no offensive succeeded in budging the Western Front by as much as ten miles.

> . . . the ruddy clouds of brick-dust hang over the shelled vil-lages by day and at night the eastern horizon roars and bubbles with light. And everywhere in these desolate places I see the faces and figures of enslaved men, the marching columns pearl-hued with chalky dust on the sweat of their heavy drab clothes; the files of carrying parties laden and staggering in the flickering moonlight of gunfire; the "waves" of assaulting troops lying silent and pale on the tapelines of the jumping-off places.
>
> I crouch with them while the steel glacier rushing by just overhead scrapes away every syllable, every fragment of a message bawled in my ear. . . . I go forward with them . . . up and down across ground like a huge ruined honeycomb, and my wave melts away, and the second wave comes up, and also melts away, and then the third wave merges into the ruins of the first and second, and after a while the fourth blunders into the remnants of the others, and we begin to run

forward to catch up with the barrage, gasping and sweating, in bunches, anyhow, every bit of the months of drill and rehearsal forgotten.

We come to wire that is uncut, and beyond we see grey coal-scuttle helmets bobbing about. . . . and the loud crackling of machine-guns changes as to a screeching of steam being blown off by a hundred engines and soon no one is left standing. An hour later our guns are "back on the first objective," and the brigade, with all its hopes and beliefs, has found its grave on the northern slopes of the Somme battlefield.[15]

With strategy paralyzed and tactics narrowed to the search for ever bigger bombardments, the war became a simple matter of attrition. New weapons like poison gas only increased the casualties without breaking the deadlock. By 1916 despairing Allied generals were sometimes reduced to the ghastly argument that since they had more men than the Germans, if they traded life for life, they would still have some men left alive when all the Germans were dead. So they would have won.

That was the real meaning of battles like the Somme. The point was not that the British captured only forty-five square miles in a five-month battle at a cost of 415,000 men—over 8,000 men for each useless square mile—but that the Germans were also compelled to sacrifice men and equipment at a similar rate. Battles had become an industrial operation in reverse, in which the rates of destruction at the front matched the rates of production in the industries at home.

———

It is significant that the term "home front" came into use during World War I, when the role of munitions workers, and of civilian production more generally, was becoming as important to victory as the soldiers in the trenches. Without a constant flow of supplies

A very long way from the Dani. French soldiers being decorated for gallantry in a trench, World War I.

equal to the vast consumption at the front, the soldiers would soon be helpless. And since the mobilization of so huge a number of men left vast gaps in the normal workforce—France put 20 percent of its entire population into uniform, Germany 18 percent, and the other major powers not much less—the remaining adult civilians had to be directed by government into whatever jobs were needed to keep production going. In effect the civilian economy was conscripted too. The governments of Europe quickly took control over labour and raw materials, imposed rationing on all scarce goods, and created true war economies. Women flooded into factories to replace the men at the front, and most production beyond the basic needs of subsistence was diverted into the war effort.

From early in the war, both sides resorted to economic warfare, imposing blockades on each other's seaborne trade. The British did it in the traditional way, by stopping all ships bound for German ports, and their blockade was very nearly leakproof. It took a long time for the full effect to be felt, but in the last two years of the war it is estimated that undernourishment caused an excess of eight hundred thousand civilian deaths in Germany over the peacetime mortality rate.[16] The Germans, denied use of the sea's surface, resorted to submarines in their counter-blockade of Britain. They sank over fifteen million tons of shipping during the war, but only once came close to cutting Britain's vital flow of food and raw materials from overseas. As soon as the Royal Navy brought back the old convoy system to protect the merchant ships, the danger passed—and Germany's campaign of unrestricted submarine warfare in 1917 played a big part in bringing the United States into the war against it, thereby tilting the manpower balance decisively against the Central Powers.

If the entire civilian population of a nation was now an essential part of its war effort, however, it could be argued that the home front was now a legitimate target not merely for the slow-acting weapon of blockade, but for direct armed attack. And by

And just as far from the Yanomamo. Women assembling shell fuses in Montreal, 1916.

1915, technology had at last produced a weapon that could strike directly at the enemy's cities and factories: the aircraft.

> The idea was to equip from twelve to twenty Zeppelins and drill their crews to function as a co-ordinated task force. Each ship would carry about 300 fire bombs. They would attack simultaneously at night. Hence, as many as six thousand bombs would be rained upon [London] at once. . . . When asked for my technical opinion, morality aside, I agreed it was definitely workable.
>
> *Capt. Ernst Lehman, German army*
> *Zeppelin service*[17]

> We who strike the enemy where his heart beats have been slandered as "baby-killers" and "murderers of women." . . . What we do is repugnant to us too, but necessary. Very necessary. Nowadays there is no such animal as a non-combatant; modern warfare is total warfare. A soldier cannot function at the front without the factory worker, the farmer and all the other providers behind him. You and I, Mother, have discussed this subject, and I know you understand what I say. My men are brave and honourable. Their cause is holy, so how can they sin while doing their duty? If what we do is frightful, then may frightfulness be Germany's salvation.
>
> *Letter from Capt. Peter Strasser, head of*
> *the German navy's airship division*[18]

Bombing civilians in cities—not by accident while trying to hit military targets, but with the deliberate purpose of killing civilians and breaking their morale—was the final step in the brutal logic of total war. If the civilians producing the weapons of war were now the real foundation of a nation's armed strength, then they were actually the most important target of all. It was Germany, whose huge zeppelins were the only aircraft with the range and bomb-carrying capacity to reach an enemy's capital when the war broke out, who initiated the twentieth century's most characteristic form of warfare, but it was just as inevitable as the trenches.

Legitimate targets at last. Houses wrecked in a Zeppelin raid, London.

The first major air raid on London came little more than a year after the war's outbreak, on 8 September 1915. Zeppelin L-15 left north Germany late in the afternoon under the command of Captain Heinrich Mathy, crossed the English coast in Lincolnshire, and followed the main railway line south to London. About 10:40 in the evening he dropped a few bombs on the north London suburb of Golders Green and continued south until he was over Russell Square. Then the rest of the bomb-load—fifteen high-explosive bombs and fifty-odd incendiaries—rained down from eight thousand feet, walking a path of destruction through Bedford Place, Queen's Square, Lamb's Conduit Passage, Red

Lion Street, and on to King Edward Street. The worst casualties were at the Dolphin public house on Red Lion Street, where a bomb fell just outside. The front blew in and the roof came down on the astounded drinkers, leaving seventeen of them dead and injured beneath the rubble. In all, the raid caused seventy-two casualties and destroyed $2.5 million worth of property.

But both the technology and the spirit of the enterprise retained an amateurish air, on both sides.

> Well the first job I had after a total of twelve hours in so-called duo and solo was as a night pilot, anti-zeppelin. I was asked by the adjutant if I could fly in the dark. I said I didn't know—I couldn't fly in the daylight, maybe it was easier in the dark. The first night I was there the commanding officer of the station went up on duty and killed himself before he'd got a hundred yards beyond the end flare, so that was my introduction to the game.
>
> And then after a flight or two I was sent to start Hornchurch air station as a night-flying anti-zeppelin station. I landed there and the aerodrome consisted of a large field full of sheep, an infuriated farmer; and a still more infuriated dog. So when we'd cleared off the sheep and I'd appeased the farmer and been billeted on him, I formed a flight there which contained amongst others Leefe Robinson—and when I was away on a four-day leave doing something much more dangerous, which was getting married, he went up and he bagged the first zeppelin.
>
> *Sir Arthur Harris, later air marshal and*
> *head of RAF Bomber Command*
> *1942–45*

The German raids on Britain in World War I, by Zeppelins and later by large two- and three-engine bombers, were tiny by later standards: only four thousand British civilians were killed and wounded throughout the war. But the raids were the precedent and the prototype for Rotterdam, for Dresden, for Hiroshima, for all the cities that were destroyed from the air in the twentieth century—and for the strategy of nuclear deterrence as well. The delay was due only to inadequate technology. After 1915, everybody was a legitimate target.

———

The transformation of mass warfare in the French revolutionary style into total war in the modern style took little more than a century. Since the Dolphin pub, there have been no barriers of behaviour left to breach, only more and more destructive weapons to be used according to principles now universally accepted. And what the governments of Europe that found themselves trapped in the first total war discovered to their dismay was that if the means used to fight a war are total, then so must be the ends; it was almost impossible to stop short of total victory for one side, and unconditional surrender for the other.

The commercial jealousies, military anxieties, and territorial disputes that caused World War I were not significantly different from those that caused the Seven Years War a century and a half before. In the old style of war, the small armies of the two alliances would have fought each other sporadically for a few years (while the vast majority of the citizens of all countries concerned went about their daily affairs undisturbed). Eventually, when one side had proved to be militarily stronger for the moment, a few concessions would have been made by the losers and peace would have returned. A few hundred thousand soldiers would be dead, but no governments would fall, no country would be occupied. The cost may already have been disproportionate to the issues at stake, but at least the governments were able to control it.

The disputes between the rival governments were no more important in 1914, but the techniques of war had completely outstripped the ability of governments to limit their commitment to it. The axiom that force can be overcome only by greater force drove them to make the war total, and the scale of the sacrifices they then had to demand of their citizens required that the purposes of the war must also be great. When sixty million men have been ordered into uniform and sent off to risk their lives; when in

France, for example, one in three of the male population (including infants and old men) has been killed or wounded in a period of four years; when the people's willingness to go on making sacrifices has been sustained in every country by hate propaganda that depicts the war as a moral crusade against fathomless evil—then governments cannot just stop the fighting, sort out the petty and obscure Balkan quarrel that triggered it, swap around a few colonies and trade routes, and thank the surviving soldiers and send them home. Total war requires the goal of total victory; and so the propaganda lies become the truth: the future of the nation (or at least the survival of the regime) really does depend on victory, no matter what the war's origins were.

So those in power, even when they could foresee military collapse or social revolution, even if they could remember what the war had been about when it started (and most of them could not, for they ended up believing their own propaganda), were unwilling and unable to look for a compromise peace. The collapses and revolutions duly came.

The collapse of the Russian army in the field and near-starvation at home brought the (first) Russian revolution in March 1917; in April, fifty-four divisions of the French army (half the total) mutinied after another futile offensive, and nearly twenty-five thousand men were court-martialled after order was restored; in May, four hundred thousand Italian troops simply abandoned the battlefield at Caporetto; and later that month the Chief of the Imperial General Staff in London wrote to General Sir Douglas Haig, the commander of the British army in France: "I am afraid there is no getting away from the fact that there is some unrest in the country now as a result partly of the Russian revolution."[19] Meanwhile German occupation troops in Russia were fraternizing with the Bolsheviks, and the Austro-Hungarian empire was teetering on the brink of dissolution into its various national components. But no government stopped fighting voluntarily; they were rightly convinced that by that time their only hope of survival was a total military victory.

Some of the governments on the winning side did survive, but none of the losers. Four great empires—German, Russian,

Austrian, and Ottoman—were destroyed by the war, and the latter two were completely dismantled into a welter of new countries and territories. About half the people of Europe, the Middle East, and Africa underwent a radical change of regime or even of citizenship as a result of the war. And several of the new regimes that emerged—in Russia at once, in Italy and Germany later on—preserved in peacetime much of the apparatus of total state control over the citizens and the economy that had been invented in order to fight the first total war.

———

Attrition, in the end, was the main factor that decided who won the war. The Entente powers simply had more men and resources than Germany and its allies (though they had some anxious moments between the time their Russian ally fell out of the war in mid-1917 and the arrival of large numbers of American troops on the Western Front in mid-1918). The scale of losses dwarfed those of any previous war in history. Over eight million soldiers were killed and about twenty million wounded, and it is estimated that around three million civilians also died, mostly from malnutrition and disease. But toward the end of the war there appeared a new weapon that gave some professional soldiers hope that there might be an alternative to the grinding war of attrition in the trenches. It was called the tank.

> Panic spread like an electric current, passing from man to man along the trench. As the churning tracks reared overhead the bravest men clambered above ground to launch suicidal counter-attacks, hurling grenades onto the tanks' roofs or shooting and stabbing at any vision slit within reach. They were shot down or crushed, while others threw up their hands in terrified surrender or bolted down the communication trenches towards the second line.
>
> *German infantryman's first encounter*
> *with a tank, 1916*[20]

No sooner had the obstacle of the trenches suddenly appeared in late 1914 than the solution occurred to a British staff officer, Colonel E. D. Swinton. What was needed, obviously, was a vehicle armoured against machine-gun bullets and carrying its own guns, which could roll over shell holes, barbed wire, and trenches on caterpillar tracks. Against much opposition from military conservatives, the idea was adopted by Winston Churchill (even though he was then running the navy), and the earliest production models of the "landships," as they were first called, reached the Western Front in the autumn of 1916.

They were huge, primitive, and horribly uncomfortable vehicles. The eight-man crew, stripped to their waists in the hundred-degree heat, shared the interior with an exposed 105-horsepower Daimler engine. The fumes from the engine and from hot shell cases rolling around on the floor made the atmosphere inside almost unbreathable in combat. There were no springs in the suspension, the noise made voice communications impossible, and it was hard to see hand signals in the semi-darkness, as the only light came through the vision slits. The tanks' top speed was only three and a half miles an hour, and they broke down on average every five or ten miles.

But the first time the tanks went into battle in really large numbers, at Cambrai in November 1917, where 476 were committed, they enabled the British army to advance six miles in six hours, at a cost of four thousand dead and wounded. Earlier the same year, at the Third Battle of Ypres, the British had taken three months to advance a similar distance, and they had lost a quarter-million men doing it. But there was more to the success at Cambrai than just tanks. There was also, for the first time ever, a comprehensive plan for indirect artillery fire to engage the German defences simultaneously through the full depth of the defended zone, all the way back to the furthest reserve positions. One thousand British guns were deployed on a six-mile front, but the 150 batteries that reinforced the sector arrived secretly and did not open fire even to observe and adjust the fall of their shells until the moment of the offensive, so as not to give the Germans any warning. It was the first large-scale use of "predicted fire,"

They were called "tanks" in the development stage to hide from German intelligence the fact that they were actually weapons. They might just as easily have been code-named "boilers" or "furnaces"—anything that used a lot of steel. But British infantry saw them as salvation. Behind the British front line, July 1917.

relying on aerial reconnaissance, accurate mapping and ballistic calculations, and—with the help of the tanks and 289 aircraft used as artillery spotters, ground-attack aircraft and bombers—it almost broke through the German lines completely. Only a very rapid and ferocious German counterattack closed the breach.

The old trench stalemate was over, for the Germans had just solved the breakthrough problem in the same way, though with less reliance on tanks. Beginning with an offensive at Riga on the Russian front in September 1917, a Germany artillery officer named Colonel Georg Bruchmüller had independently come up with the same formula for surprise and rapid penetration: massive amounts of indirect and predicted artillery fire that gave no warning beforehand, and infantry "storm-troops" who bypassed enemy strongpoints that were still resisting and just kept moving ever deeper into the defended zone, spreading confusion and dismay and ultimately driving the enemy into a major retreat.

Although German tanks never matched British ones in number or quality, it was Germany that took the offensive in the spring of 1918 (after three years on the defensive), in an all-out gamble to win the war before large numbers of American troops arrived in France. At Arras in March 1918, 6,608 German guns fired 3.2 million rounds on the first day of the offensive—and the Germans gained more ground in two weeks than the Allies had gained in every offensive during the whole war. Further fast-moving offensives followed, and the Allies nearly lost the war in the spring of 1918, but the Germans failed to reach either Paris or the Channel coast—and they lost a million men between March and July of 1918.[21]

After that the Allies went over to the offensive, mainly using British and Canadian troops to spearhead the attacks, and showed the same ability to gain ground. Tanks never did play a decisive role, but the plans for 1919, had the war continued, called for a force of several thousand tanks closely supported by aircraft to smash through the enemy's front, with infantry following closely in armoured personnel carriers. Confronted with an unprecedented military problem, the soldiers of World War I had solved the trench stalemate. They did not, however, escape from the phenomenon of the continuous front.

During the "twenty-year armistice" between the two wars, numbers of theorists worked on how best to exploit the mobility of tanks, and in 1939—41 it looked as if the Germans, at least, had found a foolproof formula. "Blitzkrieg" (lightning war) involved rapid penetration of an enemy's front by a large force of tanks, closely assisted by ground-attack aircraft and followed by motorized infantry and artillery. Once through the defended zone, the tanks would push on at high speed to the enemy's higher command posts and vital communications centres deep in the rear and spread chaos behind the front, which would then collapse almost of its own accord when the troops holding it found themselves cut off from their own headquarters and supplies.

Using the blitzkrieg formula, the Germans destroyed the entire Polish army in three weeks in 1939 at a cost of only eight thousand dead, and the following spring in France they were equally successful. Despite the fact that the French and British had more and on the whole better tanks than they did, the Germans' superior tactics allowed them to conquer the Low Countries and France in only six weeks, at a cost of 27,000 dead, 18,000 missing, and 111,000 wounded. The continuous front and its slaughterhouse battles of attrition seemed a thing of the past. But it was all an illusion. What tanks had really done was just to set the continuous front in motion, with disastrous consequences for civilians.

No innovation in warfare stays a surprise for very long, and by the middle of the war, when German forces were fighting deep inside the Soviet Union, attrition had returned with a vengeance. The solution to the blitzkrieg tactic of rapid penetration was to make the defended zone deeper—many miles deep, with successive belts of trenches, minefields, bunkers, gun positions, and tank traps that would slow down the armoured spearheads and eventually wear them away. Sometimes the defence would hold; sometimes there would be a successful breakthrough, but even then, the continuous front would not disappear. It would roll back some dozens or hundreds of miles all along the line and then stabilize again.

The consumption of men and machines in the new style of war was enormous—the Soviets, for example, built approximately 100,000 tanks, 100,000 aircraft, and 175,000 artillery pieces during the war, of which at least two-thirds were destroyed in the fighting—but the ability of fully mobilized industrial societies to absorb enormous punishment and still maintain production was seemingly endless. So was the willingness of whole nations in arms, stiffened by patriotism and propaganda and harnessed by totalitarian controls (which were imposed in almost every warring country regardless of its peacetime political system) to accept the most terrible sacrifices without flinching. The Germans ended up with two-thirds of all males between the ages of eighteen and forty-five in the armed forces and lost three and a half million military dead,[22] but their army was still fighting in April 1945 when the two fronts facing the Soviet advance from the east and the Anglo-American advance from the west were practically back to back down the middle of a devastated Germany.

All this would have amounted only to a repetition of World War I with even higher military casualties (except for the English-speaking countries, which got off quite lightly because their armies only saw heavy fighting in Europe in the last year of the war), but for the fact that the continuous front was now in motion. And as it ground across whole countries, it destroyed almost everything in its path.

> Guts splattered across the rubble and sprayed from one dying man onto another; tightly riveted machines ripped like the belly of a cow which has just been sliced open, flaming and groaning; trees broken into tiny fragments; gaping windows pouring out torrents of billowing dust, dispersing into oblivion all that remains of a comfortable parlour . . . the cries of officers and non-coms, trying to shout across the cataclysm to regroup their sections and companies. That is how we took part in the German advance, being called through the noise and dust, following

the clouds churned up by our tanks to the northern out-skirts of Belgorod. . . .

The burnt-out ruins of Belgorod fell into the hands of [our surviving troops] on the second evening. . . . We had been ordered to reduce the pockets of resistance in the ashes of a suburb called Deptreotka, if I remember correctly. . . . When we reached the end of our sweep, we collapsed at the bottom of a large crater and stared at each other for a long time in dazed silence. None of us could speak. . . . The air still roared and shook and smelled of burning. . . . By the fourth or fifth evening, we had gone through Belgorod with-out even knowing it.

> *Guy Sajer, an Alsatian conscript in the German army*[23]

Near a smashed Russian city like Belgorod, survivors search for their families.

Belgorod, a city in southern Russia, had a population of thirty-four thousand people before the front moved east across it for the first time in October 1941—and that time it was lucky. Von Reichenau's Sixth Army took it "on the run," and although there were two days of fighting around the city, most of the buildings and most of the citizens survived. Twenty months later it was liberated by Soviet troops as the front moved west again after the Sixth Army was destroyed at Stalingrad, and again it was relatively lucky: the Germans did not have time to destroy it as they retreated.

But then Belgorod was retaken by the "Gross Deutschland" Division (in which Sajer was serving) at the beginning of the great German offensive around Kursk in July 1943, in which 6,000 tanks, 30,000 guns and 2 million men fought along a front of hundreds of miles. When the German tanks had finally been halted by the deep Russian defences, the Soviet counterattack began with 70 tanks and 230 guns to each kilometre, and in mid-August Belgorod was liberated for a second time, after street-fighting (or rather, fighting in the ruins) that killed another 3,000 soldiers within the city limits. And at the end of all that, only 140 of Belgorod's 34,000 people were left; the rest were refugees, conscripts, or dead.

Belgorod had no military importance; it just got in the way. The front moved across it four times, and it was practically extinguished. And what happened there happened to tens of thousands of other towns and villages. World War II killed at least twice as many soldiers as World War I, but it also killed almost twice as many civilians as soldiers. It was the first European war since the Thirty Years War in which the civilian casualties outnumbered the military. Most of the civilians died more or less by accident, as an incidental by-product of the fighting. The continuous front moved through every city and hamlet in entire countries, sending tens of millions of civilians into flight as refugees or killing them in the rubble of their own homes. So great was the destruction and disorganization that the casualty figures are not reliable even to the nearest million, but on average the countries from Germany eastward, where the fighting was most intense and prolonged, lost about 10 percent of their populations killed.

Civilian casualties of roughly the same order have occurred on the few occasions since 1945 (like Korea) when regular armies in continuous fronts have fought their way through heavily populated territory.

————

The disintegration of nations in the last war was brought about by the actions of the armies in the field. [In the future] it will be accomplished directly by . . . aerial forces. . . . War will be waged essentially against the unarmed populations of the cities and great industrial centres. . . . A complete breakdown of the social order cannot but take place in a country subjected to this kind of merciless pounding. . . . It will be an inhuman, atrocious performance, but these are the facts.
Gen. Giulio Douhet, 1921[24]

There are a lot of people who say that bombing can never win a war: Well, my answer to that is that it has never been tried yet, and we shall see.
Air Marshal Sir Arthur Harris, head of
RAF Bomber Command, 1942−45

At least 97 percent of the forty-five million people who were killed in World War II were *not* killed by air raids on cities, and it is very hard for even the most devoted admirers of "strategic bombardment" to make a convincing argument that it won the war. It was only due to technological shortcomings that the bombers took so long to fulfil their promise of instant, decisive destruction from the skies; the will to do it was certainly there.

Bombing is the natural weapon—the *reductio ad absurdum*—of total war, and it was particularly attractive to those theorists between the wars who wished to avoid another bloody struggle in the trenches. The earliest and most influential was an Italian general called Giulio Douhet, who had proposed an independent Italian bombing force of five hundred multi-engine aircraft to attack Austro-Hungarian communications as early as

1915. (Italy had been the first country to use aircraft for bombing, in its war against the Turks in Libya in 1911.) General Douhet became commissioner of aviation after Mussolini's coup in Italy in 1922, but his greatest influence was in Britain and the United States, technologically oriented countries that would rather spend money than lives in war. The principal American bomber of World War II, the B-17, was flight-tested in 1935, and the Royal Air Force's four-engined bombers were designed in the same year.

The first major air attacks on cities during World War II, however, were made by the Luftwaffe—on Warsaw, Rotterdam, and then on most of the major British cities—although the German air force had never been primarily intended or designed for that role.

> There was a mist over the town as men and women began to crawl out of their shelters, look for their friends and survey the ruins of their city. They could hardly recognise it. . . . Hardly a building remained standing. It was impossible to see where the central streets we knew so well had been. Fires were still raging in every direction and from time to time we heard the crash of a fallen roof or wall. . . . It seemed so hopeless with our homes and shops and so much of our lovely old city in ruins. You might say we were dazed.
>
> *BBC interview after the bombing of*
> *Coventry, 14—15 November 1940*[25]

Forty thousand civilians were killed in the German blitz on British cities between September 1940 and May 1941, but casualties on this scale (one in a thousand of the population) had none of the effects predicted by Douhet. Indeed, the losses were one-fourteenth of what the British had expected and had been prepared to accept. (The government had made plans for mass graves.) German bomber technology was simply not up to the job.

Neither were British and American bombers in 1942—43. They lacked the numbers, and the freedom to operate at will in German skies, needed to achieve the purpose for which they were created—the wholesale destruction of German cities and industry. But there was no question, in the minds of the British and American advocates of strategic bombardment at least, that that was the quick and efficient road to victory. In 1942, Lord Cherwell wrote: "Investigation seems to show having one's house demolished is most damaging to morale. People seem to mind it more than having their friends or even relatives killed. At Hull, signs of strain were evident, though only one-tenth of the houses were demolished. On the above we should be able to do ten times as much harm to each of the fifty-eight principal German towns. There seems little doubt that this would break the will of the people."[26]

Up to that time the British air force, in its raids on Germany, had been trying to hit specific industrial targets (for efficiency's sake, not out of moral compunction), although even then the policy was not very strictly observed—especially since the strength of German air defences forced the bombers to fly at night.

> We didn't worry too much about not hitting the military targets we were after.
>
> Really, I suppose one thought we were at war with Germany and so long as we dropped our bombs we were doing some damage somewhere, although the ruling was that if we couldn't see our target we were to bring our bombs back, but nobody did this. . . . If the target was covered in cloud but you knew you were over a town somewhere you dropped the bombs, and when you got back at the debriefing you said there was a hole in the cloud and you bombed through the hole—the next raid after Coventry we were briefed not to bring our bombs back. . . . That was the first time we were briefed to do that, after Coventry.
>
> *Rupert Oakley, Canadian pilot in*
> *RAF Bomber Command (seventy-three*
> *missions)*

In early 1942, Air Marshal Harris took over Bomber Command and dropped the pretense that the bombing had any more precise objective than the German civilian population. His stated reasons were technical, but the new policy conformed entirely with the ideas first expressed by Douhet:

. . . a fellow called Butt was asked to report on the examination of photographs taken by bombers and he came to the conclusion that the average bomb never hit within five miles of its target. . . . With my experience in night flying which was, compared with most people in the service in those days, rather more than most, it was only what I expected, and I realized that the answer to it was simply to mass-bomb large targets, and not try to pick out targets where they make ball-bearings or knitting machines or tie-pins or anything. . . .

The policy of "mass bombing" that Harris initiated with the thousand-bomber raid on Cologne in April 1942 resulted in the progressive devastation, over the next three years, of almost every major city in Germany: 593,000 German civilians were killed and over 3.3 million homes destroyed. But the cost to Britain was also high: 46,000 British aircrew were killed, and as much as one-third of British military and civilian manpower and industrial resources was devoted to supporting Bomber Command in the latter years of the war.[27]

It seemed as though the whole of Hamburg was on fire from one end to the other and a huge column of smoke was towering well above us—and we were on 20,000 feet!

Set in the darkness was a turbulent dome of bright red fire, lighted and ignited like the glowing heart of a vast brazier. I saw no streets, no outlines of buildings, only brighter fires which flared like yellow torches against a background of bright red ash. Above the city was a misty red haze. I looked down, fascinated but aghast, satisfied yet horrified.

It was as if I was looking into what I imagined to be an active volcano. . . . There were great volumes of smoke and, mentally, I could sense the great heat. Our actual bombing was like putting another shovelful of coal into the furnace.

RAF aircrew over Hamburg,
28 July 1943[28]

The British bombers on this occasion were using the standard mix of bombs: huge numbers of four-pound incendiaries to start fires on roofs and thirty-pound ones to penetrate deeper inside buildings, together with four-thousand-pound high-explosive bombs to blow in doors and windows over wide areas and fill the streets with craters and rubble to hinder firefighting equipment. But on a hot, dry summer night with good visibility, the unusually tight concentration of the bombs in a densely pop-ulated working-class district created a new phenomenon in history: a firestorm.

Eventually it covered an area of about four square miles, with an air temperature at the centre of eight hundred degrees Celsius and convection winds blowing inward with hurricane force. One survivor said the sound of the wind was "like the Devil laughing," and another compared the noise of the firestorm to "an old organ in a church when someone is playing all the notes at once." Practically all the apartment blocks in the firestorm area had underground shelters, but nobody who stayed in them survived; those who were not cremated died of carbon monoxide poisoning. But to venture into the streets was to risk being swept by the wind into the very heart of the firestorm.

> Mother wrapped me in wet sheets, kissed me, and said, "Run!" I hesitated at the door: In front of me I could see only fire—everything red, like the door to a furnace. An intense heat struck me. A burning beam fell in front of my feet. I shied back but then, when I was ready to jump over it, it was whirled away by a ghostly hand. The sheets around me acted as sails and I had the feeling that I was being carried away by the storm. I reached the front of a five-storey building . . . which . . . had been bombed and burned out in a previous raid and there was not much in it for the fire to get hold of. Someone came out, grabbed me in their arms, and pulled me into the doorway.
>
> *Traute Koch, fifteen in 1943*[29]

Twenty thousand people died in Hamburg in about two hours. If the Royal Air Force had been able to produce that result every time, its bombers would have defeated Germany in six months. But only once more, at Dresden in 1945, were all the circumstances right to produce a firestorm. The usual consequences were far less impressive. Over the whole war, the average result of a single British bomber sortie with a seven-man crew was less than three dead Germans, of whom perhaps one might be a production worker—and after an average of fourteen missions, the bomber crew themselves would be dead or, if they were lucky, prisoners. Moreover, since the damage was done piecemeal over a long period of time, German industrial production for military

Stalingrad, 1943. By this stage in World War II, at least a million people were being killed each month.

purposes actually managed to continue rising until late 1944. The theory of strategic bombardment was sound, but the practice as applied by RAF Bomber Command was a very expensive aerial equivalent of trench warfare. American bombers had just as much effect on German war production by concentrating on daylight precision bombing of "bottleneck" industrial targets.

In the war against Japan, where the United States used huge B-29 bombers and more "British" tactics, the flimsy wooden buildings and crowded conditions of Japanese cities produced a thoroughly satisfactory result. Soon after Dresden, on 9 March 1945, General Curtis E. LeMay ordered the first mass low-level night raid on Tokyo, using incendiary bombs. "The area attacked was . . . four miles by three . . . with 103,000 inhabitants to the square mile. . . . 267,171 buildings were destroyed—about one-fourth of the total in Tokyo—and 1,008,000 persons were rendered homeless. In some of the smaller canals the water was actually boiling."[30]

By 1945, at least in the particular case of Japan, strategic bombardment was actually working the way the theorists had envisaged: only three hundred thousand civilians were killed by the bombing, but about twenty-two million—a third of the population—were living in temporary shelters amid the burnt-out cities or had fled into the countryside. "The Twentieth [U.S.] Air Force was destroying cities at . . . [a] cost to Japan [that] was fifty times the cost to us . . ." reported General "Hap" Arnold, head of the U.S. Army Air Force.[31] But even in these dire circumstances the almost limitless resilience and determination of the fully mobilized modern nation-state would have prevented a Japanese surrender and necessitated a full-scale invasion of the home islands, costing millions more lives—if an almost magical American weapon had not broken the spell imposed on the Japanese government by total war.

> We were not expecting an air raid, but high up in the sky I heard an American bomber; a B-29. I thought it was strange.
> *Mrs. Ochi, Hiroshima*

I saw a perfectly outlined city, clear in every detail, coming in. The city was roughly about four miles in diameter: By that time we were at our bombing altitude of thirty-two thousand feet. The navigator came up—looking over my shoulder; he said: "Yes, that's Hiroshima, there's no doubt about it." We were so well on the target that the bombardier says: "I can't do anything, there's nothing to do." He says: "It's just sitting there."

Col. Paul Tibbetts, pilot, Enola Gay

The U.S. government had begun the Manhattan Project in June 1942 after repeated warnings from refugee scientists that they suspected Germany was working to develop an atomic bomb. That worry was mistaken, in fact, but it was not unjustified, for it was a reasonable assumption by the mid-twentieth century that any scientific or technological development with military implications would be exploited for use in total war. The British certainly were investigating nuclear weapons already (though they and the Canadians accepted subsidiary roles in the Manhattan Project after 1942), and both the Russians and the Japanese had nuclear weapons programs by 1944.[32] And the Germans, though neglecting nuclear weapons, were busy developing the ancestors of the devices that would later become the principal means of delivering nuclear weapons: the cruise missile (v-1), of which they launched 10,500 against Britain in 1944, and the long-range ballistic missile (V-2), of which 1,115 fell on or near London. Given the context of total war and the certainty that every potential weapon would be used with utter ruthlessness, it is scarcely surprising that most scientists everywhere placed their services at the disposal of the country of their birth (or their choice).

Even so, some of the nuclear physicists who had worked on the Manhattan Project for three years had second thoughts when, in July of 1945, they moved into an old ranch house in the New Mexico desert to do the final assembly and testing of the first atomic bomb. But it was too late to change their minds. They had delivered into the hands of the government a weapon that would at last fulfil all the promises of the strategists of aerial bombing about cheap and reliable mass destruction from the air. At 5:50 in the morning, the test went off perfectly, and the awestruck scientists contemplated what they had done.

> We knew the world would not be the same. A few people laughed. A few people cried. Most people were silent. I remembered a line from the Hindu scripture—the Bhagavadgita. Vishnu is trying to persuade the prince that he should do his duty and to impress him, takes on his multi-armed form and says, "Now I am become Death, the destroyer of worlds." I suppose we all felt that, one way or another.
>
> *Robert Oppenheimer, leader of the*
> *scientific team at Los Alamos*

Scientifically the atomic bomb was an advance into unknown territory, but militarily it was simply a more cost-effective way of attaining a goal that was already a central part of strategy: a means of producing the results achieved at Hamburg and Dresden cheaply and reliably every time the weapon was used. (Even at the time, the $2-billion cost of the Manhattan Project was dwarfed by the cost of trying to destroy cities the hard way, using conventional bombs.) And there was no moral question in most people's minds about the ethics of using weapons of mass destruction against defenceless cities; that question had effectively been foreclosed over the Dolphin pub thirty years before.

> In those days when one was told, "This is what you're going to do . . . you just saluted and said, "Yes, sir!" We had worked so long and so hard to perfect the weapon, to adapt the airplanes to carry that weapon, and to train ourselves to do the job—it seemed to be routine.
>
> *Col. Paul Tibbetts*

On 6 August 1945, Colonel Tibbetts's crew dropped the weapon on Hiroshima, and total war came fully into its inheritance: seventy thousand people were killed in less than five minutes by a single aircraft carrying a single bomb. Afterwards, he said, "I couldn't see any city down there, but what I saw was a tremendous area covered by—the only way I could describe it is— a boiling black mass."

It was as if the sun had crashed and exploded. Yellow fireballs were splashing down. [Afterward, on the riverbank], there were so many injured people that there was almost no room to walk. This was only a mile from where the bomb fell. People's clothes had been blown off and their bodies burned by the heat rays. They looked as if they had strips of rags hanging from them. They had water blisters which had already burst, and their skins hung in tatters. I saw people whose intestines were hanging out of their bodies. Some had lost their eyes. Some had their backs torn open so you could see their backbones inside. They were all asking for water.

Mrs. Ochi

If I were given a similar situation in which this country was at war, risking its future, the circumstances being as they were at that time, I don't think I would hesitate one minute to do it over.

Col. Paul Tibbetts

Colonel Tibbetts is unusual only for what he did. His attitudes toward war are those that still dominate the world, although the weapons of mass destruction have grown still more efficient in the six decades since he dropped his relatively puny bomb on Hiroshima. The disproportion between ends and means in warfare has widened into an unbridgeable chasm: the causes and the various national aims of modern wars are no more profound or complex than those that sent Tuthmose III's army marching into Palestine three thousand years ago, but the means by which wars can now be fought have placed the whole human race on a permanent notice of extinction.

As General Douglas MacArthur testified to the U.S. Congress at the end of his career: "You have got to understand the history of war. . . . With the scientific methods which have made mass destruction reach appalling proportions, war has ceased to be a sort of roll of the dice. . . . If you have another world war . . . only those will be happy that are dead. . . . I understand . . . that you cannot abolish war unless others do it. . . . The only way that you can meet force is by force . . . and you have to provide for that. But sooner or later, if civilization is to survive, . . . war must go."[33] But there was clearly a long way to go. Only two years before, MacArthur himself had sought permission to use nuclear weapons on the Chinese during the Korean War.

Every era dramatizes its own dilemmas, and half the ages of mankind have believed the end of the world was nigh. Nevertheless, war, an ancient institution and an even more deeply rooted cultural tradition, is clearly nearing the end of the road. Small countries and non-state groups can still achieve some of their political goals through organized violence, but in conflicts between large industrialized states war has become a suicidal activity—which partly explains why such conflicts have not been allowed to end in war for the past sixty years.

But crisis management, however necessary, is bound to fail sooner or later; only profound institutional change can provide long-term safety, for the technologies of total war cannot be unlearned. That change has not yet been accomplished in practice, but one of the vital preconditions for change had come to pass by 1945. As a result of the two world wars, a majority of people everywhere have ceased to see war as an opportunity for personal and national glory, and come to see it instead as a very big and ugly problem.

8

A Short History of Nuclear War, 1945–90

Can one guess how great will be the toll of casualties in a future war? Possibly it would be a third of the 2,700 million inhabitants of the entire world—i.e. only 900 million people. Of course it is most terrible. But even half would not be so bad. . . . If one half of humanity were destroyed, the other half would remain, but imperialism would be destroyed entirely and there would be only Socialism in all the world.

Mao Tse-tung, speech in Moscow, 1957

I'm not saying we wouldn't get our hair mussed, Mister President, but I do say not more than ten or twenty million dead, depending on the breaks.

General "Buck" Turgidson (George C. Scott) in
Stanley Kubrick's 1963 film *Dr. Strangelove; or,
How I Learned to Stop Worrying and Love the Bomb*

GENERAL TURGIDSON WAS A FICTIONAL CHARACTER, OF COURSE, but Kubrick intended him as a caricature of General Curtis E. LeMay, long-serving commander of the U.S. Air Force's Strategic Air Command, who really did want a nuclear war. "LeMay believed that ultimately we're going to have to confront these people with nuclear weapons, and by God, we'd better do it when we have greater superiority than we will have in the future," explained former U.S. defense secretary Robert S. McNamara in the 2003 documentary film *Fog of War*. For LeMay, as for Mao, nuclear weapons had not really changed anything fundamental about the way that power worked in the world: one believed that the Marxist dialectic still guaranteed the victory of socialism even if a nuclear war wiped out half the world's population, the other thought that a seventeen-to-one U.S. "advantage" over the Soviet Union in the number of nuclear weapons (in the early 1960s) was a meaningful strategic asset. You might say that they were both victims of cultural lag.

The most dangerous part of the Cold War was the early years, when men like these still occupied positions of power in large numbers. As time passed, they were gradually replaced by people who had assimilated the basic idea of deterrence, however unwillingly, and the world became a somewhat safer place. But it remained a very dangerous place, because the belief that deterrence can ensure peace over the long run is as shaky historically as it is questionable psychologically.

> You may reasonably expect a man to walk a tightrope safely
> for ten minutes; it would be unreasonable to do so without
> accident for two hundred years.
>
> *Bertrand Russell*[1]

The assumption that lies at the root of all deterrence theory, either nuclear or conventional—that great military strength is the surest guarantee that a country will be left in peace—is demonstrably false and is indeed the exact reverse of the truth. The bigger and more powerful the state, the more frequent its wars.

During the entire period of modern European history from 1480 to 1940, it has been calculated that there were about twenty-six hundred important battles. The only country that was a leading military power during the whole of that period, France, participated in 47 percent of those battles, and Germany (Prussia), Russia, and Britain all fought in between 22 percent and 25 percent of them. By contrast Spain, which ceased to be a major military power at the beginning of the nineteenth century, soon afterwards dropped out of Europe's wars almost entirely and can only offer an attendance record of 12 percent over the whole period, and the Netherlands and Sweden (great powers only for brief periods) were present at only 8 percent and 4 percent of Europe's battles respectively. Indeed, Sweden has not used its armed forces in war for 170 years.[2]

By any other yardstick—the amount of time a given European country has spent at war, the number of wars it has participated in, the proportion of its population that has been killed in war over the years—the result is the same. There is a steep and consistent gradient of suffering, in which the most powerful nations fight most often and lose most heavily in lives and wealth. The solace that inoffensive small nations can take from this, however, is somewhat limited by the fact that the great-power wars of the twentieth century swept almost all the smaller countries into the conflagration too.

World War I spread to all the European great powers and Japan within a year, pulled the United States in after two and a half years, and had involved thirty-three belligerents—half the independent states then in existence—by its end; World War II spread to every great power in just over two years, and by 1945 all but six of the world's independent countries were at war. The increasingly rapid and uncontrollable spread of great-power wars was partly due to the sheer technological reach of modern war machines, but it was also undoubtedly related to the growing interdependency of states in trade and to the emergence of a single worldwide market in political ideas. These latter phenomena may slowly be laying the foundations on which an international system that does not depend on war will one day be built, but their short-term consequence has been to produce not world peace, but true world wars.

The post-1945 period, however, has seen a striking change in the pattern of wars between states. *None* of the great powers has fought any other great power directly for the past six decades. Most of them have fought wars in or against smaller countries, so they haven't changed their spots entirely, but this is a new and important factor in international affairs. It is certainly connected to the fact that all the great powers now possess nuclear weapons or are closely allied to those who do: they spend a fortune on their nuclear weapons, but they have not so far dared to use them in war even once since 1945. Indeed, they dare not fight one another directly at all (though they do engage in proxy wars from time to time), since any fighting could so quickly escalate into nuclear war. Perhaps this is only a lengthy pause in the historical pattern before normal service is resumed, but it is nevertheless remarkable. There has been no other sixty-year period when no great power has fought any other since the emergence of the modern Western state system in the seventeenth century, and quite possibly since the rise of the Mesopotamian city-states.

Moving down a notch, however, wars between middle-rank neighbouring countries—Israel and the Arab countries, Pakistan and India, Iran and Iraq—have continued to occur fairly regularly. There has been no general outbreak of pacifism in the international system. These wars are now known as "conventional" wars, to distinguish them from nuclear war, and they can be quite destructive—but they also tend to be short. This is partly because the high cost and great efficiency of modern weapons mean that countries can afford relatively few weapons and run out of them quickly after the fighting starts, but it is also because the United Nations is usually quick to propose ceasefires and offer peace-keeping troops. The losing side, at least, will generally grab at this, making it hard for the winning side to continue the war. As a result, the total fatal casualties in wars where both sides were using conventional World War II–style heavy weaponry—May 1945 with laser sights and precision-guided missiles, so to speak—have not exceeded ten million people in six decades. Since the Korean War ended, the average has been fewer than a million per decade.

The majority of the people killed in war since 1945 have died in quite different and seemingly new kinds of struggle: guerrilla warfare, "revolutionary war," counter-insurgency campaigns, terrorism, and the like. Mostly they have been killed by their own fellow citizens, yet few of these conflicts fit the classic model of civil war either. At one point these wars seemed to be breaking out everywhere, but they turned out to be mainly associated with anti-imperial liberation wars and post-colonial power struggles, and they have now subsided in most parts of the world. Terrorism, the weapon of the weak, continues to flourish in a variety of contexts, but when divorced from a territorially based guerrilla war, it is rarely a major threat (though it certainly succeeds in getting people's attention).

For all the differences between these three distinct styles of post-1945 conflict, they do have one new factor in common: military power is becoming less effective in achieving decisive and politically satisfactory results at every level of conflict. The ability of either governments or insurgents to achieve a clear win in the low-intensity guerrilla and terrorist wars that now account for most of the world's actual killing has steadily declined to the point where it is perfectly normal for such a struggle to drag on indecisively for decades. Similarly, conventional wars between countries generally end quickly these days, but they do not often end in peace treaties. They are much likelier to sputter out inconclusively in a morass of ceasefire lines, peacekeeping troops and unresolved issues that will still be hanging around decades later (as in the case of Kashmir since 1947, the DMZ in Korea since 1953, the Golan Heights since 1967, and Cyprus since 1974). And nobody has yet figured out how to win a war by using nuclear weapons, even though both the United States and the Soviet Union spent the whole of the Cold War trying.

———

> Any military commander who's honest with himself . . . will admit that he's made mistakes in the application of military power. He's killed people unnecessarily, his own troops or other troops, through mistakes, through errors of judgment—a hundred, or thousands, or tens of thousands; maybe even a hundred thousand. But he hasn't destroyed nations. And the conventional wisdom is: don't make the same mistake twice. . . .
>
> But there'll be no learning period with nuclear weapons. You make one mistake and you're going to destroy nations.
>
> *Robert S. McNamara, U.S. defence secretary, 1961–68*[3]

Nuclear weapons are the dominant military fact of our era, and yet we know practically nothing about how they would actually work in war when used in large numbers. Two quite small ones were dropped on Japanese cities well over half a century ago, and none have been used in war since. Just as well, of course, but it does mean that strategists discussing nuclear war are like virgins discussing sex. They have theories and hypotheses and even doctrines about nuclear war, but they do not *know* how it would work, except that it would be very bad. They are equally ignorant of the psychological effects, the electromagnetic effects, and the climate effects—and with any luck, they will long remain so. But all the useful evidence we have on these questions comes from the forty-five-year confrontation between the United States and the Soviet Union that is generally known as the Cold War.

The Cold War already seems like ancient history, but we are still relatively ignorant about the strategic debates and internal policy struggles that took place on the Soviet side. However, we know a great deal about the comparable debates and struggles that raged in the United States during that long and often terrifying confrontation, and it is a most instructive tale. In essence, it was a forty-five-year argument between those who believed that nuclear weapons must never again be used in war, and should be reserved solely for the purpose of deterring the other side's use of nuclear weapons; and those others, more numerous by far and driven by technological curiosity, careerist ambition, or ideological fervour, who continually sought ways to make them usable in war.

> The writer . . . is not for the moment concerned about who will win the next war in which atomic bombs are used. Thus far the chief purpose of our military establishment has been to win wars. From now on its chief purpose must be to avert them. It can have almost no other useful purpose.
> *Bernard Brodie, 1946*[4]

Bernard Brodie was a promising young scholar who had just joined the Institute of International Studies at Yale University when the first atomic bomb fell on Hiroshima in August 1945. While the rest of the American academic community resounded with calls for world government as the only possible way of containing the awesome destructive power of the new weapon, Brodie and a small group of like-minded colleagues who recognized the realities of power and the unlikelihood of reaching such an objective in the short or medium term set about working out the ground rules for survival in a world of stubbornly independent nation-states armed with nuclear weapons. In two conferences in September and November 1945, and in innumerable private arguments, they created the theory of nuclear deterrence—complete, definitive, and incontestable.

It was Brodie who formulated the key concepts. "Everything about the atomic bomb is overshadowed by the fact that it exists and that its destructive power is fantastically great," he wrote, and that had changed the nature of war and the conditions of peace beyond recognition. There could be no effective defence against

Bernard Brodie, the first of the civilian defence intellectuals. Right at the start, wrong for fifteen years, and right again by the end.

atomic weapons, since all defence in aerial warfare works by attrition, and only a relatively small number of nuclear weapons had to get through for the destruction to be utterly unacceptable. British defences against V-1 missiles aimed at London had shot down 97 out of 101 on their single best day, letting only four V-1s get through, but, he pointed out, "if those four had been atomic bombs, London survivors would not have considered the record good."

Moreover, there was a limited number of targets in any country—mostly cities—that were worth using a nuclear weapon on, and the destruction of those targets would be effectively the same as the destruction of the society. Therefore, beyond a certain point the relative numbers of nuclear weapons each side had did not matter. The atomic bomb was an absolute weapon: "If 2,000 bombs in the hands of either party is enough to destroy entirely the economy of the other, the fact that one side has 6,000 and the other 2,000 will be of relatively small significance."[5]

The unavoidable conclusion flowing from these facts was that military victory in total war was no longer possible. The only sensible military policy was the deterrence of war. The actual use of nuclear weapons to attack the enemy was pointless, since each side "must fear retaliation, [and] the fact that it destroys the opponent's cities some hours or even days before its own are destroyed may avail it little. . . ." The main goal of military preparations in peacetime should be simply to ensure that a country's ability to retaliate with its own nuclear weapons against an attack would survive the attack, which would be achieved by dispersing the weapons well away from cities and perhaps storing them underground.[6]

And there it was—there really was nothing important left to say. By February 1946, Bernard Brodie and his colleagues had given a complete description of the grim and precarious terms on which the peace might be kept in a nuclear-armed world until, someday, the international system that breeds war could itself somehow be changed. But at the time, nobody in power was listening to this little band of civilians who presumed to offer opinions on military affairs.

To be fair, there was no compelling reason for the U.S. government to accept the conclusions of Brodie and his friends in 1946, for it was not yet a nuclear-armed world. It was a conventionally armed world that contained one nuclear power, the United States, so deterrence was a one-way street. The first U.S. plan for a nuclear attack on the Soviet Union was drawn up in October 1945—not because the wartime alliance had begun to break down yet, but simply as part of the contingency planning that all great powers reflexively indulge in against potential rivals. It envisaged delivering twenty atomic bombs on the largest Soviet cities. By late 1947, when the Soviet Union was clearly identified as the enemy, Emergency War Plan "Charioteer" called for the newly formed Strategic Air Command (SAC) to drop 133 atomic bombs on seventy Soviet cities in the event of war (though the actual U.S. arsenal at that date was less than 50 bombs, none of them assembled, and SAC only had thirty aircraft that had been modified to carry these primitive ten-thousand-pound monsters).[7]

In these early years, the confidence induced in the U.S. government by its monopoly of nuclear weapons was so great that its actual preparations for war verged on the lackadaisical. There was no sense of urgency in the production of more bombs and bombers, and nobody outside SAC gave any thought to the actual choice of targets in the Soviet Union. Even the creation in early 1949 of the NATO alliance, which was essentially a device for strengthening the nerves of shaky Western European governments by underwriting their security with an American nuclear guarantee, was not accompanied by any major measures of conventional rearmament on either side of the Atlantic or by any acceleration in American nuclear programs. The U.S. nuclear monopoly was regarded as a magical and virtually effortless solution to the West's military security problems.

All that changed with the first Soviet nuclear test in 1949, which came as a great shock to the United States (although it should have been obvious that the Russians would make any sacrifice necessary to break the American monopoly as soon as possible). The outbreak of the Korean War only a year later was generally interpreted by Western governments as a Soviet-sponsored initiative that grew directly out of Moscow's new nuclear-armed confidence, intended as a strategic feint to draw America's limited conventional forces into Asia prior to an all-out Soviet invasion of Western Europe. NATO's response was a massive program of rearmament (defence budgets doubled or tripled in most Western countries from 1950 to 1952), and Washington plunged headlong into an expansion of its nuclear forces to preserve the "deterrent" that backed up NATO's troops on the ground.

In reality, this was the point where Brodie's rules for nuclear deterrence became relevant. Once an opponent had the ability to retaliate with its own nuclear weapons, any attempt to exert political or military leverage by threatening to drop atomic bombs would be both unconvincing and extremely dangerous. There were those in the U.S. government who recognized this. George Kennan, then director of policy planning at the State Department, wrote papers in 1950 warning against the danger of allowing nuclear weapons to become a central element of Western defence policy. Instead, they should be divorced from normal military calculations and reserved for what he called "deterrent-retaliatory purposes" (that is, solely to deter the Soviet Union from using its nuclear weapons on the United States). That way, everybody would be much safer, and only a few hundred bombs would be ample to devastate the Soviet Union and thus deter it from attacking America. Moreover, Kennan added (echoing Brodie), the number of U.S. nuclear weapons needed to provide that assurance could be determined quite independently of how many bombs the Russians had.

It was a brave but doomed attempt to apply rationality to strategic affairs. "Minimum deterrence," as it later became known, was the only logical policy for two hostile powers with an equal ability to hurt each other: actually using nuclear weapons in war would simply be a form of mutual suicide. It was still possible for American strategists to evade that reality, however, for the United States and the Soviet Union did not yet have an equal ability to hurt each other. Moscow was starting the nuclear arms race from far behind both in weapons and in delivery systems, and it could not hope to achieve the capability to devastate the United States in a retaliatory strike for some years.

> Basically, American nuclear policy has been a stated policy
> of war-fighting with nuclear weapons from the beginning.
> Robert McNamara, U.S. secretary of
> defense, 1961–68[8]

In the beginning, when only the United States had nuclear weapons, it was rational to plan to use them in war. As time passed and the Soviet Union gradually acquired a limited ability to strike the United States with nuclear weapons, it became less rational, but Soviet retaliatory capability grew only slowly through the 1950s, and the United States had a large financial incentive to keep its nuclear weapons usable in war. The focus of the military confrontation in the Cold War was in Central Europe, and the Soviet Union was a lot closer to that theatre than the United States. If nuclear weapons were removed from the equation, then the United States (and its NATO allies) would have to spend vast amounts of money building up their conventional forces on the ground in Central Europe to counter the Soviet geographical advantage. There were no "Soviet hordes"—the NATO countries actually had twice the population of the Warsaw Pact nations—but conventional forces are very expensive (soldiers have to be fed and housed and trained and paid), whereas nuclear weapons are relatively cheap. Rather than pay for bigger conventional forces, therefore, Washington embarked on a frantic buildup of its nuclear forces to maintain its lead over the Russians. The number of U.S. nuclear weapons reached one thousand in 1953, and by 1960 it had grown to some six or seven thousand thermonuclear bombs, all of them dozens of times more powerful than the Hiroshima-scale atomic bombs of 1953.[9]

Until 1960 the United States maintained at least a ten-to-one lead over the Soviet Union in nuclear weapons. Its bomber bases ringing the Soviet borders and its far superior and more numerous bomber aircraft gave it an even bigger advantage in the amount of destruction it could wreak on its opponent's society. At the same time, to ensure that Moscow understood its strategy, the United States made it abundantly clear that it was willing to use nuclear weapons first, and to use them directly on Soviet cities, in response to any unacceptable Soviet act. Secretary of State John Foster Dulles formally enshrined this policy in the doctrine of "massive retaliation" in a speech of January 1954, announcing that the United States would "depend primarily upon a great capacity to retaliate, instantly, by means and at places of our own choosing."

Massive retaliation meant the massive use of American nuclear weapons on the Soviet homeland not solely in retaliation for a Soviet nuclear attack on the United States (which was almost inconceivable in the 1950s, given the huge disparity between the two sides' nuclear arsenals), but in response to any Soviet military operation that threatened American interests anywhere in the world. It was the exact opposite of the policy of minimum deterrence advocated by Brodie and Kennan, and it was adopted mainly to save the large amounts of money that would have to be spent if the United States and NATO chose to build up their ground and air forces to match Soviet conventional forces. A few weeks after Dulles announced the policy, Vice-President Richard Nixon stated it even more bluntly: "Rather than let the Communists nibble us to death all over the world in little wars, we would rely in the future primarily on our massive mobile retaliatory power, which we could use at our discretion against the major source of aggression at times and places that we could choose."[10]

In practice, massive retaliation had already been tacit U.S. strategic policy for almost a decade (though it had not been invoked in the one big conventional war of that period, in Korea, which says a lot about how usable a strategy it really was even when the U.S. had a virtual nuclear monopoly). By the time Dulles codified it in 1954, however, massive retaliation was already beginning to run out of time, for precisely the reason Brodie had pointed out at the beginning of the nuclear era: it simply wouldn't matter what numerical superiority the United States enjoyed in nuclear weapons once the Soviet Union achieved the ability to deliver a quite limited number of thermonuclear bombs on U.S. cities.

The response of the civilian defence analysts to this development was not to push for a policy of minimum deterrence along the lines that Brodie had sketched out in 1945 and Kennan had advocated in 1950. The defence intellectuals were by now well on the way to becoming a distinct profession in the United States—especially those gathered at the RAND (Research and Development Corporation) think tank in Santa Monica, California, which was founded and supported by the U.S. Air Force—and they were no longer contemplating the implications of nuclear weapons in a theoretical context. They were the citizens of a country involved in acute confrontation with a nuclear-armed opponent, and at least partly infected themselves by the anti-Soviet hysteria that reigned in America in those years, so they bent their efforts instead to finding ways of keeping U.S. nuclear weapons usable.

As the Soviet Union began to approach a marginal capability to attack the United States directly, Albert Wohlstetter of RAND conducted a massive study of the vulnerability of SAC's bombers to a Soviet disarming surprise attack. In 1957, however, the Air Force was not interested. In response to Wohlstetter's elaborate charts and calculations showing how Soviet bombers might "Pearl Harbor" SAC on the ground, the Gaither Committee, appointed by President Eisenhower to examine U.S. strategic security, sent a delegation to interview SAC commander General Curtis LeMay. LeMay, however, simply replied that U.S. reconnaissance planes were flying secret missions over Soviet territory twenty-four hours a day.

If I see the Russians are amassing their planes for an attack, I'm going to knock the shit out of them before they take off the ground. I don't care [if it's not national policy]. It's my policy. That's what I'm going to do.
Gen. Curtis LeMay[11]

Given General LeMay's diligence when he was charged with the fire-bombing and subsequently nuclear bombing of Japanese cities in 1944–45, there is no reason to doubt that he would have done a thorough job—nor that he would have finished the job by destroying Soviet cities at the same time, since this sort of thing is bound to leave a grudge and you wouldn't want the Russians coming back later for revenge. It is not clear whether he would have apologized if (a) it subsequently became clear that his intelligence people had misinterpreted Soviet dispositions and they weren't really planning an attack after all, or (b) the whole world went dark and cold.

The U.S. Air Force's confidence in its ability to launch a preemptive nuclear attack on the Soviet Union left it utterly uninterested in the theories of "limited nuclear war" that Bernard Brodie, now also at RAND, was starting to produce. As early as 1948 he had begun to move away from the simple deterrence doctrine that he had formulated in the winter of 1945–46, publicly suggesting that there was "more strategic leverage to be gained in

A month after the bomb hit Hiroshima, a man stands by the tiled fireplace where a house once stood. Nobody has warned him (or the photographer) about radiation.

holding cities hostage than in making corpses." The most instructive (and discouraging) element in the forty-five-year history of this nuclear-war-that-never-quite-happened is how *everybody* was seduced sooner or later into trying to make nuclear weapons usable in war.

Brodie and some colleagues with similar concerns set up the Strategic Objectives Committee at RAND in 1952, and over the next seven or eight years they elaborated subtle and complex theories both for limiting the use of nuclear weapons to the battlefield and, if the fighting escalated to an exchange of nuclear weapons between the homelands, for limiting it to "no-cities" strategies that would deliberately leave the enemy's urban centres untouched. This "counterforce" strategy, which proposed using nuclear weapons to attack mainly military targets while leaving most of the enemy's population alive, would allegedly give the victor the ability to blackmail an opponent into surrender by subsequently threatening its cities. Its proponents argued that it had the equally important advantage of encouraging the Soviet Union to refrain from hitting American cities for fear of losing its own.[12]

These RAND theories for keeping U.S. nuclear weapons usable after the Soviet Union achieved a capacity to strike back at the United States depended on Soviet cooperation, of course, which was unlikely to be forthcoming. Soviet nuclear doctrine, as befitted the inferior power that would surely lose in a limited nuclear exchange, never wavered in asserting that no limitations would be observed once a war had escalated to the nuclear level. The theories also gained no favour during the 1950s with RAND's principal customer, the U.S. Air Force. Eventually, Wohlstetter's concerns about vulnerability and Brodie's ideas on limited nuclear war would both be used by the U.S. forces as arguments for more numerous and more sophisticated nuclear weapons, but in the 1950s they made no progress whatsoever against the strictly offensive, total-war tradition of strategic bombardment that dominated the U.S. Air Force.

Among themselves, the RAND analysts mocked this hidebound attitude, and Brodie circulated an internal memorandum likening war plans and sex, in which his "no-cities" restraint was coitus interruptus compared to the SAC war plan's blind terminal frenzy. His colleague Herman Kahn told SAC staff officers to their faces: "Gentlemen, you don't have a war plan, you have a war orgasm."[13] But it was all to no avail.

The civilian political authorities in Washington, however, were getting anxious about the implications of U.S. strategy as the 1950s neared their end. In November 1957, when the Gaither Committee presented the results of its inquiry into the future of massive retaliation and the likely consequences of a nuclear war, President Eisenhower simply responded, "You can't have this kind of war. There just aren't enough bulldozers to scrape the bodies off the streets."[14] Exactly a year later, John Foster Dulles went to the Pentagon and formally told the Joint Chiefs of Staff that he was abandoning massive retaliation: "Dulles, in a most solemn manner, recalled that he had been the father of the massive retaliation doctrine—it had served the nation well, he said, deterring aggression for years. But he had reluctantly concluded that it was a wasting asset. With increasing Soviet nuclear forces, it would become less credible and the U.S. military should start preparing plans and weapons systems for alternative strategies."[15]

But Dulles revealed none of this to the public, and down to its end the Eisenhower administration resisted any suggestion that it should build up U.S. conventional forces to fight the wars that it no longer believed massive retaliation could deter. Eisenhower once told Army Chief of Staff General Maxwell Taylor, who was urging an expansion of the ground forces, that larger conventional forces were not needed for overseas operations, but that "the Army will be truly vital to keeping order in the United States . . . after the big war, the force that pulls the nation together again."[16] He resisted with equal firmness SAC's attempts to stampede the Department of Defense into accelerating its programs for new bombers and missiles by blatantly manipulating intelligence reports to predict a looming "bomber gap" in the Soviet favour from 1955 to 1957, and then an equally mythical "missile gap" from 1957 to 1960. Eisenhower, a former career soldier wise in the ways of the services and equally experienced in discounting alarmist interpretations of the international situation, saw no likely major war on the horizon and simply refused to embark on any kind of crash program to build up further a military establishment that was already terrifying enough to the Soviets for any practical purposes. "If it ain't broke, don't fix it."

———

No country without an atom bomb could properly consider itself independent.

French president Charles de Gaulle,
1968[17]

Britain and Canada had voluntarily merged their considerable resources of scientific talent, technology, and uranium ore
with the U.S.-based Manhattan Project during the frantic wartime
drive to develop atomic bombs before (as they feared) the
Germans got them, and there had been no agreement about sharing the actual nuclear weapons that emerged from that project.
Naturally, the U.S. government had no intention whatever of sharing them—which produced markedly different responses in the
other two countries. Canada, despite the significant role it had
played in the war—in 1945, with most of the world's traditional
great powers in ruins, it was the fourth-largest industrial economy
in the world—had no pretensions to a global military role and was
far away from any potential military threats, so it decided virtually
without debate that nuclear weapons were irrelevant to its security.
Britain, on the other hand, looked at the Soviet army sitting in the
middle of Germany, less than four hundred miles away, and concluded that it urgently needed nuclear weapons of its own in case
things went wrong.

As soon as France, occupied for most of the war by Germany,
had stabilized its economy and rebuilt its government apparatus,
it reached exactly the same conclusion and launched its own
nuclear weapons program. Once the Chinese Communist regime
fell out with Moscow in the late 1950s, it too launched a nuclear
weapons program that was designed to deter a Soviet nuclear
attack—and in every case, these were "minimum deterrent"
forces. None of these nations had the ability to place a nuclear
weapon on every missile silo and small town in the Soviet Union,
as the United States had, but they did not think it necessary.

The French spoke in terms of their ability to "tear an arm off
the Soviet bear." The British had an explicit "Moscow criterion"
for their nuclear forces: so long as Britain had the ability to oblit-
erate Moscow, they reasoned, the Russians would not be likely to
use nuclear weapons against United Kingdom targets even if the
United States were somehow neutralized. But there was also a
deeply cynical calculation behind the French and British nuclear
striking forces. Both countries privately believed that their own
nuclear forces could serve as "triggers" for the far larger American

nuclear striking force, whether the United States was willing to wage a nuclear war or not.

The British and the French were both understandably concerned that Washington's nerve might fail in the face of a Soviet victory in a conventional war in Europe. Despite all its promises, it might decide on the night to let Western Europe go under rather than fulfil its threats of "massive retaliation" and launch a nuclear war in which American cities might also burn. Independent British and French nuclear forces were a way to make sure that didn't happen.

If either Britain or France were able to hit the Russians with a relatively small number of nuclear weapons, the Soviet Union would be hopelessly crippled in any subsequent nuclear confrontation with the United States. Knowing this, the planners in Moscow would be forced to strike all Western nuclear forces at once—American, British, and French—to pre-empt that possibility. And American planners, knowing that, would in turn be forced to launch a first strike against the Soviet Union, as massive retaliation doctrine decreed, in order to avoid a Soviet pre-emptive attack. The reasoning was convoluted but ruthlessly rational: we cannot trust the Americans to sacrifice New York City to save Paris or London. Indeed, when push finally comes to shove, they would be irrational to make that sacrifice. So we must equip ourselves with weapons that will force the Russians to attack Americans targets with nuclear weapons at the same time that they hit us. *Then* we can trust the Americans to keep their promises.

This cold-blooded rationality did not preserve the Western European great powers from succumbing to the "rage of numbers" themselves. During the 1980s, both Britain and France embarked on a "modernization" (i.e., expansion) of their respective nuclear forces that gave them the ability to destroy close to a thousand targets each. China, while showing more restraint on the numbers issue, followed the British and French examples in sending at least some of its deterrent forces out to sea in submarines, as a policy of minimum deterrence dictates. Israel, whose first nuclear weapons were probably built in the mid-1960s, did not follow suit, largely because it had no reason to fear that it might lose its weapons to an Arab surprise attack: no Arab country then possessed nuclear weapons, nor indeed possesses them even forty years later. This allows Israel to pursue an undeclared strategy of "massive retaliation," in the sense that all Arab states know that an Israeli military defeat in a conventional war could trigger the use of Israeli nuclear weapons. Anecdotal evidence strongly suggests that Israel was actively preparing to use its nuclear weapons during the first few panic-stricken days of its 1973 war with Egypt and Syria.

The signature of the Nuclear Non-Proliferation Treaty of 1968, in which the declared nuclear weapons powers agreed not to transfer their weapons to other countries, and over a hundred other countries agreed not to develop nuclear weapons themselves, put an end to this twenty-year period when the number of countries possessing nuclear weapons jumped from one to six. The likeliest remaining candidates for nuclear weapons mostly declined to sign the treaty, but thirty years passed before another country openly went nuclear.

———

I thought they were the most dangerous, depraved, essentially monstrous people. They really had constructed a doomsday machine.
Daniel Ellsberg, 1961

When the Kennedy administration came to office in 1961 (much helped electorally by the "missile gap" myth), it brought hundreds of bright, youngish technocrats to Washington, including a whole group of analysts from RAND who came to work in the Department of Defense. One of them, Daniel Ellsberg, was given a classified briefing on SAC's war plan. What he was shown was the first of the Single Integrated Operational Plans (SIOPs), a plan to coordinate the use of nuclear weapons by all the various branches of the U.S. armed forces, and he recoiled from it in horror. It contained only one option: the immediate launch of all U.S. nuclear delivery vehicles against every city and significant military target in the Soviet Union and China, and most of those in the Eastern European countries as well, at the very outbreak of a nuclear war. There was no provision for strategic reserves, no way of exempting China or Eastern Europe from the carnage even if they were not involved in the crisis—and SAC coolly calculated that the strike would kill between 360 and 425 million people.

Ellsberg thought the plan simply crazy, pointing out that the SIOP provided for the delivery of a total of 170 atomic and hydrogen bombs on Moscow: "Everybody who could put a weapon on Moscow did so. If you could somehow jury-rig a weapon so that your unit could have a weapon on Moscow, you did it." And Ellsberg also realized something that even the RAND analysts, not to mention the U.S. public, did not know. SAC, aware of America's overwhelming nuclear superiority over the Soviet Union, invariably assumed that the United States would use its nuclear weapons first in a war. The Air Force, in its quest to justify more bombers and missiles of its own, had manipulated intelligence reports to produce a more impressive Soviet nuclear force than actually existed. They had been so successful that the civilian authorities had begun to back away from the strategy of nuclear first strike, considering it no longer feasible. But SAC itself knew that the Soviets had only four operational intercontinental ballistic missiles (ICBMs) in 1961, and so "massive retaliation"—a U.S. nuclear first strike—lived on in the actual war plan.[18]

Robert McNamara, the new secretary of defense, had the same SIOP briefing and was similarly appalled. He was thus open to persuasion when the U.S. Navy revealed its proposal for a "minimum deterrence" policy that would have put an end to any thought of a first strike—as well as to most or all of SAC's forces. During the late 1950s the Navy had begun developing its own strategic nuclear force: the Polaris missile, based in submarines. Its greatest virtue was its invulnerability to Soviet attack, since the submarines could hide anywhere in the oceans. Its major defect was that it was not accurate enough to hit anything smaller than a city. So the Navy, seeking to advance the cause of its own weapons system against the Air Force's rival bombers and land-based missiles (which were more accurate but vulnerable to surprise attack), abandoned its earlier abhorrence for attacks on cities and adopted the policy of minimum deterrence wholeheartedly.

In a 1958 report, the Navy argued that the emerging counter-force strategic doctrines (which would obviously help to perpetuate the Air Force's strategic weapons) would lead only to an endless arms race without offering any real prospect that the United States could successfully fight a nuclear war. Instead, the United States should abandon any attempt to deal with non-nuclear problems by using nuclear weapons and "avoid the provocative overinflation of our strategic forces; their size should be set by an objective of generous *adequacy for deterrence alone* [i.e., for an ability to destroy the enemy's cities], not by the false goal of adequacy for 'winning.'" For that limited goal, the Navy's submarine-launched missiles alone would be quite sufficient, being both invulnerable and unstoppable. It was a return to Brodie's 1946 strategy of minimum deterrence, pure and simple, and it would have meant the end of the Air Force's strategic nuclear role. As a senior naval officer had boasted to his Air Force counterpart in 1958, "We've got something that's going to put you guys out of business."[19] And for a moment, at the very beginning of the Kennedy administration in January 1961, it looked as if the Navy might succeed.

Robert McNamara was a brilliant administrator imported from the business world who had neither expert knowledge nor any preconceptions in the field of nuclear strategy. Within a week of his arrival at the Pentagon, he had been captivated by the relative sanity of the Navy's minimum deterrence proposals (renamed "finite deterrence" so as not to sound too skimpy), in which the threat of retaliation by a mere two hundred submarine-launched missiles would secure the United States against the threat of a Soviet nuclear attack. It would mean building up expensive conventional forces to protect the interests of the United States and abandoning the pursuit of strategic superiority over the Soviet Union, but it would be a great deal safer than the existing U.S. strategy.

However, the Air Staff, which thought much more broadly than the closed fiefdom of SAC, had foreseen this challenge from the Navy's Polaris missiles, and all through 1960 a team of RAND

Robert S. McNamara briefing reporters at the Pentagon during the Cuban Missile Crisis, October 1962.

analysts led by William Kaufmann had been working on a counterforce targeting strategy. As the Air Force chief of staff, General Tommy White, wrote to the SAC commander, a continuation of the Air Force's policy of indiscriminately targeting cities "would not only be used as further justification of Polaris but . . . would be used as a strong position (which is already emerging) to eliminate virtually any strategic requirement other than Polaris, i.e., SAC."[20]

The more politically sophisticated Air Force senior officers realized that a no-cities strategy, which offered the hope that a nuclear war could be fought (and won) without a holocaust, was bound to appeal to political leaders who wanted to retain the possibility of using U.S. nuclear weapons first, despite the inevitable growth of Soviet retaliatory capability. So, only a month after McNamara had become secretary of defence, the Air Force arranged for him to be briefed by William Kaufmann.

"Within a week he had reversed himself," Kaufmann later said about McNamara's short-lived temptation to settle for minimum deterrence: "I talked him out of it." The core of Kaufmann's briefing was to contrast three scenarios. The first envisaged a Soviet surprise attack aimed solely at destroying American strategic forces, followed by an all-out retaliation on Soviet cities by the surviving U.S. nuclear forces, and the destruction of American cities by the Soviet reserve forces—results: 150 million Americans and 40 million Soviets dead. The second, corresponding to the existing SIOP, saw a "max effort" U.S. nuclear attack on the Soviet Union in a crisis, followed by retaliation against U.S. cities by the surviving Soviet missiles and bombers—results: 110 million Americans and 75 million Soviets dead. (The higher number of American casualties in both cases was due to the fact that the United States was much more urbanized than the Soviet Union in 1960.)

Kaufmann was presenting worst-case examples, based on the Air Force's grossly inflated intelligence estimates of Soviet missile strength. But it was perfectly obvious that the Soviet Union would eventually achieve the kind of retaliatory capability Kaufmann described, so his third scenario was still very attractive to McNamara. In it, the United States, unable to hold a Soviet attack in Western Europe with conventional forces, strikes at Soviet bomber fields, missile sites, and submarine pens with nuclear weapons but avoids hitting Soviet cities and holds part of its force in reserve. The Soviets, knowing that their own cities are hostages to the United States, strike back but avoid attacking U.S. cities. The United States wins the counterforce exchange and then tells the Soviets to surrender or it will pick off their cities one by one. Moscow surrenders, and the total cost of the war is "only" three million American lives and five million Soviet lives.

McNamara bought the concept hook, line, and sinker and promptly issued instructions for the development of policies for counterforce strikes and a doctrine that "would permit controlled response and negotiating pauses" in the event of thermonuclear war. By the end of the year, the SIOP had been drastically revised, dividing the list of Soviet targets into five categories from which the United States could pick and choose in a nuclear war. The options and sub-options contained in the revised U.S. strategic plan, SIOP-63, together with technical changes that enabled the U.S. military command to reprogram the targets of American missiles on short notice and fire them singly or in small numbers (rather than in minimum batches of fifty) made it theoretically possible for the United States to fight a "limited" nuclear war — *if the Russians agreed*.[21]

When McNamara went public with his new strategy in 1962, the Soviet response was uniformly negative. Marshal V. D. Sokolovskiy rejected McNamara's "rules for waging a nuclear war" and described his no-cities doctrine as a strategy for first strike, pure and simple. He neglected to mention, of course, that the official Soviet strategy was also first strike. The principal published source of Soviet military doctrine of this era, *Marxism-Leninism on War and Army*, plainly stated that "mass nuclear missile strikes at the armed forces of the opponent and at his key economic and political objectives can determine the victory of one side and the defeat of the other at the very beginning of the war. Therefore, a correct estimate of the elements of supremacy over the opponent and *the ability to use them before the opponent does* [emphasis added] are the key to victory in such a war."[22]

McNamara's strategy for a limited and controlled nuclear war proved equally unpopular with America's NATO allies when he revealed it to them at a secret meeting of the alliance's defence ministers in Athens in the summer of 1962. McNamara told them that "the U.S. has come to the conclusion that, to the extent feasible, military strategy in general nuclear war should be approached in much the same way that more conventional military operations have been regarded in the past." Most of the allies, who had shamelessly acquiesced in the policy of massive retaliation, concluded in great alarm that the American nuclear deterrent which had guaranteed their security by threatening (however implausibly) to blow up the world in their defence was becoming even more incredible.

President Kennedy had told McNamara that he should "repeat to the point of boredom" at Athens that on the one hand the United States was not contemplating a first strike, and on the other hand, the Europeans should not believe they could gain the ability to drag the United States into a general nuclear war simply by being able to fire their own independently controlled nuclear weapons at Soviet cities. But it remained obvious to the French (who said so publicly) and to the British (who have always been more tactful) that they could do precisely that, which undermined the whole concept of limited nuclear war.

Public reaction was equally negative when McNamara gave an unclassified version of the Athens speech at the University of Michigan in June 1962. The new strategy was almost universally interpreted as making nuclear war more possible. But the most powerful factor in forcing McNamara to retreat from his no-cities strategy was the way the U.S. armed forces seized upon the counterforce doctrine as a justification for demanding huge numbers of new strategic weapons to hit the almost numberless new targets that now became militarily relevant. By late 1962, the U.S. Air Force was seeking a new strategic bomber, the B-70, and talking about an eventual total of ten thousand Minuteman missiles. In January 1963, McNamara told his staff to inform the military that they were no longer to use a counterforce strategy as a rationale for asking for new weapons.[23]

Overwhelmed by the insatiable demands of his armed forces for new nuclear weapons, McNamara resorted to the bureaucratic tactic of compromising on a level of forces far higher than he thought necessary, but much lower than they wanted—and then fortified himself against further demands by devising a strategic doctrine that ratified that level of forces on arbitrarily chosen theoretical calculations of how much destructive power the United States needed for deterrence.[24] It was an extraordinarily high level, however. As one beleaguered assistant secretary at McNamara's Pentagon observed to Sir Solly Zuckerman, chief scientific adviser to the British Ministry of Defence:

> First, we need enough Minutemen to be sure that we destroy all those Russian cities. Then we need Polaris missiles to follow in order to tear up the foundations to a depth of ten feet. . . . Then, when all Russia is silent, and when no air defenses

are left, we want waves of aircraft to drop enough bombs to tear the whole place up down to a depth of forty feet to prevent the Martians recolonising the country. And to hell with the fallout.[25]

The doctrine McNamara adopted to satisfy his NATO allies, calm public opinion, and contain his own armed forces was known as Assured Destruction. As McNamara explained it to Congress in early 1965, "It seems reasonable to assume the destruction of, say, one-quarter to one-third of its population and about two-thirds of its industrial capacity . . . would certainly represent intolerable punishment to any industrialized nation and this should serve as an effective deterrent."[26]

Assured Destruction was officially a purely retaliatory strategy—minimum deterrence with far more weapons than necessary—and it became the only publicly acknowledged U.S. nuclear doctrine. With the derisive addition in 1969 of the word *mutual* (by Donald Brennan, a disgruntled campaigner for counterforce, so that he could ridicule the doctrine as "MAD"), Mutual Assured Destruction remained the declared U.S. strategy well into the 1980s. It was never explained how this allegedly retaliatory strategy was compatible with NATO's policy in Europe of "flexible response," which threatened a Western first use of nuclear weapons in response to a Soviet conventional attack. But the contradiction existed only in public, for the actual target plan, SIOP-63, was not changed in any significant way for over a decade.

> All public officials have learned to talk in public only about deterrence and city attacks. No war-fighting, no city-sparing. Too many critics can make too much trouble (no-cities talk weakens deterrence, the argument goes), so public officials have run for cover. That included me when I was one of them. But the targeting philosophy, the options and the order of choice remain unchanged from the McNamara speech [at the University of Michigan in 1962]."
>
> *Unnamed assistant secretary of defence in*
> *private correspondence to Desmond Ball*[27]

What had really happened was a split between declaratory U.S. strategy and the real war plan. Assured Destruction was there to deter a Soviet nuclear attack on the United States (a highly improbable eventuality given the existing balance of forces) and more importantly to contain the voracious appetite of the U.S. armed forces for new weapons. But behind this facade of minimum deterrence was a quite different real strategy. If war actually came, it would be fought largely according to the "counterforce" rules and limitations that McNamara had announced in Athens and Michigan in 1962. The most that could be said for Assured Destruction was that it formally dropped the idea of a disarming first strike against the Soviet Union. McNamara had never believed that a first strike could succeed anyway, and privately advised both President Kennedy and President Johnson that they should never use nuclear weapons first under any circumstances. But the SIOP never abandoned the expectation that restraint and rationality could prevail even after nuclear weapons had begun to explode over the homelands.

Moscow publicly continued to insist that nuclear war, if "imposed" on it by the "aggressor," would be waged without limitations, but American strategists assumed that there was a similar split between declaratory strategy and the real war plan in the Soviet Union, on the grounds that all reasonable men would reach the same conclusion. This view received apparent confirmation when a Russian general revealed in 1966 that the Soviet targeting plan contained five categories of targets almost identical to the "options" in SIOP-63.[28] Even as assumptions about the possibility of fighting a controlled and limited nuclear war were becoming entrenched in U.S. war plans, however, events were demonstrating how far removed they were from reality.

During the Berlin crisis of 1961, in which the West was at a huge disadvantage in conventional forces at the point of confrontation, a special task force headed by Paul Nitze was created by President Kennedy to examine his options. It considered and almost instantly rejected the idea of a nuclear warning "shot across the bow," on the grounds that it could lead to a tit-for-tat exchange of symbolic nuclear shots that one side might suddenly escalate into something more serious to prove its determination. "When that happens then you know that you're in for keeps, and you've lost a hell of a lot," observed Nitze.

More seriously, some of the RAND experts on the task force looked into the possibility of a disarming first strike against the Soviet Union (avoiding cities as far as possible) and discovered that it was eminently feasible. American intelligence, depending on the newly available reconnaissance satellites, had discovered that Soviet nuclear forces were in truly dreadful shape: far weaker than Americans had assumed and in an extremely low state of readiness. So they designed a "clever first strike," which they estimated had a 90 percent chance of catching almost all the Soviet weapons on the ground—and found that nobody wanted anything to do with it. "It was amazing how people who had no mathematical background discovered distribution," William Kaufmann noted. "Very quickly they'd come to understand that . . . there was also a 10 percent chance it will all go haywire," and then "they'd lose interest in fifteen minutes."[29]

It was a comforting outcome: by the early 1960s, the idea of a "disarming" nuclear surprise attack against the Soviet Union no longer commanded any support in Washington, and the principle of minimum deterrence had achieved some kind of official acceptance (even if the actual war plans were still counterforce). Rationality was at least still in the game, even if it had not won a decisive victory over the constant pressure to make nuclear weapons more "usable" in war. But nobody had yet gone through a full-scale military confrontation in which both sides were prepared to use nuclear weapons.

————

The Berlin crisis had petered out in late 1961 when Khrushchev realized that the United States had discovered that his loudly advertised

"Deliver twelve nuclear weapons and get out to do it again"? What undamaged air base were they planning to reload at? And what would their targets have been on the second trip?

EAT DEATH, COMRADES!

By Henry Zeybel

Today's SAC crews can get in under the radar, deliver twelve nuclear weapons and get out to do it again.

Pltz! The lenses of these goggles contain 21 layers of lead-lanthanum zirconate-titanate ceramic. Sudden bright light causes the lenses to turn opaque so quickly that light beams never reach the wearer's eyeballs. Used in wartime by pilot and copilot, the pltzes prevent flash blindness whenever the flash curtains are down, such as during takeoff and air refueling.

claims of growing Soviet nuclear striking power and, in particular, of a large intercontinental rocket force were mostly bluff. But this discovery put Khrushchev under great political pressure at home and internationally, and in the following year he took the gamble of secretly deploying shorter-range missiles on the territory of his new ally, Cuba, in order to put the United States within range of a substantial Soviet missile force and thus close the strategic gap. The U.S. discovered the missiles, and the Cuban crisis erupted. The United States declared a blockade of Cuba, and began preparations for an invasion if Khrushchev refused to withdraw his missiles.

What was most significant about the Cuban missile crisis from the point of view of nuclear strategy was that nobody paid the least attention to the idea of a limited nuclear war. Khrushchev may have been strategically inferior, but there was little doubt that at least a few of his bombers and missiles could get through to devastate American cities no matter what the United States did. By late 1962 the new SIOP was in existence, with all its options for selective and limited nuclear attacks, but in the face of a real crisis everybody fled back to the relative sanity of Brodie's original deterrent formula. On 22 October Kennedy declared that the United States would regard "any nuclear missile launched from Cuba against any nation in the Western Hemisphere as an attack by the Soviet Union on the United States *requiring a full retaliatory response upon the Soviet Union* [emphasis added]."[30]

The one consolation in the midst of this crisis, according to the assurances President Kennedy was getting from American intelligence sources, was that the Soviet missiles in Cuba were still without their nuclear warheads. Kennedy therefore concentrated on intercepting Soviet ships heading for Cuba that might be carrying the warheads, while pushing ahead with the plan to invade Cuba if Moscow did not back down. And in the end, Moscow did: Khrushchev withdrew the Soviet missiles from Cuba in return for an American promise not to invade the island and the withdrawal of similar American missiles from Turkey a few months later. After thirteen days of intense anxiety, the world again drew breath. But nobody on the American side realized at the time just how close they had come to a nuclear war.

Had Khrushchev not sent the key letter to Kennedy proposing a compromise, the United States might well have gone ahead with the invasion of Cuba, but everybody in Washington assumed that there would be at least a few more steps in the dance before nuclear weapons were used. The missiles in Cuba weren't live yet, and the fighting would stay conventional unless Moscow took the momentous, almost unthinkable step of launching a first strike from the Soviet Union against the United States. It was thirty years before Robert McNamara found out that everybody in Washington had been dead wrong.

> It wasn't until January, 1992, in a meeting chaired by Fidel Castro in Havana, Cuba, that I learned that 162 nuclear warheads including 90 tactical warheads were on the island at this critical moment of the crisis. I couldn't believe what I was hearing, and . . . I said, " . . . Mr President, I have three questions to you. Number one, did you know the nuclear warheads were there. Number two, if you did, would you have recommended to Khrushchev in the face of a U.S. attack that he use them. Number three, if he used them, what would have happened to Cuba?"
>
> He said, "Number one, I knew they were there. Number two . . . I did recommend to Khrushchev that they be used. Number three, what would have happened to Cuba? It would have been totally destroyed."
>
> That's how close we were . . . and he went on to say, "Mr McNamara, if you and President Kennedy had been in a similar situation, that's what you would have done." I said, "Mr President, I hope to God we would not have done it. Pull the temple down on our own heads? My God!"[31]

Threatening to pull the temple down on your own head and everybody else's is the very essence of nuclear deterrence, but there is a measure of reassurance to be had from these events. The Cuban crisis demonstrated that the penalties for miscalculation in a nuclear confrontation are so terrifyingly huge that theories of controllability carry little weight when political leaders face real decisions in a crisis. They become extremely cautious and conservative in their actions; people *do* recognize the difference between simulation and reality.

On the other hand, it also demonstrated that intelligence will always be imperfect and that decisions that seem to be rational may actually be fatal. If the United States had decided to launch a conventional invasion of Cuba to deal with the missiles before they were operational (as it thought), its troops would have been obliterated on the beaches by tactical nuclear missiles launched by local Soviet commanders who had been pre-authorized to act without reference back to Moscow. The United States, as McNamara concedes, would have responded with nuclear weapons of its own, and World War III would have begun. President Kennedy later estimated that the chance of the Cuban crisis ending up in a nuclear war was one in three.[32]

The Cuban missile crisis ought to have killed the notion of a limited nuclear war for good in American strategic circles: nobody seriously considered "signalling their resolve" with a few selective nuclear strikes when they were actually immersed in a real crisis. To the extent that people did believe in such a notion, it would just make it easier for the nuclear war to get started, as frightened and desperate leaders seized on the promise of controllability as drowning men clutch at straws. It also served as a justification for the creation of ever more complex and sophisticated strategic systems, both offensive and defensive, whose reliability and interactions in real war could not, in the nature of things, be fully tested beforehand. The story of the next twenty years of American nuclear war policy is largely the story of the great split in the fraternity of U.S. defence intellectuals between the believers who continued to pursue the holy grail of making nuclear weapons usable in limited nuclear wars and those who had finally lost the faith.

> Everything we know about Soviet military thinking indicates rejection of those refinements of military thought that have now become commonplace in this country, concerning, for example, distinctions between limited war and general war, between "controlled" and "uncontrolled" strategic targeting,

and between nuclear and non-nuclear tactical operations. . . .
Violence between great opponents is inherently difficult to
control, and cannot be controlled unilaterally. . . . Once hostilities begin, the level of violence has in modern times
tended always to go up.

Bernard Brodie, 1963[33]

After fifteen years of wandering in the swamps of limited
nuclear war, Bernard Brodie returned after the Cuban crisis to
his original conclusion that nuclear weapons had changed everything, and that their only rational use was to deter war, not to
fight it. For this apostasy he was virtually ostracized at RAND,
where most of the civilian intellectuals who then dominated
American nuclear war doctrine saw his abandonment of the
effort to make nuclear war into a rational instrument of policy as
a rank betrayal. They were simply not willing to acknowledge the
huge role that emotions play when life-and-death issues are at
stake, or the fact that cultural and ideological differences would
make their Soviet opposite numbers come to different conclusions and render meaningless their notions of a limited nuclear
war in which each side signaled its intentions by selecting different categories of targets.

Part of the problem was RAND's hyper-rational house style,
most spectacularly embodied in Herman Kahn, author of a book
that aspired to replace Clausewitz's classic *On War* which he
boldly entitled *On Thermonuclear War*. "I don't understand
people who aren't detached," Kahn said, and cultivated a style of
cold-blooded analysis that dealt in millions of deaths as others
might deal in dozens of eggs. On one occasion, when his coolness
was criticized, he replied: "Would you prefer a nice warm mistake?" Others, more sensitive to the horrors they were analyzing
and planning, frankly admitted to being both intellectually
intrigued by the complexities of nuclear war planning and
seduced by the sense of power and responsibility that came with it.
William Kaufmann remarked that once he slipped into the deep,
dark pit of nuclear strategy, "it was easy to become totally
absorbed, living, eating, breathing the stuff every hour of every

day"—but that once he had emerged from that realm and could see it from a distance, it all seemed crazy and unreal.[34]

Shortly before his death in 1978, Bernard Brodie told me he believed that most of the thinking on limited nuclear war by civilian strategists was, in effect, simple careerism. The theory of minimum deterrence, the only one appropriate to nuclear weapons, had been worked out and was virtually complete within a year of the Hiroshima bomb. It was simple, robust, and not susceptible to fine-tuning—but later entrants to the field of nuclear strategy had to establish their reputations by making some new contribution to the theory, which therefore led to a lot of "hypersensitive tinkering" with the basic assumptions. The best way for ambitious strategic analysts to advance their careers, he pointed out, was to identify some "flaw" in the existing deterrent theory and to provide some solution to it that enlisted the support of powerful interests in the military establishment and/or defence industry because it required new weapons. It would have been churlish to point out that he had spent many years travelling that road himself—and besides, sitting there in his living room overlooking Santa Monica Bay at the end of a remarkable career, he was clearly filled with regret about it.

Brodie's eventual rejection of the new orthodoxy and his return to his original insight put him in distinguished company. Robert McNamara also ultimately ceased to believe that nuclear war was controllable at all. Far from defending the war plan he had left behind in 1968 as his legacy, he later said of it: "If you never used the SIOP—or any one of the SIOPs—to initiate the use of nuclear weapons, then they weren't as inappropriate as they might have seemed. But if you were responding to a conventional force or movement by [escalating to the selective use of nuclear weapons] then it was totally inappropriate, because it would just bring suicide upon yourself."[35]

Henry Kissinger, President Richard Nixon's national security adviser, who spent the years from 1968 to 1976 struggling to achieve the goal McNamara had abandoned, ultimately admitted to him that he had also been unable to make U.S. nuclear strategy any more "appropriate" to the facts. In 1957, as an academic,

Kissinger had written that the central problem in nuclear strategy was "how to establish a relationship between a policy of deterrence and a strategy for fighting a war in case deterrence fails" but by 1974, after six years of experience in shaping the actual foreign policy of a nuclear power, he too had lost the faith: "What in the name of God is strategic superiority?" he asked. "What is the significance of it, politically, militarily, operationally, at these levels of numbers [of nuclear weapons]? What do you do with it?"[36]

The nuclear planners in the old Soviet Union were never torn by similar arguments. Civilians were rigidly excluded from questions of nuclear strategy in the Soviet system, and both the Russian military tradition and Marxist methods of analysis pushed doctrine in rather different directions from those it took in the United States. Limitations in warfare, once a war has begun, were almost incomprehensible to this intellectual tradition. In any case, until the early 1970s the Russians were so grossly inferior in nuclear forces that their only available strategy was all-out retaliation—or a first strike, if they saw an American attack coming and had a chance to pre-empt it. Even after McNamara "capped" American nuclear forces at about 2,250 delivery vehicles and the Soviet Union gradually caught up with and then somewhat surpassed that figure, it is highly improbable that Soviet strategists ever toyed with the notion of a limited or controlled nuclear war.

The Soviet Union's passionate attachment to massive nuclear firepower was a consistent impediment in the series of U.S.-Soviet arms control negotiations that began in the later 1960s—though certainly no greater an obstacle than the United States's mostly successful attempts to exclude from the negotiations whichever technological innovation it was currently counting on to restore its strategic superiority: MIRVs (multiple independently targetable reentry vehicles) from the SALT I treaty, the MX and cruise missiles from the SALT II treaty, and Star Wars from the START talks.[37]

The most intractable element in the push for new weapons on both sides was the fear of being left behind by technological change. Even as the first full generation of American intercontinental ballistic missiles, the Minuteman I missiles, began to go into their silos in 1963, the next step in the game of technological leapfrog was already underway. The Limited Nuclear Test Ban Treaty of that year had forced the cancellation of a U.S. Air Force test of how well those fortified silos could protect their missiles from a nuclear attack—the Air Force had planned to build a sample silo in Alaska and explode a nuclear weapon over it—and so the question of missile vulnerability seemed destined to remain permanently in doubt. The official Defense Department line was that it didn't matter, because there was no strategic advantage to be gained by using one Soviet missile to destroy one American missile. However, one physicist at RAND, Richard Latter, had a disturbing idea: what if a single missile carried numerous warheads, each able to strike a different target?

He told his idea to the Pentagon's director of Defense Research and Engineering, Harold Brown (later secretary of defense in the Carter administration), who agreed to put money into investigating it. But the potential Soviet threat of the future quickly turned into the real American threat of the present: new guidance technology and a "space bus" developed by the civilian National Aeronautics and Space Administration (NASA) to dispense several satellites from a single rocket launcher were quickly married to provide a workable system for delivering multiple nuclear warheads to separate targets. In 1965 the Department of Defense approved a program for equipping American ICBMs with MIRVs.

In secret memoranda, Defense Secretary McNamara admitted that this amounted to a counterforce system (designed to go after the enemy's missiles), but he was also using MIRVs as a weapon in his bureaucratic and diplomatic battles. Having restricted the Air Force to only one thousand Minuteman missiles, he was now able to offer it a compromise that more than doubled the number of nuclear warheads its missiles could deliver. At the same time, he could deflect the growing Air Force pressure for anti-ballistic missile (ABM) defences to protect its missile fields by pointing out that MIRV technology could cheaply saturate any ABM defence system. Above all, he saw MIRVs as a diplomatic lever with which he could persuade the Soviets not to pursue the costly and ultimately futile path of ABM deployment: "We thought we could get by without deployment . . . that the Russians would come to their senses and stop deploying ABM—in which case we would not have deployed MIRV."[38]

But as usual, the bargaining chip ultimately became a technological reality, and when the Soviet Union did finally follow the example of the United States and install MIRVs, the American defence establishment used that as a justification for the next large advance in missile technology.

> I've long been an advocate of getting all the accuracy you possibly can in ballistic missiles. . . . if the evidence is overwhelming that you're about to get hit, the advantages of pre-empting under those conditions are very substantial. . . .
> I don't think there'll be an Armageddon war; but I'll put it this way. There has never been any weapon yet invented or perfected that hasn't been used.
>
> Gen. Bruce Holloway, commander-in-chief, SAC, 1968–72[39]

When General Holloway submitted SAC's request to the Nixon administration in 1971 for a new, very large ICBM with a high degree of accuracy (the missile that later became known as MX), the "undead" doctrine of limited nuclear war was already struggling out of its shallow grave. National security adviser Henry Kissinger had already sponsored a study that advocated an American nuclear capability for early "war termination, avoiding cities, and selective response capabilities [that] might provide ways of limiting damage if deterrence fails." In early 1970 President Nixon, addressing Congress, asked, "Should a president, in the event of a nuclear attack, be left with the single option of ordering the mass destruction of enemy civilians, in the face of the certainty that it would be followed by the mass slaughter of Americans?"— and Mutual Assured Destruction, to the extent that it had ever been the real U.S. strategy, fell stone dead.[40]

Much of the thinking about U.S. nuclear strategy that went on during the next decade was considered too upsetting for the American public's delicate sensibilities, and MAD continued to be invoked rhetorically as a proof of the U.S. government's devotion to a purely retaliatory nuclear strategy. But the Foster Panel, set up by the Department of Defense to review U.S. nuclear strategy in early 1972, recommended "a wide range of nuclear options which could be used . . . to control escalation." It envisaged a limited nuclear war in which the United States would achieve its political objectives and avoid destruction of its cities by adopting a strategy that would "(a) hold some vital enemy targets hostage to subsequent destruction by survivable nuclear forces, and (b) permit control over the timing and pace of attack execution, in order to provide the enemy opportunities to reconsider his options." Its recommendations were incorporated in National Security Decision Memorandum 242, signed by President Nixon in January 1974 after Secretary of Defense James Schlesinger publicly disclosed that he was changing the targeting strategy to give the United States alternatives to "initiating a suicidal strike against the cities of the other side."

The resulting revision of the U.S. nuclear target plan, SIOP-5, explicitly took Soviet residential areas off the target list, and even changed some aiming points in ways that reduced the effectiveness of nuclear strikes against Soviet military targets in order to reduce damage to heavily populated areas. At the same time, the plan made elaborate provisions for attacking all elements of the Soviet leadership — party, army, and technocrats — in order to ensure that "all three of those groups . . . would individually and personally and organizationally and culturally know that their part of the world was not going to survive," as General Jasper Welch of the Foster Panel put it. Finally, SIOP-5 paid great attention to ensuring that at any level of nuclear exchange, the Soviet Union should not emerge as the more powerful economy in the postwar world.

> If we were to maintain continued communications with the Soviet leaders during the war and if we were to describe precisely and meticulously the limited nature of our actions, including the desire to avoid attacking their urban industrial bases . . . political leaders on both sides will be under powerful pressure to continue to be sensible. . . . Those are the

circumstances in which I believe that leaders will be rational and prudent. I hope I am not being too optimistic.

Secretary of Defense James Schlesinger
to Congress, March 1974[41]

James Schlesinger, yet another RAND product, was well suited by intellect and temperament to implement such a policy. He admitted that he did not share the "visceral repugnance" of Robert McNamara, his predecessor, to even the selective use of nuclear weapons. They could be extremely effective in influencing Soviet behaviour in a crisis, he believed, and he was confident (or said he was) that the consequent nuclear exchange could be controlled. Of all the defense secretaries who strove to keep American nuclear forces usable for purposes beyond that of deterring a direct nuclear attack on the United States, he was the most persuasive and sophisticated.

Schlesinger put no stock in simpleminded yearnings for a full counterforce strategy aimed at disarming the Soviets (he knew that Soviet missile-launching submarines, at the very least, would survive): "I was more interested in selectivity than in counterforce per se. Going after selected silos might be a way of delivering a message."[42] He was a paid-up member of that school of American strategic thinkers who believed that national leaders could remain "rational and prudent" even after nuclear warheads had exploded on their territory, and that it could be strategically sensible to bargain by "taking out" certain Soviet military or industrial installations as a demonstration of U.S. determination to prevail in a crisis.

Or perhaps Schlesinger did not really believe that and merely wanted the Soviets to think that he believed it. From quite an early stage, the RAND style of thinking on nuclear strategy incorporated large elements of psychology. (Consider Thomas Schelling's classic formulation of how "pre-emptive" attacks could happen: "He thinks we think he'll attack; so he thinks we shall; so he will; so we must."[43]) Schlesinger was well aware of the role that prior declarations of strategic intentions by either side could play in influencing the calculations of decision-makers in an actual crisis. "Occasionally the Russians should read in the press that a 'counterforce attack may not fall on silos that are empty,'" he once remarked. "Why give the Soviets that assurance?"[44] The same calculation, of course, applied to any other declaration of U.S. strategic intentions, such as Schlesinger's assertions of willingness to respond to some local Soviet military initiative with selective U.S. nuclear strikes. Credible is not necessarily the same as true.

However, the need for credibility impelled Schlesinger to approve the requests of the U.S. armed forces for new nuclear weapons—the Air Force's B-1 bombers and MX and cruise missiles, and an "improved accuracy program" for the Navy's missiles that would lead to the Trident II—all of which featured an increased ability to strike Soviet counterforce targets. It was all tied up with the importance of perceptions: Schlesinger's estimate of what Soviet strategists would perceive as convincing evidence of U.S. strategic resolve. Thus, when it became clear that the Soviet Union would follow the United States's example by MIRVing Soviet missiles—which were larger than American missiles and could carry more and bigger warheads—Schlesinger felt compelled to approve an equivalent large U.S. missile, the MX. "I ordered MX to be designed in the summer of 1973," he said, "as a way of showing the Soviets that we meant to make up the gross disparity in throw weights between their missiles and ours. My purpose was to persuade the Soviets to get their throw weights down. MX was my bargaining chip."[45]

For those who genuinely believed in the feasibility of a disarming first strike, the appearance of MIRVed Soviet missiles that could carry many more warheads than existing U.S. land-based missiles was an alarming development. The large "throw weight" of Soviet missiles and their growing accuracy led these American strategists to imagine a Soviet counterforce first strike that would destroy almost all of America's land-based missiles in a surprise attack and thus force the United States to choose between strategic surrender and engaging in a hideous counter-city war with its surviving, less accurate weapons. This hypothesis, which led to the

A Trident I missile launch from the submerged nuclear submarine *USS Ohio*, 1982.

prediction of the notorious "window of vulnerability" that plagued the subsequent Carter administration, assumed a positively heroic Soviet faith in American rationality—since this sort of Soviet first strike would kill at least ten million Americans, and the United States would retain the ability to strike back at Soviet cities with its submarine-launched missiles and its surviving bombers. But it was much favoured by those who supported the big, accurate MX missile as a means of acquiring an equivalent American capability.

For a brief instant at the beginning of the Carter administration in 1977, the idea of abandoning the whole massive edifice of nuclear war-fighting technology and withdrawing to a strategy of minimum deterrence was raised once again at the highest level. President Jimmy Carter, a former submariner who had had no direct contact with orthodox U.S. military thinking on nuclear war for two decades, was taken aback when he was shown the U.S. war plan at a pre-inaugural briefing and learned that the SIOP now listed forty thousand potential targets in the Soviet Union. The U.S. Joint Chiefs of Staff were even more shocked, however, when Carter responded by suggesting that a mere two hundred missiles, all kept in submarines, would be sufficient to deter a Soviet attack on the United States.[46]

But it was not necessary this time for the defenders of American strategic orthodoxy to resort to emergency measures to convert the heretic, as William Kaufmann had seduced Robert McNamara with theories of limited nuclear war in 1961. Carter himself was swiftly drawn into the deep, dark pit, betrayed by his technocratic fascination with the elegance of the engineering and the theories that supported U.S. nuclear strategy. By the end of his term, all the developments implicit in the limited nuclear war theories of the early 1960s had become explicit doctrine.

This doctrine was enshrined in Carter's Presidential Decision 59 of July 1980 and the accompanying revision of the targeting plan, SIOP-5D. One of the authors of that revision, General Jasper Welch, explained that the purpose "was to make it perfectly clear that nuclear weapons have a very rightful place in a global conflict, not just in a spasm of tit-for-tat." Thus the SIOP had to provide a wide menu of selective and limited "nuclear options" permitting the use of nuclear weapons in an almost boundless and partly unforeseeable range of military contingencies: "Fighting may be taking place halfway between Kiev and Moscow, for all I know. Maybe it's taking place along the Siberian border—which is a fairly likely place for it—with Americans, Chinese and Russians. But for the planning and construction of the thing, it doesn't matter."[47]

Zbigniew Brzezinski, President Carter's national security adviser, claimed that the meaning of the new strategic policy was that "for the first time the United States deliberately sought for itself the capability to manage a protracted nuclear conflict." He also took personal credit for introducing a new distinction into the SIOP, which gave the United States the option of choosing to kill ethnic Russians—the "real enemy"—while sparing other Soviet nationalities. (Brzezinski was of Polish descent.) But Defense Secretary Harold Brown insisted that the Carter administration's changes were mainly a clarification and codification of existing U.S. strategic doctrine: "PD-59 . . . is not a radical departure from U.S. strategic policy over the past decade or so."

His predecessor as defense secretary, James Schlesinger, disagreed, claiming that PD-59 represented a shift in emphasis "from selectivity and signaling to that of victory . . . in a way that was still barely plausible on paper, but in my guess is not plausible in the real world." After he left the Pentagon, Brown virtually conceded Schlesinger's accusation, explaining that the administration had been divided between those who believed in the possibility of winning a protracted nuclear war and those who did not. The argument revolved around what was necessary to deter the Soviet Union effectively, with many people arguing that the Soviets had to believe that if they started a war, the United States would win it. "We started down that path and got into that morass," said Brown. "And PD-59 was the result."[48]

———

By the early 1980s U.S. doctrine for fighting a nuclear war had become a structure of such baroque and self-referential complexity that it had only a distant relationship with the real world. It was almost as separated from reality as the missile crews who sat the long watches underground in their reinforced concrete command bunkers.

Q. How would you feel if you ever had to do it for real?

Well, we're trained so highly in our recurrent training that we take every month in simulators like this, so that if we actually had to launch the missiles, it would be an almost automatic thing.

Q. You wouldn't be thinking about it at the time?

There wouldn't be time for any reflection until after we turned the keys. . . .

Q. Would there be reflection then, do you think?

I should think so, yes.

Conversation with Minuteman ICBM crew commander, Whiteman Air Force Base, 1982

Even bomber pilots used to see the cities burning beneath them (though not the people), but the commander of a Minuteman launch capsule is separated from the targets of his missiles by six thousand miles. The pleasant young Air Force captain who would not have had time for reflection until after he had turned the key that would send fifty nuclear-tipped missiles toward the Soviet Union was intellectually aware of the consequences, but they were so remote and hypothetical that imagination failed to make them real. His principal reason for volunteering for missile duty—like many of his colleagues—was that the uneventful twenty-four-hour watches in the capsule gave him ample time to work on a correspondence course for a master's degree in business administration.

Time for reflection? A US Air Force officer ("combat crew") in the launch
simulator of a Minuteman III missile field.

He wore a neatly pressed uniform, an amber scarf with lightning bolts, and a label on his pocket that said "combat crew," but
he did not fit the traditional image of the warrior. His job more
closely resembled that of the duty engineer at a hydroelectric
power plant, and even launching the missiles—"going to war," as
they quaintly put it—would have involved less initiative and activity than the duty engineer would be expected to display if a turbine
overheated: "We're taught to react, and we are not part of the
decision-making process ourselves. We simply react to the orders
we receive through the messages that come to us, and then reflect
after we have taken our actions."

Tens of thousands of clean-cut young men like him had their fingers on some sort of nuclear trigger during the Cold War. None of them seemed very military compared to your average infantryman, but then nuclear war is not really a military enterprise in any recognizable sense. By the early 1980s, the five nuclear powers had accumulated a total of over twenty-five hundred land-based ballistic missiles, well over a thousand submarine-launched ballistic missiles, and thousands of aircraft capable of carrying nuclear bombs, plus land-, sea-, and air-launched cruise missiles and a panoply of battlefield nuclear weapons that ranged down to a fifty-eight-pound portable atomic explosive device intended to be carried behind enemy lines by commando teams. The large missiles could carry numerous separate warheads, and the sum of nuclear warheads in the world was over fifty thousand. During President Ronald Reagan's first term of office from 1981 to 1984, the United States alone was building eight new nuclear warheads a day (though many were recycled from obsolete warheads).

The Reagan administration pretended to be more radical in its desire to confront the Soviet Union, but in nuclear matters it really just picked up the baton passed to it by Carter. Defense Secretary Caspar Weinberger's Defense Guidance of 1982 talked frankly of the need for U.S. nuclear forces that could "prevail and be able to force the Soviet Union to seek earliest termination of hostilities on terms favorable to the United States . . . even under the conditions of a prolonged war." Still greater stress was put on attacking the Soviet leadership by the revised SIOP-6, and RAND veteran Andrew Marshall, who presided over that revision of the war plan, even talked of protracted nuclear wars in which the opponents might launch nuclear strikes at each other at intervals of as much as six months.[49]

But the radicalism of the Reagan administration is easily overdone: these were mere refinements of a basic strategic policy that was already in place, as was the Reagan administration's strong support for the guerrilla war being waged by Afghan rebels and Arab Islamist volunteers against the Soviet-backed government of Afghanistan. The decision to intervene in the Iran-Iraq war to save the Saddam Hussein regime from defeat, even though it was Iraq that had invaded Iran, was driven by an acute U.S. hostility to the Islamic revolution in Iran that also dated back to the Carter administration. The "anti-Communist" crusading in the Caribbean and Central America—the subsidization of "Contra" guerrillas waging a terrorist war against the Nicaraguan government, the unstinting support for right-wing regimes fighting left-wing guerrillas in El Salvador and Guatemala, the ridiculous invasion of Grenada—were simply a faint echo of the Kennedy administration's obsession with overthrowing Castro in the early 1960s. The only truly new departure of the Reagan administration was the Strategic Defense Initiative ("Star Wars")—and that was new only in technology, not in its basic intent.

The real goal of Star Wars was never to provide the United States with an impenetrable defence to a nuclear attack, for Bernard Brodie's 1946 definition of the problem still held true: all air (and space) defence operates on the principle of attrition, which means that some portion of the attacking weapons will always get through—and if they are nuclear weapons, even a very small fraction is too many. American space-based defences could never hope to deal with the thousands of incoming warheads and accompanying penetration aids that would be involved in a Soviet first strike against the United States, and the more realistic supporters of SDI were well aware of this fact. But space-based defences *might* eventually be good enough to deal with a ragged retaliatory strike after the Soviet Union had already been devastated by a largely successful American first strike. As the Defense Science Board put it in 1981, "Offensive and defensive weapons always work together. . . ."[50] The goal, as usual, was to make an American war-fighting nuclear strategy more credible and enhance its political utility.

To be fair to President Reagan, he seems never to have grasped this fact: the people who sold him on the concept of Star Wars played on his genuine aversion to nuclear weapons and his longing for some magical release from the threat of nuclear war. But people who had already been around this track several times sounded the alarm. "Such systems would be destabilizing if they provided a shield so you could use the sword," stated Richard

Nixon in 1984, and William Kaufmann simply described SDI as the latest manifestation of the search for the lost "nuclear Arcadia" of American nuclear superiority.[51] Since the United States was also seeking to introduce intermediate-range Pershing missiles into Western Europe at this time in order to cut Soviet warning time of a surprise attack, the Russian leadership was understandably alarmed.

> On the face of it, laymen may find it even attractive as the President speaks about what seem to be defensive measures. . . . In fact the strategic offensive forces of the United States will continue to be developed and upgraded at full tilt [with the aim] of acquiring a first nuclear strike capability. . . . [It is] a bid to disarm the Soviet Union. . . .
> *Soviet leader Yuri Andropov, 1983*[52]

It was not Reagan's harmless rhetoric about the "evil empire" that worried the Soviets, but the confrontational nuclear weapons policies pursued by Reagan's hardline secretary of defense, Caspar Weinberger, and the Cold Warriors around him. The danger was that this confrontation might abort the promising developments in the Soviet Union, which had begun a race for reform triggered by the death of long-ruling dictator Leonid Brezhnev in 1982.

The Soviet Union had experienced virtually no real economic growth (despite all the millions of tonnes of concrete that were poured) since the late 1960s. The Communist political and economic system had proved incapable of making further growth happen once the early days of virtually free labour flooding in from the countryside were over, and it would have crumbled under the burden of sustaining a global strategic confrontation with the United States at some point in the 1980s or the 1990s regardless of what the various administrations in Washington did. In practice, it was the steep decline in oil prices after 1981 that triggered the Soviet reform efforts: suddenly, the regime's main source of foreign exchange collapsed, and coincidentally Brezhnev died.

In a bid to stave off imminent economic collapse, reformist leader Yuri Andropov was raised to power in Moscow, only to die unexpectedly in 1983. After a brief return to the old order under Konstantin Chernenko, who also died after only months in office, another reformer, Mikhail Gorbachev, was brought to power in 1985. At first his reforms were to be only economic, but Gorbachev realized that the stagnation had a political dimension, too, and initiated the political opening that ultimately (and to his lasting regret) swept the Communists away. Reagan's "evil empire" speech and his defence budgets had virtually nothing to do with it—but it is hard to imagine that the process of reform that ultimately led to the freeing of Eastern Europe and the dismantling of the Soviet Union could have succeeded, or that Gorbachev could even have survived, if the Reagan administration's intense hostility had not abated. Happily, it did.

In November 1986, only a year and a bit after Gorbachev came into power, the Iran-Contra scandal broke. It was revealed that members of the administration had secretly orchestrated the sale of arms to Iran (even though the U.S. was actively backing Saddam Hussein's Iraq in its war with Iran), in order to raise funds for the Nicaraguan "Contras" in defiance of a Senate ban on U.S. support for them. "Cap" Weinberger and his hard-liners were summarily dismissed (eleven junior members of the administration were ultimately convicted of felonies), and Reagan's popular approval rating dropped from 65 percent to 46 percent in a month, the steepest drop any president has ever experienced. He successfully maintained that he could not recall if he had been aware of the Iran-Contra deal, but he desperately needed to change the subject. One way was to embark on a reconciliation with the Soviet Union.

Despite his frequent inattention to detail, Ronald Reagan had always been genuine in his desire to end the threat of catastrophic nuclear war that had hung over his country and the world for most of his life, and he was willing to be far more radical in pursuit of that objective than any other post-war American president. He was not always equally clear on how that objective might be achieved—at his first meeting with Gorbachev in 1985, he had puzzled the Soviet leader by talking about how they might work together if there were an invasion of aliens from outer space—but even his Strategic Defence Initiative was well meant. The people behind Star Wars were seeking a partial defence not for American cities, but for the more defensible missile fields and other strategic installations from which the United States might one day try to wage and win a limited nuclear war—but in Reagan's mind it truly was a program to protect American citizens from nuclear weapons. Moreover, he genuinely believed that the technology for Star Wars, once developed, should be made available to the Soviet Union as well.

> *Secretary General Gorbachev:* Excuse me, Mr. President, but I don't take your idea of sharing SDI seriously. You don't want to share even petroleum equipment, automatic machine tools or equipment for dairies, while sharing SDI would be a second American Revolution. And revolutions do not occur all that often. Let's be realistic and pragmatic. That's more reliable.

> *President Reagan:* If I thought that SDI could not be shared, I would have rejected it myself.

> *Reagan-Gorbachev summit, Reykjavik,*
> *Iceland, 11 October 1986*[53]

At the Reykjavik summit, Reagan proposed the elimination of all offensive ballistic missiles (to the horror of his advisers), arguing that basing nuclear deterrence only on slow-moving bombers and cruise missiles would make the world a far safer place, but his unwillingness to abandon the Star Wars project aborted the deal. Once the Iran-Contra scandal broke the next month, however, he changed course radically. He never formally abandoned Star Wars (and Gorbachev, having realized that it was a technological pipe-dream that was very unlikely to happen, eventually dropped his opposition to it), but on every other issue Reagan was willing to make a deal. On Gorbachev's first visit to the United States in 1987, the two men signed the Intermediate Nuclear Forces treaty, ending the panic over the introduction of a new generation of nuclear missiles in Europe. By the time

Reagan visited Moscow in June 1988, he declared that "of course" the Cold War was over, and that his "evil empire" talk was from "another time." Even before the fall of the Berlin Wall in the following year, the United States and the Soviet Union were no longer strategic adversaries, though it took a while longer for the nuclear forces of the two countries to get over the habit of regarding each other as the enemy.

So the first lengthy military confrontation between two nuclear-armed powers ended peacefully, but it offered little consolation for those who were concerned about the future, for it came close to the actual use of nuclear weapons a number of times, and the very process of technological development continually unleashed new instabilities into the system. The stronger rival, the United States, had made almost continuous efforts to retain or regain some kind of numerical or technological superiority that would make its nuclear weapons usable. The Soviet Union, as befitted the weaker rival, clung to a more purely deterrent strategy of all-out nuclear retaliation, but it was determined to get its retaliation in first if it concluded that war was inevitable.

There is no evidence that either side ever intended to launch a surprise nuclear attack against the other, but the fact that no nuclear weapons were used during the four decades that the confrontation lasted owed more to good luck than to good judgement. And it was only at the very end of the confrontation that everybody found out what would actually have happened if all those weapons had ever been used.

We have, by slow and imperceptible steps, been constructing a Doomsday Machine. Until recently and then, only by accident—no one even noticed. And we have distributed its triggers all over the Northern Hemisphere. Every American and Soviet leader since 1945 has made critical decisions regarding nuclear war in total ignorance of the climatic catastrophe.

Carl Sagan[54]

At the time of the Cuban missile crisis in 1962, President John F. Kennedy controlled over six thousand nuclear weapons, many of them of even greater explosive power than those the United States deploys today; General Secretary Nikita Khrushchev probably had in the vicinity of eight hundred nuclear bombs and warheads under his command. For two weeks they hovered on the brink of nuclear war, acutely conscious that a single false step could condemn tens of millions of their countrymen to death. But they had absolutely no inkling that the use of those weapons might precipitate a global catastrophe; they were thinking in terms of a super–World War II. Casualties might be three or four times greater, and it would all happen much quicker thanks to nuclear weapons—but there are not, to be crude, all that many ways to die, and apart from radiation sickness there were not many agonies that could befall the residents of cities hit by nuclear weapons that had not been experienced already by those who were caught in the Hamburg and Tokyo firestorms.

It was only in the early 1980s that scientists began to realize that since the early 1950s the world had been living under the permanent threat of a "nuclear winter." The discovery of what a nuclear war would really do to our planet began in 1971, when a small group of planetologists who had gathered to analyze the results of the Mariner 9 observations of Mars found, to their intense frustration, that the entire planet was covered by an immense dust storm that lasted three months. With nothing better to do, they set about calculating how such a long-lasting dust cloud would alter conditions on the Martian surface. They concluded that it would lower the ground temperature drastically.

Intrigued, they then examined meteorological records here on earth to see if the relatively small amounts of dust boosted into the upper atmosphere by exploding volcanoes produced similar effects. They found that every time a major volcano has gone off over the past few centuries, there has been a small but definite drop in the global temperature, lasting a year or more. So they went on to examine the consequences of stray asteroids colliding with the earth and blasting vast quantities of dust into the atmosphere, as happened from time to time in the geological past—and found evidence of temporary but huge climate changes that caused mass extinctions of living things. Subsequently other scientists have concluded that up to half a dozen "extinction events" involving the disappearance of a large proportion of the species in existence at the time have occurred over the past billion years, and that the leading suspect in most of these events is a prolonged period of worldwide dark and cold caused by the dust thrown up by very big asteroid strikes.

The original, informal group of scientists who had been involved in the Mariner project in 1971 (they called themselves TTAPS, after the first letters of their last names) went their separate ways but stayed in touch. In early 1982 they were shown an advance copy of a paper written by two scientists working at the Max Planck Institute for Chemistry in West Germany that calculated that massive forest fires ignited by nuclear blasts would inject several hundred million tons of smoke into the atmosphere in a nuclear war, and that the smoke "would strongly restrict the penetration of sunlight to the earth's surface." That paper had not even considered the smoke from burning cities and the dust from groundbursts, but the American group saw the significance at once. In 1983 they published their results.

A major nuclear exchange, the TTAPS group concluded, would cover at least the northern hemisphere, and perhaps the entire planet, with a pall of smoke and dust that would plunge the surface into virtual darkness for up to six months and cause the temperature to drop by up to 40 degrees centigrade (up to 72 degrees Fahrenheit) in the continental interiors (which would be far below the freezing point in any season) for a similar period. And when enough of the dust and soot particles had drifted down out of the stratosphere to let the sun's light back in, the destruction of the ozone layer by thermonuclear fireballs would allow two or three times as much of the harmful portion of ultraviolet spectrum (UVC) to reach the surface. This could cause lethal sunburn in exposed human beings in less than half an hour and would cause blindness in a short time. However, the scientists added comfortingly, "we have tentatively concluded that a nuclear war is not likely to be followed by an ice age."[55]

The anticipated and accepted consequences of a major nuclear war already included several hundred million dead in the NATO and Warsaw Pact countries, plus the destruction of most of the world's industry and the artistic, scientific, and architectural heritage of mankind. Fallout and the disruption of the existing infrastructure were expected to damage northern hemisphere agriculture to the point where hundreds of millions more would succumb to famine and disease in the aftermath. It was hardly a pleasant prospect, but most of humanity would survive, and in the southern hemisphere most societies would probably emerge from the ordeal basically intact. Perhaps the new great powers—South Africa, Brazil, Indonesia, and Australia—would find a way to avoid repeating the experience in another couple of generations. At any rate, history would not come to an end, although that would be small consolation to the surviving Russians and Americans.

But the prospect of a "nuclear winter" transformed these calculations. Now the cold and the dark were forecast to persist worldwide for half a year after a major nuclear war, killing off entire species of animals and plants already gravely weakened by high doses of radioactivity—and when the gloom finally cleared, ultraviolet radiation, starvation, and disease would account for many others. In April 1983, a symposium of forty distinguished biologists considered the effects of the predicted post-nuclear climate changes on living things and concluded that

> Species extinction could be expected for most tropical plants and animals, and for most terrestrial vertebrates of north temperate regions, a large number of plants, and numerous freshwater and some marine organisms. . . . Whether any people would be able to persist for long in the face of highly modified biological communities; novel climates; high levels of radiation; shattered agricultural, social, and economic systems; extraordinary psychological stresses; and a host of other difficulties is open to question. It is clear that the ecosystem effects alone resulting from a large-scale thermonuclear war could be enough to destroy the current civilization in at least the Northern Hemisphere. Coupled

DISTANCE FROM GROUND ZERO (MILES)

A hypothetical one-megaton nuclear explosion over New York showing the blast (1); shock waves and high winds (2); and a full-scale firestorm (4) and (5). The smoke and dust boosted into the upper atmosphere (6) would blot out the sun. A "nuclear winter" could follow the explosion of only 100 such bombs over cities.

343

with the direct casualties of perhaps two billion people, the combined intermediate and long-term effects of nuclear war suggest that eventually there might be no human survivors in the Northern Hemisphere.

Furthermore, the scenario described here is by no means the most severe that could be imagined with present world nuclear arsenals and those contemplated for the near future. In almost any realistic case involving nuclear exchanges between the superpowers, global environmental changes sufficient to cause an extinction event equal to or more severe than that at the close of the Cretaceous when the dinosaurs and many other species died out are likely. In that event, the possibility of the extinction of *Homo sapiens* cannot be excluded.[56]

The basic physical processes that would produce these consequences were not in question. As to how many nuclear weapons would be needed to produce these effects, the "baseline" case of a war in which five thousand megatons of nuclear weapons were exploded, 57 percent as groundbursts against "hard targets" like missile silos and 20 percent as airbursts over urban and industrial targets, would probably suffice. (The total stockpile of the United States and the Soviet Union in the mid-1980s was about thirteen thousand megatons.) Calculations were complicated, however, by the fact that the overcast screening out the sun would have two components: dust from soil particles vaporized in groundbursts, and soot from burning cities, forests, and grasslands ignited by airbursts.

It takes considerably more dust than soot to produce the same screening effect: two thousand to three thousand high-yield groundbursts would probably be needed. However, that was precisely the range of detonations that would be needed for one side to make a successful first strike on the other's missile silos, so even a "splendid first strike" that utterly disarmed the enemy, with no attacks on cities and no retaliation, was likely to result in a nuclear winter in the conditions prevailing during the Cold War. The millions of tons of soot given off by burning cities would be a far more efficient screening agent, especially if firestorms produced huge convection columns that drew most of the soot up into the stratosphere where it would remain for many months, and in that case as little as one hundred megatons on one hundred cities could be too much.[57] Even India and Pakistan could be approaching that threshold within the next decade or so—and it is unrealistic to imagine that cities would really be spared in a nuclear war: too many of the vital leadership, command and control, and industrial targets are embedded in them. Cities would be struck, and they would burn.

There was a great deal of research done on "nuclear winter" in the later 1980s, and the hypothesis held up despite major official efforts to discredit it. In 1990 the TTAPS group summarized the research in *Science*,[58] and reported that "the basic physics of nuclear winter has been reaffirmed through several authoritative international technical assessments and numerous individual scientific investigations." In a book published in 1990, Carl Sagan and Richard Turco concluded that the situation was in some respects even worse than their first estimates: "The industrial, urban and petroleum targets are characterized by combustible materials highly concentrated at relatively few sites; this is why global nuclear winter may be generated with only a few hundred detonations or less. . . . Indeed, with something like a hundred downtowns burning . . . even a substantial nuclear winter seems possible."[59] But no further research of any kind has been done on the subject of nuclear winter since 1990. It is symptomatic of the sudden and total loss of interest in the subject of nuclear war after the collapse of the Soviet Union—as though the nuclear weapons themselves had been abolished. But they have not. Most of them are still there, just as lethal as ever.

We are currently enjoying an extended holiday from the reality that war between great powers, in our technological era, means nuclear war. Unless there is a major change in the current international system, however, great-power military confrontations are bound to recur in the decades and centuries to come, and those new nuclear confrontations—between Indians and Pakistanis, between Israelis and Arabs, perhaps eventually between the present great powers once again in some new alliance constellation—will unfold with all the doctrinal mismatches, cultural misunderstand-ings, and technological hubris that marked the first one. It is no longer possible for the major powers to achieve anything useful against each other by means of war, but both their institutions and their mentalities still presume that military action is an option.

The problem we face was bound to arrive eventually: war is deeply ingrained in our culture, but it is lethally incompatible with an advanced technological civilization. Six decades after Hiroshima we have a clearer grasp of the precise nature of our fate if we fail to solve the problem, but the essence of our dilemma was already obvious to Albert Einstein in 1945: "Everything has changed, except our way of thinking."

9

Keeping the Old
Game Alive

Because of their capacity for large-scale slaughter, [nuclear weapons] may be able to cause such sudden and startling reversals of military fortune as to increase the uncertainty and irrationality that are always so pervasive in conflict situations. If we employ them on the enemy, we invite retaliation, shock, horror, and a cycle of retaliation with an end that is most difficult to foresee. . . . We are flung into a straitjacket of rationality, which prevents us from lashing out at the enemy.

Warfare must be returned to its traditional place as politics pursued by other means. We may not be able to create the refined distinctions that characterized the politics of the seventeenth and eighteenth centuries . . . but we may at least be able to approach the relatively compartmentalized pattern of the nineteenth century, and that itself would be a significant gain. Whatever the nature of the situation, we will . . . want to ensure our ability to go on playing the game. . . .

William Kaufmann, RAND analyst, 1955[1]

THE VERY IDEA THAT THERE IS A GAME OF NATIONS IN WHICH war plays an indispensable part may seem either absurd or obscene to outsiders, but it is the firmly held conviction of most of those people who run the foreign policies of sovereign states or serve in their armed forces. The advent of nuclear weapons threatened to make the game unplayable, so they responded by coming up with the notion of wars fought with everything except the nuclear weapons that would ruin the game: "conventional war." It's a concept that didn't even exist before 1945, and is explicitly designed to keep the old game alive. But why did so many people—most of whom were neither wicked nor stupid—feel that they must go on playing it? There is a historical answer, and also an institutional one.

——

The post-1945 confrontation between the United States and the Soviet Union that became known as the Cold War was perfectly predictable (and widely predicted) as soon as the probable outcome of World War II became clear around 1943. The victorious alliance quickly fell apart after 1945 because such alliances almost always do. After their opponents have been crushed, the winners are the biggest players left on the board, and as such they automatically become the greatest potential threats to each other's power. On average, they would then have been about half a century away from the next world war.

There is no issue at stake in our political relations with the
Soviet Union—no hope, no fear, nothing to which we aspire,
nothing we would like to avoid—which could conceivably be
worth a nuclear war.

*George Kennan, former U.S. ambassador
to Moscow*

The two victorious powers that emerged from World War II
as "superpowers," the United States and the Soviet Union, had
every reason to be satisfied with the outcome, as they essentially
divided Western and Central Europe, the centre of world power
for the previous three centuries, into spheres of influence whose
borders ran roughly along the line where their armies had halted
in 1945. But why did they identify each other as enemies and enter
into a long and extremely dangerous military confrontation?
There is no evidence that either ever intended to invade the other.
Ideological differences do not really explain what happened
either, for the two countries had not been enemies before 1945
despite their differing ideologies, and both found it possible to
cooperate with other nations that espoused the opposite ideology—consider the strategic collaboration that grew up between
the United States and the People's Republic of China in the 1970s,
for example, or the Soviet Union's near-alliance with India.

One possible explanation (a deeply cynical one) would be
that the continued division of Europe into Soviet and American
zones of influence *depended* on there being a military confrontation between the superpowers. That confrontation, sanctified by
universalist ideologies, was what legitimized their military presence in countries far beyond their borders and the division of
much of the world into two rival blocs led by Moscow and
Washington. This is not to suggest that either superpower had a
strategy of deliberately seeking conflict with the other in order to
justify its domination over its sphere of influence, but very often in
human affairs, people act in ways that objectively advance their
interests without ever consciously admitting it to themselves.

But even if the leaders of the two superpowers saw some
advantages in this confrontation—and some of them did—they

were still so afraid that it would end up in a devastating nuclear war that they were willing to invest in notions of "conventional war." Why? Because they knew how history worked.

We normally count only the two great wars of the twentieth century as "world wars," but what distinguished them was merely the fact that the weapons technology was much better than before. A *political* definition of a world war would be one in which all the great powers of the time are involved. That will generally guarantee that it is actually fought all over the planet, but the key factor is not geographical; what makes it a world war is that all the great powers become involved in two great rival alliances, and that the war ends up being about practically everything.

By this criterion, there have been six world wars in modern history: the Thirty Years War of 1618–48, the War of the Spanish Succession in 1702–14, the Seven Years War of 1756–63, the Revolutionary and Napoleonic wars of 1791–1815, and the two wars that actually bear the name of World War, in 1914–18 and 1939–45. The War of the Spanish Succession and the Seven Years War stand out less prominently from other wars of their era than the other four world wars because the level of "background noise" was much higher during the eighteenth century, when the dynasties of Europe engaged in almost perpetual limited wars among themselves. Nevertheless, both these wars qualify for inclusion as world wars not only on the grounds of their all-embracing cast of participants and the fact that they were the largest wars of their respective periods, but also because they each represented the culmination and comprehensive settlement of a long series of preceding lesser wars and disputes between the great powers. Contemporary observers themselves regarded these wars as having "settled" things conclusively, and having defined the relative status of the great powers in the ensuing period of comparative peace. This is precisely the function of world wars in the present international system.

The most striking thing about this list is that it has an alarmingly cyclical character. The great powers have all gone to war with each other about every fifty years throughout modern history, with only one gap in the sequence—and even the "long peace" of the nineteenth century is deceptive. Right on schedule, between 1854 and 1870, practically every great power fought one or several others: Britain, France, and Turkey against Russia; France and Italy against Austria; Germany against Austria; and then Germany against France. On several occasions it looked likely that one of these wars would expand to embrace all the great powers, but none of them lasted long enough. (Generally speaking, the longer a war between any two great powers lasts, the likelier it is to drag in the others.)

Instead, this anomalous series of smaller wars brought about changes in the international distribution of power as big as those usually accomplished by world wars. A united Italy and a powerful German empire emerged in the heart of Europe, while the relative decline of Austria was confirmed and France irrevocably lost its previous position as the greatest continental power. The great power system, having thus adjusted to the new realities of power that had been created in the preceding half-century by different rates of population and industrial growth in various parts of Europe, then settled into a long period of peace. The Treaty of Frankfurt in 1871, like the Congress of Vienna in 1815, was followed by four decades in which no European great powers fought each other.

So why did the great powers all go to war about every fifty years? It is almost certainly because the most important international facts in any inter-war period are determined by the peace treaty that ended the last war. Each world war reshuffles the pack, and the situation is then more or less frozen by the peace settlement: that is what fixes all the sensitive, disputed frontiers and allocates the various great powers their positions in the international pecking order.

At the instant it is signed, the peace settlement is generally an exact description of the true power relationships in the world. It is easily enforceable, because the beneficiaries have just beaten the losers in war. But as the decades of peace pass, some powers grow rapidly in strength and others face relative decline. After half a century or so, the real power relationships in the world are very different from those prescribed by the last peace settlement. And it is at that point that some frustrated rising power whose allotted role in the international system is too confining, or some frightened nation in decline that sees its power slipping away, initiates the next reshuffle of the deck.

There is no magic in the figure of fifty years. That just seems to be how long it usually takes for the realities of power to get out of kilter with the relations prescribed by the previous peace settlement. That World War II came only twenty years after World War I seriously distorts our perception of the normal historical rhythm, but the unusually brief interval of peace after World War I is probably due mainly to the fact that it was the first total war. Total wars tend to end in draconian peace treaties, since even the winners have suffered so greatly that they are in no mood for compromise, so the Treaty of Versailles in 1919, with its extreme terms, was a less accurate description of the real power relationships in the world than are most peace settlements. "Tremendous victories make bad peaces," as Guglielmo Ferrero remarked.

Not everybody in power after 1945 shared this precise analysis of the cyclical nature of world wars, but almost all the senior people in the governments, the foreign services and the military services of the great powers had at least a strong suspicion that history was being driven by some phenomenon of this sort—so even if the invention of nuclear weapons meant, as Einstein put it, that everything had changed, they had little confidence that it really would change. Warfare seemed to persist no matter how the circumstances surrounding it changed over time.

Warfare had played a key role in the relations between civilized states from the earliest times, and at the start it seemed a perfectly rational pursuit. Since land was the main source of wealth, conquest generally increased the wealth of a society. With proper management, this fed back into more military power, greater security, and the prospect of further conquest. Those who were good at war prospered; those who were not often ended up dead or enslaved.

Even in early modern times, the basic equations still held true: eighteenth-century European wars were still explicitly about increasing the state's wealth and power through territorial expansion. There were enormous benefits for those states that were very

good at war—English did not become the world's second language because the English were pacifists—and the cost of engaging in war was not particularly high. Indeed, until the late nineteenth century hardly anybody saw war as a problem. Losing a war could be a problem, certainly, but few questioned the validity of the institution itself.

Then the new science and technology and productive capacity began to transform the ancient institution of war, industrializing and rationalizing it in accord with the spirit of the age, which was to seek efficiency in all things. But the core business of war is killing, and the European countries began to discover the cost of industrializing and rationalizing killing in World War I, which killed eleven million people. Most of the rest of the world discovered that cost in World War II, which killed forty-five million (or even sixty or sixty-five million, if post–Soviet-era estimates of Russian casualties are accurate).

At the same time that the casualties were going up, the benefits of war were going steeply down. The wealth of industrial societies is *not* based on land, and they have little to gain from war that they could not just buy far more cheaply. Yet rather than turning away from war as it became less profitable, nations full of the best-educated people in history had fought worse wars than ever before. In the face of such massive and recent evidence of the persistence of old reflexes despite new realities, who could have confidence that war would not happen again? So wouldn't it be prudent to try to find a way to fight a war without using nuclear weapons, at least for long enough to give everybody a chance to think about their options, just in case war did come again?

The advocates of conventional war were accused by those who had greater faith in the effectiveness of nuclear deterrence of trying "to make the world safe for conventional war." It was a reasonable position to take if you could truly believe that the fear of nuclear war would be enough to prevent all wars between nuclear powers forever, but a great many people did not. The latter group

The killing gets efficient. British dead in trench at Spion Kop, South African War, 1900.

won the argument, but not really on rational grounds. They won it because nuclear war reduced all other forms of warfare to irrelevance, and thereby made the efforts and even the existence of the large majority of professional officers who served in non-nuclear branches of the armed forces irrelevant as well. People do not like being irrelevant, and there are few trade unions more powerful than the professional officer corps.

———

If you believe the doctors, nothing is wholesome; if you believe the theologians, nothing is innocent; if you believe the soldiers, nothing is safe.
Lord Salisbury

Professional military men always want to prepare for war, for "nothing is safe." Soldiers are not, on the whole, warmongers, but the "military mind"—the professional military perspective on human affairs—nevertheless exercises an enormous influence on how the business of mankind is conducted. Professional military officers understand in their bones the role of power, compulsion, and brute force in human affairs. The perspective is not merely self-serving; it is grounded in the military officers' recognition of the unpleasant realities of their profession.

The birth date of the military profession as an autonomous body with its own corporate views and interests, derived from its professional responsibilities and not from mere personal ambitions, was 25 November 1803, when the first true general staff was created in Prussia. Its job was to apply to war the same principles of rational organization and planning that were already transforming civil society in Europe: to develop fundamental principles for military operations that would give guidance for commanders, and to prepare detailed war plans for every possible conflict with other states.

Only a few years later, the transformation took another step forward when the shock of defeat by Napoleon drove the Prussian army to follow the example of the French revolutionaries and end the aristocratic monopoly on jobs in the officer corps. The Prussian military reformers realized that the "art of war," like law or medicine or any other profession, was actually a body of technical knowledge and practical experience that could be taught in such a way that men of ordinary intelligence and personality could become extremely competent in it.

> The only title to an officer's commission shall be in time of peace, education and professional knowledge; in time of war, distinguished valor and perception. From the entire nation, therefore, all individuals who possess these qualities are eligible for the highest military posts. All previously existing class preference in the military establishment is abolished, and every man, without regard to his origins, has equal duties and equal rights.
>
> *Decree on selection of officers, Prussian army, 1808*[2]

Two years later, in 1810, the Prussian army founded a staff college (the *Kriegsakademie*) where a small number of gifted middle-rank officers attended a demanding one-year course in subjects ranging from military history, tactics, and military administration to foreign languages, mathematics, geography, and geology. (One of the *Kriegsakademie*'s first directors was Karl von Clausewitz, who wrote the first general study of the theory and practice of war, called simply *On War*, during his term there.) In due course, it became the rule that only *Kriegsakademie* graduates could be promoted to high rank or appointed to the general staff.[3]

In less than a decade, Prussia had laid the foundations for the first truly professional officer corps, and the military became a profession in the full sense of the word. That is, they were granted a monopoly on the exercise of their special skills by the state, just as doctors and lawyers are, and they were also given the right to set the standards and select the candidates for entry into their profession themselves. At most levels they even had the right to make their own decisions about who would be promoted up through the ranks of their profession, although at the highest ranks the state, their only client, insisted on keeping final control.

The countries that took the lead in institutionalizing military excellence in this way reaped major advantages from it for a long time. As late as World War II, over a century after the creation of the *Kriegsakademie* and the Prussian general staff, the German army, more or less successor to the Prussian army, continued to display a consistent combat superiority over all its enemies when units of similar size and type were engaged.

> One of the things that emerged from our study of operations on the Western Front and in Italy in World War II was that there was a consistent superiority of German ground troops to American and British ground troops. As a retired American army officer this didn't particularly please me, but I can't deny what my numbers tell me. . . . In combat units, one hundred Germans in mid-1944 were the equivalent of somewhere around 125 American or British soldiers. . . . At about the same time a hundred Germans were the equivalent of about 250 Russians. . . .
>
> Now this doesn't mean that the average German was any more intelligent, any braver, any stronger, any more motivated than the average Russian, but it means that when they were put together in combat units . . . the Germans used their weapons and equipment 2.5 times better than did the Russians. . . . More than any other single factor, it was the German general staff that made the difference. . . . There were generals in World War II, Russian generals, American generals, British generals, who were as good as the best of the Germans, but the Germans had about ten times as many very good generals.
>
> Col. T. N. Dupuy, USA (ret'd), director,
> Historical Evaluation and Research
> Organization, Washington, D.C.

In the end, every other major power imitated the Prussian innovations and professionalized its own armed forces, although in some cases it took almost a century. But the emergence of this new

The downside of professionalism: officers as managers, war as a statistical operation. The managerial delusion at work in Vietnam.

military profession had some large and undesirable side effects. Since it is the professional duty of military officers to identify threats to the security of the state, they are constantly searching for potential dangers abroad—and virtually every other state within military reach constitutes such a threat simply by virtue of having armed forces of its own. The planning reflex of general staffs provides governments with detailed and regularly updated scenarios for conflicts in unlikely places with improbable enemies. (As late as the 1920s, military planners in the United States and Canada were maintaining carefully worked out plans to invade each other.)

In addition to the general propensity of the military to see threats everywhere, there are invariably rivalries among the three or more separate armed services maintained by most countries. These frequently lead to an exaggeration of the alleged threats facing a country in order to justify the acquisition of some new weapon by a particular service, or generally to advance its cause in the perennial inter-service competition for resources. And there are always civilians who are willing to help the service to make its case—for a price.

When I was in the Pentagon I had as many as fifty contracts under my supervision to think tanks around Washington to give us advice on strategy and tactics and even how to deploy various weapons systems. . . . If they didn't answer the mail, in the sense of providing reasons for our weapons systems, I wouldn't renew the contract. . . .

One day I met a young man from one of the most prestigious of the think tanks, and he said he was doing a study for the Navy on aircraft carriers. I said, "Why in the world are you doing a study for the Navy? The Navy is the world's expert on aircraft carriers." He said, "Well, I don't know, but we've got a $50,000 contract from the Navy, and all we did was to tell them that we thought we could show that the Navy needed eighteen carriers rather than fifteen."

Adm. Gene LaRocque, USN (ret'd),
former director, Center for Defense
Information

The matrix of interlocking interests that drives this process has become known in the United States as the "military-industrial complex," so named by President Dwight Eisenhower in his famous farewell speech in 1961. A large part of U.S. defence spending, for example, is due to an informal alliance between military officers in the Pentagon, whose prospects of further promotion depend on their success in defending their own service's interests and in acquiring new weapons, roles, and resources for it; ambitious scientists and technologists who provide ideas for new weapons; defence consultants who come up with strategies that justify the need for those weapons; and private industry, which provides a large part of the political clout necessary to sell the package. Defence contractors have not only the influence conferred by the possession of large amounts of money, but the direct political influence that comes from being the providers of a great many jobs. It is a formidable combination, and it usually gets its way.

Much the same combination of factors is in play in every other major power: a professional military propensity to see threats everywhere, intense competition for resources between the various armed services, and an alliance between the military and the civilian players who live off military contracts. Even in countries like the former Soviet Union where there was no commercial nexus, the same interest groups created the same basic alliance driven purely by careerist motives: the Soviet equivalent of the military-industrial complex was known as the "metal-eaters' alliance." And while the branches of the military specializing in nuclear weapons extracted vast sums from their governments to build even more of the things, the rest of the armed forces, who hated and feared nuclear weapons because they threatened to make their branches of the military profession irrelevant and obsolete, waged a generation-long, more or less successful campaign to keep the possibility of conventional war alive.

———

Soviet tanks are sweeping across western Europe. The British army, routed by Russian forces and in retreat, has one last chance for survival—the deployment of its high-tech weapon of last resort: the chicken-powered nuclear bomb. . . .

Downing Street was forced to put its faith at the height of the Cold War in a giant plutonium landmine kept functioning by a detachment of German poultry. The seven-ton weapon, code-named Blue Peacock, was a state-of-the-art munition to be buried on the plains of northern Germany during a British retreat and detonated by remote control or timer to destroy advancing Russian forces in the event of the Third World War. But its inventors at the Aldermaston Atomic Weapons Research Establishment . . . were concerned at the effects of the central European winter on their Doomsday armament and resorted to fowl tactics. A 1957 memo recommended burying a flock of chickens with the landmine in order to keep it warm.

The Independent, 1 April 2004[4]

There was always an element of black comedy in the forty-five-year confrontation between the NATO and Warsaw Pact armies in central Europe, since the idea that conventional military forces could fight for long in that part of the world before their owners went nuclear and blew up much of the world was inherently incredible. Indeed, in the early days of the Cold War the doctrine of "massive retaliation" formally promised to do just that. If the Russians attacked in Europe, there would be no preliminary shilly-shallying with conventionally equipped armies: the bombers of U.S. Strategic Air Command would simply destroy the Soviet Union with nuclear weapons. But the actual soldiers on the ground never liked that idea even one little bit.

> The theory was that as soon as the other side established beyond a doubt that they were invading, you then let loose the American strategic arm and blasted, incinerated, irradiated enough of the people on the other side to make them stop what they were doing, whatever it was. Well, that was the raving of a feverish child, but I lost a lot of friends by saying this, particularly among the airmen. . . .
>
> *Gen. Sir John Hackett, former commander, NATO Northern Army Group*

> We know that since 1945 nineteen nuclear strikes have been considered in Washington—four against the Soviet Union.
>
> *Marshal Oleg A. Losik, Malinovsky Armored Forces Academy, Moscow*

Massive retaliation was the simplest, surest, most satisfying strategy imaginable for the West, so long as it had an effective monopoly of nuclear weapons. For the Russians, it was a nightmare of impotence and dread until they attained a nuclear capability roughly comparable to that of the United States. In strictly logical terms, the probability of a war between the United States and the Soviet Union should then have diminished to zero, since it was obvious that both countries would be destroyed in such a war. Yet since few people really believed that war was impossible, it was in precisely this period after 1960 that the West in particular began to give serious attention to its non-nuclear forces in Europe, and elaborated theories for how they might be used in circumstances short of all-out nuclear war.

Most people believed, probably correctly, that there was greater danger of war growing out of a confrontation in Central Europe, where millions of NATO and Warsaw Pact troops directly confronted each other on the ground, than of any premeditated "first strike" against the superpowers' homelands—so it was important to be able to conduct non-nuclear warfare in Europe, at least for a brief period, to give the diplomats a chance to stop the drift into disaster. (No doubt Indian and Pakistani strategists are now wrestling with the very same questions.) The doctrine that put conventional war back on the map was "flexible response," and in practice it was NATO policy in Europe by 1962, though it was not officially proclaimed until 1967. It was never formally adopted by the Warsaw Pact, but it was also the policy of the Soviet forces by the early 1970s.

"Flexible response" didn't actually promise that NATO would not use nuclear weapons at the start of a war—it was deliberately ambiguous about that, and NATO always insisted that it might go nuclear first—but the soldiers all intended to stay "conventional" for as long as they possibly could: re-fighting World War II was a lot more attractive than fighting a real World War III. The problem they simply could not solve was that sooner or later one side was bound to start losing—and at that point it was very likely that the nuclear weapons would come out. Either the losing side would launch them to signal that it would not accept defeat, or the winning side would anticipate that act and decide to pre-empt it. Even then, however, they hoped to buy a little more time before Armageddon by restricting their initial escalation to the use of only "battlefield" nuclear weapons.

About six thousand of the twenty-five thousand nuclear weapons in the U.S. nuclear arsenal in the mid-1980s were relatively low-yield devices kept in Western Europe. (The Soviet Union kept a somewhat smaller number of tactical nuclear warheads in Eastern Europe.) If it were NATO that decided to escalate, the Supreme Allied Commander Europe would probably have begun by requesting political permission from NATO and the White House for the release of one or more "packages" of nuclear weapons for use on defined areas of the front where collapse was imminent or had already occurred. A typical package, as defined by U.S. Army Field Manual F 100–5, would have consisted of two atomic demolition land mines, thirty rounds of W48 warheads (plutonium fission, yield: under 1 kiloton) and W33 warheads (enriched uranium, variable yield up to 10 kilotons) for 155mm and 8-inch artillery shells, ten Lance or Pershing surface-to-surface missiles for deeper nuclear strikes, and five B-43 air-delivered bombs (yield: between 500 and 1,000 kilotons). A modest start: forty-seven nuclear explosions in the vicinity of the Fulda Gap, say, with a total yield of around 3,000 kilotons.

For purposes of comparison, the Hiroshima bomb was under 20 kilotons. A limited or "theatre" nuclear war on the Central Front would not only have destroyed most of the armies that were engaged; it would also have caused millions or tens of millions of civilian deaths in central Europe in a matter of days. And even that level of escalation was seen principally as a last opportunity for reflection and second thoughts, so to speak, before the opponents moved on to the employment of "strategic" nuclear weapons and the devastation of the entire northern hemisphere.

No sane leader on either side would ever have planned and executed a deliberate attack against the other side in Europe. There was nothing to be gained by it, and a world to be lost. Yet the presence of large conventional forces on either side of the border, and their natural propensity to practise for the war they hoped to avoid, succeeded in creating the impression in the minds of each side's soldiers and politicians that the other side might well attack if they thought they could get away with it.

Q. All our exercises in Central Europe assume a Soviet attack. In Soviet staff colleges, do they really run exercises in which NATO is on the offensive from the start?

A. That's exactly what they do: their scenarios, their equivalents to ours, always start with a NATO offensive, then after twenty-four hours or so they sort of turn this around and they start plodding through to the Rhine very quickly to counter this.

Adm. Robert Falls, chairman of the
NATO military committee, 1980–83

It was an extraordinary interlude. For over four decades, a period that covered the entire working lives of a generation of soldiers, there was a sustained attempt to turn Central Europe into a kind of game park where the great powers could preserve an endangered species, conventional war. The problem is that the line they drew between conventional and nuclear war was, in the end, an artificial distinction, and probably a pretty flimsy one. If either side started to win a conventional war, the other would almost certainly have brought out its nuclear weapons, and a stalemate would also have brought strong pressures for escalation. Win, lose, or draw, conventional war in Europe would probably have led to nuclear war, probably in only a couple of weeks.

It has always frightened me to death, ever since I was to command a division in Germany in the late Fifties and the nuclear weapon appeared for the first time as a cotton-wool cloud on the sand table. The assumption that you can control a nuclear war is pure fantasy. From the moment the nuclear weapon is released on the European battlefield, you open Pandora's box and you don't know what's coming out. But one thing you can count on is that there will be a very high probability of early and steep escalation into the strategic all-out exchange that nobody wants. So you mustn't use the things.

Gen. Sir John Hackett

Everybody's intentions were good, but if the shooting had ever actually started, it's likely that most of Europe would have been destroyed. In Wintex '83, one of the last of NATO's annual command and staff exercises before the Cold War began to shut down, the script had the Warsaw Pact forces crossing the border into West Germany on 3 March. On 8 March, NATO's commanders requested authority to use their nuclear weapons to stop the Soviet breakthrough, and the first nuclear strike against the Warsaw Pact was ordered on 9 March. The conventional war lasted six days.

———

Pakistan is not a democratic country and we don't know their nuclear threshold. We will retaliate and must be prepared for mutual destruction on both sides.

Yogendra Narain, Indian Defence
Secretary, 2002

But nuclear weapons capacity put the same shackles on conventional military power in their new owners as it did in the five declared nuclear powers of long standing. A recent University of Illinois study concluded that a nuclear war in the Indian subcontinent would result in 17 million deaths in Pakistan and 30 to 35 million in India, and these numbers can be expected to rise as the current number of nuclear weapons—around a hundred for India, and probably fewer than fifty for Pakistan—grows. As a result, the two subcontinental powers have been flung into the same "straitjacket of rationality" that William Kaufmann wrote about with reference to the U.S.-Soviet conflict in 1955 and can expect to achieve nothing more by war. Like Moscow and Washington during the Cuban missile crisis of 1962, Islamabad and New Delhi were forced to acknowledge this reality during the grave military confrontation over Kashmir in the spring of 2002, when they mobilized more than a million men along their common border and then carefully stood them down again ten months later.

As the post-1962 history of Soviet-American relations shows, the recognition of total mutual vulnerability does not necessarily

Ceci n'est pas un symbole phallique. Pakistani officers and scientists with nuclear-capable missile, June 2004, at an undisclosed location. Pakistani President General Pervez Musharraf is third from right.

lead to the instant reduction of military tensions, and India and Pakistan are still in the extremely dangerous phase that the Russians and the Americans were passing through in the early 1960s. Each side's small number of nuclear weapons is vulnerable to destruction in a surprise attack by the other side, so false warnings of attack, whether technological or diplomatic, can cause pressures for preemption on the "use 'em or lose 'em" argument. (India's current plan to move part of its nuclear deterrent out to sea on Russian-built nuclear submarines carrying Indian-built BrahMos cruise missiles is years away from realization, and in any case will not eliminate the hair-trigger aspect of the relationship unless Pakistan can make its nuclear weapons invulnerable too.) But all this notwithstanding, the risk of a nuclear exchange does force Indian and Pakistani policy-makers to abandon any residual fantasies of decisive military victory over the other side.

But they were already fantasies: India and Pakistan had already demonstrated to any reasonable person's satisfaction that military power could not impose a lasting political settlement on their conflict anyway. Pakistan was defeated in war by India three times before nuclear weapons entered the equation—hardly astonishing, since it has only a seventh of India's population—but modern states, by any previous historical standards, are very hard to destroy. Contemporary Pakistan has an efficient centralized government, considerable wealth, and millions of highly educated people, and it has access to all the technological and scientific capabilities of the era it lives in. It dedicated itself to catching up with India's development of nuclear weapons as soon as New Delhi tested its first "peaceful nuclear explosive" in 1974, and by 1998 it was instantly able to match India's defiant series of six nuclear weapons tests (carried out mainly to affirm India's great-power status to the world) with five nuclear tests of its own. The result of over half a century of military confrontation is a permanent stalemate in which India's seven-to-one population advantage is no longer a meaningful advantage at all.

If we lose this war, I'll start another in my wife's name.
Moshe Dayan (attributed)[5]

Precisely the same thing is true of the Arab-Israeli confrontation, which began only a year after the Indian-Pakistani one. An Arab victory, unlikely from the start, was absolutely precluded once Israel developed nuclear weapons in the early 1960s, but a four-decade-long nuclear weapons monopoly in the Middle East has not yielded Israel any tangible advantages either. As a Western country with a classic European mobilization system, Israel has been able to put more troops on the battlefield than its Arab opponents in four out of its five wars, and in all of its wars except for the 1948–49 independence war, it has had major technological advantages as well. Israel's successful attack on Egypt in collusion with Britain and France in 1956 was followed by an unassisted Israeli victory in 1967 that put the entire Sinai peninsula in Israeli hands and closed the Suez Canal for a decade. But Israel's military triumphs never delivered lasting political success.

Only after Egypt's limited attack in the 1973 war somewhat restored the military balance between the two states was an Egyptian-Israeli peace settlement possible—precisely along the 1948 border. Similarly, three Israeli military victories over Syria left much of the Golan Heights in Israeli hands, but no Syrian government could accept a peace settlement that did not restore the 1948 border either. And after twenty years of fruitless occupation and mounting Israeli casualties, Israel unilaterally withdrew from southern Lebanon in 2002. None of Israel's neighbours have serious pretensions to being able to take it on militarily any more—but even with the unstinting support of the United States, the world's sole remaining superpower, Israel has been unable to translate its overwhelming military power into regional political power; that is, the ability to control outcomes.

It is not a question of a fight between one government and another. It is a question of an invasion by an Iraqi non-Muslim Ba'athist [regime] against an Islamic country, and this is a rebellion by blasphemy against Islam.

Ayatollah Ruhollah Khomeini, in
Tehran, 20 October 1980[6]

Nowhere was the sheer resilience of the modern state more vividly demonstrated than in the biggest war of the late twentieth century, the Iran-Iraq war of 1980–88. Iraq's attempt to exploit the turmoil following the Iranian revolution of 1978–79 and seize Iran's oil-rich and largely Arabic-speaking southwestern province was an act of folly: Iran has three times as many people as Iraq and the revolution had already aroused Iranian nationalist fervour, whereas Iraq was a crude dictatorship ruling over a population deeply divided by ethnicity and religion. Nevertheless, Tehran ultimately proved unable to defeat Baghdad: Iraq's Shias, a majority of the population, mostly remained loyal to the Iraqi state despite the appeals of their co-religionists in Iran, and a Kurdish rebellion in northern Iraq was brutally and successfully crushed.

Once the United States, smarting from the overthrow of its collaborator in Iran, the Shah, concluded a de facto alliance with Saddam Hussein's regime in 1983, the Iran-Iraq struggle became mired in bloody trench warfare that closely resembled the Western Front stalemate of World War I—even including the extensive use of poison gas by the Iraqis. The Reagan administration tried hard to bring about an Iraqi victory: it organized an informal arms embargo against Iran, encouraged its allies to sell modern weapons to Iraq, provided satellite intelligence data and U.S. Air Force photo interpreters to help Iraq plan its offensives against the Iranian trenches, and even tried to cover up Saddam Hussein's use of poison gas against his own Kurdish citizens by instructing the State Department to blame it on Iran—but it proved impossible to break Iran's will to resist either. The war ended in 1988 in mutual exhaustion and the restoration of the *status quo ante.*

The failure of conventional military power to deliver decisive results, even in confrontations where nuclear weapons do not impose strategic paralysis, has become chronic, and so the world in the early twenty-first century presents an unfamiliar aspect. Cross-border wars, the staple of international politics down the ages, have virtually disappeared from the Americas, Europe, Oceania, and most of Asia. If you leave out the troubled southwest quarter of Asia, extending from Kashmir through Afghanistan and Iraq to Israel—the greater Middle East, so to speak—the only international wars that have been fought in the past thirty years anywhere in these vast regions, home to over 80 percent of the world's population, were the Vietnamese invasion of Cambodia in 1979 and the Anglo-Argentine war of 1982.

Sub-Saharan Africa continues to be ravaged by wars: it has only 10 percent of the human population, but in the past decade it has accounted for at least half the deaths in war on the entire planet. The worst in the past few years has been the many-sided war in the Democratic Republic of Congo, second only to Nigeria in population, in which six foreign African armies became involved and over a million people were killed. But that was the only African war of recent years that had a significant international dimension; most are internal affairs driven by Africa's uniquely complex ethnic politics.

Of all the inhabited continents, Africa is the only one which has experienced neither the millennia of imperial rule that gradually ground the multitudinous ethnic groups of Eurasia into a relatively manageable number of large ethnic groups—75 per cent of Europeans speak only eight languages, and half of all Asians speak only three—nor the genocides that drastically reduced ethnic complexity in the Americas and Australasia and replaced it with a small number of European-derived cultures. Africa, by contrast, retains most of its original ethnic complexity—over 200 ethnic groups numbering over a quarter-million, but only a handful of over 10 million—and so experiences far more internal wars.

These African wars contribute heavily to the false impression that the entire world is ravaged by war. In fact, more countries elsewhere are at peace, with little expectation of war in their neighbourhood in the foreseeable future, than at any time in modern history. It is hard to judge how much the growing inability of military force to produce satisfactory results has contributed to this phenomenon, but it has certainly played a role: there are few if any recent examples of military victories that have had permanently profitable results for the victor. This even applies to the cheap and easy victories that occur when rich and technologically advanced countries turn their armed forces loose on corrupt and incompetent dictatorships in the developing world.

The history of the modern military establishment can be
described as a struggle between heroic leaders, who embody
traditionalism and glory, and military "managers." . . .
Military managers . . . are aware that they direct combat
organizations . . . but they are mainly concerned with the
most rational and economic ways of winning wars or avoiding
them. . . . Heroic leaders . . . would deny that they are anti-
technological, but for them the heroic traditions of fighting
men, which can only be preserved by military honor, military
tradition, and the military way of life, are crucial.

Morris Janowitz, The Professional
Soldier[7]

The traditional soldier's conviction is that battle is not a statistical operation and that it cannot be won with a managerial
approach. Military officers have traditionally seen themselves as
warriors, not administrators, even though they have always been a
mixture of both. To accept that technology is more important than
human will is to reduce their own efforts, and perhaps their own
deaths, to insignificance, so combat officers in every army tend to
reject the notion strongly. Today, however, armies also contain
many officers whose bent is managerial rather than "heroic," and
the temptation to believe that all the human imponderables of
combat can be reduced to simple equations is very seductive. If it
were true, ground combat would become a predictable science,
not an arcane art in which the good commander's chance of success is only about the same as the good poker player's chance of
winning on a given evening (for the same sort of reasons).

But the technological and logistical elements of warfare,
being much more amenable to the planning process, tend to get
an undue share of attention in peacetime. This has led a number
of armed forces—most notably those of the United States, the
ultimate technological society—to exalt the role of the manager
and the planner over that of the traditional fighting commander,
whose worth cannot be evaluated until the shooting starts, and so

to grant competent administrators and technocrats greater resources and more rapid promotion. There is such a thing as national style in armies (whose members, after all, share most of the basic values and assumptions of the civilian society from which they are drawn). In the particular case of the U.S. Army, the "managers" have almost entirely taken over on several occasions.

> The technology that is available to the U.S. military today and now in development can revolutionize the way we conduct military operations. That technology can give us the ability to see a battlefield as large as Iraq or Korea—an area 200 miles on a side—with unprecedented fidelity, comprehension and timeliness, by night or by day, in any kind of weather, all the time.
> *Admiral William A. Owens, former vice-chairman, U.S. Joint Chiefs of Staff*[8]

The technological hubris that infects many people in the American military-industrial complex, where speculation about a "Revolution in Military Affairs" hardened to confident assertion in the aftermath of the walk-over against Iraq in 2003, has two sources. One is the so-called "information revolution," a combination of sophisticated sensors and real-time data-processing that encourages some military ideologues to imagine that the "fog of war" can finally be dispelled and the "friction of war" eliminated. The other source is found in the new generations of guided weapons with a "one-shot-kill capability," which allegedly allow the commanders to act on all this information promptly and with reliable results—and hold out the further promise of not exposing their operators to serious danger. Together they engender the delusion that combat operations can be reduced to a managerial process conducted according to rational calculations, with predictable results, in which the best technology will always win.

Sometimes, against a sufficiently backward and incompetent opponent, it does actually work like that for a while, as in the brief American-led conventional wars against Iraq in 1991 and 2003. But the same technologies that made the new weapons possible have also created new forms of mass media that bring the realities of war home to a public that never before had to deal with them, and that has created a whole new vulnerability for the armies of developed countries: the acute reluctance of the civil population to accept high casualty tolls in wars that seem less than vital to the survival of the nation. The first time this phenomenon had a large impact on events was in the Korean war of 1950–53.

> The President observed that the quicker the operation [of using atomic bombs against China] was launched, the less the danger of Soviet intervention.
>
> *National Security Committee minutes,*
> *May 1953*

President Dwight D. Eisenhower's willingness to use nuclear weapons, if necessary, to break the stalemate in the Korean truce talks in 1953 was less shocking in an era just emerging from a total war than it would be today, but it was certainly an extreme position for a generally moderate leader to take. Nevertheless, he felt obliged to, because he had been elected on a promise to end a conventional war in Asia that had already cost almost 50,000 American lives since the North Korean invasion of South Korea three years before.

After surging back and forth the whole length of the Korean peninsula, the front had stabilized fairly close to the previous frontier between North and South Korea along the 38th parallel, and by 1953 units of "volunteer" Chinese troops sent in by the recently established Communist regime in Beijing had largely replaced North Korean troops on the front facing the U.S. and other United Nations troops. It was obviously time to declare a draw and move on, but the American public was already in revolt against the war and so the North Korean and Chinese negotiators at the ceasefire talks at Pyongyang felt that they had Eisenhower over a barrel. All they had to do was stall some more, and he would be forced to give them better terms. So Eisenhower upped the ante by threatening a nuclear attack on China.

Americans had borne four years of war and a third of a million dead during World War II without complaint, because they were convinced that great moral and national security issues were involved. Less than a decade later, they turned against a three-year war that had killed less than a sixth of the American toll in World War II simply because they didn't believe that it was necessary. Perhaps they were wrong, for the Korean War was the first serious test of the new United Nations rules banning acts of aggression, but they were the voters and they had spoken. Eisenhower's threat worked and a ceasefire ended the fighting in Korea soon after, but it was the start of a new phenomenon: popular dissent with a war even as the fighting continues. Fifteen years later in Vietnam it was far worse.

The American war in Vietnam from 1965 to 1973 is still widely viewed as a counter-guerrilla war, but in fact it was nothing of the sort. A minority of American troops and a majority of South Vietnamese forces were involved in the classic and extremely tedious task of counter-insurgency and internal security operations, but most U.S. combat units were fighting a semi-conventional "limited war" almost from the day they arrived in the country. This was due primarily to the fact that the North Vietnamese chose to make it that way:

> Americans had an image of war. . . . which equated guerrilla warfare with a certain very small set of images: basically any kind of jungle warfare must be guerrilla warfare. The guerrilla warfare image and television led everyone to think that everything that was going on in Vietnam was a guerrilla war. They saw newsreel footage of only a few stock images week after week, year after year: people slogging through rice paddies, people going through jungle so thick that you couldn't believe that there could actually be another unit in there fighting you, film footage of villages being bombed.
>
> In all cases you couldn't see the enemy, which seemed to confirm the image of the guerrilla as being very elusive. There you are with a lot of heavy forces moving around trying to find him. He fires; he gets you; you don't get him; he runs away—and you've mashed a village or something but you don't get any results.

375

In fact, quite frequently you had very large and very conventional North Vietnamese forces operating against the
Americans just when this newsreel footage was being taken.
But the point about newsreel footage is that you virtually
never see the enemy, in any war. So the whole Vietnam war
seemed to be an anti-guerrilla war while of course it was
nothing of the kind. The American units went into the jun-
gles, up into the highlands in the western part of the country
where the enemy lived, going straight for battle against the
main enemy in classical old military style, and once they got
there it was a conventional American force fighting against a
lightly equipped but conventional Asiatic enemy.

> Tom Tulenko, former U.S. military
> adviser, Vietnam

American strategy aimed to stop the rot in South Vietnam by
committing enough combat troops on the ground to take the pressure off the South Vietnamese army (which was very near collapse
in 1965), while the offensive element consisted of "limited" but
large-scale aerial bombardment of North Vietnam. This theory of
escalation involved bombing an expanding list of targets until
Hanoi's "threshold of pain" had been reached and it desisted from
sending regular units south along the Ho Chi Minh trail into South
Vietnam. "I can't believe that a fourth-rate power like Vietnam
doesn't have a breaking point," US National Security Adviser
Henry Kissinger said to his staff in 1969—but the threshold of pain
of an intensely nationalistic and ruthlessly totalitarian regime like
North Vietnam's was not even reached when the Americans had
escalated all the way to bombing Hanoi and Haiphong.

The American strategy was founded on the argument, based
on ideological preconceptions rather than fact, that the threat to
the South Vietnamese regime in 1965 came not from local guerrilla forces (the Viet Cong) enjoying a certain amount of logistical
support from the North—which was in fact the case—but rather
from the large-scale infiltration of regular North Vietnamese army
units down the Ho Chi Minh trail. It was therefore argued that if
Hanoi could be forced to stop the infiltration, the problem in

Propaganda in the jungle, South Vietnam.

South Vietnam would go away. In fact, however, the dispatch of large numbers of American combat troops to South Vietnam served to turn Washington's mistaken assessment of the situation into an accurate one, for Hanoi responded by sending large forces of its own into South Vietnam.

By the end of 1968 the North Vietnamese army was in effective charge of all operations in the south, most of the Viet Cong guerrilla cadres had been replaced by regular North Vietnamese military officers, and whole divisions of the North Vietnamese army were operating in the Central Highlands. In thus providing the Americans with precisely the hard targets they wanted, and standing up to U.S. forces in open battles that cost them huge casualties, the North Vietnamese were contravening all the traditional rules of rural guerrilla warfare. But they were no longer fighting that kind of war. They were instead working from the analogy of their 1954 battle with the French at Dien Bien Phu, and it hardly mattered whether they won their battles, as they had done in that case, or lost, as they did in the comparable siege of Khe Sanh in 1967–68. The point was that by engaging Americans in fierce combat – even accepting loss ratios of as much as ten-to-one, which was an inevitable consequence of the vastly superior American firepower – the North Vietnamese could exact that steady and large toll of American casualties that would destroy the American public's will to continue.

> "You know," [Colonel Harry] Summers told a North Vietnamese colonel [at the Paris peace talks in 1973], "you never defeated us on the battlefield." To which his Communist counterpart replied, "That may be so, but it is also irrelevant."[9]

It worked precisely as Hanoi had calculated. American troops hardly ever lost a battle in Vietnam, but it took only three years of combat, culminating in Hanoi's purportedly "suicidal" Tet offensive of 1968, for the North Vietnamese to win the battle on the American home front. Only fifteen thousand American fatalities in Vietnam were incurred before Tet[10] and in purely military terms Tet was a victory for the U.S. forces. But even that scale of loss, when combined with the relentless television coverage of the war, proved more than the American public was willing to bear in such a doubtful cause. After Tet and the victory of Richard Nixon in the presidential election at the end of that year, the U.S. government stopped looking for fights and started looking for a way out— though it took five more years to find the famous "decent interval" that let American forces leave in 1973 without overt military humiliation and pretend that it was not a defeat for the U.S. Army when Hanoi collected its victory two years later.

The acute political sensitivity of Western electorates to casualties has been a major constraint on foreign military interventions since Vietnam, and even the dramatically cheap and easy victory

The last day of South Vietnam. People scaling the wall of the U.S. embassy in Saigon in the hope of evacuation by helicopter from the roof.

won by American air power in the Gulf war in 1991 failed to erase the "Vietnam syndrome" (although President George H.W. Bush believed it had done so at the time). Only eighteen American soldiers killed in a single day in the Somalia intervention in 1993 had such an impact on U.S. public opinion (thanks mainly to videotaped footage of a dead American soldier being dragged through the streets before cheering Somali crowds) that American troops were withdrawn from Somalia by President Bill Clinton a few months later. He subsequently refused to allow a UN intervention to stop the genocide in Rwanda in 1994 for fear of a similar public reaction to casualties there in a U.S. election year.

Popular concern about casualties is not exclusively American; it was also a major factor in the former Soviet Union's eventual retreat from its 1979 intervention in Afghanistan. Former U.S. National Security Adviser Zbigniew Brzezinski claims that he successfully lured Moscow into invading Afghanistan by feeding arms and money to the pro-Soviet regime's fundamentalist opposition during the late 1970s, with the specific intention of creating "Russia's Vietnam" and destroying the Soviet Union. "What is more important to the history of the world?" he asked triumphantly in 1998. "The Taliban or the collapse of the Soviet empire? Some stirred-up Muslims or the liberation of central Europe and the end of the Cold War?" The assumption underlying Brzezinski's strategy was that Russians were as vulnerable as Americans to the demoralization and public disaffection that comes with taking endless casualties in a seemingly futile and purposeless war—and although it is very much to be doubted that his strategy had anything to do with the collapse of Soviet power, it certainly did produce Vietnam-like effects on Russian public opinion and force Moscow to end its military involvement in Afghanistan.

This new and acute political allergy to military casualties has shaped most U.S. research and development on conventional weapons for the past several decades. Priority has been given to weapons systems that will allow American troops to apply force while limiting their own casualties to an absolute minimum, almost regardless of the cost of the weapons in

Captured mujahideen in Afghanistan during the Soviet occupation. Later on, some of them would be fighting Americans as the Taliban, but at this point the U.S. was backing them.

question. All the rest of the money spent on an army will have been wasted if public opinion will not let you use it for fear of taking casualties. The American-led military interventions in former Yugoslavia in the later 1990s — Bosnia in 1995, and Kosovo in 1999 — were specifically structured not just to minimize but actually to avoid any American casualties in the "war." In the case of Kosovo, pilots were ordered not to fly below ten thousand feet in order to reduce their vulnerability to anti-aircraft fire, even though that seriously degraded their ability to hit their targets. And no American or other NATO ground troops were committed to combat at any time during the campaign for the same reason: to lose even a few soldiers might undermine fragile popular support for the operation.

During the 1990s, people talked in Washington about the "Mogadishu line": an unwritten understanding that no American military intervention abroad that was not directly and clearly connected to the vital national interests of the United States should be undertaken unless its advocates could guarantee that it would not cost the lives of more than twenty American soldiers—two more than the number of Americans killed in 1993 in the badly planned raid in the narrow streets in southern Mogadishu that inspired the major Hollywood movie *Black Hawk Down*. Post 9/11, the acceptable number of American casualties in a conflict in Iraq that many Americans believe is somehow connected to the "war on terror" is clearly higher than that. It may even be a hundred times higher now, which would take it up to two thousand fatal casualties. It is certainly not a thousand times higher. It is easy and cheap for a technologically advanced country to invade a ramshackle Third-World dictatorship, but occupying it for any lengthy period of time starts to cost soldiers' lives, which is politically crippling at home.

This is not a bad thing. It is regrettable that people do not really start to be upset about sending their young men and women into combat until television pictures rub their noses in what actually happens to them when they get there, and that they are not equally moved by the deaths of the foreigners whom their sons and daughters may kill, but this popular aversion to casualties does raise the bar for foreign military interventions in a way that may make some of the more foolish and cynical ones impossible to defend. It is currently confined to the richer countries where nationalist reflexes are somewhat eroded and the media are better developed, but the same phenomenon is already beginning to spread to other parts of the world. What it actually shows is that while people may support the idea of war from time to time— rightly or wrongly—they find the reality of war shocking and repulsive. We may be in the midst of a profound cultural change here, although of course it is partial, ragged, and inconsistent, as cultural change always is.

The understandable obsession with nuclear weapons during the Cold War has obscured another new reality that had been creeping up on soldiers: even a purely conventional war fought with state-of-the art weapons has become rather problematic if the opponents are equally matched. Maybe the battlefield surveillance systems and the "fire-and-forget" weapons are transforming conventional war—maybe there really is a "Revolution in Military Affairs"—but it is more likely to produce stalemate than quick and decisive victory if the great powers ever fight one another again.

It was not just in Europe that the armies never actually got to try out their new weapons against each other. We are as short of useful evidence about what would happen when fully modern military forces clash as the great European powers were on the eve of 1914. The last time that modern armies fought a serious conventional war was the 1973 war between Israel and two of its Arab neighbours, more than three decades ago, and the lessons one can draw from that are limited by the fact that the Egyptian and Syrian armies were comparatively poorly led and trained. More recent conventional conflicts have been either between armies using mostly previous-generation weapons like the Iran-Iraq war of 1980–88, "colonial" conflicts like the Falklands War between Britain and Argentina in 1982 that merely showcased the abilities of some particular weapons system (sea-skimming anti-ship missiles, in that case), or hopelessly one-sided struggles like the two wars between the United States and Iraq. None of them tell us what would happen if two armies that were both equipped and trained like the U.S. armed forces were to fight each other—but there is reason to suspect that they would be facing a surprise as great as the one that the armies of the European great powers stumbled into in 1914.

The most striking fact about conventional military forces in the post-World War II era is that the armies have got small again. If war had come to Europe in the last decade of the Cold War, for example, the NATO commander on the Central Front would have had approximately a million men and two thousand combat aircraft under his command. His Soviet counterpart would have had comparable forces at his disposal, although with rather more tanks and other armoured vehicles. These were the largest mechanized armies that could be found anywhere in the world—at least half the world's advanced conventional weaponry was concentrated in a relatively small area—and the forces of both sides would have received substantial reinforcements in the first weeks of a war. Yet most planners assumed that loss rates would be so high that neither side's front-line troops would exceed their initial numbers at any point in the proceedings—and although million-man armies are nothing to be sneered at, these forces did not remotely compare with the armies that the great powers deployed during either of the world wars of the twentieth century.

This drastic shrinkage in the scale of conventional military forces has happened worldwide, and the main reason is money. Conventional weapons have grown so expensive that most nations cannot justify producing very large numbers of them in peacetime, and see little point in paying extra soldiers for whom they cannot afford to buy state-of-the-art weapons. They would be willing to spend more if they found themselves in a major war against another great power, but modern weapons systems are so complex and the production rates so slow that there would be no time to expand production significantly after a war had begun. On the contrary, both sides would immediately start losing their major weapons systems like tanks and aircraft at a rate they could not hope to replace.

> It used to be you could send up hundreds of aircraft, and they weren't too successful in combat: nobody shot too many people down. Whereas now the lethal rate is very, very high, so consequently the war probably won't last very long. . . . You'll have to fight with what you have right now, and the war will go at such a pace that it will be difficult to use your industrial capacity to replace airplanes lost on the battlefield because the lead time to produce that airplane may be longer than the war lasts. It's a very difficult situation, in that you want a sophisticated airplane that will do a lot of roles, but you need quite a few of them because that's what you're going to fight with—and they come very expensive.
>
> *Jack Krings, flight operations head,*
> *McDonnell-Douglas Corp., 1982*

The F-15 Eagle is a case in point. It first entered production in 1972, and continued to be built into 2004, but in all that time total production for the US Air Force was 1,065 aircraft. Each F-15 took about eighteen months to build, and it cost $42.5 million per copy—the cost being mainly a reflection of the tens of thousands of man-hours of highly skilled labour that went into building it. Even today it remains a very impressive and lethal machine—but it is also very scarce.[11]

The increase in the cost of weapons since World War II has been staggering. The Spitfire, probably the best fighter in the world in 1939, cost £5,000 to build. When its current equivalent, the air defence version of the Tornado, entered service with the Royal Air Force in the early 1980s, each one cost £17 million: one hundred and seventy-two times more expensive *after* allowing for inflation. Subsequent price rises have been gentler, but that doesn't help much: the total program cost for the next-generation Eurofighter, of which the Royal Air Force has ordered 232 for production between 2002 and 2014, is £15.9 billion, or about £68 million each. No country is several hundred times richer than it was at the beginning of World War II, so far fewer weapons can be built. Approximately the same amount of factory space was devoted to the construction of military aircraft in the United States at the height of the Reagan defence build-up in the 1980s as was devoted to the same purpose in Germany during World War II. But whereas in 1944 Germany was building three thousand planes a month (and losing them at about the same rate), American production of military aircraft in the 1980s averaged about fifty a month.

Recent generations of fighters are far better than those of World War II, of course. They can fly three times as fast and carry five or six times the weight of munitions; they can detect an opponent hundreds of miles away and attack at a hundred times the range a Spitfire could manage. They are also much more likely to destroy their opponent, because their weapons are far more accurate and lethal. But that simply makes the problem worse: not only can air forces afford fewer aircraft, but they are going to lose them at a faster rate.

This phenomenon is not confined to military aircraft, although they are the most extreme case. All military technology, from tanks and warships to communications gear and night-vision equipment, has undergone the same transformation. It has become so expensive that the number of items bought must be severely curtailed, and at the same time the weapons have become so lethal that loss rates in battle are dramatically higher.

> We started out with eleven tanks . . . and we lost five in the space of thirty minutes.
>
> Q. Is that normal?
>
> A. It will be if they come at us. We had about three combat teams come at us then, that's about thirty or forty tanks, and that would be normal—half our force would be knocked out. . . . Normally we would be expected to last in a tank battle about two hours.
>
> *British tank commander on NATO exercises*

In the Middle East war of 1973, both the Arabs and the Israelis lost close to half their total stock of tanks in less than three weeks of heavy fighting. If there had been a conventional war in Europe in the 1980s, loss rates in all major items of weaponry would probably have been even higher. Each day's fighting might easily have seen the destruction of a thousand tanks and several hundred aircraft—and unlike the Middle East in 1973, there would have been no outside source of supply to which the combatants could turn for replacements. It would have been a "come as you are" war: the weapons that had already been built would have been the only ones available. The problem of attrition has become paramount.

> [There might have been] an extraordinarily short burst of mutual wiping out of first-line equipment, leaving the armies dependent on quite simple weapons—a return to an earlier

Very expensive, not too numerous, and very hard to replace. An Israeli F-16 on duty.

phase of warfare. We had that in 1914: all the sides had gone to war with stocks quite inadequate for the scale of the fighting that took place, and there was then the famous "winter pause" which was partly to lick their wounds. . . . and very much to gear up the shell factories. Because the inventory of weapons is so much larger [it would have been] a pause for the replacement of almost everything: tanks, aircraft, missiles, missile launchers, armoured vehicles of all sorts. . . .

Sir John Keegan, military historian

What was true at the end of the Cold War is probably even truer today. No country, not even the richest, can afford to equip an old-style mass army incorporating most of the young male population with modern weapons. Israel came close for a while, but it was spending around 30 percent of its GNP on defence, got vast amounts of U.S. military aid as well, and ended up bankrupt.

None of the major industrialized nations attempted such a feat even at the height of the Cold War. In the mid-1980s, NATO and the Warsaw Pact together, with a combined population of almost a billion people, had enough first-line conventional military weapons to equip fewer than ten million troops: under 1 percent of their population. Today, the same countries have fewer than five million regular soldiers.

The bright side of all this is that none of the major industrial powers currently anticipates fighting a serious conventional war against any of the others, and so issues like building up adequate "war stocks" of key military equipment to allow for very high consumption rates can be safely ignored. The great powers continue to maintain nuclear deterrent forces, but even the greatest military power of all, the United States, has only enough ground forces for short wars against relatively small and weak countries—what historian Emmanuel Todd calls "theatrical micro-militarism." And although these forces are quite adequate to deliver quick and easy military victories against opponents like Iraq, their ability to convert military success into long-term political success is far less impressive. Just as nuclear weapons are essentially irrelevant to the pursuit of traditional military goals like "victory," there has also been a severe erosion in the political usefulness of conventional military forces.

10

Guerrillas and Terrorists

The advantages are nearly all on the side of the guerrilla in that he is bound by no rules, tied to no transport, hampered by no drill-books, while the soldier is bound by many things, not the least by his expectation of a full meal every so many hours. The soldier usually wins in the long run, but very expensively.

Archibald Percival, Lord Wavell[1]

The ability to run away is the essence of the guerrilla.

Mao Tse-tung[2]

Karl von Clausewitz wrote little about guerrilla war though he certainly knew about it, but his most famous dictum applies: "War [including guerrilla war] is not only a political act, but also a real political instrument, a continuation of political commerce, a carrying out of the same by other means." Guerrilla war has political goals, and strategies for achieving them; its main difference from other kinds of war is that it is not usually being carried out by a state, and so is not legal in terms of the law currently in force on the territory where it is fought. However, the guerrillas almost always aim to become the legal government in the end, and if they succeed then the boot suddenly shifts to the other foot. Most early guerrilla struggles were waged against foreign occupiers who had effectively decapitated the insurgents' state and destroyed its army, but they are now more commonly fought by political groups or ethnic minorities in rebellion against their own national government.

The conduct of guerrilla war almost always involves a good deal of what is now called terrorism, and legitimate states have therefore consistently tried to paint it as immoral—except, of course, when they are sponsoring it on some other country's territory, as they have frequently done. Since most of the bigger states have shown no reluctance in using terror techniques themselves in war—consider the rationale behind the doctrine of "strategic bombardment" in World War II, or the "balance of terror" that was at the heart of the Cold War—their views on the matter may safely be dismissed as self-serving hypocrisy, but very serious moral questions nevertheless arise with regard to guerrilla war.

While conventional armies seek contact with the enemy and decisive victory, guerrilla forces deliberately avoid fighting regular forces that they cannot hope to match and concentrate instead on "soft" targets whose destruction may ultimately undermine the government's control over the country. In practice, this often means torturing local officials and slaughtering their families in front of the assembled community—and the counter-insurgency specialists are not too squeamish either. Operation Phoenix, the U.S.-run campaign of assassination to eliminate Viet Cong cadres after the Tet offensive in 1968, killed between twenty and fifty thousand people, most of them inevitably innocent civilians, but it also effectively gutted the Viet Cong infrastructure in much of South Vietnam.

For a time in the 1950s and early 1960s, guerrilla war seemed to be a virtually infallible technique for overthrowing governments. But like the first of the modern methods for seizing state power, the urban uprisings of nineteenth- and early twentieth-century Europe that drew their inspiration from the French Revolution in 1789, guerrilla warfare proved to be a technique that flourished only in a specific environment.

———

Wherever we arrived, they disappeared; whenever we left, they arrived. They were everywhere and nowhere, they had no tangible centre which could be attacked.

French officer fighting
Spanish guerrillas, 1810[3]

Guerrilla warfare as a form of resistance to foreign occupation or an unpopular domestic government had been around for the better part of forever, but it gained particular prominence in the Napoleonic wars, when the Spanish who gave the technique its name (*guerrilla* = "little war") and the Germans waged large guerrilla campaigns against French occupying forces. As is almost normal in guerrilla war, systematic atrocities designed to terrorize the other side were routinely employed by the French army as

Counter-insurgency tactics,
Spain, ca.1810 by Francisco Goya,
from *Los desastres de la Guerra*.
Clockwise from top: "Tampoco"
(Nobody knows about this one
either), "Por que?" (Why?), and
"Lo mismo" (The same).

much as they were by the Spanish guerrillas: the savagery of the struggle in Spain from 1808 to 1814 was indelibly captured in Francisco Goya's *The Disasters of War*. But guerrilla warfare was not generally regarded as a decisive military technique even as late as World War II, when it was widely employed against German and Japanese occupation forces, primarily because it lacked an adequate strategy for final victory.

So long as the guerrillas remained dispersed in the hills, forests, or swamps and indulged in only hit-and-run raiding against the government or the foreign occupiers, they could make an infernal nuisance of themselves. They could also carry out what would today be called "terrorist" attacks in the cities—but they could never clear their opponents out of the urban centres of power. If they came down from the hills and attempted to do so in open combat, they gave their opponents the target they had been hoping for, and the enemy's regular forces would smash them. Even the Yugoslavs, the most successful European guerrilla fighters of World War II, could not have liberated their country unaided; the Germans finally pulled out of Yugoslavia mainly because the victorious Red Army was sweeping through the Balkans toward them.

> By May 1928 . . . the basic principles of guerrilla warfare, simple in nature and suited to the conditions of the time, had already been evolved; that is, the sixteen-character formula: "The enemy advances, we retreat; the enemy camps, we harass; the enemy tires, we attack; the enemy retreats, we pursue."
>
> *Mao Tse-tung*[4]

The one great exception to all the rules was Mao Tse-tung. After the Chinese Communist Party lost its urban Shanghai base in the massacres of 1927, he led the surviving Communist cadres in an eighteen-year rural struggle against the Nationalist government of China, and later against the Japanese invaders, that literally wrote the book on modern guerrilla warfare. It is unlikely that there has been any guerrilla commander of any nationality or ideology in the past seventy-five years who has not read Mao's works. However, there have not been many guerrilla commanders who have done what Mao did, which is to start with a handful of rural guerrillas and end up by overthrowing and replacing a well-established government with local roots. As time passed, his victory has come to look more and more like a one-of-a-kind.

This was not immediately evident after 1949, however, because similar rural guerrilla techniques were successfully deployed against the European colonial empires at a time when the imperial powers had lost their nerve and were in a gravely weakened economic condition. As in the occupied countries of Europe during the war, the guerrillas in Asian and African colonies after the war had no difficulty in mobilizing many of their newly nationalistic fellow countrymen against their foreign occupiers. As in the occupied countries of Europe, they still had

The first time it worked. People's Liberation Army propaganda truck in Shanghai as the Chinese People's Republic is declared, 1949.

virtually no prospect of winning a military victory against the well-equipped regular forces of the imperial power, but they could turn themselves into an expensive and ineradicable nuisance. What was different was that whereas the Germans in Yugoslavia were fighting a great war in which the very survival of their own regime was at stake, and so were willing to bear the cost of fighting the Yugoslav guerrillas virtually indefinitely, the European powers had no such stake in retaining control of their colonies.

> You may kill ten of my men for every one I kill of yours, but even at those odds, you will lose and I will win.
> Ho Chi Minh, ca. 1948 (to the French)

> The conventional army loses if it does not win. The guerrilla wins if he does not lose.
> Henry Kissinger[5]

It came down in the end to the fact that if the guerrillas could make it very expensive for the colonial power to stay, and could go on doing so indefinitely, they didn't have to worry about gaining a military victory. The colonial power would eventually decide to cut its losses and go home. This was a reality that had already been demonstrated by the Irish war of independence in 1919–20 and the Turkish war of national resistance against attempted partition by the victorious Entente powers in 1919–22 (the struggle for which the Bolsheviks originally coined the phrase "national liberation war"). The pattern was repeated many times in the two decades after 1945, in Indonesia, Kenya, Algeria, Malaya, Cyprus, Vietnam, South Yemen, and many other places. In a few cases, like Malaya, the imperial power managed to hand over control to some local group other than the guerrillas themselves (but this depended mainly on the unusual racial split in Malaya). In most cases, it was the guerrilla leaders themselves who inherited power: Sukarno in Indonesia, Jomo Kenyatta in Kenya, the FLN in Algeria, and so on. And once the European imperial powers finally grasped their own fatal vulnerability to this technique, the decolonization process in most of their remaining colonies was achieved without need for a guerrilla war.

At the time, the apparently irresistible spread of rural guerrilla wars caused great alarm and despondency in the major Western powers—partly, of course, because it was their own oxen that were being gored. There was also an ideological element, however, in that most of the post-1945 guerrilla movements followed some version of the same Marxist ideology preached by the West's main international rival, the Soviet Union. (And naturally, being Marxists, the guerrillas attributed their successes to ideology rather than to the particular environment they were operating in, and announced this conviction loudly.) This led to a belief in the West that it was Soviet and/or Chinese expansionism, and not simply local resentment of foreign rule, that lay behind these guerrilla wars. This, in turn, led to the creation of special counter-insurgency forces, especially in the United States, and ultimately to the commitment of U.S. troops to Vietnam under a total misapprehension as to what the war there was about.

In fact, the guerrilla revolutionaries had adopted a Marxist ideology partly because of the powerful influence of Mao's successful example in China, but mainly because it was the principal revolutionary ideology on offer at the centre of the empires that ruled them: the Third World revolutionaries of the fifties and sixties learned their Marxism in London and Paris, not in Moscow. After all, they could scarcely be expected to adopt the liberal democratic ideology (for domestic consumption only) of the imperial powers they were seeking to expel. In opting for the leading opposition ideology that prevailed at the imperial centre, Marxism, they were following the example of an earlier generation of anti-imperialist revolutionaries who had borrowed the then-fashionable revolutionary ideology of liberalism from the European left and used it as the ideological basis for their own revolutions in Turkey in 1908, in Mexico and Iran in 1910, and in China in 1911. Nonetheless it did create the wrong impression in Western capitals.

The full-scale U.S. military commitment to Vietnam in 1965 was made not only for the wrong reason—to thwart perceived Soviet expansionism acting through the Chinese—but at the wrong time. For by 1965 the wave of guerrilla wars in what used to be called the Third World was coming to its natural end, as most of the countries there had already received their independence. Apart from Indochina, only southern Africa and South Yemen were still the scenes of active guerrilla campaigns against imperial rule by 1965. And although it had scarcely been noticed yet, the rural guerrilla technique hardly ever worked against a locally based government supported by the local majority ethnic group. The natural antipathy against foreign rule that would attract recruits to the guerrillas' cause was lacking, and more importantly, a locally based government could not simply give up and go home if the cost of fighting a counter-insurgency campaign got too high. It already was home, and had nowhere else to go.

There are a few minority ethnic groups that are sufficiently large, cohesive, and determined that they might eventually make the "decolonization" model work against an independent Third World government—the Eritreans won their independence from Ethiopia, and the Tamil Tigers and the Chechens might one day succeed against Sri Lanka and Russia—but this is essentially a wave that has passed. For the most part, rural guerilla groups without a distinct ethnic base who are fighting against their own national government have to solve the question of how to win final military victory in open battle against the government's regular armed forces. Generally, they cannot solve it.

> Make wiping out the enemy's effective strength our main objective; do not make holding or seizing a place our main objective. . . . In every battle, concentrate an absolutely superior force, encircle the enemy forces completely, strive to wipe them out thoroughly and do not let any escape from the net.
>
> *Mao Tse-Tung*[6]

Mao was an effective guerrilla leader in the 1930s and the early 1940s, but he would never have issued those instructions then. In those days he followed the standard rules of guerrilla warfare: ambush small groups of the enemy, but never stand and fight against his main forces. By the time he gave the above orders, however, the Japanese had surrendered to the Allies and the Chinese

Communists were moving into the last phase of their struggle with the Nationalist regime that still controlled all the cities and most of the population: open warfare using large regular formations. Between August 1945 and August 1947, the People's Liberation Army grew fourfold, to two million men, and came out into the open to beat the corrupt, divided, and incompetent Nationalist army in a series of full-scale battles. Indeed, it was a detachment of exactly the same army, using standard light infantry tactics and burdened by few heavy weapons, that infiltrated across the Yalu River into Korea in late 1950 and drove a numerically equal American and United Nations army in panic down almost the whole length of the Korean peninsula.

Mao achieved the Holy Grail of guerrilla war: he built his party cadres into an alternative government, turned his guerrilla soldiers into a real army, and then beat the existing government in open battle. And he did it with no support from outside and no help from ethnic grievances. It was a brilliant accomplishment, and innumerable revolutionary groups tried to follow his example, but only two succeeded: Fidel Castro's little band of brothers who came down from the Sierra Maestre in 1959, and the Sandinistas in Nicaragua in 1979. In both cases they benefitted from having as opponents governments that were so extraordinarily iniquitous, incompetent, and politically isolated that they made even the Chinese Nationalists look good. They could also appeal to the anti-American sentiment that ran strongly in those countries after so much American intervention. Both the Batista regime in Cuba and the Somoza family in Nicaragua were widely seen by their fellow-countrymen as American puppets, and so the revolutionaries were not in a radically different position from those who waged success-ful anti-imperial struggles in the colonies of the European empires.

Even today the world remains littered with rural guerrilla movements, most of them representing minority ethnic groups and hanging on in the more rugged parts of Third World coun-tries, but they generally have little prospect of success against local governments that can credibly invoke nationalism on their own side. If they ever try to move up from the low-intensity busi-ness of assassinations, car bombs, and hit-and-run raids to more

Africa: Every river an ethnic frontier.

ambitious operations involving large units that stand and fight, they simply give the government forces the targets that they have been hoping for.

The most dramatic demonstration of how ineffective rural guerrilla warfare was outside the specific late colonial environment in which it had flourished was provided by the Cubans. They made a concerted effort in the middle and late 1960s to export the technique to the independent states of Latin America in the hope of bringing about Marxist revolutions there. Rural guerrilla movements sprang up in almost all the states of South America, Marxist in orientation and enjoying tacit or even open Cuban support. Without exception, they failed disastrously. The epitome of this failure was "Che" Guevara's own tragicomic attempt to start such a movement in Bolivia, which ended in his own death.

Our isolation continues to be total; various illnesses have undermined the health of some comrades . . . our peasant base is still underdeveloped, although apparently a program of planned terror will succeed in neutralizing most of them, and their support will come later. We have not had a single recruit (from the peasantry). . . . To sum up, a month in which all has evolved normally considering the standard development of a guerrilla war.

"Che" Guevara, Bolivia, April 1967[7]

Six months later Guevara was dead and his little guerrilla band had been broken up—and the same fate eventually attended almost all the other attempts to copy the Cuban experience that had sprung up in Latin America. This is not to say that the technique can never work in independent countries, but rural guerrillas in Latin American countries had been eliminated or reduced to a merely marginal nuisance by 1970 except in Colombia (where they had their roots in a terrible civil war that had involved the whole country) and in Peru (where the Maoist "Shining Path" guerrillas drew their support from the ethnic Indian population of the highlands). Those two movements survive to this day, but another generation has brought them no closer to power. The inescapable conclusion—which was accepted by most Latin American revolutionaries—was that rural guerrilla warfare was another revolutionary technique that had failed.

———

It is necessary to turn political crisis into armed conflict by performing violent actions that will force those in power to transform the political situation of the country into a military situation [i.e., carry out a military coup]. That will alienate the masses, who, from then on, will revolt against the army and the police and blame them for this state of things.

Carlos Marighella, Minimanual of the Urban Guerrilla[8]

Fidel Castro and victorious Sandinista soldiers, Havana, 1979. But usually it doesn't work.

The failure of classic rural insurgency in the Latin American countries drove numbers of disappointed revolutionaries into random terrorism (or rather, urban guerrilla warfare, as it came to be known). In effect, the strategy of the Latin American originators of this doctrine, most notably the Montoneros of Argentina, the Tupamaros of Uruguay, and Brazilian revolutionaries like Carlos Marighella, was aimed at driving the target regimes into extreme repression. It was what French Marxists have long called *la politique du pire* (the policy of making things worse, in the hope of provoking a crisis and a decisive break with the status quo).

By assassinations, bank robberies, kidnappings, hijackings, and the like, all calculated to attract maximum publicity in the media and to embarrass the government to the greatest possible extent, the "urban guerrillas" sought to provoke the displacement of moderate, more or less democratic governments by tough military regimes, or to drive existing military regimes into even stricter and more unpopular security measures. If the regime resorted to counter-terror, torture, "disappearances," and death squads, all the better, for the goal was to discredit the government and alienate it from the population.[9]

> First we kill all the subversives; then, their collaborators; later, those who sympathize with them; afterward, those who remain indifferent; and finally, the undecided.
>
> *General Iberico Saint Jean, governor of*
> *Buenos Aires province during the Terror*[10]

In a number of Latin American countries, the urban guerrillas did accomplish the first phase of their strategy: the creation of thoroughly nasty and brutally repressive military governments dedicated to destroying them. But what then happened was that these governments proceeded to do precisely that. In Argentina, perhaps the worst-hit country, the military seized power from an ineffectual and discredited civilian government in May 1976, and instituted a reign of terror that ultimately killed between 15,000 and 30,000 people. Most of them were kidnapped off the streets or from their homes, tortured for some days in military bases, and then killed, their bodies buried in unmarked graves or dumped into the sea. The majority of those murdered by the military regime were not guilty of any crime, a fact of which the soldiers were well aware. They, too, were pursuing a strategy of deliberate terrorism, but with all the resources of a modern state behind it. In every Latin American country where the urban guerrilla strategy was attempted, the vast majority of the revolutionaries ended up dead or in exile. Their principal achievement was to cause a military reign of terror that blighted the lives of a whole generation in a number of South American countries.

As in the case of rural guerrilla warfare outside the colonial environment, the fatal flaw in the urban guerrilla strategy was that it lacked an effective end-game. The theory said that when the guerrillas had succeeded in driving the government into a sufficiently repressive posture, the populace would rise up in righteous wrath and destroy its oppressors. But even if the population should decide that it is the government and not the guerrillas that is responsible for its growing misery, just how is it to accomplish this feat? By the urban uprisings that have rarely succeeded since the nineteenth century? Or by the rural guerrilla warfare that has just demonstrated its ineffectiveness?

The faint and even more foolish echo of these Latin American terrorist strategies were the terrorist movements espousing mostly "Trotskyist" ideologies that flourished in Western Europe and North America during the 1970s and 1980s. Their main ideological guru was American academic Herbert Marcuse, who wrote about the need to "unmask the repressive tolerance of the liberal bourgeoisie" through creative violence that forced them to drop their liberal mask and reveal their true repressive nature—standard Latin American Marxist rhetoric from the previous decade—whereupon the revolutionary masses would rise up and overthrow them. As Richard Huffman wrote of the leading West German group of urban terrorists:.

> The Baader-Meinhof Gang certainly didn't expect to win their war by themselves. They assumed an epic proletarian backlash would be the Revolution's true engine. They assumed their wave of terror would force the state to respond with brutal, reflexive anger. They assumed that West German civil liberties and civil rights would be quashed as the state turned the clock back 25 years. They assumed that the proletarian West Germans would react in horror as the true nature of their own government was revealed. They assumed that factory workers, bakers and miners, would be inspired to smash their own oppressors. They assumed that they would be the vanguard of a movement where millions of Germans brought Revolution home. They assumed a lot.[11]

"Anarchist Criminals" Wanted poster for the Baader-Meinhof Gang. Note that almost half the members are women.

▬ Anarchistische Gewalttäter ▬
– Baader/Meinhof-Bande –

Wegen Beteiligung an <u>Morden</u>, <u>Sprengstoffverbrechen</u>, Banküberfällen und anderen Straftaten werden steckbrieflich gesucht:

Meinhof, Ulrike, 7. 10. 34 Oldenburg	Baader, Andreas Bernd, 6. 5. 43 München	Ensslin, Gudrun, 15. 8. 40 Bartholomae	Meins, Holger Klaus, 26. 10. 41 Hamburg	Raspe, Jan-Carl, 24. 7. 44 Seefeld
Stachowiak, Ilse, 17. 5. 54 Frankfurt/M.	Jünschke, Klaus, 6. 9. 47 Mannheim	Augustin, Ronald, 20. 11. 49 Amsterdam	Braun, Bernhard, 25. 2. 46 Berlin	Reinders, Ralf, 27. 9. 48 Berlin
Barz, Ingeborg, 2. 7. 48 Berlin	Möller, Irmgard, 13. 5. 47 Bielefeld	Mohnhaupt, Brigitte, 24. 6. 49 Rheinberg	Achterath, Axel, 15. 4. 35 Hannover	Hammerschmidt, Katharina, 14. 12. 43 Danzig
Keser, Rosemarie, 31. 8. 17 Ebersberg	Hausner, Siegfried, 24. 1. 52 Selb/Bayern	Brockmann, Heinz, 1. 3. 48 Gütersloh	Fichter, Albert, 18. 12. 44 Stuttgart	

Für Hinweise, die zur Ergreifung der Gesuchten führen, sind insgesamt **100 000 DM** Belohnung ausgesetzt, die nicht für Beamte bestimmt sind, zu deren Berufspflichten die Verfolgung strafbarer Handlungen gehört. Die Zuerkennung und die Verteilung erfolgen unter Ausschluß des Rechtsweges.

Mitteilungen, die auf Wunsch vertraulich behandelt werden, nehmen entgegen:

Bundeskriminalamt – Abteilung Sicherungsgruppe –
53 Bonn-Bad Godesberg, Friedrich-Ebert-Straße 1 – Telefon: 02229 / 53001
oder jede Polizeidienststelle

Vorsicht! Diese Gewalttäter machen von der Schußwaffe rücksichtslos Gebrauch!

This was designer terrorism by celebrity terrorists, as much about radical chic as about real politics. The Red Army Faction (the formal name of the Baader-Meinhof Gang) was so well known for its preference for BMWs when stealing cars that their favourite model became popularly known in West Germany as the "Baader-Meinhof-Wagen." The urban guerillas who flourished in the 1970s and 1980s in West Germany, Italy, the United States and a few other countries in the developed world killed several hundred people and generated several hundred thousand headlines during their relatively brief moment in the limelight, but they never threatened any government anywhere. Leonard Cohen captured their naïveté and narcissism perfectly in his sardonic song "First We Take Manhattan":

> I'm guided by a signal in the heavens.
>> I'm guided by this birthmark on my skin.
> I'm guided the beauty of our weapons.
>> First we take Manhattan. Then we take Berlin.
>>> *From* Famous Blue Raincoat

If the Baader-Meinhof Gang in Germany, the Red Brigades in Italy, the Symbionese Liberation Army and the Weathermen in the United States, the Japanese Red Army and the like had any influence at all on events, it was chiefly as handy bogeymen useful to right-wing governments seeking to vilify their legitimate left-wing opponents, but even in that humble role they were not very useful. Nationalist urban guerrillas operating from a religious or ethnic minority base like the Provisional Irish Republican Army in Northern Ireland and Euskadi ta Askatasuna in Spain's Basque provinces have shown greater staying power and killed more people—"It's not the bullet with my name on it that worries me. It's the one that says 'To Whom It May Concern,'" said an anonymous Belfast resident[12]—but they could almost certainly have made more progress towards their political goals in less time by the politics of non-violent protest.

There have been two terrorist groups that did find a way to make an impact on events, however. Both of them made their mark with international operations, both had political aims that did not require the overthrow of the target governments—and both were Arab.

———

Palestine is the cement that holds the Arab world together, or it is the explosive that blows it apart.
Yasser Arafat[13]

The Palestine Liberation Organization was founded by Yasser Arafat in 1964 as an umbrella organization that would co-ordinate a strategy for the many and ideologically disparate armed groups that were forming in the refugee camps that were home to most of the Palestinians who had fled or been driven from Israel in 1948. Most Palestinians were politically quiescent for a long time, waiting for the Arab states to restore them to their homes by war, but in the aftermath of the catastrophic Arab military defeat of 1967 they recognized the hopelessness of depending on other Arabs for help. Arafat's key insight was to realize that while Palestinian armed groups stood no chance of defeating Israel and regaining their homes by force—they were even weaker than the Arab states and could do nothing except launch futile terrorist attacks—their energies might produce useful results if directed at a different goal.

Arafat and his colleagues had come to understand that their most important task was to re-brand the "refugees" as "Palestinians." So long as they were seen by non-Arabs (and even by some Arabs) as merely generic "Arab refugees," then they were only pawns in other people's games. They could theoretically be resettled—at least in the eyes of the West and in the insistent view of Israeli propaganda—anywhere in the Arab world. If they were ever to have any chance of going home, therefore, the first prior-ity must be a campaign to convince the world that there was such an identity as "Palestinian"—for merely to call people by that name is implicitly to accept that they have some legitimate claim to the land of Palestine. (Some Zionists seize upon this fact to suggest that the Palestinian identity is artificial, but it would be fairer to say that the transformation of the word "Palestinian" from purely a regional description to a genuine national identity was a result of the experience of loss and exile. It is probably also true to say that the Palestinians have come increasingly to resemble their enemy, as long-term opponents often do: longing for the lost land is a familiar theme in Jewish culture and a large part of Israeli identity.)

So what kind of campaign might convince the world that there really are Palestinians? Not an advertising campaign, certainly, but a campaign of international terrorism might do the job. Carry out shocking acts of newsworthy violence and they'll have to report them—and to explain them, they'll have to talk about Palestinians. In September 1970, the Popular Front for the Liberation of Palestine (one of the groups

A demonstration in the desert. The PFLP blows up hijacked airliners in Jordan, September 1970.

operating under the umbrella of the PLO) organized the simultaneous hijacking of four airliners, which they then flew to a desert airfield in Jordan and destroyed before the world's television cameras after the passengers had been removed. Subsequent attacks cost many lives, but this was international terrorism with a rational and achievable objective: not to bring Israel to its knees, let alone all of the West, but simply to force everybody to accept that there is a Palestinian people and that they must be active participants in the discussion of their own fate. And once that objective was achieved in the late 1980s, the PLO called off the terrorists (though some maverick small groups continued to wage a private and pointless campaign on their own).

It wasn't pretty, but it was effective—and for more than a decade the PLO essentially avoided terrorism while pursuing the goal of a negotiated peace settlement with Israel. Unfortunately, Arafat proved to be a maddeningly indecisive negotiator, and both he and his key negotiating partner, Israeli prime minister Yitzhak Rabin, found their freedom of action increasingly circumscribed by the "rejectionist" forces in their own community: Likud and the religious parties in Israel; Hamas, Islamic Jihad, and some of the smaller secular Marxist movements among the Palestinians. These parties and groups refused to contemplate the kinds of concessions (on land, and on the right of return for refugees) that would be needed for a peace settlement.

After Rabin was assassinated by a Jewish right-wing extremist in 1995, Palestinian terrorist attacks resumed, this time in Israel itself in the midst of an election campaign—but the authors of these attacks were the rising Islamist movements that flatly rejected the idea of a territorial compromise with Israel that would create a Palestinian state in only a small part of the former British mandate of Palestine. It was another terrorist operation with limited and achievable political goals, but this time directed as much at thwarting Arafat as at killing Israelis. The purpose of the Hamas and Islamic Jihad bombing campaign, which particularly targeted buses to produce high casualties, was to drive Israeli voters away from Rabin's successor Shimon Peres, who was widely expected to win easily on a sympathy vote after the assassination, and into the arms of the Likud Party's Binyamin Netanyahu, a closet rejectionist who could be counted on to stall indefinitely on peace negotiations with Arafat.

It worked: the bombs swung the election to Likud, and there was virtually no progress on a peace settlement for the next three years. The rejectionists on the two sides do not exactly collaborate to thwart the realization of a "two-state solution" where Israeli and Palestinian states live side by side between the Jordan River and the sea, but they are (in the favourite term of the older generation of Marxists) "objective allies"—and their principal tool for thwarting moves in that direction is violence.

———

The nations of infidels have all united against Muslims. . . . This is a new battle, a great battle, similar to the great battles of Islam like the conquest of Jerusalem. . . . [The Americans] come out to fight Islam in the name of fighting terrorism. These events have split the whole world into two camps, the camp of belief and the camp of disbelief.

Osama bin Laden, October 2002

Terrorism is still not a useful tool for overthrowing governments directly, but it has been developed in recent decades into a quite flexible tool for achieving other, less sweeping political objectives. An appalling but very effective example of this was the terrorist attacks carried out against the United States by al-Qaeda on September 11, 2001.

The "Islamist" project that animates al-Qaeda and its many clones and affiliates starts from the proposition that the current sorry plight of the Muslim countries is due to the fact that they are half-Westernized and lax in their observance of Islam. This has caused God to withdraw his support from his people, and it can be regained only when Muslims are once again living their faith as God truly intends it to be lived—in the Islamists' rather extreme view of how Muslims should live.

On this analysis is built a two-stage project for changing the world. In stage one, all the existing governments of the Muslim countries must be overthrown so that the Islamists can take over their places and use the power of the state to bring Muslims back to the right ways of believing and behaving. Then, once all of the world's Muslims are living properly, God will be on their side again, and it will be possible to move on to stage two and unite the whole of the Muslim world in a single, borderless super-state that will take on and overthrow the domination of the West. In the more extreme formulations, this will culminate with the conversion of the entire world to Islam.

Relatively few Muslims accept this analysis or support this project, but the proportion is greater in the Arab world than elsewhere because those are the countries where rage and despair at the current situation are strongest. As a result, there have been active Islamist revolutionary groups in most of the larger Arab countries for over a quarter-century already. Their first goal is to overthrow the existing governments and take power themselves in order to get on with stage one of the Islamist program, and their main tool is terrorism. Ever since the late 1970s countries like Egypt, Saudi Arabia, Syria, and Algeria have been the scene of numerous terrorist attacks—and unsurprisingly, the Islamists have failed to win power anywhere. Terrorism on its own does not overthrow governments: it didn't work for the Tupamaros, it didn't work for the Baader-Meinhof Gang, and there is no reason that it should work for the Islamists either.

What *can* overthrow a government (apart from a military coup, which is an unlikely way for Islamists to come to power) is a million people in the street. Then a real revolution may happen, either in the old-fashioned violent way or even in the more recent non-violent style, but first you have to get the million people out—and for Islamists they just won't come. They simply don't like or trust the Islamists enough to risk their own lives to bring them to power. The result in several Arab countries has been a long and bloody stalemate between Islamists and governments, with most people sitting out the struggle and wishing a curse on both their houses. The deadlock was already well established when Osama bin Laden founded al-Qaeda in Afghanistan at the beginning of the 1990s.

From the beginning, al-Qaeda's goal was to attack not Arab governments—that could be left to the existing Islamist movements in the various Arab countries—but to go after the West directly. Yet we must assume that al-Qaeda's militants have not forgotten that their real goal is still to bring about revolutions in the Arab and other Muslim countries that will raise Islamists to power and get stage one of the project—the reformation of their people in the true path of Islamic observance—off the ground. So how would attacking the West directly help to bring those revolutions any nearer? How will it get the mobs out in the streets?

Terrorists will never tell you their strategies, but almost certainly it was the *politique du pire* all over again, this time in an international context. Only a very ignorant person would have believed that a terrorist attack on the United States that caused three thousand deaths would make the U.S. government withdraw from the Muslim world and abandon all its client governments there, and there is no sign that bin Laden and his associates were either ignorant or stupid. Any sensible person would have known that the U.S. government's reaction was bound to be one or more large, armed incursions into the Muslim world in an attempt to stamp out the roots of the terrorism, and that it would not be too careful about who got hurt in the process. There was a reasonable chance that America's actions would alienate so many Muslims and drive them into the arms of their local Islamist organizations, especially in the Arab countries, that the people might finally revolt against their pro-Western governments and bring Islamists to power instead.

> It is going to be a great battle, and we are going to defeat the enemy. The fighting should be in the name of God only, not in the name of nationalist ideologies, nor to seek victory for the ignorant governments that rule all Arab states, including Iraq.
> *Osama bin Laden, just before the U.S. invasion of Iraq*[14]

Walking into the trap. British Commandos invading Iraq, March 2003.

If tricking the United States into marching into one or more Muslim countries was the strategic purpose of al-Qaeda's 9/11 attacks on New York and Washington, it has to be admitted that bin Laden has had a reasonable return on his investment: within twenty months, the United States had invaded and occupied two Muslim countries containing fifty million people. The images that accompanied the invasions caused great humiliation and distress to Muslims, especially in the Arab world, and the inevitable brutalities and mistakes of the subsequent military occupations of Afghanistan and Iraq produced a steady flow of further images in the same vein. The anger these caused no doubt pushed millions of Muslims into the arms of the Islamist revolutionary organizations, but at the time of writing this had not succeeded in producing any revolutions that actually brought Islamists to power in a Muslim country.

It is easy to overestimate the insight of the al-Qaeda planners and the power that their mastery of terrorist techniques confers

413

upon them. While they undoubtedly expected the United States to respond to 9/11 by invading Afghanistan to eliminate their bases there, they probably counted on a prolonged Afghan resistance of the sort that greeted the Soviet invasion of 1979. In fact, the United States rapidly conquered and subdued the entire country by making alliances with various local warlords who opposed Taliban rule and destroyed al-Qaeda's camps without ever putting very large numbers of American soldiers on the ground as targets. This did not go well with the announced American aim of bringing "democracy" to Afghanistan, but it did minimize Afghan opposition to the occupation and also American casualties (always a major political consideration given the extreme aversion to casualties back home).

The loss of al-Qaeda's bases in Afghanistan was a nuisance for the organization, no doubt, but not a disaster, as it was already a highly decentralized network with very small logistical requirements. Since it presented no further military targets of any significance after the occupation of Afghanistan, the logical thing for the United States to have done after the end of 2001 was to shift from military mode to a more traditional anti-terrorist operation: terrorists are civilians, not an army, and the appropriate tools for dealing with them are normally police forces, intelligence gathering, and security measures, not armoured brigades. Al-Qaeda's planners could not have anticipated that the United States, instead of concentrating on terrorism, would then proceed to attack Iraq as well—al-Qaeda began the process of planning 9/11 almost two years before the U.S. election of November 2000, and in any case its leaders were probably unaware of the neo-conservative agenda of those who would subsequently populate the cabinet of President George W. Bush. But it is that further invasion which may yet bring the balance sheet on the 9/11 operation into the black for al-Qaeda.

How big might the "international terrorist threat" get? So far, al-Qaeda is still operating in the same technological universe that the PLO exploited thirty years before (although with radically different political objectives). It discovered a new use for hijacked airliners that depended on the unforeseen innovation of teams of suicide hijackers, including trained pilots, but that was a one-time-only surprise and there do not appear to be dozens of further unexplored techniques of similar power lying around waiting to be tried. All al-Qaeda's subsequent attacks to date have been thoroughly conventional low-tech bombings that caused no more than a couple of hundred deaths at worst.

These attacks can have significant political effect when they are well-timed, like the bombs on Madrid commuter trains three days before the Spanish election of March 2004, which may well have swung the election outcome against the incumbent conservative government that had supported the U.S. invasion of Iraq. This is not exactly a brand-new tactic, however: two of the three major North Vietnamese offensives were staged in the U.S. election years of 1968 and 1972, and the third was timed to take advantage of the Watergate crisis of 1975. As for the possibility of terrorism with so-called weapons of mass destruction, it is neither new, nor would it utterly transform the situation. It is known that one faction of the Baader-Meinhof Gang in Germany was experimenting with biological weapons in the 1980s, and in the United States a terrorist (now believed to be an American extremist rather than an Islamist) sent letters dusted with weaponized anthrax spores in late 2001; only four or five people were killed. The Japanese sect Aum Shinrikyo actually released sarin-type nerve gas on the Tokyo subway in 1995; only twelve people were killed. The practical problem with both chemical and biological agents is dispersal; the attackers listed above would all have got better results for less effort out of nail bombs.

A nuclear weapon in terrorist hands would be a much bigger problem, of course, and has been the subject of relentless speculation and dozens of novels and films over the past twenty years. But a single nuclear weapon is a local disaster, comparable in scale to the Krakatoa volcanic explosion of 1883 or the Tokyo earthquake of 1923. We should obviously strive very hard to prevent it, but even a nuclear detonation in some unhappy city some time in the future, if it were to occur, should not stampede the world into doing what the terrorists want—and what they almost always want is an over-reaction of some sort. Terrorism is a kind of political jiu-jitsu in which very small, weak groups use the limited amounts of force that they can bring to bear in ways that trick their far more powerful opponents — usually states — into responding in ways that harm the opponent's cause and serve the terrorists' own purposes.

The world lived for forty years with the daily threat of a global nuclear holocaust that would have destroyed hundreds of cities and hundreds of millions of lives at a stroke. It can live with the distant possibility that some terrorist group some day might get possession of a single nuclear weapon and bring horror to a single city. The point is not to panic, and not to lose patience. The "war on terror" is a deeply misleading phrase, for wars can sometimes be won. It makes more sense if we regard it as a metaphor similar to the "war on crime" that is declared from time to time: it may succeed in getting the crime *rate* down, but nobody expects that all the criminals will come out with their hands up one day, after which there will be no more crime.

> I'm afraid that terrorism didn't begin on 9/11 and it will be around for a long time. I was very surprised by the announcement of a war on terrorism because terrorism has been around for thirty-five years . . . [and it] will be around while there are people with grievances. There are things we can do to improve the situation, but there will always be terrorism. One can be misled by talking about a war, as though in some way you can defeat it.
>
> *Stella Rimington, former director-general of MI5, September 2002*[15]

11

The End of War

The good news for humans is that it looks like peaceful conditions, once established, can be maintained. And if baboons can do it, why not us?

Frans de Waal, Yerkes Primate Center, Emory University

ABOUT TWENTY YEARS AGO, A DISASTER STRUCK THE FOREST Troop of baboons in Kenya. A tourist lodge was within their range, and the biggest and toughest males in the troop would regularly go to the garbage dump there to forage for food. Subordinate males, however, did not go, because there were regular fights with the Talek Troop of baboons who also patronized the dump. So when the brutal and despotic alpha males of Forest Troop all ate meat that was infected with bovine tuberculosis at the dump and promptly died, the less aggressive 50 percent of the group's males survived. And the troop's whole culture changed.

Male baboons are normally so obsessed with status that they are always on a hair-trigger for aggression—and it isn't just directed at male rivals of equal status. Lower-ranking males routinely get bullied and terrorized, and even females (who weigh half as much as males) are frequently attacked and even bitten. Chimpanzee males can be nasty and status-obsessed, but compared to baboons they are pacifists—and human beings are practically saints. You really would not want to live your life as a baboon.

Yet after the biggest, baddest males of Forest Troop all died off at once, the whole social atmosphere changed. When it was first studied by primatologists from 1979 to 1982, it was a typical, utterly vicious baboon society, but after the mass die-off of the bullies, the surviving members relaxed and began treating one another more decently. The males still fight even today—they are baboons, after all—but they are much more likely to quarrel with other males of equal rank rather than beating up on social inferiors, and they don't attack the females at all. Everybody spends much more time in grooming, huddling close together, and other friendly social behaviour, and stress levels even for the lowest-ranking individuals (as measured by hormone samples) are far lower than in other baboon troops. Most important of all, these new behaviours have become entrenched in the troop's culture; it's no longer just a bunch of gentle, wimpy individuals who were liberated from their oppressors by an accident.

Male baboons rarely live more than eighteen years: the low-status survivors of the original disaster are all gone now. All the current adult males of the Forest Troop are baboons who joined it as adolescents after 1982. (Female baboons live in their birth troop all their lives and inherit their mother's rank; males have to leave at puberty, wheedle their way into some other troop, and work their way up the social ladder from the very bottom.) By now, the range of male personalities in Forest Troop must have returned to the normal distribution, from dominance-oriented alphas to timid and submissive losers who would never normally stand a chance. But the behaviour of the troop has not returned to baboon-normal: levels of aggressiveness remain relatively low and random attacks on social inferiors and females are rare. "We don't yet understand the mechanism of transmission," said Robert Sapolsky, a biology and neurology professor at Stanford University who co-authored the 2004 report on the Forest Troop phenomenon, "but the jerky new guys are obviously learning: 'We don't do things like that around here.'"[1]

All of us primates are very malleable and adaptive in our cultures; even baboons are not shackled by their genes to the viciously aggressive norms of baboon society. Human beings are less aggressive and more cooperative than baboons or even chimpanzees, and a thousand times more flexible in our cultural arrangements. Most of us now live quite comfortably in pseudo-bands called nations that are literally a million times bigger than the bands our ancestors lived in until the rise of civilization. War is deeply embedded in our history and our culture, probably since before we were even fully human, but weaning ourselves away from it should not be a bigger mountain to climb than some of the other changes we have already made in the way we live, given the right incentives. And we have certainly been given the right incentives.

You can say more truly of the First World War than of the
Second or of the Third that if the people had known what
was going to happen, they wouldn't have done it. The
Second World War—they knew more, and they accepted it.
And the Third World War—alas, in a sense they know everything about it, they know what will happen, and they do
nothing. I don't know the answer.

A. J. P. Taylor, historian, author of The
Origins of the Second World War

When Alan Taylor talked like that in 1982, it resonated
strongly with a generation that had spent its life waiting for World
War III to happen. Now, nobody talks like that: the collapse of the
Soviet Union and the end of the Cold War convinced most people
that World War III isn't ever going to happen, as if there were no
systemic causes and the only reason that it ever might have happened was the wicked Soviets. During the 1990s people fretted
about the savage wars of ethnic cleansing that ensued in various
parts of the old Communist world and the equally terrible ethnic
wars of Africa, and latterly they worry about terrorism, too, but the
apocalyptic edge has gone. World War III has apparently been
cancelled. The little wars that still happen don't really threaten the
developed countries and can be dealt with or not as the moral
mood of the moment dictates. The only people who remember
that it was the structure of the international system itself, not just
bad regimes, that produced the cycle of great-power wars we now
call world wars, are some of the professionals who work within or
study the system—quite a few diplomats and professional soldiers,
some statesmen, and a few historians.

Our current holiday from history, dating from the end of the
Cold War, has been a splendid opportunity to make some progress
on global governance. None of the great powers sees any of the
others as a dangerous enemy at the moment, and the only international violence that threatens the developed countries is the
occasional bit of terrorism. The opportunity wasn't entirely wasted,
either. The U.S.-led United Nations campaign to expel the Iraqi
invaders from occupied Kuwait in 1991 was the first time that UN

rules against aggression had been enforced by military action and with the full legal authority of the Security Council since the Korean war forty years before. In response to the ethnic wars of the 1990s, the UN rules that protect the absolute sovereignty of independent states were bent several times to allow international military interventions to prevent genocides (although the worst case, Rwanda/eastern Congo, was ignored). But little was done to increase the authority of the Security Council and entrench the habit of multilateralism, for the unilateralist current was already running strongly in the United States, now the sole global superpower.

A certain amount of hubris was to be expected after the apparent victory of the United States in the Cold War, and the glorification of national military power had already become part of the political culture in Washington. The two fused in a project for benevolent American hegemony commonly called "pax americana" whose neo-conservative proponents ended up controlling U.S. military and foreign policy in the administration of President George W. Bush in 2001. The Bush administration launched a sustained assault on multilateral institutions, abandoning the Anti-Ballistic Missile treaty, attempting to sabotage the International Criminal Court, rejecting long-negotiated amendments that sought to make the conventions against chemical and biological weapons more enforceable, and using the terrorist attacks of 11 September 2001 as the pretext for an invasion of Iraq in 2003 that was also a deliberate attack on the authority of the Security Council. It is not yet clear how much damage the neo-conservative adventure has done to the United Nations, but any progress made in the nineties, particularly with regard to trust among the great powers, has probably already been lost. If the United States returns to its traditional commitment to multilateral institutions fairly soon, before other states also start to abandon them, then the UN will emerge from this episode basically intact, but much time has been wasted and the holiday from history may be almost over. Harsher times are coming.

———

Three great changes are due to arrive in the next decades that could tip the international system back into the old anarchy: the environmental challenge of climate change, the political challenge of the rise of new great powers, and the technological challenge of nuclear proliferation. In combination—and they will probably arrive more or less together—they will put the ramshackle system we have designed to keep the peace in the world under acute stress. It will be very difficult to get through all these changes without a catastrophic war.

Over the next two or three generations, the full implications of what we have done in the past two centuries—increasing the human population sixfold and industrializing most of the planet at the same time—will be working their way through the system, and the consequences will not be small. The average human being in the early twenty-first century has at least five times the impact on the environment of the average person in 1800, in intensive land use for meat production, increased per capita water consumption for domestic and industrial purposes, increased consumption of raw materials, and increased production of waste. (The lighter environmental footprint of the global poor is included in the average.) So six times the population multiplied by five times the per capita environmental impact gives a total human pressure on the environment that is now *thirty* times greater than it was only two hundred years ago.

That is bound to have major global effects, and though we cannot predict exactly what they will be or when they will hit, we can be sure that most of them will be unpleasant. Global climate change; the decline of the world's fisheries; freshwater resources failing to meet demand in many regions; forests shrinking and fertile topsoil eroding; ten thousand new chemical and biochemical substances released into the environment with largely unknown consequences; mega-cities drowning in old and new forms of pollution and generating new diseases—you can argue about the details of any of these phenomena, but major regional and system-wide disruptions are clearly on their way. Some of them will have grave political implications, including a very high potential for conflict.

At the same time, the international system over the next twenty or thirty years must adjust to the arrival of new great powers and the relative decline of some of the existing powers. By the year 2040, according to a long-range economic forecast made by investment bankers Goldman Sachs in late 2003, China will be the world's largest economy, followed closely by the United States (which may still be China's equal in technological innovation) and at a not very great distance by India. The second tier of powers, quite a long way behind, will be Brazil, Russia, and Japan. Bringing up the rear will be the five other big industrial economies of the West—Britain, Germany, France, Canada, and Italy.[2] Though the Goldman Sachs study does not go into it, even at this level there will be new entrants into the major-power stakes. Mexico, South Africa, Pakistan, and Indonesia will probably be in the same range of GDP as the five lesser Western powers by 2040, as will Korea (especially if it is reunited by then) and perhaps Turkey and Thailand.

These forthcoming changes in the international system are practically graven in stone. One or two countries might not live up to expectations, and details of timing are obviously open to change: another outbreak of political madness like the Great Leap Forward or the Cultural Revolution could cost China ten years of growth and delay its arrival to the top of the heap until 2050, or the rapid spread of AIDS in India could cut a percentage point or more off that country's high economic growth rate. But even that sort of disaster would only slow the process of transformation a bit, not change its broad outlines or halt it permanently. What guarantees China and India an economic growth rate more than twice as high as that of the United States over the coming years is not the details of the political system or the economic strategy, but the availability of large amounts of cheap and easily trainable labour plus the fact that the middle rungs of the economic ladder— between $1,000 and $5,000 per capita annual income, say—can be scaled without the need for major social change. China and India are virtually guaranteed to become the first and third economic powers in the world in the next generation.

There is nothing surprising about this. China and the Indian subcontinent were the two largest concentrations of economic activity in the world before the European countries stole a technological march on the rest of the world four or five centuries ago, and it's only natural that they should regain their leading positions now that the technological gaps are closing. The ticket to superpower status in the world of 2040 will be brutally simple: you must be a country of subcontinental scale with a population near to or over half a billion people. Only three candidates will meet that criterion: America, China, and India. The jostling crowd of new and old lesser powers at the bottom of the heap may cause a certain amount of turbulence in the system, but what could really send it spinning out of control is the change of rankings at the top.

The last time the world went through such an upheaval in the ranking of the great powers was at the end of the nineteenth century. As late as 1850 Britain was still the sole and undisputed global superpower, with almost half of the entire world's manufacturing capacity located on British soil. By 1890 the United States had already overtaken Britain in industrial production and Germany was catching up fast. Other countries like Russia and Japan were starting to follow the same trajectory of rapid industrial development, while France, once the dominant European power, was slowly and resentfully drifting down the league tables. Most other kinds of power are mainly a function of economic power, so the existing international system, built on the assumption of overwhelming British dominance ("pax britannica"), was going to have to adjust to the new realities.

Unfortunately, the nineteenth-century system proved unable to make the necessary adjustments peacefully. Some of the rising powers were impatient and pushed too hard, the declining powers resisted their gradual loss of status, and the whole system ultimately tumbled into the calamity of World War I—which was far more about the pecking order of the great powers than it was about specific quarrels between them. Nothing surprising about that, either: war was the normal way that the international system adjusted to accommodate the demands of rising powers at the expense of declining ones. But we definitely do not want to go through that again with twenty-first century weapons.

To complicate matters further, those weapons—and particularly the nuclear weapons—are proliferating into the hands of more and more countries. Between 1945 and 1964, the "Permanent Five" great powers on the UN Security Council, the United States, the Soviet Union, Britain, France, and China, all tested their first nuclear weapons, and one other country, Israel, secretly developed them without openly testing them. These six countries all now possess many hundreds or thousands of nuclear (and in most cases thermonuclear) warheads, but there was a lengthy delay before other nuclear weapons powers emerged.

India tested its first "peaceful nuclear explosive" in 1974, ostensibly for civil engineering projects but really to create a deterrent against Chinese nuclear weapons (the two countries had fought a brief border war in 1962). Pakistan, which had fought and lost three wars with India in the previous quarter-century, felt obliged to match Indian nuclear weapons—Prime Minister Zulfikar Ali Bhutto declared that Pakistanis would "eat grass," if necessary, to restore the balance between the two countries—and embarked on its own secret nuclear program. As Soviet and Cuban troops began showing up in "confrontation" countries to the north, the apartheid South African regime began developing nuclear weapons. Argentina and Brazil, under their respective military regimes, started working on them as well, theoretically for use on each other, but in reality mostly just as badges of national prowess. At some point in the late 1970s or 1980s, Iraq, Iran, and North Korea also set up nuclear weapons programs.

The list of the countries that didn't go nuclear is equally instructive. Countries like Canada, Italy, and Australia could have developed nuclear weapons within two years from the word "go" at any time since the early 1950s, but chose to rely instead on the American nuclear umbrella because they believed that further proliferation would set a dangerous example to the world. Japan and the Federal Republic of Germany essentially came to the same conclusion. They would have faced greater political obstacles to developing nuclear weapons because of World War II, but they would have done so anyway, regardless of legal and political constraints, if they had really felt the need. They, too, were dissuaded by the U.S. nuclear guarantee, as were Taiwan and South Korea. The Swiss and the Swedes, who were also easily able to develop nuclear weapons in a year or two, held occasional debates on whether they were necessary to defend their neutrality, but always decided against them. The point is that all the countries that decided to go nuclear, with the exception of the South American ones, faced real enemies already armed with nuclear weapons whom they wished to deter. Proliferation happens for rational reasons.

It didn't work out as badly as it might have done. South Africa did build half a dozen nuclear weapons, but dismantled them again and closed its whole program down after the end of apartheid in 1994. Brazil and Argentina both shut down their nuclear weapons programs without ever building an actual bomb after the fall of the generals. Iraq, after an initial setback caused by the Israeli bombing of its Osirak nuclear reactor in 1981, made considerable progress on nuclear weapons in the later 1980s, only to have its entire program comprehensively dismantled by United Nations inspectors after its defeat in the Gulf War of 1991. American inspectors seeking evidence of a revived nuclear weapons program after the U.S. invasion of Iraq in 2003 found nothing at all.

But the North Korean regime, truthfully or not, claims to have developed nuclear weapons, partly to deter an American attack and partly in the hope of getting bribed handsomely to relinquish them. Iran almost certainly does have a secret nuclear weapons program: Israel regards Iran as its most dangerous remaining enemy, and almost any Iranian government would be urgently seeking nuclear weapons as a deterrent to the current Israeli ability to launch a nuclear strike against Iran with impunity. India and Pakistan came out into the open in 1998 with rival series of nuclear tests and are now immersed in a 1950s-style "use 'em or lose 'em" nuclear confrontation that is particularly self-defeating from the Indian perspective. Before it forced Pakistan into a nuclear arms race, India's sevenfold population advantage and far larger industrial base guaranteed it victory in any conventional war with Pakistan, but nuclear weapons are the great equalizer: now India and Pakistan are equally vulnerable to nuclear strikes.

In absolute terms, the world's record on nuclear proliferation over the past forty years is not that bad. Only two more countries are known for certain to have nuclear weapons, for a total of eight plus two possibles. But as the number of those powers approaches double figures, the likelihood that one of them will use nuclear weapons sooner or later grows, particularly because the countries that seek them are mostly those that anticipate military confrontations. An equal or even greater danger is the constant pressure within the U.S. military-industrial complex to build smaller and more "usable" nuclear weapons for purposes so obviously marginal to any serious strategy—penetrating deep into the earth to destroy hardened bunkers, for example—that the naked careerism of all those involved is impossible to ignore. But newly nuclear neighbours and a superpower openly discussing nuclear-weapons use against non-nuclear states provide powerful incentives for further countries to consider developing their own nuclear weapons.

The "firebreak" against actual nuclear weapons use that we began building after Hiroshima and Nagasaki has held for well over half a century now, and it has created a strong presumption among the existing nuclear weapons powers that they should not and will not be used. It is hard to predict what the impact of crossing that firebreak would be, but it would be much better not to find out.

Just the proliferation of nuclear weapons alone is a major challenge to the stability of the system. So are the coming crises, mostly environmental in origin, which will hit some countries much harder than others and may drive some to desperation. Add in the huge impending shifts in the great-power system, and it will be hard to keep things under control. With good luck and good management, we may be able to ride out the next half-century without the first-magnitude catastrophe of a global nuclear war, but the potential certainly exists for a major dieback of human population.

We cannot command the good luck, but good management is something we can choose to provide. It depends above all on preserving and extending the multilateral system that we have been building (with many interruptions and failures) since the end of World War II. The rising powers must be absorbed into a system that emphasizes cooperation and makes room for them, rather than one that deals in confrontation and raw military power. If they are obliged to play the traditional great-power game of winners and losers, then history will repeat itself and everybody loses.

Our hopes for mitigating the severity of the coming environmental crises also depend on early and concerted global action of a sort that can happen only in a basically cooperative international system. When the great powers are locked into a military confrontation, there is simply not enough spare attention, let alone enough trust, to make deals on those issues. Concerns about the environment began to grow forty years ago, for example, but apart from the urgent deal on the ozone hole, there were no international agreements that addressed those concerns until after the end of the Cold War. So the highest priority at the moment is to keep the multilateral approach alive and avoid a drift back into alliance systems and arms races. And there is no point in dreaming that we can leap straight into some never-land of world government and universal brotherhood; we will have to confront these challenges and solve the problem of war within the context of the existing state system.

———

We must get the modern national state before it gets us.
Dwight MacDonald, 1945[3]

Justice without force is a myth.
Blaise Pascal

The solution to the state of international anarchy that compels every state to arm itself for war was so obvious that it arose almost spontaneously in the aftermath of the first total war in 1918. The wars by which independent states had always settled their quarrels in the past had grown so monstrously destructive that some alternative system had to be devised, and that could only be a pooling of sovereignty, at least in matters concerning war and peace, by all the states of the world. So the victors of World War I promptly created the League of Nations.

But the solution was as difficult in practice as it was simple in concept. Great nations with long traditions of absolute independence and deep-rooted suspicions of their neighbours do not easily abandon all their habits just because they have created some new institution that will allegedly take care of their security problems. The idea that all the nations of the world will band together to deter or punish aggression by some maverick country is fine in principle, but who defines the aggressor, and who pays the cost in money and lives that may be needed to make him stop?

More specifically, every member of the League of Nations was well aware that if the organization somehow acquired the ability to act in a concerted and effective fashion, it could end up being used against them. No major government was willing to give the League of Nations any real power in practice, and so they got World War II instead. That war was so bad that the victors made a second attempt in 1945 to create an international organization that really could prevent war. They were badly frightened people, and so the United Nations was a much more radical initiative than the League of Nations. They literally changed international law and made war illegal.

This had already been done symbolically once before, in the Kellogg-Briand Pact of 1928, an initiative by U.S. president Calvin Coolidge's secretary of state, Frank B. Kellogg, in which all the major powers (except the Soviet Union, which most of them weren't speaking to) agreed to renounce war as an instrument of national policy. There were no mechanisms for enforcing the new rule, so everybody was happy to sign, and it made no difference at all to the approach of World War II—but it wasn't a waste of time, either, for now the idea that war could be banned was out in the marketplace and the great powers had already agreed to it in principle. Apparently futile gestures like the Kellogg-Briand Pact are one of the main ways that radical new ideas infiltrate into the system and gain wider acceptance.

When they sat down to negotiate the Charter of the United Nations in San Francisco in 1945, therefore, the winners of World

War II could start by combining the total renunciation of war as a tool of policy that was the legacy of the Kellogg-Briand Pact with the policing and enforcement role of the great powers that had been the core of the League of Nations, and come up with something radically new: a theoretically enforceable ban on war. The UN charter forbids the use of force against another country except in strict self-defence or in obedience to the Security Council's orders—and those orders would be issued only in order to stop some country that was breaking the UN rules by attacking some other UN member. So there it was: from the bad old days to a new world of law where war was banned in a single breathtaking leap.

Not really. Everybody understood that the creation of the United Nations was the launch of a hundred-year project. The states of the world have fought wars for many thousands of years. War permeates all our institutions, our cultures, even our mentality. The survivors of the worst war in history could rationally agree that war had now become lethal and must be abolished, but they were well aware that all of that history and all those reflexes were not going to vanish overnight. They weren't the least bit naive about what they were trying to do, and the proof of that is the brutal realism they brought to the job of writing the rules for enforcement.

Normal international treaties always keep up the pretense that all sovereign states are equal; the UN rules simply make all five victorious great powers of 1945 permanent members of the Security Council, while other countries must rotate through on two-year terms. The great powers must convince enough of the temporary members that there has been a breach of the peace to win a majority vote in the fifteen-member Security Council before they can order military action against a country accused of aggression—but any one of the great powers can veto action even if the majority in favour is fourteen-to-one. Nobody took the League of Nations or the Kellogg-Briand Pact seriously enough to offend diplomatic propriety by making rules that frankly acknowledged that the great powers are more equal than the others, but the founders of the UN really meant it to work.

It's never been hard to persuade small and middle-sized countries to sign up for a project to ban war: they had little to gain by war, and a great deal to lose if the big powers decided to expand at their expense. Getting the great powers to sign up to the same rules was a lot harder, because they were being asked to give up a tool, military power, that often let them get their way in the world. They understood that in another great-power war they, too, were likely to be destroyed, and that changing the international rules was therefore also in their own long-term self-interest—otherwise they wouldn't have been willing to contemplate an organization like the United Nations at all—but they were being asked to give up a bird in the hand for one in the bush.

There had to be a deal to get them over this hurdle, and it was the device of the veto—a get-out-of-jail-free card that allowed each great power to prevent the UN ever from taking action against it, and in effect exempted them all from the ordinary functioning of the new international law. Other countries had to obey it: if the Security Council agreed that their actions represented a danger to peace, they could face enforcement by an international army operating under the UN flag. It happened to North Korea in 1950, and to Iraq in 1990. The great powers were expected to obey the law, too, and might face heavy moral pressure if they didn't, but they could never be brought to book for their actions; they could simply veto any Security Council resolution that condemned them.

And despite all that, it still didn't work. Realistic though the founders of the UN were, they could not guard against the high probability that the great powers would fail to agree among themselves and thus cripple the organization's work. That's exactly what happened, with the five permanent members of the Security Council dividing into two hostile military blocs in just a few years, as victorious nations often do after a great war. As the largest surviving military powers in the world, they automatically represent the greatest potential threats to each other's security.

> If the permanent members [of the Security Council] had stuck together as the wartime alliance in peacetime, they would have constituted, for better or worse, a very genuine, powerful authority in the world . . . but of course, there was never any chance of that. . . .

It's going to be a very long time before governments are prepared in fact to submit to limitations on their national policies by an international body. Of course, in theory they've all said they would do that in the Charter; and they're all for everybody else doing it—but when it gets to a particular government having to do that, it's not so easy. Not least because you've got a tremendous domestic opposition to it, very often.

Brian Urquhart, former under secretary-general, United Nations

It would be futile and depressing to catalogue the many failures of the United Nations, but it would also be misleading. The implication would be that this was an enterprise that should have succeeded from the start and has instead failed irrevocably. On the contrary; it was bound to be a relative failure at the outset, and that is no reason to despair. It was always going to be hard to persuade sovereign governments whose institutions have served them and their predecessors well for ten thousand years to surrender power to an untried world authority that might then make decisions that were against their particular interests. Progress will necessarily be measured in small steps even over a period of decades.

In the words of the traditional Irish directions to a lost traveller: "If that's where you want to get to, sir, I wouldn't start from here." But here is where we must start from, for it is states that run the world. There is no point in yearning for some universal Gandhi who could change the human heart and release us from our bondage to considerations of national interest and power. We do not behave as we do for stupid or paltry reasons: those considerations really matter. We can no longer afford to settle our conflicts by war, but there is no simple solution to the problem of war that magically bypasses the existing structure of power in the world.

That structure exists to defend the many conflicting interests of the multitude of separate human communities in the world. It is true that the present nature of the international system, based on heavily armed and jealously independent states, often exaggerates the element of conflict in relations between these communities and sometimes even creates perceptions of conflict and threat where genuine interests are not at stake, but the system does reflect an underlying reality. Namely, we cannot all get all we want, and some method must exist to decide who gets what. That is why neighbouring states have lived in a perpetual state of potential war, just as neighbouring hunter-gatherer bands did twenty thousand years ago.

If we now must abandon war as a method of settling our disputes and devise an alternative, it can be done only with the full cooperation of the world's governments. That means it certainly will be a monumentally difficult and lengthy task, but it is the only relevant one. It is the absolute independence of national governments that makes war possible, but the short-term disadvantages that might ensue from a surrender of sovereignty to the United Nations have deterred every national government from making any serious gesture in that direction. Mistrust reigns everywhere, and no nation will allow even the least of its interests to be decided upon by a collection of foreigners. Even the majority of states that are more or less satisfied with their borders and their status in the world would face great internal opposition from nationalist elements if they were to consider even a limited transfer of sovereignty to the United Nations.

Nobody is thinking of a "world government" that would collect the garbage and decide on local speed limits, but the nationalists of all countries are quite right to worry about what a powerful United Nations might mean. The United Nations was created to end war—"not to bring mankind to Heaven, but to save it from Hell," in Dag Hammarskjöld's words—and its founders were fully aware that in order to do that it had to be able to guarantee each country's safety from attack by its neighbours, and to make decisions on international disputes *and enforce them.* Neither order nor justice can be imposed without at least the threat of superior force, if not its actual use, so a functional United Nations would need to have powerful armed forces under its own command. (Indeed, the UN Charter makes provisions for member countries to contribute contingents to just such an armed force.)

That is why the United Nations has never worked as designed: a truly effective United Nations would have the ability to coerce national governments, so naturally they refuse to give it the powers it would need to do so. They all know what they must do to end international war, have known it since 1945 at the latest, but are not yet willing to do it. The possibility of their own interests being damaged somewhere down the line by the decisions of a United Nations grown too powerful to resist is so great a deterrent that they prefer to go on living with the risk of war. (That is, until the risk of some particular war involving them grows too great, or a war in which they are directly involved goes badly wrong. Then national governments are very glad to appeal to the United Nations' fictitious authority to get themselves off the hook.)

> People often wonder why it is that one continues to batter away here in the UN. In the first place, it's extremely interesting. If you want to watch the human tragicomedy unfold, this is a terrific front-row seat, and every now and then you can do something about it. You can stop somebody from being executed, you can prevent somewhere from being destroyed. It's a drop in the bucket, but . . . you can sometimes control a conflict—and the most important thing is to provide a place where the nuclear powers can get out of their confrontations. . . . As Hammarskjöld once said, while none of us are ever going to see the world order we dream of appear in our lifetime, nonetheless the effort to build that order is the difference between anarchy and a tolerable degree of chaos.
>
> *Brian Urquhart*

The United Nations as presently constituted is certainly no place for idealists, but they would feel even more uncomfortable in a United Nations that actually worked as was originally intended. It is an association of poachers turned gamekeepers, not an assembly of saints. One of the implications of a powerful United Nations that is rarely discussed by its advocates (for obvious reasons) is that a world authority founded on the collaboration of national governments would inevitably try to freeze the existing political dispensation in the world in the interests of its members, or at least drastically slow down the rate of change. As a result, national and ethnic communities that do not already have states of their own would lose almost all chance of getting them in the future, simply because they didn't make it under the wire in time. If the established sovereign states of the world had created some equivalent of the United Nations with real power in the mid-eighteenth century—a mutual protection association that guaranteed their territories—the United States might never have won its independence from Britain. If they did it today, Tibetans, Kurds, and Basques might as well forget their hopes of ever achieving it.

Even as presently constituted, the United Nations places legitimacy above all other considerations. It continued to recognize the Khmer Rouge as the legitimate government of Cambodia after the Vietnamese invasion of 1979, despite its horrific record of genocide against its own citizens, because it had been displaced by the illegal method of foreign invasion. Eventually a deal was done that acknowledged the new reality in Cambodia, but the more power the United Nations is granted by its members, the more it will have to reciprocate by acting to defend their existing interests and possessions.

The consequences would be quite oppressive to many people and some would rebel. Guerrilla wars, terrorism, and other forms of armed protest against the existing distribution of power would not only continue, but might well increase. The most that could be expected, even from a United Nations with teeth, for a century or so, is an end to large-scale international war. Internal conflict would not vanish from the world even if all legitimate governments signed their armed forces over to the United Nations tomorrow.

There is a further, even more distasteful, implication to a United Nations with real power: it would not make its decisions according to some impartial standard of justice. There is no impartial concept of justice to which all of mankind would subscribe and, in any case, it is not "mankind" that makes decisions at the United Nations, but governments with their own national interests to protect. To envision how a functioning world authority might reach its decisions, at least in its first century or so, begin with the arrogant promotion of self-interest by the great powers that would continue to dominate UN decision-making and add in the crass expediency masked as principle that characterizes the shifting coalitions among the lesser powers in the present General Assembly. It would be an intensely *political* process. The decisions it produced would be kept within reasonable bounds only by the overriding shared recognition that the organization must never act in a way so damaging to the interest of any major member or group of members that it forced them into total defiance, and so destroyed the fundamental consensus that keeps war at bay.

There is nothing shocking about this. National politics in every country operates with the same combination: a little bit of principle, a lot of power, and a final constraint on the ruthless exercise of that power based on the need to preserve the consensus on which the nation is founded and to avoid civil war. In an international organization whose members represent such radically different traditions, interests, and levels of development, the proportion of principle to power is bound to be even lower. It's a pity that there is no practical alternative to the United Nations, because otherwise nobody would dream of creating the kind of cumbersome and meddlesome monster that a powerful world authority will probably prove to be.

> There are two possibilities, it seems to me. The first one is that we run into another global disaster, which doubtless, if there's anything left, will finally change people's minds about the benefits of unlimited national sovereignty. The second alternative is something much more gradual and slower; which is that we convince governments that, just as they have given up sovereignty in certain specialized fields—for example, radio frequencies or postal systems or something like that—that they have to do this also in the political field.
> *Brian Urquhart*

We consent to all the impositions and inconveniences of a distant and unwieldy government apparatus at the national level because, in the final analysis, its benefits outweigh its costs. For all its drawbacks, it provides us with civil peace, a measure of protection from the rival ambitions of other national communities, and a framework for large-scale cooperation in pursuing whatever goals we set ourselves as a national society. All the same arguments theoretically operate with equal strength in favour of an international authority, but there is not widespread popular support for the surrender of sovereignty to the United Nations in any major country in the world. Most people are reluctant to accept that war and national sovereignty are indissolubly linked, and that to be rid of one they must also relinquish much of the other. The belief in the need for complete national independence is very strong in most people.

Curiously (or maybe not so curiously), that belief tends to be less strong in governments than in the people they govern. The United Nations was not founded by popular demand. It was created by *governments* who were terrified of the path they were on and who could not afford to ignore the grim realities of the situation. The people who actually have the responsibility for running foreign policy in most countries, and especially in the great powers, know that the present international system is in potentially terminal trouble, and many of them have drawn the necessary conclusion.

It goes against the grain to speak well of diplomats, but if they didn't have to worry about the enormous domestic political resistance to any surrender of sovereignty, the foreign policy professionals in almost every country (without regard to ideology) would immediately make the minimum concessions necessary to create a functioning world authority, because they understand the alternative. Many of the more reflective military professionals would concur for the same reason. But it is politicians who are in charge of states, and even if they understand the realities of the situation themselves (which many of them do not, for their backgrounds and their primary concerns are usually in domestic issues, not international affairs), politicians cannot afford to get too far ahead of the people they lead. Nevertheless, progress has been made.

If the abolition of great-power war and the establishment of international law is a hundred-year project, then we are running a bit behind schedule but we have made substantial progress. We have not had World War III, and that is thanks at least in part to the United Nations, which provided the great powers with an excuse to back off from several of their most dangerous confrontations without losing too much face. The rule that no border may be changed by force has been observed, in the sense that no change achieved by force has gained international recognition, and in at least one case, East Timor, such a change has subsequently been reversed under UN auspices. The wars between middle-sized powers that have broken out from time to time—Arab-Israeli wars and Indo-Pakistani wars, mostly—seldom lasted more than a month, because the UN's offers of ceasefires and peacekeeping troops provided a quick way out for the losing side.

There have also been spectacular failures, like the eight-year war between Iraq and Iran in the 1980s, which was deliberately prolonged by American and Russian aid to Saddam Hussein in the hope that he would be able to destroy the revolutionary Islamic regime in Iran. Great-power interventions in Third World countries like the Soviet invasion of Afghanistan in 1979 and the U.S. invasion of Iraq in 2003 were illegal but could not be dealt with by the UN because of the veto system. (It was always clear that the great powers would be the last countries to accept the new international rules as binding on themselves.) Most of the deaths in war in the past thirty years have been in internal wars, mainly in Africa, that the UN has neither the legal standing nor the political incentive to get involved in.

If you were to assess the progress that has been made since 1945 from the perspective of that terrifying time, the glass would look at least half-full. The enormous growth of international organizations since 1945, and especially the survival of the United Nations as a permanent forum where the world's states are committed to avoiding war (and often succeed), have already created a context new to history. The present political fragmentation of the world into more than 150 stubbornly independent territorial units will doubtless persist for some time, but it is already becoming an anachronism, for in every other context, from commerce, technology, and the mass media to fashions in ideology, music, and marriage, the outlines of a single global culture (with wide local variations) are visibly taking shape.

———

There is a serious question as to whether civilization was a wise experiment. Human beings were doing quite nicely without it, compared to other large land animal species, and seemed set for a successful run of some millions of years. Here we are, only ten thousand years into the experiment, facing a crisis of vast proportions that we can now see was inevitable once we took the civilized road. War and the state were centrally important elements in our strategy for gaining more control over our environment, but they have brought us inescapably to our present dilemma, which involves the potential extinction of the human species.

> [The prospect of a nuclear winter] raises the stakes of nuclear war enormously. . . . A nuclear war imperils all our descendants, for as long as there will be humans. Even if the population remains static . . . over a typical time period for the biological evolution of a successful species (roughly ten million years), we are talking about some 500 trillion people yet to come. By this criterion, the stakes are one million times greater for extinction than for the more modest nuclear wars that kill "only" hundreds of millions of people.
> *Carl Sagan*[3]

> Nature has no principles; she furnishes us with no reason to believe that human life is to be respected—or any particular species either: just look what happened to the ammonites and pterodactyls.
> *Victor Hugo*

If the laws of physics were such that nuclear fission was not possible, we would still not be much better off at this stage of our history. Instead of nuclear weapons, we would have developed alternative weapons of mass destruction, probably of various chemical and biological varieties, in order to produce much the same dilemma. We would not be facing the final abyss of a nuclear winter, perhaps, but the scale of destructiveness that can be achieved with scientific weaponry would not diminish much. At bottom, the problem of war is political, but modern scientific weaponry has turned it from a bearable affliction into a potentially terminal crisis. And science and technology have not yet ceased to advance; the day could come — if we last long enough — when we look back on the era of nuclear weapons with nostalgia.

High intelligence, at least in the form represented by the human species, may prove not to be an evolutionary trait favourable to survival. The potentially fatal flaw is that our intelligence tends to produce technological and social change at a rate faster than our institutions and emotions can cope with — and this tendency becomes more pronounced the deeper we get into the experiment of civilization, because innovation is cumulative and the rate of change accelerates. We therefore find ourselves continually trying to accommodate new realities within inappropriate existing institutions, and trying to think about those new realities in traditional but sometimes dangerously irrelevant terms.

It is very likely that we began our career as a rising young species by exterminating our nearest relatives, the Neanderthals, and it is entirely possible we will end it by exterminating ourselves, but the universe is not in the business of dealing out poetic justice. The fact that we have always had war as part of our culture does not mean that we are doomed always to fight wars. There are other aspects of our behavioural repertoire that are more encouraging. Consider, for example, the fact that we are in the process of reclaiming our old heritage of egalitarianism.

The most important behavioural difference between pre-civilized human beings and most other social primates was the absence of a fixed hierarchy. The humans, indeed, were so determined to preserve the absolute equality of every adult male that they had well-established social strategies for bringing down those who got too big for their boots. Some individuals in a hunter-gatherer band would inevitably be more influential and more eloquent than others, but they had no authority beyond that of persuasion: every adult male, and in some cultures every adult of either sex, had an equal right to participate in the band's decision-making process. Decisions were reached by prolonged discussion in which each band member could speak as long and as often as they wished, and consensus was often achieved only by exhaustion. Even then, an individual who dissented could just walk away from the band.

Egalitarian values have been so universal among hunter-gatherer groups studied by anthropologists that they are presumed to have been universal among our more distant ancestors as well. The likeliest explanation for this divergence from the primate norm is that the requirements of raising big-brained proto-human young with long dependent childhoods required more male input. This favoured stronger male-female bonds and a diversion of male energies and loyalty from the old male pecking order to the newly invented family. But whatever the reason, human beings lived as equals for thousands of generations—and then we dropped it practically overnight when we invented civilization.

Everywhere, the move into the mass societies was accompanied by a social revolution: their people ended up living in rigid hierarchies as steep as the pyramids they built, with a god-king at the top and peasants and slaves at the bottom. The hierarchies were functionally necessary, because these new mass societies simply could not go on making decisions in the old egalitarian way any more. A million people could not sit around the fire and debate the decision, or even (in the absence of mass media of any kind) know what the issue to be decided was. The problem of numbers meant that egalitarianism had to go: orders had to flow down from the top, and everybody at the bottom had to be forced to obey.

Since human beings also had access to their older primate heritage of exactly that sort of hierarchy, they were easily able to shift into that mode of behaviour (with some prodding from local bullies who aspired to be god-kings). Not surprisingly, all these new mass societies were heavily militarized, and though the reason given was usually some foreign threat, it's hard to avoid the suspicion that the military were also there to preserve the hierarchy. But what is interesting and hopeful is that human beings did not really surrender themselves to the tyrannies and internalize their monkey-king values.

Everywhere the old values of fairness and equality were preserved in the way people behaved among their small social circle of family and friends. When the new populist religions of the mass civilizations arose between 1,500 and 2,500 years ago, they embodied precisely those values, not those of the state. Down the thousands of years of legally enforced inequality and systematic oppression when the mass societies treated most people like worker ants, human beings never forgot who they really were — and when the new technologies of mass communications eventually began to create the possibility that millions of people could make collective decisions for themselves, they immediately demanded their equality back.

Hobbes and Rousseau barely saw the start of it. By the late eighteenth century, in a few rich and technologically advanced countries, the printing press and mass literacy were giving around half the population access to a running debate about the nature and purposes of society, and it became possible to imagine a society of millions of equals where decisions were made in common — a mass democracy. From the imagining to the doing was only a short step, and the revolutions began. And although the people of the eighteenth century knew little about the human past and nothing about the long pre-human past, the very word they coined, "revolution," embodied their conviction that they were "turning back" to the true egalitarian values of humankind.

It took over two centuries, with many false starts and lengthy detours, for most of the West to democratize itself, and for most of that time almost everybody believed that what they were seeing was a purely Western cultural phenomenon rooted in Christian and/or classical Greco-Roman values. This mistake lives on today in the belief that the West has a mission to "bring" democracy to the rest of the world, as if they would never get it on their own, but the reason for the early Western monopoly on democracy was purely technological, not cultural.

Few non-Western societies had broad access to mass media in their own language until after World War II, when decolonization began, so the conditions for a democratic transformation simply did not exist in what was then called the Third World. Once they did arise, it was less than a generation before the democratic revolutions began there too. The new democrats even figured out how to do their revolutions non-violently, unlike their Western predecessors: from the Philippines, Thailand, South Korea, and Bangladesh in the later 1980s to Tiananmen Square, the Berlin Wall, and the end of the Soviet Union at the turn of the decade, and on to the fall of apartheid in South Africa in 1994, the Indonesian revolution of 1998, and the Georgian revolution of 2003, people of every culture and religion showed that they wanted democracy, and that they could get it (in most cases) without violence.

We are in the midst of a large and seemingly irreversible transformation, made possible by the new technology of mass communications, in which human beings are reclaiming their ancient egalitarian heritage. The surprisingly frequent success of non-violent techniques against repressive regimes seems also to be related to mass communications: tyrants are often deterred from using massive force against unarmed people when the whole world is watching them. And although becoming democratic ought not logically make people more peaceful—egalitarian hunter-gatherers were not exactly peaceful, after all—it seems to have that effect nevertheless: democratic countries continue to fight wars, but they almost never fight *each other*.

We will have to go on working at the institutions, or else our more egalitarian, more connected world could still be toppled back into war by just a few countries that insisted on playing the old games, but we do seem to have some profound social and philosophical changes helping us along. There is, in fact, a slow but quite perceptible revolution in human consciousness taking place: the last of the great redefinitions of humanity.

At all times in our history we have run our affairs on the assumption that there is a special category of people (our lot) whom we regard as full human beings, having rights and duties approximately equal to our own, and whom we ought not to kill even when we quarrel. Over the past fifteen or twenty thousand years we have successively widened this category from the original hunting-and-gathering band to encompass larger and larger groups. First it was the tribe of some thousands of people bound together by kinship and ritual ties; then the state, where we recognize our shared interests with millions of people whom we don't know and will never meet; and now, finally, the entire human race.

There was nothing in the least idealistic or sentimental in any of the previous redefinitions. They occurred because they were useful in advancing people's material interests and ensuring their survival. The same is true for this final act of redefinition: we have reached a point where our moral imagination must expand again to embrace the whole of mankind, or else we will perish. Both the necessary shift in cultural perspective and the creation of political institutions that will reflect the new perspective are clearly changes that must take a very long time: it is hard to believe we are even halfway to our goal yet, though we have been immersed in this change for most of a century already.

As for the argument that there will never be universal brotherhood among mankind, and so any attempt to move beyond the current system of national states is foredoomed: of course we aren't going to end up loving one another indiscriminately, but that isn't necessary. There is not universal love and brotherhood within national states either. What does exist, and what must now be extended beyond national borders, is a mutual recognition that everybody is better off if they respect each other's rights and accept arbitration by a higher authority, rather than killing one another when their rights or interests come into conflict.

It's no coincidence that the period in which the concept of the national state is finally coming under challenge by a wider definition of humanity is also the period that has seen history's most catastrophic wars, for they provide the practical incentive that drives the process of change. There would be no change without the threat of war, but the transition to a different system is a risky business. The danger of another world war which would cut the whole process short and perhaps put a permanent end to civilization is tiny in any given year. Cumulatively, given how long the process of change will take, the danger is extreme. That is no reason not to keep trying.

However deficient in many ways the United Nations may be, I think it's an absolutely essential organization. There is no way in which this effort cannot be made—it has to be made—knowing perfectly well that you're pushing an enormous boulder up a very steep hill. There will be slips and it will come back on you from time to time, but you have to go on pushing. Because if you don't do that, you simply give in to the notion that you're going to go into a global war again at some point, this time with nuclear weapons.

Brian Urquhart

Our task over the next few generations is to transform the world of independent states in which we live into some sort of genuine international community. If we succeed in creating that community, however quarrelsome, discontented, and full of injustice it probably will be, then we shall effectively have abolished the ancient institution of warfare. Good riddance.

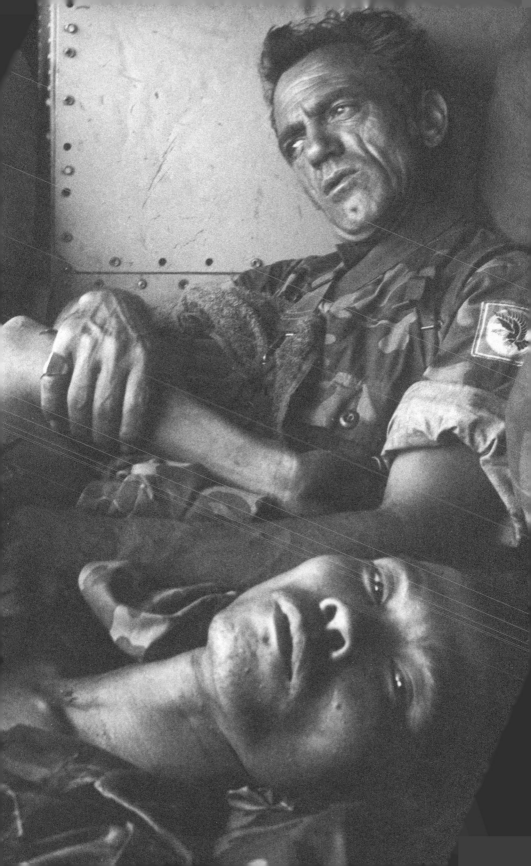

Notes

Chapter 1

1. Martin Middlebrook, *The Battle of Hamburg* (London: Allan Lane, 1980), 264–7.
2. James Wellard, *By the Waters of Babylon* (London: Hutchinson, 1982), 147.
3. Leonard Cottrell, *The Great Invasion* (London: Pan, 1961), 83.
4. Anthony Swofford, *Jarhead: A Soldier's Story of Modern War* (New York: Simon & Schuster, 1997), 197–99.
5. *Ibid.*, 230–31.
6. Robert Blake, ed., *The Private Papers of Douglas Haig, 1914–1919* (London: Eyre and Spottiswoode, 1952), 70.
7. M. Lindsay, *So Few Got Through* (London: Arrow, 1955), 249.
8. John Ellis, *The Sharp End of War* (North Pomfret, Vermont: David and Charles, 1980), 162–64; Richard Holmes, *Acts of War: The Behaviour of Men in Battle* (London: Weidenfeld and Nicolson, 1986), 350.
9. Samuel P. Huntington, *The Soldier and the State* (New York: Vintage, 1964), 79.
10. S. Bagnall, *The Attack* (London: Hamish Hamilton, 1947), 21.
11. S.A. Stouffer et al., *The American Soldier*, vol. II (Princeton, New Jersey: Princeton University Press, 1949), 202.
12. Lt. Col. J.W. Appel and Capt. G.W. Beebe, "Preventive Psychiatry: An Epidemiological Approach," *Journal of the American Medical Association* 131 (1946), 1470.
13. Bagnall, *op cit.*, 160.
14. Appel and Beebe, *op. cit.*
15. Col. S.L.A. Marshall, *Men Against Fire* (New York: William Morrow and Co., 1947), 149–50.
16. *Ibid.*, 191.
17. *Ibid.*, 191, 182, 153.

Chapter 2

1. Leonard Cottrell, *The Warrior Pharaohs* (London: Evans Brothers, 1968), 52.
2. Samuel Rolbart, *The Israeli Soldier* (New York: A. S. Barnes, 1970), 206.
3. Rolbart, *op. cit.*, 58.
4. S.L.A. Marshall, *Men Against Fire* (New York: Wm. Morrow, 1947), 56–57.
5. *Ibid.*, 79.
6. Dave Grossman, *On Killing: The Psychological Cost of Learning to Kill in War* (New York, Little, Brown & Co., 1995), 18–28.
7. *Ibid.*, 10–11.
8. G. Gurney, *Five Down and Glory* (New York: Putnam's, 1958), 256.
9. Peter Watson, *War on the Mind: The Military Uses and Abuses of Psychology* (London: Hutchinson, 1978), 45.
10. Grossman, *op. cit.*, 178–79.
11. *Ibid.*, 259–60, 264–66, 281–89.

Chapter 3

1. M.J. Meggitt, *Desert People*, Chicago: University of Chicago Press, 1960, 245.
2. J. Morgan, *The Life and Adventures of William Buckley: Thirty-Two Years a Wanderer Amongst the Aborigines* (Canberra: Australian National University Press, 1979 [1852]), 49–51.
3. Richard Wrangham and Dale Peterson, *Demonic Males: Apes and the Origins of Human Violence* (Boston: Houghton Mifflin, 1996), 17.
4. Stephen A. LeBlanc and Katherine E. Register, *Constant Battles: The Myth of the Noble, Peaceful Savage* (New York: St. Martin's Press, 2003), 81–85. Many of the following sources are referenced in LeBlanc's and Wrangham's ground-breaking books, which have played a large part in shaping my argument in this chapter.
5. Morgan, *op. cit.*, 82.
6. W.L. Warner, "Murngin Warfare," in *Oceania* I: 457–94 (1931).
7. E.S.Burch Jr., "Eskimo Warfare in Northwest Alaska," *Anthropological Papers of the University of Alaska* 16 (2): 1–14 (1974).
8. E. Biocca, *The Yanomama: The Narrative of a White Girl Kidnapped by Amazonian Indians* (New York: Dutton, 1971), quoted in LeBlanc, 154.
9. N.A. Chagnon, *Studying the Yanomamo* (New York: Holt, Rinehart and Winston, 1974), 157–61; N.A. Chagnon, *Yanomamo*, 4th edition

(New York: Harcourt and Brace Jovanovic College Publishers, 1994), 205.

10. LeBlanc, *op. cit.*, 94–97.

11. Quincy Wright, *A Study of War* (Chicago: University of Chicago Press, 1965), 63.

12. Wrangham, *op. cit.*, 65. Much of the following discussion is based on Wrangham's arguments in Chapter 8, "The Price of Freedom," in this book.

13. The account of the killing of a lioness is taken from Wrangham, *op. cit.*, 160–61. The makers of the film, Beverly and Dereck Joubert, wrote an accompanying article, "Lions of Darkness," which appeared in *National Geographic* 186 (1994), 35–53. Deaths of this sort are rare in confrontations between prides, which are generally confined to much roaring and other threat displays followed by retreat. It was the isolation of the old Maomi female that made her killing likely.

14. Charles Darwin, *The Descent of Man: and Selection in Relation to Sex* (originally published in London by John Murray in 1871; most recent edition London: Gibson Square Books, 2003), 132.

15. LeBlanc, *op. cit.*, 45–49, 113.

16. Robert L. O'Connell, *Ride of the Second Horseman: The Growth and Death of War* (Oxford: Oxford University Press, 1995), 28–29; ibid., 49, 113, 175–76.

17. The original "blitzkrieg" theory to account for the mass extinction of large North American fauna was proposed by Paul Martin of the University of Arizona in 1967. Articles in *Science* of June 2001 by evolutionary biologist John Alroy of the University of California, Santa Barbara, regarding the North American extinctions, and by an Australian, French, and U.S. team regarding the Australian extinctions ended the debate in favour of Martin's hypothesis for most people. Shepard Krech's book, *The Ecological Indian: Myth and History* (New York: N.W. Norton & Co., 1999) is a detailed investigation of the claims to superior environmental wisdom of North American Indians based mainly on the copious historical records of the fur trade and other commercial enterprises engaged in by a wide variety of tribes during the eighteenth and nineteenth centuries.

18. J. Woodburn, "An Introduction to Hadza Ecology," in R.B. Lee and I. De Vore (eds.), *Man the Hunter* (Chicago: Aldine, 1968), 49–55.

19. Margaret Mead (ed.), *Ruth Benedict: An American Anthropologist at Work* (Boston: Houghton Mifflin, 1959), 374. Ironically, I used both

this and the next quote in naive support of the "Rousseau" position in the first edition of this book.

20. Ernest Wallace and E. Adamson Hoebel, *The Comanches* (Norman, Oklahoma: University of Oklahoma Press, 1952), 247. The story was told to the authors in the 1930s by Post Oak Jim, an old Comanche who as a youth had been the friend waiting outside the Ute encampment.

21. Natalie Angier, "Is War Our Biological Destiny?" *New York Times*, Nov 11, 2003.

Chapter 4

1. Homer, *Iliad*, tr. Richard Lattimore (Chicago: University of Chicago Press, 1951), 15, 322—28.

2. Xenophon, *Agesilaus* ii, 9. The Battle of Coronea (394 BC) is far closer in time to us than to the earliest kingdoms, but this slaughterhouse style of infantry warfare was fairly standard by the late second millennium BC, and remained so until halfway through the second millennium AD.

3. Homer, *op. cit.*, 16, 345–50.

4. *Holy Bible, New Revised Standard Version, Anglicised Edition* (Oxford: Oxford University Press, 1995), Joshua 6: 20–21.

5. Robert L. O'Connell, *Ride of the Second Horseman: The Growth and Death of War* (Oxford: Oxford University Press, 1995), 55–60.

6. Jared Diamond, *Guns, Germs and Steel: The Fates of Human Societies* (New York: W.W. Norton, 1997), 112.

7. *Ibid.*, 135–140.

8. *Ibid.*, 137–38, 141–42, 159–68.

9. *Ibid.*, 176–91.

10. O'Connell, *op. cit.*, 64–66; John Keegan, *A History of Warfare* (New York: Vintage, 1994), 124–26.

11. O'Connell, *op. cit.*, 68–76.

12. W.B. Emery, *Egypt in Nubia* (London: Hutchinson, 1965), 105.

13. O'Connell, *op. cit.*, 133–41; LeBlanc, *op. cit.*, 182–83; and Keegan, *op. cit.*, 130–32, 141–42.

14. Keegan, *op. cit.*, 130–32; O'Connell, *op. cit.*, 187–88.

15. Homer, *op. cit.*, 5, 65–84.

16. Samuel Noah Kramer, *History Begins at Sumer* (Philadelphia: University of Pennsylvania Press, 1981), 30–32.

17. Boris Piotrovsky, *The Ancient Civilisation of Urartu* (London: Barrie and Rockliff: The Cresset Press, 1969), 47.

Chapter 5

1. Leonard Cottrell, *The Warrior Pharaohs* (London: Evans Brothers, 1968), 80.
2. *Ibid.*, 99.
3. *Ibid.*, 81–82; Yigael Yadin, *The Art of Warfare in Biblical Lands*, trs. by M. Pearlman (London: Weidenfeld and Nicolson, 1963), 100–03.
4. Witold Rodzinski, *A History of China* (Oxford: Pergamon Press, 1979), 164–65.
5. Robert L. O'Connell, *Ride of the Second Horseman: The Growth and Death of War* (Oxford: Oxford University Press, 1995), 71–76.
6. *Ibid.*, 77–83; Keegan, *op. cit.*, 156–57.
7. Keegan, *op. cit.*, 161.
8. *Ibid.*, 166.
9. A. Friendly, *The Dreadful Day* (London: Hutchinson, 1981), 27.
10. O'Connell, *op. cit.*, 121, 165–66; Keegan, *op.cit.*, 168.
11. O'Connell, *op. cit.*, 161–64, 170–73.
12. H. Saggs, *The Might That Was Assyria* (London: Sidgwick and Jackson, 1984), 258.
13. O'Connell, *op. cit.*, 145–58.
14. Cornelius Tacitus, *The Histories*, trs. Kenneth Wellesley (London: Penguin Books, 1982), 156.
15. *Ibid.*, 165.
16. E.R. Chamberlin, *The Sack of Rome* (London: Batsford, 1979), 176–78.
17. *Ibid.*
18. Virgil, *The Aeneid*, trs. W.F. Jackson Knight (London: Penguin Books, 1968), 62–65.
19. The eyewitness account of Polybius itself is lost, but this account by Appian is directly based on it. Susan Rowen, *Rome in Africa* (London: Evans Brothers, 1969), 32–33.
20. *Ibid.*
21. Graham Webster, *The Roman Imperial Army* (London: Adam Charles Black, 1969), 221.
22. Thucydides, *History of the Peloponnesian Wars* (London: Penguin, 1954), 392.
23. Herodotus, describing the battle of Marathon in *The Histories*, trs. Aubrey de Selincourt (London: Penguin, 1954), 428–29.
24. F.E. Adcock, *The Greek and Macedonian Arts of War* (Berkeley: University of California Press, 1957), 14.
25. Aeschylus, *The Persians*, trs. by Edith Hall (Warminster, England:

Aris and Phillips Ltd., 1996), lines 409–423. For dramatic purposes, Aeschylus was describing the battle from the Persian side.

26. Thucydides, *op. cit.*, 182–83. Here Phormio addresses the crews of the Athenian fleet before the Battle of Naupactus, 429 BC. As it turned out, Phormio was lured into the gulf and lost eleven of his twenty ships there in half an hour.

27. *Ibid.*, 523–24.

28. Keith Hopkins, *Conquerors and Slaves: Sociological Studies in Roman History*, vol. 1 (Cambridge: Cambridge University Press, 1978), 33.

29. *Ibid.*, 28.

30. Edward N. Luttwak, *The Grand Strategy of the Roman Empire From the First Century A.D. to the Third Century A.D.* (Baltimore: Johns Hopkins Press, 1976), 15, 189.

31. Charles C. Oman, *The Art of War in the Sixteenth Century* (London: Methuen, 1937), 237–38.

32. *Ibid.*, 240.

Chapter 6

1. J.J. Saunders, *The History of the Mongol Conquests* (London: Routledge and Kegan Paul, 1971), 197–98.

2. Jared Diamond, *Guns, Germs and Steel* (New York: W.W. Norton & Co., 2003), 430–32.

3. Gavin Menzies, *1421: The Year China Discovered the World* (London: Bantam Press, 2002), 75–85.

4. Malcolm Mallet, *Mercenaries and Their Masters: Warfare in Renaissance Italy* (London, Bodley Head, 1974), 157; Malcolm Vale, *War and Chivalry* (London: Duckworth, 1981), 137–38.

5. Andre Corvisier, *Armies and Societies in Europe 1494–1789* (Bloomington, Indiana: University of Indiana Press, 1979), 28.

6. A.L. Sadler, *The Making of Modern Japan: The Life of Tokugawa Ieyasu* (London: George Allen and Unwin, 1937), 103.

7. *Ibid.*, 105.

8. Frederick Lewis Taylor, *The Art of War in Italy, 1494–1529* (Cambridge: Cambridge University Press, 1929), 56.

9. C.V Wedgwood, *The Thirty Years' War* (London: Jonathan Cape, 1956), 288–89.

10. J.F. Puysegur, *L'art de la guerre par principes et par règles* (Paris, 1748), I.

11. David Chandler, *The Campaigns of Napoleon* (London: Weidenfeld and Nicolson, 1966), 342.

12. Edward Mead Earle, ed., *Makers of Modern Strategy* (New York: Atheneum, 1966), 56.

13. Hew Strachan, *European Armies and the Conduct of War* (London: George Allen and Unwin, 1983), 8.

14. Willerd R. Fann, "On the Infantryman's Age in Eighteenth-Century Prussia," *Military Affairs* XLI, no. 4 (December, 1977), 167.

15. Lawrence Sterne, *A Sentimental Journey through France and Italy* (Oxford: Basil Blackwell, 1927), 85.

16. Christopher Duffy, *The Army of Frederick the Great* (London: David and Charles, 1974), 62.

17. Maurice, Compte de Saxe, *Les Rêveries, ou Mémoires sur l'art de la guerre* (Manheim, Jean Drieux, 1757), 77.

18. Strachan, *op. cit.*, 9.

19. Martin van Crefeld, *Supplying War: Logistics from Wallenstein to Patton* (Cambridge: Cambridge University Press, 1977), 38.

20. John Childs, *Armies and Warfare in Europe, 1648–1789* (Manchester, England: Manchester University Press, 1982), 158.

21. Edward Gibbon, *The History of the Decline and Fall of the Roman Empire* (New York: The Modern Library, 1932).

22. Maj. Gen. J.F.C. Fuller, *The Conduct of War, 1789–1961* (London: Eyre and Spottiswoode, 1961), 32.

23. R.D. Challener, *The French Theory of the Nation in Arms, 1866–1939* (New York: Russell and Russell, 1965), 3; Alfred Vagts, *A History of Militarism*, rev. ed. (New York: Meridian, 1959), 108–11.

24. Vagts, *op. cit.*, 114; Karl von Clausewitz, *On War*, eds. and trs. Michael Howard and Peter Paret (Princeton, New Jersey: Princeton University Press, 1976).

25. Vagts, *op. cit.*, 126–37; John Gooch, *Armies in Europe* (London: Routledge and Kegan Paul, 1980), 39.

26. Gunther Rothenburg, *The Art of War in the Age of Napoleon* (London: B. Batsford, 1977), 172–73.

27. Anthony Brett-James, *1812: Eyewitness Accounts of Napoleon's Defeat in Russia* (London: Macmillan, 1967), 127.

28. Christopher Duffy, *Borodino and the War of 1812* (London: Seeley Service, 1972), 135.

29. David Chandler, *The Campaigns of Napoleon* (New York: Macmillan, 1966), 668; Gooch, *op. cit.*, 39–41.

30. Vagts, *op. cit.*, 143–44.

31. *Ibid.*, 140.

32. Earle, *op. cit.*, 57.

Chapter 7

1. Guglielmo Ferrero, *Peace and War* (London: Macmillan, 1933), 63–64.
2. Karl von Clausewitz, *On War*, tr. Col. J.J. Graham (London: Trubner, 1873), I, 4.
3. Paddy Griffith, *Battle Tactics of the Civil War* (New Haven, Conn.: Yale University Press, 1987), 144–50.
4. Frank E. Vandiver, *Mighty Stonewall* (New York: McGraw-Hill, 1957), 366.
5. Col. Theodore Lyman, *Meade's Headquarters 1863–1865* (Boston, Mass.: Massachusetts Historical Society, 1922), 101, 224.
6. Mark Grimsley, "Surviving Military Revolution: The U.S. Civil War," in MacGregor Knox and Williamson Murray, eds. *The Dynamics of Military Revolution, 1300–2050* (Cambridge: Cambridge University Press, 2001), 84.
7. Frederick Henry Dyer, *A Compendium of the War of the Rebellion* (New York: T. Yoseloff, 1959).
8. *Personal Memoirs of General W. T. Sherman* (Bloomington, Ind.: Indiana University Press, 1957), II, 111.
9. Jan Bloch, *The War of the Future in Its Technical, Economic and Political Relations*. English translation by W. T. Stead entitled *Is War Now Impossible?*, 1899. Bloch died in 1902.
10. Jacques d'Arnoux, "Paroles d'un revenant," in Lieut.-Col. J. Armengaud, ed., *L'atmosphère du Champ de Bataille* (Paris: Lavauzelle, 1940), 118–19.
11. The most recent and in many ways the best book on the 1914 Christmas truce is Michael Jürgs, *Der kleine Frieden im Grossen Krieg: Westfront 1914: als Deutsche, Franzosen und Briten gemeinsam Weihnachten feierten,* (München: C. Bertelsmann, 2003).
12. André Tardieu, *Avec Foch: Août-Novembre 1914* (Paris: Ernest Flammarion, 1939), 107.
13. J. E C. Fuller, *The Second World War, 1939–1945: A Strategic and Tactical History* (New York: Duell, Sloan and Pearce, 1949), 140.
14. *Ibid.*, 170; Keegan, *op. cit.*, 309.
15. Henry Williamson, *The Wet Flanders Plain* (London: Beaumont Press), 14–16. Williamson was nineteen years old during the Battle of the Somme.
16. Arthur Bryant, *Unfinished Victory* (London: Macmillan, 1940), 8.
17. Aaron Norman, *The Great Air War* (New York: Macmillan, 1968), 353.
18. *Ibid.*, 382.
19. Sir William Robertson, *Soldiers and Statesmen* (London: Cassell, 1926), I, 313.

20. Bryan Perret, *A History of Blitzkrieg* (London: Robert Hale, 1983), 21.
21. Jonathan B.A. Bailey, "The Birth of Modern Warfare," in Knox and Murray, *op. cit.*, 142–45.
22. Theodore Ropp, *War in the Modern World*, rev. ed. (New York: Collier, 1962), 321, 344.
23. Guy Sajer, *The Forgotten Soldier* (London: Sphere, 1977), 228–30.
24. Giulio Douhet, *The Command of the Air* (London: Faber & Faber, 1943), 18–19.
25. Norman Longmark, *Air Raid: The Bombing of Coventry 1940* (London: Hutchinson, 1976), 146.
26. Max Hastings, *Bomber Command* (London: Pan Books, 1979), 149.
27. *Ibid.*, 423.
28. Martin Middlebrook, *The Battle of Hamburg* (London: Allan Lane, 1980), 244.
29. *Ibid.*, 264–67.
30. Wesley Craven and James Cate, *The Army Air Forces in World War Two* (Chicago: University of Chicago Press, 1948), vol. 5, 615–17.
31. H. H. Arnold, *Report . . . to the Secretary of War; 12 November 1945* (Washington: Government Printing Office, 1945), 35.
32. Leonard Bickel, *The Story of Uranium: The Deadly Element* (London: Macmillan, 1979), 78–79, 198–99, 274–76.
33. William Manchester, *American Caesar: Douglas MacArthur 1880–1964* (London: Hutchinson, 1979), 612, 622–23.

Chapter 8

1. D. Bagley, *The Tightrope Men* (London: Collins, 1973).
2. Quincy Wright, *A Study of War* (Chicago: University of Chicago Press, 1964), 53.
3. Errol Morris, director, *The Fog of War*, film (Los Angeles: Sony Pictures, Classics, 2004).
4. Bernard Brodie, ed., *The Absolute Weapon: Atomic Power and World Order* (New York: Harcourt Brace, 1946), 76.
5. Fred Kaplan, *The Wizards of Armageddon* (New York: Simon & Schuster, 1983), 26–32.
6. *Ibid.*
7. Desmond Ball, "Targeting for Strategic Deterrence," *Adelphi Papers*, No. 185 (Summer 1983), London: International Institute for Strategic Studies, 3, 5.
8. Gregg Herken, *Counsels of War* (New York: Knopf, 1985), 306.

9. Ball, *op. cit.*, 40.
10. Gerard H. Clarfield and William M. Wiecek, *Nuclear America* (New York: Harper & Row, 1984), 155.
11. Kaplan, *op. cit.*, 133–34.
12. *Ibid.*, 47, 79–80, 203–19; Herken, *op. cit.*, 79, 84–87.
13. Kaplan, *op. cit.*, 222–23.
14. Herken, *op. cit.*, 116.
15. Gerard C. Smith, *Doubletalk: The Story of the First Strategic Arms Limitation Talks*(Garden City, N.Y.: Doubleday, 1980), 10–11.
16. Maxwell D. Taylor, *The Uncertain Trumpet* (New York: Harper & Brothers, 1960), 123.
17. *New York Times*, 12 May 1968.
18. Herken, *op. cit.*, 143–45; Ball, *op. cit.*, 10.
19. Kaplan, *op. cit.*, 233, 235.
20. *Ibid.*, 235–45, 263–72.
21. *Ibid.*, 242–43, 272–73, 278–80; Herken, *op. cit.*, 51, 145; Ball, *op. cit.*, 10–11.
22. *Marxism-Leninism on War and Army*, quoted in Joseph D. Douglass, Jr., and Amoretta M. Hoeber, *Soviet Strategy for Nuclear War* (Palo Alto: Hoover Institute, 1979), 36.
23. Kaplan, *op. cit.*, 283–85, 316–17; Ball, *op. cit.*, 11–13; Herken, *op. cit.*, 163–65, 168–69.
24. Herken, *op. cit.*, 317–19.
25. Sir Solly Zuckerman, *Nuclear Illusion and Reality* (New York: Vintage Books, 1983), 46–47.
26. Senate Armed Services Committee, *Military Procurement Authorization, Fiscal Year 1966*, Introduction, note 1, p. 39.
27. Private correspondence to Desmond Ball from an assistant secretary of defence in the last years of the Johnson administration, quoted in Ball, *op. cit.*, 15.
28. Col. Gen. N. A. Lomov, ed., *Scientific-Technical Progress and the Revolution in Military Affairs* (translated and published by the U.S. Air Force) (Washington, D.C.: U.S. Government Printing Office, 1974), 147.
29. Herken, *op. cit.*, 157–60; Kaplan, *op. cit.*, 294–304.
30. Robert F. Kennedy, *Thirteen Days: A Memoir of the Cuban Missile Crisis* (New York: Norton, 1968), 156.
31. Morris, *op. cit.*
32. See "The Cuban Missile Crisis, 1962: A Political Perspective After Forty Years," in *The National Security Archive of The George*

Washington University (website) at http://www.gwu.edu/~nsarchiv/nsa/cuba_mis_cri/

33. Kaplan, *op. cit.*, 340.

34. *Ibid.*, 208, 373.

35. *Ibid.*, 267.

36. *Ibid.*; Henry Kissinger, *Nuclear Weapons and Foreign Policy* (New York: Harper & Row, 1957), 132; U.S. State Department *Bulletin*, 29 July 1974, 215.

37. Gerald C. Smith, *Doubletalk: The Story of the First Strategic Arms Limitation Talks* (Garden City, New York: Doubleday, 1980), 154–78, 479–80; Zbigniew Brzezinski, *Power and Principle: Memoirs of the National Security Adviser, 1977–81,* (London: Weidenfeld and Nicolson, 1983), 337; Strobe Talbott, *Endgame: The Inside Story of Salt II* (New York: Harper & Row, 1979), 35; Cyrus Vance, *Hard Choices* (New York: Simon & Schuster, 1982), 55.

38. Kaplan, *op. cit.*, 360–64; Michael Parfit, *The Boys Behind the Bombs* (Boston; Little, Brown & Co., 1983), 38–40; Herken, *op. cit.*, 201.

39. Parfit, *op. cit.*, 251–54.

40. Kaplan, *op. cit.*, 366–67.

41. *Ibid.*, 368–73; Herken, *op. cit.*, 261–62; Ball, *op. cit.*, 20; Peter Pringle and William Arkin, *S.I.O.P.: The Secret U.S. Plan for Nuclear War* (New York: Norton, 1983), 178–79.

42. Herken, *op. cit.*, 263–64.

43. Thomas Schelling, *The Strategy of Conflict* (London; Oxford University Press, 1963), 229.

44. Herken, *op. cit.*, 264.

45. James Canan, *War in Space* (New York: Harper & Row, 1982), 120.

46. Arkin, *op. cit.*, pp. 172–73; Thomas Powers, "Choosing a Strategy for World War Three," *Atlantic*, November 1982, 82–109.

47. Herken, *op. cit.*, 297–98.

48. Brzezinski, *op. cit.*, 455–56; Ball, *op. cit.*, 20–22; Herken, *op. cit.*, 301–2.

49. Herken, *op.cit.*, 320–22; Kaplan, *op. cit.*, 387.

50. Canan, *op. cit.*, 162.

51. *Los Angeles Times*, 1 July 1984; Herken, *op. cit.*, 312.

52. McGeorge Bundy, George F. Kennan, Robert S. McNamara, and Gerard Smith, "The President's Choice; Star Wars or Arms Control," *Foreign Affairs* 63, no. 2 (Winter 1984–85), 271.

53. *Cold War–Historical Documents: Reagan-Gorbachev Transcripts*, at http://www.cnn.com/SPECIALS/cold.war/episodes/22/documents/reykjavik

54. Carl Sagan, "Nuclear War and Climatic Catastrophe: Some Policy Implications," *Foreign Affairs*, Winter 1983/84, 285.

55. R.P. Turco, A.B. Toon, T.P. Ackerman, J.B. Pollack, C. Sagan [TTAPS], "Nuclear Winter: Global Consequences of Multiple Nuclear Explosions," *Science*, Vol. 222 (1983), 1283–297; and R.P. Turco, A.B. Toon, T.P. Ackerman, J.B. Pollack, C. Sagan [TTAPS], "The Climatic Effects of Nuclear War," *Scientific American*, Vol. 251, No. 2 (Aug.1984), 33–43.

56. Paul R. Ehrlich et al., "The Long-Term Biological Consequences of Nuclear War," *Science*, vol. 222, no. 4630 (December 1983), 1293–1300.

57. Sagan, *op. cit.*, 276; Turco et al., *op. cit.*, 38.

58. *Science*, Vol. 247 (1990), 166–76.

59. Carl Sagan and Richard Turco, *A Path No Man Thought* (New York: Random House, 1990), 201–03.

Chapter 9

1. Kaufmann's 1955 essays were very influential in shaping the United States army's thinking on the possibility of restricting war in Europe to conventional weapons. Fred Kaplan, *The Wizards of Armageddon* (New York: Knopf, 1984), pp. 197–200.

2. Samuel P. Huntington, *The Soldier and the State* (New York: Vintage, 1964), 79.

3. Walter Goerlitz, *History of the German General Staff* (New York: Frederick A. Praeger, 1953).

4. Cahal Milmo, "British Army Had Fowl Plan to Repel Russians," *The Independent*, 1 April 2004.

5. Justin Wintle, ed. *The Dictionary of War Quotations* (London: Hodder and Stoughton, 1989), 379.

6. *Ibid.*, 382.

7. Morris Janowitz, *The Professional Soldier* (New York: Free Press, 1964), 21, 35.

8. Admiral William A. Owens with Ed Offley, *Lifting the Fog of War* (New York: Farrar, Straus and Giroux, 2000), 4.

9. Stanley Karnow, *Vietnam: A History*, Revised Edition (London: Pimlico, 1994), 19.

10. *Ibid.*, 312.

11. From the Global Security website: http://www.globalsecurity.org/military/systems/aircraft/index.html

Chapter 10

1. From a speech at Blackdown, August 30, 1932, quoted in Justin Wintle, ed., *The Dictionary of War Quotations*, (London: Hodder and Stoughton, 1989).
2. Mao Tse-tung, *Strategic Problems in the Anti-Japanese Guerrilla War*, 1939.
3. Walter Laqueur, *Guerilla*, (London: Weidenfeld and Nicolson, 1977), 40.
4. Mao Tse-tung, "Problems of Strategy in China's Revolutionary War (5.3)," December 1936, *Selected Works of Mao Tse-tung*, (Beijing: Foreign Languages Press edition, vol. 1, 1965).
5. Henry A. Kissinger, "The Vietnam Negotiations," *Foreign Affairs*, January 1969.
6. Christon I. Archer, John R. Ferris, Holger H. Herwig, and Timothy H.E. Travers, *World History of Warfare*, (London: Cassell, 2003), 558.
7. J. Bowyer Bell, *The Myth of the Guerilla*, (New York: Knopf, 1971), 231.
8. Quoted in Robert Moss, *Urban Guerillas*, (London: Temple Smith, 1972), 13.
9. *Ibid.*, 198.
10. First quoted in the *Boletin de las Madres de la Plaza de Mayo*, May, 1985, reproduced in Robin Morgan, *The Demon Lover: On the Sexuality of Terrorism* (London: Methuen, 1989).
11. Richard Huffman, *The Gun Speaks: The Baader-Meinhof Gang and the West German Decade of Terror 1968–1977*, http://www .baader-meinhof.com/gun/index.htm
12. Quoted in *The Guardian* (London), 16 October 1991.
13. Quoted in *Time* (New York), 11 November 1974.
14. Taped broadcast on Al-Jazeera, 12 February 2003.
15. Sarah Ewing, "The IoS Interview," in *The Independent on Sunday*, London, 8 September 2002.

Chapter 11

1. Natalie Angier, "No Time for Bullies: Baboons Retool their Culture," *New York Times* (Science Desk), 13 April 2004.
2. Goldman Sachs, "Dreaming with BRICs: The Path to 2050" (October 2003), http://www.gs.com/insight/research/reports/99.pdf
3. Dwight Macdonald, *Politics*, August 1945.
4. Carl Sagan, "Nuclear War and Climatic Catastrophe: Some Policy Implications," *Foreign Affairs*, Winter 1983–84, 275.

Image Credits

Al Rockoff, vi

Al Rockoff, xi

Erich Lessing / Art Resource, NY, 7

Erich Lessing / Art Resource, NY, 9

Bettman / CORBIS / MAGMA, 16

Bettman / CORBIS / MAGMA, 34

AP / Wide World Photos. top left, 39

Getty Images. top right, 39

Getty Images. bottom, 39

CORBIS / MAGMA, 44

Getty Images, 60

Film Study Center, Harvard
University, 78

Source: [Keeley, Lawrence H.; *War
Before Civilization*; 1996], 95

Paul Almsay / CORBIS / MAGMA, 119

Erich Lessing / Art Resource, NY, 128

Erich Lessing / Art Resource, NY, 139

The British Museum (124825), 142

The British Museum (123908), 156

The British Museum (115634), 171

Erich Lessing / Art Resource, NY, 176

Alinari / Art Resource, NY, 181

Scala / Art Resource, NY, 185

Alinari / Art Resource, NY, 191

Erich Lessing / Art Resource, NY, 201

Scala / Art Resource, NY, 209

Spencer Collection / The New York
Public Library / Astor, Lenox and
Tilden Foundations, 213

Anne S.K. Brown Military
Collection / Brown University
Library, 226

Réunion des Musées Nationaux / Art
Resource, NY, 230

Bettman / CORBIS / MAGMA, 237

Victoria & Albert Museum, London
/ Art Resource, NY, 238

American Memory Collections /
Library of Congress, 244

American Memory Collections /
Library of Congress, 247

Public Archives of Canada
(PA 003683), 251

Public Archives of Canada
(PA 001326), 254

Imperial War Museum (Q 4665), 256

Hulton-Deutsch Collection /
    CORBIS / MAGMA, 258
Public Archives of Canada (PA
    024436), 261
Bettman / CORBIS / MAGMA, 263
Public Archives of Canada (PA
    003022), 269
Sovfoto / Eastfoto, 273
Sovfoto / Eastfoto, 280
Yale University Library, 295
AP / Wide World Photos, 302
AP / Wide World Photos, 310
Zeybel, Henry; *Eagle Magazine*;
    December 1984, 317
CORBIS / MAGMA, 329
Jim Sugar / CORBIS / MAGMA, 333
Worpole, Ian; *Scientific American*;
    August 1984, 343
Hulton-Deutsch Collection /
    CORBIS / MAGMA, 354
PJ Griffiths / Magnum, 359

AP / Wide World Photos, 367
Bettman / CORBIS / MAGMA, 377
AP / Wide World Photos, 379
Sovfoto / Eastfoto, 380
AP / Wide World Photos, 387
"Tampoco." Art Resource, NY, 393
"Por Que." Private Collection /
    IndexBridgeman Art Library, 393
"Lo mismo." PrivateCollection /
    IndexBridgeman Art Library, 393
Bettman / CORBIS / MAGMA, 395
Patrick Robert / CORBIS SYGMA /
    MAGMA, 400
AP / Wide World Photos, 402
Richard Huffman, www.baader-
    meinhof.com, 404
Bettman / CORBIS / MAGMA, 408
JA Giordano / CORBIS SABA /
    MAGMA, 413
Bruno Barbey / Magnum, 447
Bettman / CORBIS / MAGMA, 462

Index

All page citations appearing in *italic* refer to *quoted material* in the text. Page citations in **boldface** refer to **illustrations** in the text.